Phenomenology of the Truth Proper to Religion

SUNY Series in Philosophy
Robert Cummings Neville, Editor

Phenomenology of the Truth Proper to Religion

Edited by
Daniel Guerrière

STATE UNIVERSITY OF NEW YORK PRESS

Published by
State University of New York Press, Albany

© 1990 State University of New York

For information, address State University of New York
Press, State University Plaza, Albany, NY 12246

Library of Congress Cataloging-in-Publication Data

Phenomenology of the truth proper to religion / edited by Daniel
Guerrière.
p. cm.—(SUNY series in philosophy)
Includes index.
ISBN 0–7914–0170–7.—ISBN 0–7914–0171–5 (pbk.)
1. Religion—Philosophy. 2. Truth. 3. Phenomenology.
I. Guerrière, Daniel, 1941– . II. Series.
BL51.P514 1990
200′.1—dc19   89–4300
                                                              CIP

10 9 8 7 6 5 4 3 2 1

Contents

III. ETHICAL

IV. DECONSTRUCTIVE

V. TRANSCENDENTAL

Preface

A major orientation in philosophy, namely, phenomenology; a major phenomenon, religion; and a major issue, truth—the constellation of these became this book. It gathers together studies by scholar-philosophers in the phenomenological tradition on the issue of the truth that is proper to religion. No other work addresses the matter specifically and extensively. Here is represented the whole spectrum of phenomenology: transcendental (as exemplified in Husserl), existential (as in Heidegger), hermeneutic (as in Ricoeur), ethical (as in Levinas), and deconstructive (as in Derrida).

Each contributor was free to define the problematic as he saw fit. The only guideline was that, whatever other thinkers or issues he engage, his style remain phenomenological and his focus remain on "truth." The achievement of any one person is finite in scope, execution, and truth. Hence a collection—with its multiplicity of perspectives—would serve well to illuminate, as we individually cannot, what "truth" could possibly mean with respect to religion. The question is important for the philosophical, theological, and scientific study of religion—not to mention our personal decisions.

Introduction

The style of philosophizing known as phenomenology is, on any account, one of the major philosophical movements of twentieth-century thought. Arising in Germany at the turn of the century, it achieved new originality in France in the 1930s and in North America in the 1960s. One of the phenomena that it has interrogated in a new way has been religion. The present work focuses on the problematic of truth in this new way.

What is distinctive about phenomenology may be formulated abstractly from its concrete practice. It has shown itself to be a progressively primordial reflection. Specifically, it has been:

1. the articulation of the *correlative* structures of objectivity and subjectivity;

2. the evincement of *foundational* objectivity and subjectivity; and

3. the circumscription of the *primordial unity* out of which objectivity and subjectivity differentiate.

The earlier moments may be and have been practiced independently of the latter. Let us briefly discuss each moment in turn.

First, phenomenology is the articulation of the structures of subjectivity in correlation with the structures of objectivity. To avoid the arbitrariness of introspectionism, the internal structure of the subject is to be "read off of" the structure of objectivity, starting with the world of quotidian praxis and proceeding to its microingredients and macrocontexts.

In this articulation, phenomenology opposes itself, on the one hand, to "empiricism" or "objectivism," which regards the world as merely in-itself and consciousness as merely a passive receptor; and, on the other hand, to "idealism" or "subjectivism," which regards the world as merely for-consciousness and consciousness as merely an active producer. A popular version of the former is the view that "physical reality" is simply "there without us," and of the latter the view that numbers are simply "in the head" and then "applied to reality." Rather, for phenomenology, objectivity of whatever type does not lie "out there," waiting to be mirrored by an isolate mind whose representations may or may not correspond to it. Nor does subjectivity of any kind lie "in here," looking out upon isolate things that may or may not impassively subsist. Phenomenology affirms that objectivity *means* presence-for the subject, and subjectivity *means* presence-toward the object.[1]

Phenomenology aims to retrieve the truth in both objectivism and subjectivism, and to retain the tension between them. The subject does not arbitrarily invent but rather constitutes the object, and the object does not indifferently occur but rather accords itself to the subject. Of course, some of the objects are other subjects; we are each a (presence-)toward-others and a (presence-)for-others at once. In any case, the philosopher may not dissolve the tension between the bestowal of meaning by the subject and the offer of meaning by the object. The thesis of the correlativity of sense-bestowal and sense-offer has long been recognized by nonphenomenological philosophers of science in their insistence that there is no scientific world without a scientific attitude or, otherwise put, that facts are theory-laden. And just as the Gestalt psychology of the 1930s discovered that the world is a humanly constituted world, so the cognitive science of the 1980s has discovered the same thing.[2] The philosopher must always understand subjectivity and objectivity, throughout their structures, in their correlativity.

Next, phenomenology not only retains the tension between the two but also tries to uncover the foundational levels of subjectivity and objectivity. It is the regress to the radical. Layer by layer, phenomenology brings to light the constituting activity of the subject until it can conceive the fundamental achievement of subjectivity and, correlatively, sedimentation by sedimentation, it brings to light the self-givenness of the object until it can conceive the fundamental evidence of objectivity. This regress may be called genetic analysis, or archaeology, or the exhibition of the a priori, and so on. The radix may be characterized in various ways. Foundational subjectivity may be called the synthetic self, the unconscious, the subjective a priori, and so on. Foundational objectivity may be called the original world, synthetic materiality, the objective a priori, and so on. Of course, the subject is always already social, and the world a co-world. For most phenomenologists, this radical self and radical otherness are the most proper issues of phenomenological philosophy. However, this moment of phenomenology may transcend itself into a more primordial problematic.

Finally, phenomenology not only tries to evince the foundational levels of subjectivity and objectivity but also aims to comprehend them as poles of a primordial One. Phenomenology may extend its radical questioning to the very *Unity* in the unity of reciprocal implication, to that Unity *in* which the correlation is what it is. Phenomenology would finally circumscribe and bring to the fore that primordial Presence which differentiates itself into presence-toward and presence-for. This original Oneness may be called, with Heidegger, Disclosure *(Erschlossenheit)*, Time *(Zeit* or *Temporalität)*, the Not-a-thing *(das Nichts)*, the Disconcealment-process *(das Wesen der Unverborgenheit)*, *Alētheia* or Truth, the enduring-Presencing *(Anwesen)*, the Enownment-process or Event-of-enownment *(Ereignis)*, or simply Being. It may be called, with Merleau-Ponty, wild Being *(l'Être sauvage, l'Être brut)* or Nature. It may be called, with Dufrenne, the Apriori of the aprioris, or Nature. It is the Issuance of beings, their process of be-ing (in the participial sense) what and how they are, their Emergence *(Aufgehen)*. All beings are in the process of be-ing, and this process may be called Beingizing. This neologism serves to emphasize that at issue is precisely that process which is *beings* be-ing, whether the being be subject or object. Phenomenologists speak sometimes as if this Being-process were nothing other than beings-in-process, and sometimes as if it were beyond beings and has priority over them.[3] Evidently these two characterizations are not incompatible if we understand them to be given from different standpoints—the former from the second moment, the latter from the third moment of phenomenology. For the second moment, this one Beingizing is the unity of the subject and object. For the third moment, this one Presencing is what dualizes or polarizes itself into subjectivity and objectivity.

Sometimes phenomenologists have complicated matters by naming this Beingizing in terms of one or the other side of its duality. On the one hand, it can be thought in terms of the object-pole as World. In that case, World encompasses the pole of consciousness as well as the pole of world. Beingizing is then thought as the inexhaustible Latency of the world, which in turn is the "there" where Being advents; the world is Being adventing, the advent of Being. Hence as Being fragments, the subject-pole appears as the self-presence of the world, its doubling back upon itself. The difficulty here is that "world" becomes ambiguous; it is the Whole and one of the "total parts" of it. The late Merleau-Ponty clarified this approach. On the other hand, Beingizing can be thought in terms of the subject-pole as transcendental Subjectivity. In that case, the transcendental Ego encompasses the pole of the world as well as

the pole of consciousness. Beingizing is then thought as the indom-
itable Power of consciousness, which in turn is the "there" where
Being advents; man is Being adventing, the advent of Being. Hence
as Being fissures, the object-pole appears as the transcendent component of the subject, its doubling of itself into an other. The difficulty is that "consciousness" becomes ambiguous; it is the Whole
and one of the "total parts" of it. The middle Husserl stayed within
and the early Heidegger developed out of this approach. In either
case, Being remains the Medium of the simultaneous opposition
and chiasm of subject and object, the Presencing that does not immediately present itself but that differentiates itself into presence-
toward-objects and presence-for-subjects.

This Presencing, as Heidegger and then the whole phenomenological movement has recognized, is not traditional Being.

Articulated explicitly by Parmenides for the first time, traditional Being is necessary, absolute or infinite, unique, ungenerable,
imperishable, and eternal. But beings are contrarily contingent, finite, multiple, generable, perishable, and temporal. If they *are*,
however, then they can only *be* Being; they are nothing other than
it. But Being "is" not merely they. As Plato first articulated, absolute Being must, so to speak, do itself in and as them, but incompletely so; in other words, beings both are and are-not.[4] It "is
present" in and as them (i.e., they are), but incompletely so (i.e.,
they are not). The Absolute, the Infinite, the Eternal—to give it a
few of its traditional names—*emerges* (though incompletely so) in
and as beings. The Eternal "becomes" or emerges; and this process
is Becoming, or Emergence, or the World.

It is possible to think Emergence—that is, absolute Being
emerging in and as beings—*as if* it were "independent," as if *it*
were *not* precisely the Absolute emerging. And this Emergence or
Presencing-process of beings is what phenomenological ontology—
the third moment of phenomenology—puts at issue. This is clear
enough in Heidegger, Merleau-Ponty, and Dufrenne.

But does traditional absolute Being come to any recognition in
phenomenology? Indeed it does, in two major thinkers. The first is
Heidegger himself: the *Alētheia*-process happens in and out of a
prior *Lēthē*. This *Lēthē* is precisely the Hidden whose self-disclosure
is the Disclosure-process that phenomenology reaches in its third
moment.[5] The second is Levinas: the Infinite, or the Good, is beyond or transcendent to Being in the sense of Emergence. This
Emergence may be credited with such finality, however, that it
would appear as the Totality that allows nothing exterior to itself.
But in the countenance of the other person *(l'autrui)*, the phenome-

nologist must recognize the Exteriority of this Totality.[6] The difficulty of these philosophers matches their originality. In any case, the Being-process or Presencing that phenomenology reaches through the duality of subjectivity and objectivity is itself the "trace" of its "otherwise," the infinite Being of traditional philosophy.

From the beginning, philosophers have identified the traditional Infinity with the God of religion. That is one possible way to bring religious experience to philosophic judgment. The core of this assimilation is the "proofs for the existence of God." They all affirm infinite Being under one title or another, and then affirm that "this is what we call God." The conclusion from these premises is that "God exists." But how does "what we call God" arise in the first place? What in experience could be called God? And why should this be identified with the Being of philosophic reflection?[7] In order to affirm—or even to not affirm—the identity, traditional philosophy must accept as *given* something to be called God. But it is precisely this givenness that phenomenology would explore. *It* would investigate the prior experience that delivers the "God" to traditional philosophy. Phenomenology does not seek to "prove" that anything "exists," but inquires into that which presents itself for consciousness to process in the manner that it presents itself. This presence-for is not, of course, the whole of Beingizing. But the putative religious presence-for would come to pass only *within* Presencing. What makes its appearance for man that he should have identified it with absolute Being? What appears in Presencing that we would name it uniquely "God"? Only by close attention to actual experience does phenomenology proceed. It attends to the "appearance" of God.

Any philosophic movement that would be more than mere evidence of its era must find a way to illuminate, among other things, the phenomenon of religion. From the early 1920s on, phenomenology has done this in an original way.[8] Since its establishment in North America, the excellence of its work in the philosophy of religion cannot be gainsaid. Aside from the translations and shorter works of Paul Ricoeur, the major studies to appear in English have been: *The Other Dimension* (1972) by Louis Dupré, *Ecclesial Man* (1975) by Edward Farley, and *God, Guilt, and Death* (1984) by Merold Westphal. These works do not engage in vain speculation; they philosophize about the real religion of real persons.

Beyond the personal experience of the philosopher, the science of religions and theology provide the data that the phenomenologist interrogates. If one were to read Gerardus van der Leeuw's *Phänom-*

enologie der Religion [Religion in Essence and Manifestation], a scientific work, he would find in parts 1–3 a scientific phenomenology that is very close to a philosophic phenomenology (especially in its first moment).[9] Likewise, if one were to read David Tracy's *Blessed Rage for Order*, a theological work, he would find in chapters 5–8 a "theological phenomenology" that is very close to philosophical phenomenology (especially its second moment).[10] Hence the question arises as to the relation among scientific, philosophic, and theological reflection.

The science of religion *(Religionswissenschaft)*, or religious studies, or the comparative history of religions, is one of those new integrative sciences which articulate one particular reality from several different standpoints in contrast to the classical critical sciences (whether formal like mathematics, natural like physics, or human like psychology), which each articulate one aspect of reality as a whole. The scientific study of religion integrates geography, archaeology, historiography, sociology, ethnology, culturology, psychology, and philology. It integrates these into a science of religion. What, then, is the place or role of "phenomenology" in the comparative history of religions?

> All that phenomenology of religion intends to understand is the essence of the religious phenomenon, taken in the empirical sense of the invariable structure of a phenomenon that underlies every religious fact.[11]

It articulates the structural wholes, the ideal-types, in religious experience. It articulates the "empirical eidos" of the religious subject or soul and the religious object or other. Hence, while historiography, psychology, and so on, study the phenomenon in its various aspects, the scientific phenomenology of religion is what, in the science, preserves the distinctiveness of its proper object and thus does not allow the phenomenon to be reduced to an epiphenomenon. It focuses on the *identity* of the phenomenon that shows itself in its various aspects.[12]

However, a critical reflection on the science of religion will show its limitations. This science finds its limits in the issues of compactness, corruption, and illusion.

First, the issue of compactness. All sciences—refining and thus extending prescientific comprehension—posit in advance what is to count as data for them. But even when this project gets enough specificity to allow research (and thus the prospective role of science begins to dominate), still the sciences, in their explicative role, must accept as data whatever prescientific comprehension provides. If, for instance, a certain ritual counts prescientifically as "religious," then the science of religion must accept it as such.

But in the data that science initially gathers, "the religious" is largely *compact* with the social, the political, the economic, and so on. Not until recent Western experience has "the religious" been differentiated to some extent from the other dimensions of experience. (Indeed, this is what has made possible a science of religion.) How far the differentiation will continue is unknowable. In any case, for most of humankind in most of its history, the religious has been compact with the other dimensions of experience. Were the builders of Stonehenge religious functionaries (priests) or astronomers (scientists)? They were both—*compactly*.[13] Is Hinduism a philosophy or a religion or a social system? It is all of them—*compactly*.[14] The entanglement—or better, the compactness—of properly religious "ideas" with other ones is part of the initial data for the science of religion; their specification may never be complete.[15] Religious myths (i.e., symbolic stories) are, through most of history, compact with the social myths ("ideologies" or "representations") by which a people identifies itself.[16] They are compact also with the psychological myths by which we mediate to ourselves the normally unconscious dynamics of our own selves.[17] They are likewise compact with the philosophical myths by which we recognize the coexistence of what is conceptually irreconcilable (as the myth of the social contract reconciles individual and society in Rousseau, or the Phoenician myth reconciles the equality of unique, i.e., nonequal, persons in Plato).[18]

Because science must accept as religious whatever prescientific consciousness brings to it as religious, it has no way to answer a religious critic who protests its inclusions. On the question of compactness, science in itself has no resources to make a decision. To break up the compact phenomena by a simple decision is arbitrary. Prescientific judgment needs refinement by science, but science in turn has only the data that prescientific comprehension provides to it: and *that* includes compact phenomena. Science *could* make a decision only by recourse to a criterion of inclusion that is beyond science to establish. Only another discipline could justify without arbitrariness a criterion of inclusion. Only another discipline can respond to the question of what is to count as specifically or *truly* religious. The question of truth arises.

Secondly, the issue of corruption. The science of religion cannot control for corruption. It cannot quite discern the difference between the genuinely religious and the corruptly religious—

especially if corruption be, as is likely, universal. Hence the eidos of religion and its proper countereidos cannot be entirely separated by science. It must, again, accept as religious whatever prescientific comprehension provides to it. Any judgment of corruption would be arbitrary. Science *could* control for corruption only by recourse to a criterion of genuineness that is beyond science to establish. Only another discipline could justify without arbitrariness a criterion of genuineness. Only another discipline can respond to the question of what is to count as genuinely or *truly* religious. The question of truth arises.

Thirdly, the issue of illusion. The science of religion cannot decide whether the correlative "other" of human religiousness is "really there." It may well be—as the antireligious critic claims—that the divine is only a symbol of social structures, or a projection for psychic need-fulfillment, and so on. Science can proceed only in the subjunctive mood—*as if* this "other" were objective. It must accept whatever prescientific comprehension provides to it and ignore the issue of illusion. Science could decide whether the religious "other" were "really there" only by recourse to a criterion of objectivity that is beyond science to establish. Only another discipline could justify without arbitrariness a criterion of objectivity. Only another discipline can respond to the question as to whether the religious "other" is really or *truly* there. The question of truth arises.

In summary, then, scientific investigation cannot decide on the issues of compactness, corruption, and illusion. It cannot resolve the questions of specificity, genuineness, and objectivity. That work belongs to another discipline.

This other discipline is philosophy. Science articulates the "empirical eidos" of religion, while philosophy exhibits its "transcendental eidos." The difference may be put in another way: for science the *essential* is only the *general*, but for philosophy it is the *necessary*. Both begin, of course, in quotidian comprehension: they have nowhere *else* to begin.[19] Both try to find the essence of the data—in this case, religious phenomena.

Both examine the facts. But the experience of religious factuality is already the experience of the religious *Wesen* or eidos (essence, Being-way). Any fact is an instance of what can in principle appear as other instances; the eidos is not private or arbitrary but is the norm of the experience, making it an experience *of* this or that. This "what" of a phenomenon is not susceptible of "proof"; it is rather the object of an immediate grasp or "sight" *(Wesenschau)* through the fact. The essence appears in and as the fact; they are in fact inseparable.[20] Although immediate, the comprehension of the eidos is not at first self-transparent and articulate.

It is science, however inchoate, that gathers the facts and tries to become the self-transparent and articulate comprehension of this eidos. It does so by means of induction—understood as the logic of similarity (analogy), the logic of typicality (generalization), and the logic of regularity (statistics a posteriori, and probability-calculation a priori). But the science of religion cannot address the question of truth in the three senses discussed above.

This issues of specificity, genuineness, and objectivity in regard to religion may be treated only if our comprehension of the religious eidos be purified in such a way that its *necessary*, and not simply its *general*, structure become evident. Philosophy—and in particular phenomenology in its first moment—would articulate the transcendental eidos through imaginative *variation*; science may not leave the *data*. Because the data include historical compactness, probable corruption, and possible illusion, science cannot address the questions of truth. Philosophy would consider them on the basis of a determination of the necessary structure of religion, its transcendental eidos. Here "the necessary" does not have the traditional metaphysical sense of that which cannot not be or cannot be otherwise—whose opposite is the contingent, whose contrary is the possible, and whose contradictory is the impossible. Rather it means that-without-which or the exclusion of impossibility—whose opposite is the factual, whose contrary is the possible, and whose contradictory is the otherwise. Only if the *necessary structure* of the religious be known could its truthfulness become an issue. Beyond scientific investigation, it is philosophy that exhibits this eidos of the religious within the mass of facts.[21]

Of course, in as much as the transcendental eidos appears nowhere else but in the facts, philosophy must appropriate the research of science in order to be responsible. Indeed, philosophy benefits greatly by attention to the empirical eidos of the religious as science articulates it.

But what about theology? Could *it* justify the principles of specificity, of genuineness, and of objectivity that science, while perhaps presupposing, cannot justify? Theology is the intrareligious discipline.[22] As the reflective work of a particular religious tradition, it gives conceptual elaboration to religious experience and its constituent symbolizations (rites and stories). Theology is the self-comprehension of a particular manner of religiousness: faith seeking understanding.

As such, it could elaborate *universal* principles of specification, of genuineness, and of objectivity only by accident—that is, only in the course of a work with a different aim. What, from all the data, to include in "religion"? How, for religious acts and institutions in general, to filter out corruption (and indeed to account for it)? Is there, in all religions, a referent of religious acts that is more than illusory idealization? A theology is already a *commitment* to an answer to these questions—a commitment to one possible way to be religious and to that extent not requisitely universal in the face of these questions.

To put the matter otherwise: the reflections *of* a religious confession upon itself are not the same as the reflections *about* the religious in general or in its necessary structures. As faith seeking *self*-comprehension, theology can raise *universal* questions only by accident; if at all, theology would address the issues of compactness, corruption, and illusion only secondarily to its purpose. Likewise only instrumentally does it address the radical question of truth in respect of religions: How to understand the truth that is *proper* to any religion as religion? And what is its *criterion?* Religious reflection stays within the religious commitment to which it is in service.

Theology remains the self-knowledge of faith for the sake of faith. It comprises a systematic (or dogmatic) and a practical (or pastoral) endeavor, each with a methodological (or dialectical) moment. However, beyond its systematic and practical endeavors, theology may become another endeavor with three moments: an analysis of the religious dimension of common experience, an interpretation in a theistic way of the horizon of this experience, and a confessional interpretation of the theos so discerned. In that case, it is fundamental or foundational theology.[23] The aim of this foundational endeavor, in its three moments, is to argue the merits of one particular way to be religious. It is a religious commitment giving itself public justification and even persuasiveness: apologetics. However, foundational theology may be *abstracted* from the theological enterprise as a whole; and then this theology may be abstracted from its *confessional* moment. In that case, what remains would be an analysis of the structures of human existence and how they are already religious before determination into any particular way-of-religiousness (or confession). This abstraction would need only a change in key, as it were, to make it into another discipline—a discipline autonomous in status and universal in scope.

This other discipline is philosophy. In exhibiting the transcendental eidos of religion, it would establish a criterion for inclusion of data and thus address the question of truth; it would establish a criterion for genuineness and thus address the question of truth; it would establish a criterion for objectivity and thus address the question of truth. Furthermore, it would question after the very sense of "truth" in regard to religion; it would quest after the criterion for this truth. Beyond any scientific project and beyond religious commitment reflecting upon itself, philosophy would address the questions of truth.

But philosophy must be self-critical. This imports, among other things, that it take the phenomena to be interrogated as themselves, not as if they were something else. A philosophy of politics, for example, would become vain speculation if it were to take political existence not as itself but as (say) mathematical pedagogy. The elementary character of this methodological principle does not make it any the less disregarded in academic Anglophonic philosophy. The task peculiar to philosophy—contrary to academic custom—is *not* to treat religiousness as if it were a set of propositions and then to inquire whether these are "true." The task is *not* "the critical examination of basic religious beliefs and concepts."[24] Such an enterprise has little to do with the phenomenon at issue: the actual religions of actual human beings. A philosophy that conceives its task in the customary Anglophonic way would try to decide abstractly upon the "truth" of propositions about the nature of God, the existence of God, the problem of evil, immortality, mysticism, the rationality of beliefs that go beyond evidence, and the value of theism as a worldview in competition with others.[25] But the phenomenon "religion" is not a matter of propositions abstracted from life. It is a matter of concrete experience and its concomitant symbolization. The doctrinalization that is sometimes worked upon the symbols is secondary; doctrines are concrete experience become abstract, religiousness become proposition. *At best*, the ordinary approach today takes religion as if it were a matter of doctrines and, at worst, as if they were subject to "scientific verification." Thereby it ignores the way-to-be, the eidos, of religion.

In contrast to it stands phenomenological philosophy. *Its* questions on religion concern the concrete phenomenon. Since when does something about human experience get summarized as "religion"? Is this a critical concept? What is it about human existence that allows something like "religion" to arise in the first place? To what existential problem is religion a response? What has religion to do with any postvital existence? What is the meaning of "God" in religion? How does the religious God enter into philosophy? How does the religious God remain outside philosophy? What is the aim of the "proofs for the existence of God"? What do those who argue over the proofs reveal about themselves? Why would anybody profess "atheism"? Is "atheism" even a critical concept? What is it about human experience that allows something like atheism to arise in the first place? How are religions and moralities related? Is there any "religious morality"? What is truth in religion? What is truth *for* religion? Is there any truth *of* religion?

But instead of arguing whether this or that religious concretion be true, or whether some religious proposition be true, phenomenology would inquire into what it is that constitutes "truth" in the first place; it would inquire into what the foundational and derivative senses of "truth" may be, and into what the conditions may be that are the possibility for "truth" to eventuate in the first place. Phenomenology has reflected extensively on "truth"—as *alētheia*, manifestness.[26] Given "truth" understood phenomenologically, philosophy may pose questions like the following. *How* are religions true—that is, what sort of manifestness belongs to them? Are there levels of truth in religion and, if so, what are they? In general, how to conceive the truth *proper* to religion? Can one religion be more true than another? How about a criterion for religious truth? How do the good and the true relate with respect to religion, and does one have priority over the other? How does religious truth relate to other modes of truth? How about truth, meaning or sense, and referent? How about truth, symbol, and myth? What is the status of language in the truth proper to religion? What is the status of traditional concerns, for example, the arguments over "the existence of God"?

A phenomenological philosophy of religion, while primary addressing itself to the phenomenon "religion," would secondarily comprise a critical confrontation with other philosophical approaches. It would find in the phenomenon the reasons for the other philosophies of religion.

However, not everything can be said at once. The present volume gathers essays by most of the Anglophonic phenomenologists who have recently interrogated the phenomenon of religion. The aim in this collection was, first, to find whether there would be any consensus on the phenomenological notion of truth and, specifically, the truth proper to religion. That consensus has largely been established, as the essays evince. The aim was, secondly, to allow a creative elaboration of the issues of truth and religion across the whole spectrum of phenomenology. This volume offers elaboration not of all the issues but of the most important of them; and, further, it offers ways in which to raise new issues (e.g., the nontruth and the untruth proper to religion).

Because progress in philosophy is *ressourcement* rather than advancement, it would be inappropriate to summarize the research of these essays as if they now "establish" some "result." However, what may be useful to the reader is an indication of their "place" in the phenomenological enterprise. Historically, phenomenology has developed in various directions.[27]

The first group of essays moves mainly in the existential direction of phenomenology:

(1) Louis Dupré, "Truth in Religion and Truth of Religion"

(2) Philip Clayton, "Religious Truth and Scientific Truth"

(3) Edward Farley, "Truth and the Wisdom of Enduring"

(4) Daniel Guerrière, "The Truth, the Nontruth, and the Untruth Proper to Religion"

These are put first because this direction of phenomenology is the most accessible to the noninitiate. As Professor Dupré says at the beginning, traditional religious conceptions of truth stress its ontological and moral senses rather than its epistemic sense. So does phenomenology, which then develops the epistemic sense out of the more fundamental sense of truth. Dupré places the phenomenological among the various theories of truth. Professor Clayton compares the truth proper to natural science and that proper to religion; he finds parallels that aid in the articulation of the differences. Professor Farley places the phenomenological question of the truth proper to religion in its nonphilosophical context today and in the philosophical discussions of truth. Professor Guerrière makes explicit the experience in which religious truth originates and the criterion of truth; he then explores the threefold nontruth and the threefold untruth (or falsity) proper to religion. What is common to all these essays is the basic phenomenological notion of truth as *alētheia* (disclosure, manifestation, unconcealedness, manifestness, "revelation") and, further, the notion of religious truth as basically one kind of "manifestness" correlative to a particular human intentionality.

The second group of essays goes mainly in the hermeneutic direction of phenomenology:

(5) Merold Westphal, "Phenomenologies and Religious Truth"

(6) Richard Kearney, "Ideology and Religion: A Hermeneutic Conflict"

(7) John D. Caputo, "Radical Hermeneutics and Religious Truth"

Professor Westphal introduces this direction to the reader and shows how the hermeneutics of finitude and of suspicion may illuminate the truth proper to religion. Professor Kearney recounts how Paul Ricoeur supplements a hermeneutics of suspicion with a hermeneutics of affirmation; he shows how this hermeneutics may allow ideology—always a possibility for religion—to pass from prejudice to critical self-reappraisal. Professor Caputo offers a case study of the sort of upheaval that hermeneutics has effected in our understanding of religious truth in particular; he seeks, through an appropriation of the work of Emmanuel Levinas, to show the radical implications of hermeneutics. What is common to these essays is the insistence that all comprehension, indeed all experience, is already interpretation—that there is no such thing as truth without interpretation.

The next essay conducts an exploration in the "ethical" direction of phenomenology—that is, within the ambit of the work of Emmanuel Levinas:

(8) Richard A. Cohen, "The Face of Truth in Rosenzweig, Levinas, and Jewish Mysticism"

Professor Cohen, too, offers a case study in which he shows that all three of his subjects share a conception of truth that is consonant with phenomenology as a whole: truth as "revelation" (of the Infinite in the human face).

The next essay takes the deconstructive direction in phenomenology:

(9) Walter Lowe, "Freud, Husserl, Derrida: An Experiment"

Professor Lowe would take "the Derridean wager" and find whether it allows a "deeper objectivity," indeed a "deeper truth." This article especially will be more difficult for the noninitiate; but if all the articles are read in the order presented here, it should be accessible.

The final two essays move in the transcendental direction of phenomenology:

(10) James G. Hart, "Divine Truth in Husserl and Kant"

(11) Steven W. Laycock, "God as the Ideal: The All-of-monads and the All-consciousness"

These are put last because for the nonexpert in phenomenology they would be the easiest to misread. Both essays extend the previous work of each author.[28] The reader may well place them within the context suggested by this Introduction; they both take Husserlian thought as belonging to the third moment of phenomenology. In other words, although Husserl and those who move in his direction often appear to be subjective idealists, they actually think the Whole, the prior unity of subjectivity and objectivity, which from the subjective side may be called transcendental Subjectivity and from the objective side the World.[29] If that be understood, then these two investigations will not become abstract speculations.

What all the essays have in common is their hermeneutical situation: we are all late twentieth-century Western thinkers who, though perhaps knowing other traditions, have no place else to begin but in our own.

The editor has stipulated that the pronominal set *he/his/him* has its usual generic, inclusive sense unless made masculine by contrast with the feminine set *she/her/her*. One would use the feminine set and therefore make a contrast only if he had some reason to call attention to gender. But in philosophical reflection gender is hardly ever relevant.

The editor would suggest that the nonexpert in phenomenology read the essays in the order presented.

Part I

———

Existential

1

Truth in Religion and Truth of Religion

Louis Dupré

If one thing distinguishes traditional religious conceptions of truth from modern philosophical ones, it is the absence, or secondary role, of epistemological concerns. Despite their substantial differences, all religious traditions agree in stressing the ontological and moral qualities of truth over the purely cognitive ones. Truth refers to *being*, rather than to knowledge. In Sanskrit, the mother tongue of our Indo-European languages, *truth* is *satya* while *being* is *sat*. Gandhi based his life-long quest for what he called truth upon this identity. In 1932 he formulated it:

> Nothing is or exists in reality except Truth. That is why *Sat* or Truth is perhaps the more important name of God. In fact, it is more correct to say that "Truth is God" than to say that "God is Truth."[1]

The proper attitude with respect to this ontological truth consists in the first place in devotion and fidelity: the path of truth is the path of devotion *(bhakti)*—the only path that leads to God.[2] In a religious vision of this nature lies, I believe, the origin of the so-called correspondence theory, which later became so exclusively cognitive: the consistency between *what is* and one's conduct. Not to be "true" to one's self means, in fact, to descend to a lesser mode of being. Only when we are fully connected with Being shall we be able to *know*. The relation here is exactly the opposite of modern thought, which starts from the primacy of consciousness.[3]

The nature of religious truth consists in the first place in an *ontological* state whereby the relation to God defines the definitive link with Being. That relation also secures access to the source of ultimate meaning. All "true" *knowing* depends on a *being* in the

19

truth. But the transcendent pole of the relation establishes human *awareness* of the relation as well as the relation itself. Truth in religion implies more than merely admitting that an ontological bond with God exists. The recognition of that bond must itself be given. Truth, then, consists in the right relation to the ultimately real and only that transcendent reality can enlighten us concerning the nature and even the existence of that relation.

This principle summarizes the fundamental belief about truth not only in the Judeo-Christian tradition but, if I am not mistaken, in all others as well. It marks the constant factor in religious truth. Our own tradition stands out by its increasing emphasis upon the second aspect—the need for a divine disclosure, a revelation. The theology of the Word begins in the first chapter of *Genesis* and continues right through the New Testament, the Greek and Latin Fathers, medieval Scholasticism and mysticism, reformed theology and the Catholic *magisterium*. This tradition announced from the beginning that *God speaks*—that the Absolute is self-expressive. God speaks essentially and by his very nature. Christianity took this doctrine to its farthest extreme when it proclaimed that God had become Word. In doing so it also declared the reality grounded in God's Being to be self-expressive. Being as such now becomes self-illuminating, self-manifesting, self-enclosed, not opaque.

In the following pages I shall consider how this religious truth, that is, truth as conceived *within* religion for the explicit purpose of defining the Judeo-Christian revelation, at first developed into the basis and principal analogate of *all* truth. Yet rational reflection gradually emancipated this truth *in* religion from its origin until, in the Modern Age, an independent theory of truth, grounded in the human subject rather than in a divinely established reality, turned into a severe critic *of* religion. In the second part of this paper I shall consider both the legitimacy and the limits of a confrontation of religion with a notion of truth that is no longer based upon the transcendent foundation of religion.

Truth in Religion

There exists no single religious view of truth, not even within one religious tradition. Religious typology, always hazardous, is particularly risky in defining a concept as comprehensive, and hence as elusive, as truth. Chances of succeeding in such a task would require an exceptional insight into all major faiths as well as a constant concern not to impose Western categories upon unfamiliar modes of thinking. This essay will be restricted to some facets of a philosophical reflection, stretching from the Middle Ages to the modern epoch, on a notion of truth of which the New Testament (on a solid biblical foundation) had defined the basic principles. In an appendix I have outlined what I consider to be the most significant traits of the New Testament conception of truth as it emerged out of the Hebrew tradition.

Considering the radicalness with which the New Testament has transformed a terminology borrowed from Hellenistic culture, one may be surprised how early Christian thinkers came to accept the Greek gnosis. Already in the third century, theologians in Alexandria (Clement, Origen) viewed faith itself as the fulfillment of philosophical insight. Yet the new gnosis is not a philosophical rationalization of faith, nor an extension of philosophical understanding: it consists in the self-understanding *of* faith. The gnostic Christian is one who fully *appropriates* what he believes, not one who, besides being Christian, has been educated in philosophy. In insisting that the act of faith contains its own understanding, the Alexandrian and Cappadocian Fathers clearly ruled out the kind of opposition between faith and understanding that lies at the basis of much modern thought.[4]

Initially the Latin West had misgivings not only about mixing worldly wisdom with revealed truth, but even about accepting faith itself as a supreme mode of understanding. Tertullian bluntly opposed one to the other *(credo quia absurdum)*. The great turning point came with Augustine—and not without reservations. He also, after his Neoplatonic period, considered philosophical learning conducive to *impia superbia*.[5] Nonetheless, he judged the search for truth to be *intrinsically* good and salvific. Had Cicero's *Hortentius* not spurred him on toward the quest for eternal wisdom *(Conf. II, 4)*? Though Augustine excepts certain *subjects* from that virtuous search, branding the pursuit of them mere *curiositas*,[6] he attributed a divine, revelatory quality to truth *as such*.

Yet Augustine's major innovation in the conception of religious truth consists in what we may call its interior quality. Whereas originally the understanding had come with the faithful acceptance of the gospel, now God teaches each individual soul, though always *in consonance with* the objective testimony of Scripture and ecclesiastical tradition. The divine light that informs the mind, or the interior voice that addresses it, enlightens the believer with regard to not only Scripture but profane learning as well.[7] The very source and condition of truth becomes thereby sacred for Augustine. With the idea of the interior Master, Augustine achieves a new synthesis between faith and understanding. What for the early Fathers had consisted essentially in a process of explication, now becomes an illumination *simultaneously* derived from different sources (objective and subjective). By subjecting all understanding to a divine illumination that only faith properly identifies, Augustine tightened the original unity of faith and understanding.

With the immanence of divine truth comes the mandate to explore it interiorly, but also the risk of reducing a transcendent message to an acquisition of reason. Augustine always remained aware of both the need for and the limits of a rational exploration. With him the emphasis remains on the *intellectus quaerens fidem*, and faith never ceases to be the ultimately decisive argument. Thus his daring speculations about the Trinity are always accompanied by the spirit of a healthy skepticism about their final success and a cavalier lack of concern concerning their ultimate compatibility.

With Anselm the quest for truth takes a new turn. His "faith seeking understanding," despite its Augustinian tone, moves in a different direction. There is no reason to question his loyalty to St. Augustine, which he explicitly professes in the *Monologium* (preface). Augustine had written: "There are those things that are first believed and afterward understood. Of such a character is that which cannot be understood of divine things except by those who are pure in heart."[8] Anselm echoes: "right order requires that we believe the deep matters of the Christian faith before we presume to discuss them rationally."[9] Yet the very revelation in which we believe urges us to reflect on its implications and to draw its conclusions. One such conclusion consists in the *necessary* character of God's Being. This in turn influences God's relation to His creation (another revealed datum). On the basis of these *data* Anselm develops a logic of immanence and transcendence that encompasses even the historical event of Christ's incarnation. Inasmuch as God is necessary in His very Being, divine redemptive activity must also result from an inner necessity.

Yet, in deducing the inner necessity of God's dealings with the historical contingencies resulting from human decisions, Anselm goes in fact well beyond the limits of what a consistent explication of the data of revelation allows. Thus he reduces God's choice after the fall to the following: "To deal rightly with sin without satisfaction is to punish it. Not to punish it is to remit it irregularly." In attributing the need for satisfaction to divine nature itself, Anselm makes such fundamental assumptions concerning divine freedom— neither stated nor implied in the revealed text—that his theory can no longer be called an explication of that text. Indeed, it contains the seeds of all future religious rationalism. It certainly surpasses what revelation assisted by reason enables one to say about God's disposition to the world. An Aristotelian logic of propositions has manifestly impelled Anselm to give an *exhaustive* account of the relations between God and creation. Thus a project proclaimed to be based on the *data revelationis,* in an unambiguous profession of faith, changed its nature in the course of its execution.[10]

Still, Anselm's rationality remains throughout a *devout* rationality, illumined by a monastic vision, that never consciously deviates from the principle stated in the *Proslogion: Quaero credere ut intelligam, non autem intelligere ut credam.* Faith remains the basic presupposition of all genuine understanding. Yet a trend was set and the rationalism that emerged with Abelard was far less pious. No theological knowledge of Scripture was needed, he thought, to investigate the truth of religious mysteries. Logic alone sufficed to understand even such recondite dogmas as the eucharist or the Trinity. The reception of Aristotle's systematic works made the study of theology itself something it had never been before— namely, a *science* in the Aristotelian sense. With it came the epistemic distinction between two orders of knowledge: a philosophical and a theological.

In the very beginning of the *Summa Theologiae* (article 2), Thomas Aquinas raises the question: Is sacred doctrine a science? Of particular interest is the purely Aristotelian definition by which he supports his affirmative answer—namely, that "science" progresses from self-evident principles. Principles "known by the natural light of reason" appear on an even footing with principles "established by the light of a higher science, namely, the science of God and the blessed." To us such an equation may appear surprising, for it proves by means of what has to be proven. Need not the so-called science of God and the blessed itself be first established as a science? But Thomas takes the epistemic solidity of the manner in which we gather the "first principles" of sacred doctrine for granted. A little later he fully admits that they are *articuli fidei* (articles of faith), hence direct objects of revelation. "As other sciences do not argue in proof of their principles but argue from their principles to demonstrate other truths in these sciences, so this doctrine does not argue in proof of its principles, which are the articles of faith, but from them it goes on to prove something else."[11] The higher "science" then turns out to be revelation—an interpretation of his text that Aristotle would have found surprising. Because Thomas is concerned only about the formal procedure from principles (however certified) to conclusions, he unhesitatingly transplants the method from one to the other.

Such a scientific definition of religious truth differed too obviously from the one advocated by Augustine and the entire Greek Christian tradition that preceded him to remain unchallenged. The Paris condemnations of 1277 as well as the nominalist development in theology profoundly shook it. Still in the end, Thomas's "scientific" presentation of religious truth may not be as far removed from the Augustinian tradition as it seems. In themselves the articles of faith are only "external" principles: to be convincing at all they must be accompanied by an "interior light that induces the mind to assent." The principles themselves function like sense data, which do not become intelligible until the mind illumines them. The light of faith provides the formal element that converts the objective data of faith into religious truth.[12] For Aquinas as for Augustine what ultimately determines the act of faith is God's own internal witness. The truth about God can come only from God, and in faith human beings respond to God's self-witness. Aquinas moves within a well-established tradition initiated by the fourth Gospel: religious truth derives its constitutive evidence from a divine illumination. The external object of belief (the "principles") reveals itself as *true* only within the act of faith.

Nominalism soon undid the synthesis of faith and reason that Thomas and his followers had achieved. Henceforth religious truth, though still possessing the intrinsic evidence of experience, could no longer count on the concomitant support of reason. Henceforth, there would be two separate conceptions of truth. The one of reason eventually found its basis in the remarkable harmony between mind and nature; the one of theology came to rest exclusively on an authority beyond nature. The different attitude of what henceforth was to be called philosophy appears in its attempts to establish the *truth of religion*, clearly distinct from faith's own truth. These attempts gave birth to an intellectual exercise that had never existed before: arguments for the existence of God based upon reason alone. Of course, Anselm and already Augustine had construed some rational formulation of the mind's ascent to God. But medieval writers had never intended to do so independently of the religious sources (including revelation) that had provided the idea of God in the first place. They wanted to show that this idea, far from conflicting with reason, fully agreed with that of an infinite Being that they considered to be necessary for supporting the finite.

In the Modern Age the purport of the arguments was to *prove*, independently of any intrinsically religious evidence, the existence of a particular being called God. The "truth" of religion must hereby emerge from a process of reasoning from the finite to the necessity of an infinite principle. But even if the proof succeeds in establishing the independent existence of such a principle *beyond* the world—a most difficult task indeed—it still has to establish that this principle coincides with the God of religion. Aquinas, Maimonides, or Avicenna did not face such excessive challenges, for they started by accepting the God of faith, and then proceeded to show that to do so is not irrational. Once the finite's need of the infinite was established, they did not hesitate to identify this infinite with their religious idea of God: from theological reflection they knew already that, among other things, the God in whom they believed must be infinite and necessary. This procedure often leads to careless thinking. Because the authors knew the outcome beforehand, they were anxious to reach the goal and have it all over with. But in principle the method is unobjectionable.

In contrast with this method, arguments that by a process of sheer reasoning pretend to arrive at full-fledged religious conclusions assume the phenomenal world capable of yielding positive information about the nature of what transcends it. To conclude to a transcendent ground, or to postulate such a ground in order to make the real intelligible, is not yet to attain the idea of God as religious faiths have traditionally conceived it. Is the absolutely intelligible—which many philosophers require to found the intelligibility of the real—the perfect Being intended by the religious act? Karl Jaspers's philosophy of transcendence is there to prove that one does not necessarily imply the other: the philosophical idea of transcendence, though it invites further investigation, leads by itself to no specific religious content. Only from a religious confrontation with the divine in "revelation" and "grace" can transcendence acquire such a content. An autonomous study of Being or consciousness can state the problem; it cannot provide the answer.

In the arguments for the existence of God, modern thought reveals most clearly its attitude with respect to religious truth. It assumes that there is no specifically *religious* truth. Religion has been allotted a specific field of consciousness ruled by methods of its own, but the final judgment on truth has been withdrawn from its jurisdiction and removed to the general domain of epistemic criteriology. Revelation may "add" to what we "know" by natural means, but it remains subject to the general rules of truth and credibility. These rules did not originate in religion's native land: they are a creation of the modern mind, a mind unwilling to have the criteria of truth established by any source outside itself. Until the beginning of this century theology mainly followed the axioms of this rationalist epistemology *either* by reducing religion to a moral attitude or a mode of experiencing (as in liberal Protestantism), thus abandoning truth claims altogether, *or* by formulating its doctrine in a set of propositions that, if not strictly provable, were, on the sole ground of their high probability, thought to impose themselves upon the reasonable mind (as in Catholic Scholasticism). *Truth*, if still granted to religious affirmations, no longer springs from within faith but is extrinsically conveyed to faith. In the traditional view, religious truth originated in some sort of participation in the revealed mystery of divine Being. The human subject, now the source of truth, was then no more than a receptacle endowed with a divine potential for apprehending the truth as divinely revealed.

With this separation from faith, and perhaps as a cause of it, goes a gradual separation of experience *from* faith. In early centuries, faith, far from being opposed to experiential evidence, was never considered to be complete without it; but later it came to occupy an order of its own with a minimum of experiential content. Experience was more and more reserved to a small segment of believers. Mystical schools—sixteenth-century Spanish Carmelites, seventeenth-century German Pietists and French devout humanists, eighteenth-century Quietists, and nineteenth-century Russian spiritualists—continued to uphold their own form of religious truth. Quite typically, these movements became more and more marginal with respect to official theological thought.

By the middle of the eighteenth century the rationalist interpretation of religious truth began to show its serious deficiencies. They were twofold. First, it was becoming increasingly clear that the synthesis itself was faulty. Religion proved unable to "add" to the self-contained truth that originated in the subject. Truth conceived as a coherent epistemic structuring of the real by an autonomous subject is not receptive to additions derived from a different source. The existence of a necessary Being might still qualify as a necessary axiom in the mind's intellectual and moral ordering process, but a historical revelation proved to be an indigestible item. Lessing's objections against historical facts establishing necessary truths are well known. But from a religious point of view it became equally obvious that faith had nothing to gain by adopting an idea of truth so foreign to its origins and so empoverishing in its effects. Early in the nineteenth century a reaction carried by the general revolt against rationalism set in.

The leading figure in this theological *reconquista* was undoubtedly Friedrich Schleiermacher. One should not dismiss his attempt to establish religion outside the battle zone of what his Kantian contemporaries called truth as an abandonment of truth-claims. His efforts to rescue the proper identity of religion aimed at nothing less than at regaining a firm foothold for a truth proper to religion. The term "feeling," so loosely used in Schleiermacher's early work, signals in fact an attempt to escape from the kind of scientific objectivity or philosophical rationality to which truth-claims had come to be reserved. What Schleiermacher really pursued was a more fundamental truth that anteceded the subject-object split. He perceptively realized that once this dualism (with the constitutive primacy of the subject) is accepted as decisive, chances for recognizing the proper identity of religious truth have vanished. The entire realm of transcendence comes then to be drawn into the immanent circle of self-constituted truth. Whether the term *feeling* was appropriate for defining the new ground of truth may be questioned. But to Schleiermacher goes the lasting credit of having broken with the rationalist tradition.

A number of Catholic theologians, especially those affiliated with the Tübingen school, likewise moved away from a rationalist conception of religious truth toward one in which the *experience* of faith played a more important part. That experience, the *experimentum fidei* (2 Cor. 13:3–9), far from being an exceptional mystical privilege, belonged to the very core of faith itself. Indeed, until the late Middle Ages faith without experience would have been inconceivable. Because the inhabitation of God's Spirit inevitably manifests itself in the attitude and consciousness of the believer, all faith results in experience.

The return to experience begun by the theologians of the romantic epoch holds a particular significance for the believers who share the subjective attitude of modern culture. To them, the *experience of faith* provides the decisive test of its truth. But while formerly that experience was linked to the message itself, now the connection between experience and the objective message of revelation has become much looser. What Augustine posited as a *distinction* between the subjective enlightenment by the inner Master and the objective message now tends to become a *separation* between content and experience. More precisely, the experience justifies the content only in a general way while omitting substantial aspects of it from consideration, if not explicitly rejecting them. Clearly such a reliance upon an experience that is no longer solidly attached to the objective message may endanger the specific *truth* of religion. Has it not replaced a transcendental message by an immanent experience? All here depends on the manner in which experience relates to content. If the two become fully separated with only a vague moral or sentimental sympathy to connect them, the specific quality of religious truth is lost. But such a full separation does not usually occur. The act of faith in intending its transcendent object is experienced as a *being-grasped* by a higher reality rather than as an autonomous *grasping* or a self-enclosed feeling. Thus an intrinsically religious truth has generally succeeded in maintaining its transcendent character, even while adopting a specifically modern (that is, subjective) form.

Truth of Religion

If religion by its own account provides the basis of its own truth, can we move to a basis outside the domain of faith and yet hope fairly to evaluate that truth? Can faith accept any judgment critical of its truth that originates in an autonomous philosophy independently of the principles of faith itself? Can any statement be made about the truth *of* religion that does not coincide with the truth *in* religion itself without undoing or seriously distorting the latter?

This much seems certain: a critical examination that on the basis of pure reason, independently of the religious experience proper, attempts to establish or disestablish "the truth of religion" must indeed result in distortion. Because modern philosophical theories of truth were developed for the purpose of securing a foundation for scientific practice, this axiom may appear to render them unfit for evaluating the specific nature of religious truth. Yet such a conclusion would be premature and, I hope to show, in the end unjustified. The basic *models* of truth used in those theories predate the scientific concerns of the Modern Age. They may, in fact, have grown out of a religious soil. Such was, almost certainly, the case with the disclosure model. But truth as correspondence and truth as coherence were also formulated well before their modern methodic investigation started. Clearly, philosophy has developed these ancient models of truth on the basis of careful (albeit often unduly limited) analyses of the cognitive act. To compare religious claims to those models by no means commits one to the antitheological assumptions that often accompany their appearance in modern philosophy. But neither do we propose to "justify" religious truth in the light of that philosophy. Unless one assumes the basic legitimacy of the religious act on its own merits, attempts at an all-comprehensive justification inevitably fail. Truth, as Spinoza taught, must prove itself: one cannot prove it to be true by another "truth" that presumably stands outside it.

The following argument presupposes the existence of a truth proper to religion. In comparing it with the existing models of truth

I merely intend to investigate the aptitude of these models in clarifying that religious *fact* as well as the particular conditions required for successfully doing so. In a sense, then, it is philosophy—or at least its available apparatus—rather than religion, that is being examined here. To be sure, if the concept of religious truth proved to be radically incompatible with any of the existing models, the critical believer would have serious grounds for questioning the "truth of religion." For truth, in whatever manner envisaged, must, in principle, be able to accommodate all legitimate claims of truth. If recent philosophy has often rejected the legitimacy of religious claims, the *application* of the basic models, rather than the models themselves, may be at fault. If, however, the religious concept of truth were to prove intractably resistant to any *integration* with other concepts of truth (such as the scientific ones) within the existing models, this would create a serious problem in the religious truth-claims themselves. All the more so since these models originated long before any positivist restrictions were attached to them.

Even though religion unfolds its own truth, it is forced to do so within the available categories of general discourse. Revelation itself cannot be rendered intelligible unless it still proves capable of being assumed within the modern pattern of speaking and thinking. However sublime and unique, a message confronts the elementary fact that, in order to be expressed, it must adopt an *existing* language and thereby integrate itself within a *praxis* of discourse.

Western philosophy since its Greek origins has held truth to consist in an *ideal* presence, an objective quality that transcends the subjective experience of certainty. Only since the last century have philosophers begun to question this traditional position. Today certain psychological, sociological, or linguistic theories tend to reduce adherence to a particular epistemic position to unacknowledged factors in the individual or in the group to which the individual belongs. "Truth," in this view, would be attained by deconstructing the obvious surface structure and by gathering information about the building stones presumed to have been used in its construction. Obviously, within such a perspective religion is a priori banned from presenting any truth-claims at all. Since truth as demystification or deconstruction either begs the question of truth altogether or rests upon a more fundamental model to which it merely clears the access, I shall not consider it here.[13]

Correspondence

The correspondence between word and reality appears even in the earliest tradition, if not as the central core of religious truth, at least as one of its essential components. Truth, including religious truth, requires that our words or concepts conform to things as they are in themselves. Philosophy, after it took the critical epistemic turn, found nothing but insoluble problems in such a neat division between a purely "mental" concept and a purely "real" object. Precisely the invincible difficulties inherent in the unproven assumption of a harmony between the mind and the world led to Kant's radical reversal of the correspondence theory.

After his "Copernican revolution" the line that distinguishes the correspondence from the coherence theory becomes hard to draw. Thus Edmund Husserl in his basically Kantian *Logical Investigations* asserts about the relation between ideas and things:

> The connection of things, to which the thought-experiences *(Denkerlebnisse)*—the real or the possible—are intentionally related, and, on the other hand, the connection of truths, in which the unity of things *(die sachliche Einheit)* comes to objective validity as that which it is—*both are given together and cannot be separated* from each other.[14]

The famous "things themselves" *(die Sachen selbst)*, to which Husserl intends to return philosophy, prove then to be as ideal as the relations of consciousness. They constitute the invariable element in the mind's perspective variations. The very notion of intentionality—the relation between the mind and its object—is reinterpreted into one of immanent objectivity: the object *belongs* to the act of consciousness itself. It is constituted not independently of that act, but with and through it, yet with an *immanent* independence of the *experience* of the object. The intuition of truth in the end, then, is the outcome of a process in which we bring the object to givenness. A thing is given when it is *brought to* ideal presence. Clearly, in such an immanent interpretation the distinction between a theory of "correspondence" and one of coherence approaches the vanishing point.

Even without following the Kantian reinterpretation to its idealist extremes, we cannot but regard the appeal to "the facts," which some contemporary critiques of religion continue to make, as patently uncritical. No facts are perceivable without a screen of interpretation that converts data into objects or facts. To perceive a complex of data as a fact always includes seeing it through an interpretation. In the case of religion, which deals with the ultimate structure of the real itself, interpretation plays a particularly significant and inevitably controversial part. It is quite common for two persons confronted with the same state of affairs to see it *as* religious or as nonreligious, and to do so without in the least contradicting each other on the relevant observable data. Both may agree on the *basic* interpretation, but one may feel the need for a further interpretation, which the other rejects or considers unnecessary. On a practical and on a limited theoretical level, believers and unbelievers interpret the world in a manner so similar that they may intimately collaborate with one another on social or scientific projects without ever having to resolve major differences of interpretation. Basic, partial interpretations suffice for practical, scientific work, and even for a general cultural exchange. Nevertheless, the all-comprehensive, religious interpretations shed a different light on all aspects of the real. To those who hold them, they have the deepest impact upon emotional, ethical, and even motivational attitudes.

A philosophical evaluation of the "truth of religion" on the basis of a correspondence theory of truth, then, requires taking into account not only the legitimacy of separate levels of interpretation but, in addition, the possible conflict of an interpretation made on a basic level with those made on other levels. Nevertheless, there are solid reasons for continuing to speak, even in philosophical discourse, of correspondence with respect to religious truth. For truth in religion always presents itself as a *relatedness* to what ultimately *is:* a conversion, both moral and ontological, toward Being as it is in its very roots and origins, contrary to appearance and deception. The possible discrepancy between one and the other, as well as the process required to reach the state of total correspondence, suggests the existence of a separation between the mind and the ultimate reality that religious truth claims to bridge. Moreover, the "truth" thus attained is presented as *revealed*—that is, *given* to the mind from a principle or level of being that surpasses the mind's own reality. Here again the *process* of truth overcomes an initial duality between the mind and the "inner word" of revelation. It is worth noting that *both* these elements belong to the *ideal* realm (the only *locus* of truth since Kant) and hence that the correspondence theory thus applied to religious truth is not the naive-realistic one, but the modern critical one.

Coherence

Today most truth theories, implicitly or explicitly, refer to coherence. This is particularly the case with religious truth. Many, who had become disheartened about the prospect of religious truth filling the demands for empirical verification advanced by positivists and empiricists, saw in the new forms of the coherence theory an escape from their troubles. Linguistic theories, such as that found in Wittgenstein's *Philosophical Investigations*, would legitimate any discourse in its own right, independently of others, provided it *consistently* apply the rules it set itself. Undoubtedly the coherence theory has protected the realm of religious meaning against undue intrusions of other realms. Each particular system, each "significant whole" as Harold Joachim defined it in his classical *The Nature of Truth*, obeys laws of its own that differ from those of other significant wholes.[15] An internal articulation organically integrates the separate elements into a unity of meaning. In the case of religion such a recognition of a relative autonomy becomes particularly important, for it dispenses us from applying criteria derived from those epistemic conditions that determine purely objective knowledge.

Yet the theory as developed in modern epistemology requires several qualifications if it is to relate to what we have traditionally understood as *religious* truth, or even to accomplish the more modest goal of justifying the meaningfulness of religious discourse. Coherence easily turns into closedness. To make genuine truth-claims, a system must be coherent not only within itself but also with other systems. This requires at the very least that principles inherent in what may be called "basic" interpretations of experience do not contradict those implicit in a "higher" or more remote system of interpretation, where religious truth places its stake. Recent debates on religious truth tend to neglect this point. To prove that the discourses of religion and of physics substantially differ is not sufficient to exclude a priori any possible conflict.

That religion has staked out its own realm of discourse does not dispense it from having to enter into dialogue with other realms and to render its claims compatible with the "basic" interpretations of common sense and the physical sciences. Even the principles of falsifiability and verifiability that rule these interpretations should not be immediately dismissed as not applying to this "higher" realm. In withdrawing religious truth from universal criteria of meaning, we rescue it from outside criticism only to drown it in total meaninglessness.

If truth in religion were not to share some basic assumptions with other areas of truth, the term "truth" as we understand it today would cease to preserve any meaning at all. Religious truth, while being distinct, nevertheless relates to all aspects of life. Philosophical reflection tolerates neither unmediated pluralism nor epistemic relativism, since one system of truth cannot remain totally unrelated to another.[16]

Closing religious doctrines off from other realms of thought may in the end create worse problems than open conflicts with them. Precisely the failure to harmonize those doctrines with the scientific worldview has rendered religion so improbable to many of our educated contemporaries as not to deserve any serious consideration. C. C. Broad, while agreeing with the claim that nothing in modern science "refutes" the belief in miracles and in an afterlife, nevertheless dismissed it for being totally out of tune with the world picture of science: "there is literally nothing but a few pinches of philosophical fluff to be put in the opposite scale to this vast coherent mass of ascertained facts."[17] A preposterous conclusion, to be sure—but one made possible by the increasing "hermetization" of religious discourse.

To avoid the problems of modern culture, believers tend to compartmentalize their worldview. Facing social, psychological, and scientific developments that they feel unable to integrate with their faith, they disconnect their unexamined religious beliefs from the rest of their convictions, as an island of truth isolated from the mainland of modern culture. Yet the believer should know that these convictions on a basic level draw a line of probability beyond which even the most hallowed "revelation" becomes rationally inadmissable. Rather than outrightly rejecting the validity of the principle of falsifiability in religious truth, believers should question the one-sided manner in which the positivist usually applies it. They may rightly refuse to accept criteria that fail to account for the specific quality of religious beliefs. But they should at least admit the fact, supported by daily apostasies, that faith is in principle falsifiable and that the limits of probability, however different from one person to another, cannot be stretched indefinitely.

Taken by itself the theory of coherence proves insufficient to account for the most characteristic quality of religious truth—namely, that it originates *outside* the system.

A brief glance at the theory's most popular current representative should illustrate this. Reexaming the relation between the objective world and the discourse that signifies that world, structuralism concludes that a system of discourse filters each new perception through a preestablished, self-sufficient network that allows to emerge only so much as the system is able to handle. Decisive for the appearance of objects at any given time is, in the words of Michel Foucault, "the interplay of the rules."[18] Such a self-sufficient, self-referential structure excludes the world of objects or, for that matter, any other system. All assertions refer to the established communal meaning.

This is not the place to enter into the different varieties of structuralist theories. But their general tendency to have social, mostly linguistic, structures determine thought, restricts truth to a social, linguistic problem. A consistent structuralist system, if I understand it correctly, tolerates no intrusion from beyond, indeed, no genuine novelty. Since the context alone must account for any possible appearance, the form of new phenomena was a priori implied in the structure itself. Not to admit genuine difference is, of course, fatal to any idea of religious truth, which implies a transcendent revelation. Precisely because Derrida perceived the inability of a closed structuralism to admit genuine novelty, he developed a theory of language that would allow him to move beyond intrinsic socio-linguistic limitations. His philosophy of the creative *word* breaking through the given, whereby the signifier transcends the signified, appears, paradoxically, to reopen the way to religious transcendence.[19]

Having expressed these objections against the potential of the coherence theory to serve as exclusive model for a philosophical evaluation of religious truth, we must nevertheless admit its unique appropriateness for legitimating the *relative* autonomy and distinct identity of religious discourse. My objections bear only on the sufficiency of a closed theory of coherence for the purpose of justifying the characteristic truth of such a discourse.

Disclosure

The correspondence and coherence models remain indispensable for understanding the truth of religion. But the more they came to reflect the subjective turn of modern thought, the more they became removed from what religion itself has traditionally understood to be the essence of its truth. We saw how hard it becomes to accommodate the idea of revelation in theories for which the sole source of equation or of coherence is the human subject. The disclosure theory appears less tainted by modern subjectivism and therefore better suited to recognize the specific nature of *religious* truth.

In recent discussions that theory has moved once again to the front stage of the philosophical scene. But its origins lie hidden in the beginnings of Western thought. We find it in Plato and Plotinus, of course, but, before them, already in Parmenides' famous poem and, even earlier, in the dark recesses of Greek myth. In its modern form it reasserts the priority of *ontological* over epistemic truth. "Truth," Heidegger states, does not possess its original seat in the proposition but in a disclosure "through which an openness essentially unfolds." Allowing things to be, to disclose themselves in the open, is the very essence of freedom. Though the essence of truth lies in freedom, its focus is not on the subject, but on the openness within which Being itself appears.[20]

Such a theory definitely moves closer to the essence of religious truth. Indeed, its origin is clearly religious. But here, the problem presents itself rather from the opposite angle. How will a theory so obviously dependent upon the traditional idea of illumination meet the modern critical demand that truth *justify* itself? Until it does, *disclosure* may be the concept in which religion views its own truth, but philosophy will resist accepting it as the truth *of* religion.

Since the days of Heidegger and Marcel, however, hermeneutic philosophy has gone a long way in attempting to justify the disclosure theory, not, to be sure, by means of the critical method (which would soon reduce disclosure to a subjective source), but by a careful analysis of modes of cognition that illuminate Being without being restricted by the epistemic criteria of the positive science. Thus, both esthetic and historical consciousness attain truth in a manner that surpasses the subordinate moments of historical accuracy and of esthetic "imitation of nature." Obviously, to apply here the critical norms used in establishing the foundations of the positive sciences constitutes an ineffective attempt to transfer the truth proper to one domain into a different one.

Gadamer clearly defined the issue: "Our task demands that we recognize in it an experience of truth which must not only be critically justified, but which itself is a mode of philosophizing."[21] "Critical" justification (the term itself is misleading in this context!) here consists in a particular "mode of philosophizing," a retracing in *actu reflecto* of what we are actually doing in *actu exercito*, rather than in establishing the kind of critical foundation that philosophy provides for the sciences. The purpose of this immanent reflection is to uncover the light it sheds on Being and on human existence within Being. The real test of disclosure consists in establishing its ontological significance. This, according to Gadamer (in the third part of *Truth and Method*), occurs in a fundamental reflection on language.

In his discussion of the image, Gadamer refers to the ontological quality of the iconic symbol by the term *Seinszuwachs*—augmentation of Being. However one may judge this usage, the term eminently applies to the truth disclosed in religious symbols and, in the Judeo-Christian tradition, that means in the first place, religious language. Precisely in this ontological nature of religious disclosure resides its characteristic truth. This, I believe, is ultimately what Hegel had in mind when he declared the Christian religion to be essentially "true"—that is, expressing the deepest dimension of Being: "[Christian doctrine] is not merely something subjective but is also an absolute, objective content that is in and for itself, and has the characteristic of truth."[22] Rather than submitting this disclosure to antecedent philosophical criteria, Hegel subordinates this critical awareness itself to what he considers the prior, religious disclosure: "[the standpoint of religion] is the affirmation that the truth with which consciousness is actively related *embraces all content within itself.* Hence this relation of this consciousness to this truth is itself the highest level of consciousness, its absolute standpoint."[23] The absoluteness of religious truth lies in the fact that its disclosure includes all reality without having to refer to any reality outside itself, and that it implies its own necessity.[24]

But then Hegel adds that the truth of religion is fully disclosed only when religion itself loses its representational form and becomes philosophy. The *justification* of religious truth—which formerly had mostly consisted in the critical *reflection upon* an already established truth—now constitutes *itself* as truth. Hence the disclosure of religious truth is no longer completed *within faith* itself. At this point we may wonder whether Hegel is not withdrawing with one hand what he had given with the other. Nevertheless, in reclaiming ontological ultimacy for religious disclosure, Hegel supports the position of the mystics who, almost unanimously, assert that religious disclosure contains an ontological richness unparalleled by any other mode of truth.

Theologians and many philosophers were quick in appropriating the disclosure theory for their explanation of religious truth. Understandably so, since they felt they were merely returning an indigenous idea to its original habitat. Religious symbols undoubtedly disclose a unique fullness of Being. Of course, philosophers still found themselves stranded with the arduous task of *justifying* this ontological manifestation without appealing directly to a supernatural revelation. Many chose to ignore this difficult issue and were satisfied with *describing* the unique disclosure that takes place in the religious act. One need not decide on the natural or supernatural origin, they felt, in order to see in the religious act an illumination within which all previous contents and relations come to stand in a new light. Even as we suddenly perceive a picture that, without any change in the configuration, totally transforms a mere complex of lines and colors, so a religious disclosure conveys to ordinary reality a symbolic and metaphorical quality.

But does such a description philosophically legitimate the religious act? How does the ontological disclosure justify the specific beliefs and rules that provided the occasion for it? I have already indicated how the traditional requirements of verification and falsification in a general way also apply to religion. For the religious believer, the ontological disclosure occurs entirely *within* the language of revelation. In the Christian revelation, God's living Word provides, with its own disclosure, the conditions for the internal *justification* of its truth. The Spirit given with, and in, the Word testifies to the veracity of the message and enables the believer to see its evidence.

But a justification of this nature is neither available nor sufficient to philosophy today. The idea of a divine revelation, far from providing the justifying evidence that disclosure requires, has itself come to stand in dire need of support. Nor should we assume, as Gadamer does (in analogy with the way revelation justifies itself to the believing mind), that language *justifies* its own disclosure. For the disclosure of language by itself provides no adequate criteria for distinguishing truth from falsehood—an essential task in the traditional justification of truth.

One particular characteristic of the disclosure of faith appears to exclude the kind of objective, impartial justification on which philosophy insists for the legitimation of truth. This disclosure does not consist in a detached intellectual insight but requires an involved participation that philosophy cannot, and should not, reproduce. Phenomenologists experienced this when they attempted to apply to the religious disclosure Husserl's *epochē*—the bracketing of all existential elements needed to bring the phenomenon to its pure "essential" appearance. Is a method devised for grasping the object as it appears in the immanence of experience qualified to bring out the *transcendence* of that object? How can phenomenology preserve the unique transcendence of what the religious act intends? The doxic modality of faith affects not only the *real* (empirical) experience of the act but also the *ideal* (i.e., independently of the psychological conditions of the experience) status of its object. The religious act intends its object as lying essentially *beyond* the immanence of the experience. One may well wonder, then, whether the phenomenological method, restricted as it is to the ideal immanence of that object, suffices for *justifying the truth* of the disclosure. Unlike other acts of consciousness, faith never brings its intentional object to full immanence. Its object is experienced as lying *beyond attain-*

ment, and its only immanence in the experience consists in the very awareness of a lasting transcendence.

Two prominent students of the phenomenology of religion, Gerardus van der Leeuw and Max Scheler, concluded therefrom that the religious act and its intentional object cannot be understood unless one shares the faith that conditions them—that is, unless one accepts the transcendence of its object.[25] Clearly, if this implied the need to convert philosophy into faith, philosophy would *eo ipso* cease to justify the religious disclosure altogether. Yet according to another, milder interpretation, an adequate philosophical evaluation of religious disclosure would require only that the critic be *in some way* directly acquainted with its experience. This acquaintance need not consist in a full participation in the faith on which one reflects: it may be no more than the memory of an actual faith, or even no specific faith at all, but only a personal acquaintance with the religious experience in general.

Even so, the restriction prevents philosophical reflection on the religious disclosure from being universally available. But can a reflection not generally accessible be called philosophical? Does "a truth" that cannot justify itself on a universal basis still be considered philosophically justified at all?

Before answering these questions negatively, we should realize that the esthetic experience falls under the same restrictions. Only a person actually acquainted with such an experience qualifies for passing philosophical judgment on it. Rather than claiming that there is no truth in the disclosure of art and religion, one should conclude that the truth of disclosure, esthetic or religious, intrinsically differs from scientific or historical truth, even though they may share *some* rules. But this much remains certain: religion introduces its *own truth* without allowing itself to be measured *definitely* by any extrinsic or universal norm.

Other, perhaps equally fundamental, difficulties have emerged from the attempts to apply to religion the disclosure theory of truth as formulated by Heidegger. Theologians sympathetic to his distinction between Being *(Sein)* and beings *(Seiende)* have not succeeded in defining the place of God in his structure. Is God Being itself, or a being? I doubt whether the issue can be resolved on Heidegger's terms.

Whether a particular theory of disclosure fits the religious case depends very much on the mode in which it is conceived. Heidegger's disclosure clearly differs from, and is possibly incompatible with, the Judeo-Christian religious disclosure. The problem exceeds the linguistic aptitude of Greek concepts for articulating ideas mainly expressed in Hebrew concepts. When Rudolf Bultmann interpreted religious truth as existential disclosure, his superior knowledge of the Jewish background of Christianity succeeded in neutralizing, at least in part, the Hellenic orientation of Heidegger's theory. No, the more fundamental problem lies in the very assumption that the gospel *can be* exhaustively translated into existential terms. Kierkegaard, with his own intense interest in an existential realization of the gospel, remained acutely aware of the ultimate incongruity between transcendent meaning and immanent existence, and therefore considered all genuinely religious truth to remain permanently hidden from *direct communication*. Religious truth is, indeed, interiorly disclosed, but never directly. It remains, as Kierkegaard put it, a "pathetic-dialectical" message—that is, one that after having been passively received must still be dialectically interiorized. This translation into existence, essential to the religious disclosure, consists in a never-ending process of mediation.

The self-manifestation of the transcendent is, in the end, neither self-understanding nor understanding of Being. Though contributing to both, it also surpasses them in referring to the inexpressible. Mystical writers have fully accepted this paradox. John of the Cross introduces his chapter on "naked truths" with the disconcerting preface: "You should know, beloved reader, that what they in themselves are for the soul is beyond words."[26] He then proceeds by declaring the knowledge of God a subject on which "in no way anything can be said."[27] Nor is this inexpressible knowledge "manifest and clear"; rather it is "sublime" because "transcending what is naturally attainable."[28] These paradoxes of mystical knowledge affect religious truth *as such:* it discloses what can never be fully disclosed. Without accounting for this unique mode of religious disclosing, a philosophical theory of truth-as-disclosure, far from "justifying" religious truth, remains incapable of understanding it.

Religious disclosure is truth that, in its essentials, refuses to submit to external criteria. To confirm this conclusion we only have to reflect on the notion of *experience* as religion uses it. Any disclosure takes place in some mode of what we vaguely refer to as experience. If experience means no more than the various mental process by which persons, actively and passively, respond to the stimuli of their life world, then the term contains no brief for truth. Yet if, as Aristotle taught,[29] experience yields a unique form of insight that, though not scientific, nevertheless attains a kind of cumulative and never completed universality, then it is at least on the way to truth. Experience defines its own meaning: those who experience learn in the process itself *what* they are experiencing. This insight cannot claim the title of truth, however, until, beyond a mere empirical awareness, it attains some form of ideal necessity and thereby discloses a permanent feature of the real as such. Yet the truth of experience does not lie exclusively in its possible *result*, namely, the knowledge, for which it establishes the precondition, but also, and primarily as Gadamer points out, in *the process itself*.[30] Precisely in following the very course of consciousness in time, experience acquires its unique purchase on truth—namely, that it is and becomes increasingly *my own* experience. It hereby endows truth, on whichever level acquired, with some kind of *practical indubitability*, which, though not warranting freedom from error, nevertheless secures unsubstitutional evidence.

Religious disclosure occurs *within* a highly personal or intensely communal experience and, even when raised to the level of full and universal truth, retains this personal or communal quality in being a *truth-for-me* or a *truth-for-us*. Revelation discloses as much about the believer as it reveals of God: in it a transcendent message interacts with an immanent experience. This tight link between the message and the experience does not render religious disclosure a purely subjective affair. The *reality* we experience—in this case, the transcendent reality as communicated in revelation—defines the nature of the experience and endows it with its own authority—not the other way round.[31]

This, however, by no means implies that in the immanence of his experience the believer gains *direct access* to the transcendent object received by it. The experience of faith does not consist of the kind of meaning-fulfillment whereby other modes of thought render their object "personally" present. God never *appears* in the manner in which a sense object bodily presents itself, or in which the solution to a mathematical problem suddenly forces its incontrovertible evidence upon the mind.[32]

Nonetheless, faith carries an evidence of its own, which, without the manifest presence of its object, illuminates the believer's relation to it as vital to the understanding of itself and of all reality. The experience of revelation draws the *decisive* arguments for verifying its content not from external sources but from itself. Believers assume that what they know of the divine object they know through that object itself. Christians have traditionally expressed this in the doctrine of the indwelling Spirit who teaches them "the entire faith." Eckhart echoed it in his word that the eye with which we see God is the eye with which God sees God. Clearly this kind of evidence provides no scientific support for its truth, nor does it lend greater coherence to our empirical observation of the world. Neither does it provide metaphysical insight. But it opens up a different perspective on metaphysical insight as well as on empirical investigation, and brings with it a unique yet highly personal justification of its own truth.

Appendix
"Truth" from the Bible to the New Testament

The earliest articulation of truth in the Bible basically consists in a relation of faithfulness *(emet)* or firmness—a moral quality.

Not surprisingly, truth also appears as a correspondence between word and fact—a relation that even to the uncritical mind appears problematic from the start. Thus in Proverbs 12:17 we read: "He who utters the truth affirms that which will stand; but a lying witness, that which will bring disappointment."[33] But the more fundamental truth consists in God's steadfastness toward His people and in their participation in this steadfastness by fidelity to divinely revealed law.[34] In some of the Psalms (such as Ps. 119) the correlation between the law and truth appears particularly clear: the *law* reveals to us God's fidelity (truth) and its observance enables us to share in that truth.[35] With the idea that truth requires entrusting oneself to a higher authority, a cognitive quality joins the moral one. We remain in the truth to the extent that we heed the revelation of God's truthfulness as expressed in His commands, and that our deeds, values, and attitudes *correspond* to that divine disclosure. The idea of *correspondence*, then, which came to dominate the later cognitive discussion, started out as a moral-practical one.

The same could be said about the idea of *coherence*. Trust in God's providence and obedience in the Covenant unite all aspects of communal and individual existence. The sapiential literature in particular stresses the harmony of a life guided by the law. The emphasis upon trust, obedience, and receptivity in the attainment of truth distinguishes the biblical conception from that modern one according to which truth originates in the knowing subject.[36]

Yet more and more the idea of truth as *disclosure*—that is, as based on a divine revelation—gained in significance. The Septuagint translation, which facilitated an exchange with the more cognitive Hellenistic approach, may have contributed to this shift in emphasis. Still, it was not until the final period of canonical writing (most explicitly in Daniel 8:26; 10:1; 11:2) that *emet* acquired the precise meaning of *revealed truth*.

The New Testament adopted this emphasis on the *revealed* quality of truth. The Pauline notion of a *mystery* hidden in God and revealed in Christ must be understood more in continuity with Hebrew sapiential and apocalyptic literature than with Greek mystery cults. Particularly noteworthy is the absence of the modern opposition between knowledge and faith. "Truth" has been revealed, disclosed by divine power rather than by human wisdom. Yet once received in faith, revelation brings an internal evidence that renders its truth compelling. The source of evidence here lies not in the self, but in God: certainty derives from being grasped, not from grasping.[37] The idea of revelation itself attains a new significance when Christ brings it to fulfillment in his own person.

The idea that divine truth has disclosed itself in a physical person dominates the Johannine writings. This personified Truth, mostly presented as a light, transforms those who believe in Him. The truth of Christ consists in a new way of being, more than in a new mode of knowing. Only they who *do* the truth will become enlightened by it. Divine illumination becomes truth *for us* only when assimilated in our existence. The same divine Word that, according to Genesis, called creation into being has now come *to dwell* in it. Those who accept its light gain access to truth as it exists in God Himself. In faith believers internalize that truth so that it becomes their own. Yet they never acquire possession of the source of this truth, as they do with worldly learning. The Word has become totally manifest (*ephanerōthē;* 1 John 1:2) and yet it remains invisible until the "Spirit of truth" (John 14:17; 15:26) illuminates believers by His inner testimony. In John truth continues to flow from a transcendent source. Indeed, the very term "true" often serves to distinguish divine from ordinary reality, as when Christ is declared to be "the true light" (John 1:9) or "the true bread" (John 6:32). Here *true* stands for what fully *is*.

2

Religious Truth and Scientific Truth

Philip Clayton

Phenomenological studies into the nature of religious truth have revealed nothing more clearly than the elusiveness of their object. This fact suggests recourse to a negative, comparative study: Can we discover fields where truths reveal themselves in a mode clearly incompatible with religious truth? If so, we might derive the outlines of a phenomenology of religious truth by a process of negation. Comparison with scientific truth provides a particularly auspicious focus for such an inquiry. Here, it seems, we deal with the objective world rather than an all-too subjective universe of religious beings and values; with a clearly specified domain rather than one apparently resistant to all cartographic efforts; with a method productive of proven results rather than a methodless wandering through perennial (and perennially unanswerable) questions. Precisely in science's methodological self-confidence, its knowing how to pursue the truths it does not yet know, would seem to lie its appropriateness as a foil for a phenomenology of religious truth.

The methods of phenomenology free us from the need to judge between the types of truth or to arbitrate their relative epistemic merits. Still, of course, choosing the comparison with science will structure our approach to the question of religious truth in some ways. We will have to look to the attitudes of practitioners in both areas, to their modi operandi in constructing the statements they hold to be true, and to the types of statements they have made. The "truth proper to science" lies in the type of statement that scientists construct, the broader theoretical framework they presuppose and, crucially, the techniques they use to verify it. The comparison will thus predispose us to look at religious truth in terms of the methods, attitudes, and practices of religious persons, extrapolating from these to the nature of religious truth. It may be hoped that this sort of an inquiry will supplement those of other contributors to this volume's project.

My analysis will proceed dialectically via three successive modes of construing scientific and religious truth. I begin with the scientist's "natural attitude," the traditional view of science as a strictly rational practice aimed at objective truth, and with religion as its polar opposite. But the onesidedness of this picture inevitably gives rise to its opposite, a "hermeneutical" construal of science (section 2). This view, by treating science only as subjective human activity, draws science and religion much closer together than the first. Still, the attempted identification of science and religion will give rise to problems of its own: however "religious" science becomes, it remains a theoretical (albeit human) endeavor in a manner distinct from religion. Therefore, the final stage of the inquiry into religion and science will need to negate the negation of the traditional view, neither dichotomizing nor identifying their two types of truth. In the final analysis, then, we will be led to reaffirm several central distinctions between scientific and religious truth.

A quick caveat: it is common for philosophers of science to be somewhat suspicious of broad statements about the nature of "science," even to eschew any statements whatsoever about "science" as a whole. Such reticence is not misplaced: phenomenological studies have revealed important variants among scientific disciplines and subdisciplines. However, we would leave some broad features of the "scientific attitude" unnecessarily obscure were we to reject all reflection about the phenomenon of science in general; if the premise of this paper is correct, we would thereby hamper our understanding of the religious attitude as well. In the following pages "science" when used without qualifiers will refer to the natural sciences and those social sciences that proceed according to the model of the natural sciences. That very different conclusions follow from a different model of science will be argued in due course.

1. A Contrastive Theory of Religious Truth

I begin, then, with a phenomenological analysis of scientific truth along lines suggested by more traditional treatments of science. According to the "received view," successful science mirrors the way things are; it is characterized by detachment, a thoroughly rational method, and asymptotic progress toward a system of propositions that would correspond, one-to-one, with physical reality. In its nature and mode of disclosure, scientific truth so construed diverges widely from the personal involvement and concern with meaning found in religion.

This analysis portrays the scientist as in confident contact with a comprehensible world. There is an apparent paradox here: nature confronts us as other, as something standing apart from us, which is not us; and yet we approach it with more epistemic confidence than the human "other." But the paradox is only apparent, for science's strength lies precisely in its resultant ability to control. Using scientific methods, the domain under study can be closed, excluding forces and entities qualitatively different from the target domain. In accepting the law of entropy as a general law of thermodynamics, for instance, we posit the universe as a closed system, with no ordering influences from "outside." Human agency is thus "inside" the scientific framework rather than transcending it. It is the power of scientific theory to admit only that world which can be grasped using its concepts.

A second paradox catches our attention as well. Science, with its detailed specifications of domain and method, imposes an a priori structure on nature. Kant's "discovery" of the forms of intuition and categories of the understanding stemmed not by chance from his natural philosophy, his reflection on science. Science enjoys the advantages of theory because of the power of its initial binding of nature. Yet, paradoxically, its ability to set parameters in this way makes possible a more acute listening to nature. Among others, Heidegger has seen this with reference to Greek science, which was born as an observation of nature prior to the development of the concept of experimentation. *Ta mathēmata* is what can be remembered, the knowable in nature;[1] mathematics is the imposition of structure that allows natural structures to emerge. Nothing is qualitatively changed with the addition of experimentation. In fact, phenomenologically, experimentation only intensifies the same paradoxical form: it involves the move from passive observing to structured observing, to a more careful posing of the question. Yet the result is a heightened listening.

Two of the features of science that stand out within the traditional phenomenological perspective have supported the drawing of sharp distinctions between science and religion. First, the scientific attitude is said to involve the switch from viewing the world as ready-to-hand to present-at-hand, and to exclude questions about its own status. Science seeks to formulate true assertions about the world; to do so, it abstracts from questions of the mode of being of the questioner, from any features that may set this questioner apart from any other one. The central role of *replicability* means just this:

any researcher who can re-create precisely these objective conditions will observe just these consequent behaviors. Out of the de facto plurality of life-worlds, it is claimed, the scientist seeks to abstract a single underlying framework that belongs to every possible observer. Think, again, of Kant's insistence that his forms and categories (and, in the *Grounding*, the categorical imperative) would apply not just to all persons but to *all rational beings*. Here is a philosophy of the "they" par excellence!

Secondly, this "strength" of the scientific perspective has also been viewed as its weakness. To attain unambiguous access to its domain it must rule out questions that require a different (nonscientific) theoretical perspective, as well as self-referential questions. Husserl and Heidegger, Schutz and Merleau-Ponty, have variously argued that this fact makes science dependent on philosophical or phenomenological analysis for clarification of its own concepts and practices. Regarding our particular question of the truth proper to science, we can still say that science, given its domain, speaks most authoritatively about the phenomena it questions; it does "unveil" *(alēthein)* them in an adequate fashion. But that which makes it the best judge in its field may also make it incompetent to judge the nature of its own truths, their proper scope, their inherent limitations.

What, then, is the truth "proper to" science or the scientific attitude? Scientific truth, according to the present model, is the truth of correspondence, the *adequatio intellectus et rei*. It involves a picture theory of language, in which we create terms for the basic entities in the physical world ("reality as it really is") and utilize mathematical functions to express the lawlike interrelations of these real things. Prediction is possible because of the accuracy of our linguistic modeling: the "forces" that dictate the extension of an acceleration curve reflect analogous forces in nature, which act on their "real" objects in the same way.

Within this model, what catches the phenomenologist's attention about scientific truth is the striving for mastery. It expresses the will to dominance, dominance through analysis and objectification. To objectify is to put under my control, whether it be the theoretical control of "saying the truth about something" or the technological control of routine manipulation. It is the opposite pole to the experience of the other as other. In fact, we express this in a moral (or religious) context by speaking of science as "dehumanizing" the other, reducing the other to the status of an object that we can control without the encumbrance of moral strictures.

If we accept this first model, then we would have to conclude that scientific truth is objective and dispassionate; it is not person-relative but is rather the paradigm of transpersonal knowledge. Its assertions are free from perspectival corruption: they may impose a grid à la Kant, but it is one *necessarily* imposed by any rational creature who wishes to know. Since science strives for "true propositions," those elusive entities that mediate between words and world, scientific truth can only mean perfect correspondence with the nature of the way things are. It is the seeing of things as they reveal themselves to the observer (whether the seeing be structured through experimentation or not). It is the truth of disciplined observation, of questions posed for clear answers. From here, it is a short move to the conclusion that scientific method is the paradigm of knowledge, the unrivaled possessor of justified truths.

The position just sketched forces on phenomenologists of religion a straightforward *via negativa*, for it requires us to construct a point-by-point characterization of religious truth in contradistinction to science so understood. According to the contrast, religious truth can only be subjective, passionate, intrinsically perspectival. The truth of religious explanations are the truths of myth and personal disclosure, not the truths of logos. Religious persons are involved and their involvement is a matter of ultimate concern to them. Unlike scientific truth, religious truth is inseparable from questions of meaning. It does not share the cognitive goal of repicturing the world (human or divine) with objective accuracy, but the "meaninged" or semantic goal of understanding the divine (or the religious sphere) in a personal manner, as the divine encounters me and with the call to action that it makes on me.

And so on: the contrasts inspired by this *via negativa* can be extended at will (and often have been). In fact, many of the dichotomies traditionally used to characterize the religious dimension— reason vs. faith, nature vs. grace, natural vs. supernatural—owe their existence to precisely the same strategy. The reasons given for accepting this "contrastive" theory of religious truth may be heuristic or essential: one may hold that religious truth is most effectively characterized by contrasting it to a better known type of truth; or one may believe that the transcendent *can* only be described in negative terms such as these. In any event, contrastive theories of religious truth presuppose a phenomenology of science along lines similar to the ones here suggested.

2. Toward the Identity of Scientific and Religious Truth

But closer observation of the phenomena of science strongly challenges the adequacy of the traditional picture. A new face of science has been unveiled by more recent work, which supports, *at minimum*, the compatibility of scientific and religious truth. In fact, in this section we will examine the case for accepting the most extreme form of this switch, which I have entitled the "identity theory" of scientific and religious truth. The identity theory holds that there is no difference in principle between scientific and religious truth, that the two types of truth are ultimately indistinguishable. Defending this view means negating the dichotomies defended in section 1. By tightening the phenomenological cords binding science and religion to the breaking point in this manner, we will be able to ascertain where they snap—if they do—and why; the results provide, I believe, crucial parameters for subsequent work in the phenomenology of religious truth.

I begin by challenging two misconceptions that underlie the contrastive theory. First, science is not common sense made rigorous, in contrast to the religious pursuit of truth that putatively flies in the face of the everyday view of the world. Even if one held that Aristotelian or Newtonian physics naively presupposed the then generally accepted view of the world, the same can hardly be said of recent work in physical cosmology or particle physics. Like religious thought, that of science may begin with the world as we know it, but it may well conclude with a world unrecognizable to the noninitiate. Secondly, scientific work does not exhibit some sort of objectivity absent from other forms of human activity that the religious quest transcends (or falls short of). Instead, both activities can be *identical* in that both *exhibit the critical use of hypothesis and doubt within a subjective human framework pervasively influenced by personal, social, and historical factors.* The defense of the identity theory is based (1) on the content of scientific statements (the type of truth that science grasps), and (2) on the attitudes and activities of scientific researchers (i.e., the means to truth that they employ). Addressing each seriatim reveals perhaps unexpected similarities in religious and scientific activity.

As to *the content of scientific statements*, it has not been possible to interpret scientific theories as explanations obeying a certain formal structure and general criteria of adequacy.[2] Relativistic and quantum mechanical physics have made observer limitations central to the epistemology, even the ontology, of science. Attempts at a general calculus of probability or formal specifications of adequacy have floundered, leaving behind an awareness of the irreducibly pragmatic components of scientific adequacy. The "truth" of scientific statements must include intrinsically perspectival elements: my spatio-temporal frame of reference, my moment and manner of measurement, the question I am asking and the purposes for which my explanation will be used. A massive literature treats scientific theories as myths, models, narratives, stories—with the truth proper to such accounts.[3]

These new insights have stemmed not only from advances in physics. Equally important have been the attempts to isolate the social sciences as distinct disciplines operating according to their own principles. Thinkers such as Dilthey, Rickert, and Windelband at the end of the last century fought to weaken the grip of the natural scientific model on human studies, and to establish methods and a theoretical structure appropriate to the nature of human existence in the world. Under the influence of Husserl, Alfred Schutz defended an "interpretive social science" inspired by a phenomenology of the life-world, and Maurice Merleau-Ponty worked to specify the relation between subject and object in a manner congenial to the demands of both scientific research and human existence. To some extent, this research has been taken up into social scientific practice, such that it is no longer an intellectual oddity to utilize phenomenological methods as a part of one's social scientific work.[4] More recently, the fundamentally hermeneutical nature of the natural sciences has been recognized as well.[5]

Thus there is no longer any justification for labeling science as essentially objective and abstractive. Scientific statements can now be viewed as one perspective, one of many ways humans attempt to construct a coherent, comprehensible world. Epistemologists might try to argue that there is a greater probability that scientific statements are true than that religious ones are. But the phenomenologist is interested instead in the mode of manifestation, and here (it is claimed) religion and science are identical: both are symbolizing activities aimed at making the world meaningful through the creation of a unique symbolic structure or context. Each context has its own manner of speaking or type of "speech acts"; each speech act makes its particular type of validity claim; different validity claims are tested according to different criteria. Jürgen Habermas, for instance, has distinguished "constative," "expressive," and "regulative" speech acts, depending on whether the context is theoretical, expressive, or ethical. Most important for our purposes, each context has its distinctive "truth" within the broader project of human communication.[6]

These insights free our view of science from the "positivism" that infected the section 1 description. Scientific truth can only be elucidated in terms of its social context. As McHugh notes:

> There are no adequate grounds for establishing criteria of truth except the grounds that are employed to grant or con-

cede it—truth is conceivable only as a socially organized upshot of contingent courses of linguistic, conceptual, and social
behavior. The truth of a statement is not independent of the
conditions of its utterance, and so to study truth is to study
the ways truth can be methodically conferred.[7]

We know that religious beliefs about oneself and the world reflect
one's cultural and historical setting; so too the beliefs of the scientist. We know that the truths of religion are inherently historical;[8]
those of science equally so. Phenomenologically, science must
therefore be construed in terms of the totality of the contexts operative in its formulations. Science is not so much our response to the
speech of nature as it is our imposition onto nature of the dictates of
our perspective.

The foregoing analysis begins to indicate the complexity of elu-
cidating a scientific theory of truth; the barest outline of a proposal
will have to suffice here. I suspect that the phenomenology of scientific truth will have to be reconceived along coherential lines.
Scientific judgments are not made true by some sort of perfect correspondence with reality's states of affairs. Instead, as Kockelmans
has recently written, scientific "judgments state how things are as
seen from some limited context of meaning or, in the final analysis,
from the perspective of the whole of meaning of which we can
conceive."[9] It *may* be that a particular theoretical structure better allows the truth of the world to manifest itself in scientific statements,
hence that one structure is "truer" than another; but there are reasons to be skeptical that the scientist actually possesses the requisite
eidetic vision. More likely, we can judge the relative adequacy of a
given higher-order theory only on internal, coherential grounds,
since all criteria of evaluation are "theory-laden." We need only recall that our crucial experimental tests are suggested by our presently accepted theoretical structure, our data molded by it, our
conclusions interpreted by it, our anomalies explained away by it.

In short, a coherence theory reflects the abandonment of the
belief that nature is speaking in some direct and unmediated sense
through scientific statements. Instead, scientific truth is just the coherence within the various sets of statements we label "science":
coherence of sets of observations with sets of predictions (formerly
"correspondence to reality"), coherence of different levels of theory
sets with one another ("theoretical consistency"), coherence of sets
of beliefs held by various theorists ("scientific consensus").

But do we not find in this shift sufficient grounds for recognizing the structural identity of (at least) the cognitive or belief compo-

nents in science and in religion? Both are striving for unity, seeking to avoid the cognitive dissonances of incoherence; neither has unmediated access to an external, objective reality. In fact, a coherential account of religious truth has much to recommend it. Religious life is essentially characterized by its vibrant coherence of belief and practice. The criteria for successful religious existence would, I believe, all turn out to be coherential at base: for example, the coherence of personal belief and practice with the standards of one's religious community; the coherence of one's belief expectations with actual life events; the perceived coherence between religious doctrines.

As to *the attitudes and activities of scientific researchers*, the coherential understanding of truth already suggests science-religion parallels in practice as well as in theory or doctrine. As already indicated, the identity theorist holds that there are reasons for viewing science not as a basically theoretical endeavor but in the first place as a particular species of human activity, one reflecting the perspectives of its participants. Of course, practicing scientists have rarely disputed the close link between scientific knowledge and human activity. Instead, it has been philosophers of science such as Karl Popper who have maintained that science may be a purely rational project that involves "conclusive falsifications" of theories and hypotheses. Recently, the pendulum has swung increasingly toward a pragmatic and institutional view of science with the rejection of formal models of scientific explanation and rationality. When science is viewed as something that humans do, its theories cannot be viewed (as in section 1) as purely objective constructions. Science does not stand completely apart from the researcher's need to construct a meaningful context for living; it remains one of the projects that arises out of a researcher's life-world. Once again, parallels with religion demand recognition. *Our* interactions with the "world" (as structured by theoretical parameters) give rise to scientific theories; theory is a prediction of future interactions *we* will have. Likewise, the religious attitude or lifestyle usually comes before the believer's formulation of beliefs, and beliefs for their part give rise to further attitudes and actions.

This distinctive stress on science as human activity can be uncovered in two contexts: the individual and the institutional. As to *the individual context*, with the demise of the positivistic myth of science, it appears that there are no grounds for denying that scientific knowledge is personal knowledge; and scientific truth, personal truth.[10] One finds no phenomenological reason to hypostatize science, as if it were a Platonic form; "science" is simply what persons called scientists do. Research biochemists in the lab, for instance, do not exemplify some timeless "logic of discovery"; rather, their various guesses and trials are better studied by a psychology of research.[11] For anyone, scientist or otherwise, to hold a claim to be warranted is for that person to find its justifications credible— which ultimately involves an internal, if far from arbitrary, "seeing" or "finding." Science, one may say, institutionalizes the mental state of doubt; and—to continue the personalist perspective—judging is a type of skill, commitment to a theory a disposition, the quest for objectivity a passion or prejudice.

As to *the institutional context,* science is also a social activity. Like all other social or symbolic worlds, a scientific world is constructed. An individual is trained according to textbook examples and problem sets, which provide "exemplars" (T. S. Kuhn) of correct answers and problem-solving methods. When a theoretical perspective has amassed a sufficient number of anomalies (incompatibilities with new experimental data or with other firmly entrenched theories), a group of scholars will replace it with a different framework, creating a new research program or subdiscipline if necessary. Historical coincidences, such as the inability of a major theorist to form a "school" or the emergence of an attractive alternate hypothesis, can be as decisive in such shifts as any empirical observations. Factors such as the theory-dependence of observations and experimental data, and the difficulty of deciding whether recalcitrant data militate against experimental presuppositions or the hypothesis being tested, make the justification of scientific truths as knotty as that of religious hypotheses. In fact, the decisions can be so complex and highly subjective that Kuhn has referred to them as scientific "conversions."[12]

Moreover, when we view science as an institution, we begin to perceive the extent to which scientific statements express the interplay of and for power within the scientific community.[13] Science seen as "institution" includes the role of textbooks, the editorial criteria of leading journals, the better placing power of professors at top universities for their doctoral or postdoctoral students. It involves a social network with its own rites and rituals, which fosters a certain view of the world. And it considers the expressions of these power relations as they appear in journals or are presented at conventions at any given time. Under this perspective, science becomes one of many social worlds, one of many ways of socially constructing reality, and its truth is the reality that results. To take a historical example,[14] one could say that Galileo's views predominated because his experiments let the world speak as it really is. But it is equally true to say that Galilean science predominated because Galileo wrote in the vernacular, used better rhetorical techniques than his churchly opponents, offered an alternative to a then-outworn metaphysics—and because his worldview was more compatible with the humanistic, mercantile, and Reformation interests of a Europe gradually emerging from the control of the Roman Catholic Church.

In short, we obscure the "truth proper to science" if we insist on describing it in abstraction from such phenomena. *The interests of science are inseparable from its truth.* Hence, an account of scientific truth would run as follows: I decide when, where, and how to inquire of nature. On a number of different levels I handcuff nature in order to get it to speak. First, I set the most basic parameters in that I presuppose certain foundational principles of rationality, mathematicizability, and replicability. Then I place more particular requirements in choosing the specified realm and the experimental methods of my particular subdiscipline: the molecular biologist will "see" nature revealing different truths than those of the environmental biologist, the cognitive psychologist different truths than those of the social psychologist. Finally, I establish specific outlines through the group of theories that I either accept or view as live options. Taken together, these restrictions amount to a complex variety of subjective factors, not as monolithic as a single "apophantic as" that has been claimed to characterize all sciences, nor as specific as Gadamer's claim that "the knowledge of all the natural sciences is knowledge for domination."[15] Rather, the interests out of which the truth of science is constructed are highly relative to time, existing scientific institutions, specific powerful individuals, and the like.

Phenomenologists of religion will have read this last paragraph with a wry grin: Has religion's truth not been characterized in precisely these terms? Louis Dupré describes in detail the creation of symbols that, however human, then acquire the weight of the sacred.[16] Winston King writes of the often imperceptible shift from religion as effort or quest to religion as response.[17] Eliade proclaims the inevitable transition from the history of religions to the phenomenology of religion. And van der Leeuw's classic phenomenology of religion explores the manifestation of the divine or transcendent as it takes form through religious symbols and practices.

Based on the view of science described in this section, then, the identity theorist concludes that there need be no difference in the phenomenology of the truths "proper to" science and religion. Many of us can deny neither the transcendent intentionality of religious experience and practice, nor the personal and social nature of all religious words; our work in phenomenology of religion explores the complex realm of their interactions without dismissing either side. Likewise, for the identity theorist, scientific truth is approached through exactly the same two poles. Does our reflection on the commonalities in mystical experience lead us to posit an intuition of the divine through mystical consciousness? Science also, as we saw in section 1, contains its moments of waiting and listening. Does our observation of historical and cultural differences among religious phenomena force us to stress the role of communal norms and practices? Here too a scientific model exists, for it is just as difficult to separate the activity and passivity of the scientist (was their intrinsic inseparability not Kant's fundamental point?). When we interpolate from a finite number of experimental data to a smooth curve that makes claims concerning a potentially infinite number of observations, are we listening to or dictating to nature? When we understand a historical text or event, are we hearing or dominating its author? Especially in the social sciences, it is impossible cleanly to separate the hypotheses we construct about human actions from the direct understanding we have of their significance.[18]

Actually, the dichotomy between religion and science fails from the other (religious) side as well. In the modern Western context, adherence to a religious tradition and its practices often occurs side by side with various doubts about its truth or relevance. This has created a phenomenon that we may call the "secular believer." This person holds, sometimes passionately, to the beliefs and/or ritual practices of his tradition while exposing them to (active or passive) doubt. This means, in an age when the most respectable view of the world is scientific, that religious believers may evince a more tentative, hypothetical stance toward their beliefs than scientists; scientists, in turn, may remain more firmly and devoutly attached to their theories than believers.

Much can be said about the historical genesis of this surprising reversal. Its causes include the failure of the modern, Cartesian attempt to ground religious truth in the individual's subjectivity, as well as the role granted to science as authoritative source of truths about the world. Just as crucially, the secular believer reflects a certain interlinking within religion of the two intellectual arbiters of religious truth, theology and the study of religion. For our purposes, theology may be taken as religious reflection on the content of one's belief, and the study of religion as reflection about religious beliefs within the context of other disciplines. The former is therefore a first-order reflection from the perspective of the life of faith, the latter, a second-order and "external" reflection that does not presuppose the truth of the beliefs in question. I am arguing that secular believers are no longer persons for whom theology (in this sense) is arbiter of religious truth, but that their stance toward religious truth is equally the product of external moral and intellectual contexts.

It follows that doubt is a central part of the secular believer's faith. Tillich seems to have perceived this clearly:

> This element of doubt is a condition of all spiritual life. The threat to spiritual life is not doubt as an element but the total doubt. . . . [The doubting person] asks for an answer which is valid within and not outside the situation of his despair. . . . [The only answer is] that the acceptance of despair is in itself faith and on the boundary line of the courage to be.[19]

But the doubt about religious truth need not be confined to passive, passing worries; believers who admit doubt as an inevitable concomitant of their faith may also standardize its role and actively pursue its insights. The resultant ongoing dialogue between the religious and secular perspectives on one's life creates an internal tension central to the dynamics of one's faith or religious practice. We may speak of it as a possession of religious truth that is at the same time a questing for truth. The secular believer may, within the context of the life of the church or synagogue, consciously select among received teachings, comparing them with the teachings of science or other religious traditions, collecting and weighing instances that would apparently falsify his tradition's beliefs.

The activity I have been describing need not of course be pursued in a disinterested manner, any more than that of the scientist need be. In fact, it may well be that a passionate concern with the outcome is essential to the *religious* preoccupation with the truth question. Still, the phenomenon of the secular believer shows that a genuine (as opposed to "in principle") openness regarding the truth of one's own beliefs is essentially compatible with sincere religious commitment and practice. When combined with the subjective elements in scientific practice discussed above, this fact *appears* to justify an identity theory of scientific and religious truth. Or are the observations in this section, like those in section 1, also in need of a corrective?

3. Compatibilism without Identity

To recap: when we analyze the intentionality of the scientific disciplines, as revealed in the attitudes of their practitioners and the practices of the scientific community, we are struck by often unacknowledged parallels with religious truth. The parallelism gives rise to speculation on the possible identification of the two kinds of truth. Nevertheless, further reflection reveals, I believe, the ultimate untenability of the identity theory. A synthesis of the one-sided emphases in the two preceding sections returns us to several fundamental differences between the truth proper to the two fields, differences that now emerge as essential. In the following I will be able to treat only four of the clearest of these.

1. Science does still involve a theoretical attitude, at least in its intentionality. It may well be influenced by the subjective wishes of researcher and theorists, by their drive for power, hope for a particular experimental outcome, faith in their own theories, or need to receive tenure. But the nature of the activity requires one to suppress the influence of these factors—successfully, unconsciously, or in outright bad faith—in one's publications and lectures. "Objectivity" has been institutionalized (whether successfully or not) in scientific practice, and remains the binding ideal for all practitioners.

No so in religion. Here, whatever hunger for power and control may also be present, the guiding values include subjective faith and response. Geertz summarizes the fundamental contrasts:

> [The religious perspective] differs from the scientific perspective in that it questions the realities of everyday life not out of an institutionalized scepticism which dissolves the world's givenness into a whirl of probabilistic hypotheses, but in terms of what it takes to be wider, nonhypothetical truths. Rather than detachment, its watchword is commitment; rather than analysis, encounter.[20]

Geertz is basically right about the contrasts, though his distinctions may be a little bald: whatever theologians and anthropologists may say, few religious persons would be content to replace doctrinal claims with a mere "I'm feeling religious today." Concern with correct belief (orthodoxy) often necessitates careful detachment and analysis. Moreover, any reductionist account that would redefine believers' critical reflection on the content of their belief as ipso facto philosophical, political, or esthetic is certainly anathema to the phenomenologist.

Our conclusion must be carefully stated, then, for the distinctions suggested by the science-religion comparison are more quantitative than qualitative. Both science and religion share the quest for true belief. And scientists may be passionately attached to their theories as matters of ultimate concern to them. But in religion this involvement or engagement—"the assurance of things hoped for, the conviction of things unseen"—is more than an allowable concomitant of series of truth claims; it is essential to the phenomenon itself. Science, but not religion, can be played with the mind alone. In short: the "secular believers" whom I described above may treat their beliefs as conjectures, as Wolfhart Pannenberg has repeatedly suggested, and they may avoid the "immunization strategies" of which Hans Albert accuses theologians. But they will never rejoice in the falsification of their hypotheses as Karl Popper's scientists will.[21]

2. The scientific endeavor has often been characterized by the sense of a progressive mastery of nature, a piece-by-piece conquest of nature's secrets. The shifts detailed in section 2 have weakened this association by stressing the diversity of scientific motives over any monothematic equation of science with the will to dominate—think, for instance, of the role of esthetic, political, and religious motives in the activity of persons such as Copernicus, Galileo, and Einstein. Further weakening of the link has resulted from epistemic doubts about whether we can know what we have possessed, or whether there is actually any real external world for us *to* possess. Nevertheless, such doubts have scarcely invalidated the attitude of possession or control in science. The move from realism to instrumentalism, for example, heightens the awareness that theories are retained in the first place because they are useful for our purposes.

By contrast, the religious object is essentially characterized by its unpossessability; it remains always beyond, *jenseits*, all claims made about it. The religious attitude never claims to "master" the object of devotion, even in moments of greatest closeness when the divine is most clearly perceived. When worship strives after possession, religion crosses the line into the realm of magic. The religious meaning, van der Leeuw writes, is the "last word," yet one that is never spoken:

> The ultimate meaning [is] a secret which reveals itself repeatedly, only nevertheless to remain eternally concealed. It im-

plies an advance to the farthest boundary, where only one sole fact is understood:—that all comprehension is "beyond."[22]

Attentiveness, subordination, worship: concepts such as these struggle to express the sense of encounter with a Something Greater that underlies the religious attitude. Where scientific truth is "for us," religious truth remains grounded in the "beyond us."

3. The truth of religion is not found in a specific object of experience but in the *ground* of all experience. In contrast to the scientific mind-set, the religious consciousness will never countenance the divine as one object among other objects in the world. The paths for avoiding this mistake are almost unlimited in number: Tillich's move beyond ontology to the ground of Being; Duméry's use of the transcendental reduction to speak of the ground of all experience rather than mere objects of experience;[23] concentration on the meaning of religious attitudes (Louis Dupré); the subjectivism of Hick's "seeing as" or Hare's "bliks"; the "neither/nor" of Buddhism's nondualistic consciousness; and of course the mystical *via negativa* in its many forms.

This difference in the truths of religion and science is reflected in the form of expression of their truths. "Completed science," if such a notion is coherent, would be a system of propositions that reflected the totality of states of affairs. This ideal could in principle be reached by a gradual accretion of adequate theories improving upon, but not essentially changing, the way we currently formulate and test theories. By contrast, the need to negate or qualify one's statements about the divine increases almost proportionately with their correctness. When "adequate" statements are made about the divine, the believer inevitably insists that they are to be taken analogically, doxologically, maieutically, praxologically, even equivocally. There is a sense in which believers will accept their explanations of *specific* events or doctrinal teachings as adequate, while insisting that, at the more general level, holistic explanations are called for that exceed the abilities of human language. The appeal to a knowledge beyond words—or to the limited effability of parable, myth, or symbol—is the repeated temptation of the religious teacher.

4. Finally, scientific activity—and hence scientific truth—remains sui generis on account of its method, which in some way allows humans the means for moving from their particular frameworks toward intersubjective agreement. Here the strengths of scientific method explored in section 1 retain their validity even in face of the section 2 insights into the nature of scientific truth as "per-

sonal knowledge." Scientific activity may be permeated by individual perspectives and institutional influences on belief change or maintenance. But it is also characterized by significant mechanisms for avoiding, or recognizing and circumventing, errors and prejudices in the construction of theories. Whereas in art and, I believe, religion, individual or communal perspectives contribute to the richness of religious and artistic truth, in science significant means exist for eliminating perspectival differences. Where perspectives are ultimate givens, as in special relativity or cultural anthropology, mathematical functions or formal taxonomies (respectively) are always sought to specify the interrelationships between frameworks.

We thus find ourselves driven in the final analysis back toward at least some of the traditional distinctions between scientific and religious truth. The movement is not strictly circular, however, for some progress has been made. After observing the significant overlaps between scientific and religious activity in section 2, we can no longer construe the four distinctions just discussed as signs of a fundamental religion/science dichotomy, as in section 1. Though we do grant essential differences between truth in the two fields, we do so as part of a differentiated phenomenology of science and religion, one that eschews black-and-white distinctions in favor of careful gradations more truly representative of the complex realities of the phenomena themselves.

3

Truth and the Wisdom of Enduring

Edward Farley

The Diminishing Sphere of Religious Truth

Truth in theology is not a matter of a single problem; it entails a legacy of issues. Truth in other words has a history. Furthermore, in Western Christian religion and theology the direction of this history has the character of erosion, or, to change metaphors, a selling off of formerly claimed reality territories.[1] What was it that was sold off? We must acknowledge that Western Christianity is a historical reality that combines many ancient traditions, themselves containing different histories and meanings of truth. This combination brought together an authoritative written and institutional tradition (which became itself the route to truth), a comprehensive metaphysic, and an account of the origin, structure, and final destiny of the cosmos. Constituting the (authoritative) account was an official cosmology, history of the human race and its destiny, a more or less official geography, multiple historical claims (convictions) about the origin of Christianity and the church, an anthropology, ethic, and church polity.[2] *What* is true is this comprehensive cosmological narrative and the *basis* of truth is revelation as it obtains an indubitable expression in writing and institution. And both narrative and base comprise the cognitive territory that has undergone severe erosion.

The erosion of the classical synthesis of authority and cosmo-history can be traced in four steps. The Christian cosmo-history itself with its geography, planetary scheme, body-soul anthropology with all its alliance with the ancient world was challenged and displaced by the work of what came to be a group of sciences (physics, geology, biology, etc.), which obtained independence from both philosophy and religion. The conclusion of this dispute is that matters of fact about nature, about cosmos and life, are settled not by authority or by coherence of scheme but by experimental verification. The Christian message could then be interpreted as something not dependent on the "secular" cosmological and natural sciences.

A second erosion occurred when authoritative claims to *historical* matters of fact (Who wrote what book of the canon? When did such-and-such an event occur? Did Jesus of Nazareth say everything attributed to him?) were subjected to historical evidence and methods. The outcome of this dispute was that appeal to the sedimented mediators of revelation (scripture, church tradition) cannot establish or of themselves vindicate historical claims.[3] This called forth a version of the Christian message as something not dependent on history.

The third erosion began when sixteenth-century Protestant reformers attacked the metaphysical element of Catholic Scholasticism, and continued as theology allied itself with the antimetaphysical tradition of modern philosophy.[4] The outcome of this erosion was the assertion of theology's (and religion's) independence from philosophical and speculative accounts of being, the categories of being (Aristotle), the hierarchy of being (Neoplatonism), the coherence of being, and so forth. Thus, to affirm the truth of the Christian message requires no alliance with generic accounts of being and of world process.

We seem to be living now in a period where a fourth selling off of truth real estate is occurring. Surviving the erosions of cosmology, historical facticity, and metaphysics is still a kind of truth claim imbedded in the Christian message. The kerygma, narrative, primary symbols, doctrines, and theologies of Christianity do still communicate something about the way things are. This something is a specific and in a certain sense universalizable ontology of the human condition. Thus, theologians from Paul Tillich to Karl Rahner acknowledge and participate in the first three erosions but probe the legacy of Christian discourse and the reality of the Christian community for a remnant of ontology. In a certain sense contemporary hermeneutic theology does something similar. It is just this remnant of ontology that is the subject of another yet more radical phase of philosophical critique of both philosophy and theology. It was anticipated by that type of Anglo-American analytic philosophy that would reform philosophy's vocation into a therapeutic of language, by neo-Reformation theologies (Barth), which empty theology of any self-conscious moment of ontological analysis, and by the radical theology movement of the 1960s. The reason the attack on ontology is also an erosion of truth, at least in most of truth's meanings, is that ontology requires a manifesting *presence* for

its reflective verifications, plus some form of the surpassing of concrete particularity that uses *universals*, plus, again, some form of *ref-
erentiality* of words and meanings of words. But these are the very
notions that have become problematic and dispensable in "postmodern" philosophers (the later Heidegger and Derrida) and in
those who combine Marxist hermeneutics and pragmatism to argue
that ontology is always an *oppressive* and socially legitimating universalization.

Some contemporary theologians and philosophers of religion
embrace this fourth (and final?) erosion of truth and announce the
end of theology itself.[5] Reflecting the antiontology of the neo-
Reformation movement, others propose a new (and final?) restoration to religious truth claims. Religion claims a truth only within the
confines and bounds of its historical particularity. Therefore, it can
do without cosmology, history, metaphysics, and ontology, because
the truth it affirms can be maintained and measured only within
and by means of the language games of the specific historical
community.[6]

Where does religion (and theology) stand at the end of these
erosions? Its situation seems to be enviable and at once pitiable.
Enviable (from a certain point of view) is its new immunity from
criticism. Its message can now be presented without making its case
before juries of scientists, historians, and philosophers. Its situation
is pitiable because the Christian message no longer has to do with
truth at all, or at least, any state of affairs, any matter of fact, any
persisting reality. This is not so much the "question of truth" as the
situation in which reflection on religion and the truth of things now
occurs. It would surely be uncritical to grant cognitive and philosophical status to the mere fact of these erosions. As steps or stages
of diminishment they all call for analysis and assessment. But the
erosions are a present legacy that continues to shape the struggle
with the truth of things in the sphere of faith.

The Current Rending of the Body of Truth

The form in which questions or issues of truth are now
present is that of very fundamental and continuing disputes. The
legacy of the "truth question" has produced a literature of polemics
and counter-polemics so that the "body" of truth is present to us as
something torn, pulled asunder. Truth is split both into major issues
and into apparently exclusive approaches to these issues. Three issues dominate the present fray: the meaning of truth itself, the lo-
cale or path to its occurrence, and the historicity of truth.

An older and conventional typology distributes the alternatives into correspondence, coherence, and pragmatic theories.[7] This typology obscures rather than illumines the present-day discussion, because another three-cornered debate has replaced it.[8] The correspondence approach is still very much with us, presupposed by most sciences and undertakings of scholarship, and explored and maintained in Anglo-American linguistic philosophy, Thomism, and various versions of realism.[9] The correspondence *theory* of truth predetermines the meaning of truth to be a feature of assertions—to wit, the concord or harmony between their immanent meaning and the indicated state of affairs. This approach has been the target of two major types of challenge, both of which are formulated as either supplementations or replacements of the correspondence theory. One challenge has arisen in twentieth-century Continental philosophy and the phenomenological movement. In its Husserlian form this challenge occurs in connection with a turn to the *experience* of truth as the experience of evidentiality in originary form.[10]

However, it is Heidegger who, taking his cue from Brentano, gives the turn from correspondence to a more primordial sense of truth a central place. Well-known is his retrieval of the "primordial" meaning of truth as *a-lētheia* or the unconcealing of what is hidden. Truth, then, is *Dasein*'s way-of-being (*Seinsart*) in the world, and means directly the unconcealment, the uncovering of Being that attends that way-of-being, a world transaction in the mode of illumination.[11]

The second challenge (though not necessarily a displacement) of the correspondence theory arises in conjunction with various versions of the "historicity of truth." Historicity here is a comprehensive term that includes the historical, social, changing, and contextual character of truth. One version, *historicism*, has a reductionist character. That is, truth is neither correspondence, manifestness, nor liberative action, but a product of an epoch's or society's convictional system.[12] Phenomenology, existentialism, heremeneutics, and deconstruction are all moments in Continental philosophy's versions of truth's historicity; and pragmatism (Dewey, Rorty) is another. The most widespread expression of the historicity of truth is probably the Marxist hermeneutic and philosophy of action.[13] Marx, too, attacks the subject-object approach in which truth is a mere content delivered from an object in itself to a subject, or a mere mirroring of the objective world in the subject. In place of this delivery, truth is always human activity, not in the sense of the autonomous subject, but in the sense of historical, corporate action. When this rather general insight is drawn into more specific contexts of human action, contexts of oppression and its political opposition, truth names a product of liberating activity. The untrue, then, describes the cognitivity, even sciences, philosophies, "logics," and conceptualities, that advance and maintain oppressive powers.[14]

Taking Sides: Four Theses

Two themes have shaped my approach to the question(s) of (religious) truth: the gradual reduction of the sphere of truth virtually to a vanishing point, and issues posed by present-day philosophical disputes, particularly the issue of the cogency and sufficiency of the correspondence approach and the concepts (universal, meaning-reference, etc.) engendered thereby.

Before taking up the issue posed by the historical legacy, the waning sphere of religious truth, it is necessary to appraise and sift the issues engendered by the confrontation between the correspondence approach and its critics. In the scope of a brief essay, I can only do this "dogmatically" and impressionistically, through preliminary explorations that prepare the ground for the climactic two sections of this essay.

The Genesis of Truth: The Need for a Wisdom of Enduring

In all three approaches to truth, one thing is clear. Truth does not happen prior to or outside the sphere of the human and human activity. Peirce, Heidegger, Marx, Rorty and the Anglo-American philosophers agree on this. Truth describes a certain way-of-being (*Seinsart*) in the world, a kind of transaction with things. How is it that such a transaction would ever arise?

It is proper but not sufficient to say that a kind of illumining of things attends human existing. Like all actual things, human beings exist *as* complex biopsychological environments and *in* larger complex environments. Further, all actual living entities, individual and corporate, do not just endure but unflaggingly attend to the conditions of their enduring. They mount perpetual surveillance over possible detrimental or favorable changes going on about them. Not only do they live in the mode of nonindifference; one could say that in the mode of passion or eros, vis-à-vis the conditions of their well-being, they obtain and accumulate a kind of wisdom about these conditions, which endures with their enduring. This applies to everything from a protozoa to a nation-state and civilization.

This wisdom of enduring is rarely locked up inside the interior complexity of the thing, because any actual entity is never merely an interiority but a cooperative transaction and reciprocity with its environment. Hence, this wisdom pertains not simply to the well-being of the individual entity but to others of its type and even to its total environment. Thus one part of the enduring of living things, one thing that endures with them, is a wisdom pertinent to the conditions of enduring. Arctic wolves discover certain things about arctic survival (for instance, the availability of rodent populations in certain seasons), and this becomes a feature of the enduring not just of a single wolf but of arctic wolves—a wolf-wisdom, so to speak.

In the sphere of the human, wisdom pertinent to enduring becomes enormously refined and complex, and grows in complexity with the complexification of cultures. Nor is it reducible to such concepts as biological or race survival. If the sphere of the human is the sphere of *Dasein*, of imagination, time-consciousness, existence, personal reciprocities, language, and the like, the conditions of well-being will have to do with these things. The historicity of human being, the differentiating and even creative power of difference in particular entities, periods, and cultures ever destroys identical formulations of these conditions. Hence, particular individuals and socialities discern and maintain a wisdom of enduring pertinent to their particularity.

What has all this to do with truth? It discloses why truth enters and shapes the human transaction within the world. All living entities require and accumulate a wisdom of enduring pertinent to "the way things are." A self-transcending and in a certain sense present-transcending entity (toward past and future) entertains such wisdom in the mode of abstracting and symbolizing apprehension about the way things are. The way things are is "illumined," inquired into, argued, and even institutionalized. That which drives these multiple cognitive activities is the distinctive way in which a self-transcending entity pursues and enjoys a wisdom of enduring.

Truth and the Interhuman

The anomaly of an absolute skepticism about truth, knowledge, or reality apprehension is that it must appropriate what it rejects to make its case—namely, the sphere of the interhuman. There is a common element in various attempts to deny or eliminate truth as a feature of the human transaction with things. This is the initial restrictive placing of truth (and knowledge, reality) in a prereality individual whose capacities for truth must then be demonstrated. The enterprise then is to indicate a number of causalities (cultural relativities, brain physiology, genetic predispositions) whose interventions hold reality and truth in abeyance. It is obvious to the point of banality that reality-positing must occur to make the case for such interventions. But any account of truth that begins with the prereality individual can only perpetuate anomalies and puzzlements. The reason is that truth is born not only in the human transaction with things, which has the character of an illumined wisdom of enduring, but is born also in the sphere of the interhuman (*das Zwischenmenschliche*).[15]

We would be acceding to individualism if we were to say that truth originates in the bestowal of reality on the (human) other. The primordial reality behind this more derivative notion is the interhuman (dialogal, reciprocal, intersubjective) sphere that precedes and is presupposed by all individuality and individual acts.[16] That is to say, all acts, emotions, thinking, and world interventions of individuals occur in a reciprocity, a language, and an acculturation that have already shaped them. This world or sphere of the interhuman primordially there is the sphere in which the human transaction with things takes place. Thus, the experience of, inquiry into, and reflection on such things as nature, entities, events, and even human being itself take place in a sphere of accumulated language, responsibilities and obligations, agendas, and cooperative activities.

In other words, the sphere of the interhuman is the condition for the possibility of participation in the reality of things.[17] Thus, if the sphere of the interhuman is bracketed, repudiated, or ignored, there is no road from what remains to "reality." The Marxist insistence on the primacy of action to truth is a specific version of this. That is, one of the persisting realities of that primordial sphere is the reality of human oppression and its attending self-concealment by ideology and the infrastructures of institutions.[18]

The Primordial Sense of Truth

The primordial sense of truth, behind which one cannot go, and in relation to which all other senses are derivative, is *the manifestness of what is as itself.* This is the one sense of truth that applies across the board to formal, a priori matters, to the flow of actualities, to apperceived features of the self, to experimental confirmations, and so on. There seem to be no philosophies, however radical their opposition to "presence," that do not assume this sense of truth in making their case. Indeed, in their polemics philosophers target the views of other philosophers; and they do this by representing as accurately as possible what those views are, engaging in etymological and other queries that range over the larger spectrum of hermeneutics. Unending world and thing references fill the writings and orations of all philosophers. These hermeneutic acts and world-related claims invite the ordinary questions of evidence and indicate readiness to respond to challenges of an affirmations's evidence, cogency, and clarity. All philosophers who appeal to texts, to implications, invite questioners to join with them in a joint act of standing before *the manifestness* under consideration.

The primordial sense of truth as manifestness tends to be obscured when truth is postponed to some postperception moment of interpretation or reflection.[19] The emptying of perception of its truth dimension is successful only in a narrowed understanding of perception. Consider what happens in human perception. In the perception or perceptive experience of a physical object (for instance, a cloud in the sky) there is a focused, intended entity (the cloud) as *that* entity (the cloud); a meaning of that entity as its *type* (cloud); a meaning of that entity in its specific setting (time, location, etc.) and in the *type* of setting or field for that type of entity; and a meaning of that entity as a totality and synthesis of details, features (moving shapes of cloud, cloud color), and so forth. All this occurs minimally in any perception. An expanded account would have to consider postures, perspectives, practical assessments, emotions, language, and many other things as attending perception. That truth (manifestness) occurs in connection with perception becomes apparent when a perception undergoes interhuman interrogation. An affirmative response to a query about perceiving *that* cloud has imbedded in it all the above features. To say that "yes, I saw the cloud" is to say that "it is true that I saw that cloud, that *that* cloud existed in that setting, as that totality of those details." This is not to say that perception (or any other experience of manifestness) is infallible or so utterly instantaneous as to prevent further exploration, confirmation, or reflection. Reflection may uncover the embedded features of perception or other modes of the experience of manifestness, but it is not their author. Likewise with verification, which addresses a provisional and inadequate perception. But neither reflection nor verification displaces the minimal features of perception. They do not get behind them or go beyond them to some mode that has no need of the manifest reality.

There are also attempts to interpret the primordial sense of truth (manifestness) as displacing or contradicting truth as a feature of assertions such that they correspond to their references. Yet criticism of the correspondence theory, which is found both outside and within Anglo-American analytic philosophy, addresses difficulties of particular ways of understanding correspondence. Of particular concern is the splitting of assertion, linguistic expression, and meaning from referred matters in the form of subject and object so that some sort of deus ex machina must be posited to bring them back together. It would, however, be a strange mysticism of truth to so restrict truth to manifestness that it has no connection with expressions, cognitive acts, and agendas of inquiry, or with criteria of accuracy, adequacy of evidence, and the like. In other words a dualism of truth and correctness as mutually exclusive is a high price to pay for the restoration of the primordial sense of truth.

"The Orders of Truth"

If the *primordial* sense of truth is the *manifestness or illumination of* something, it is clear that truth occurs in connection with whatever is manifest, which means also whatever *type* or genre of thing is manifest. Many of the disputes over truth (and thus also knowledge, reality, and method) reflect the social and cognitive hegemony of the natural sciences, which tends to spawn a one-dimensional approach to truth. Thus, truth *means* mathematical, experimental, or perceptual verification. Such a view identifies truth with one of its derived modes and misses altogether the primordial sense of truth. For any assertion that truth *means* some particular method cannot avoid proposing the proper content or object of that method, an act that permits a selected method and its paradigm to determine in advance all possible cognitive objects. Method determines reality. But if truth is the manifestness of whatever manifests itself, its object, type, and content cannot be determined in advance or by method. Rather, method, mode of experience, and cognition will be determined by the specificity of what is manifest. This is why the primordial sense of truth gives rise to what Paul Ricoeur calls "orders of truth."[20] For manifestness occurs in connection with an open-ended variety of world transaction and world experience. It occurs in connection with political agendas, esthetic experience, moral agency, mathematical speculation, structural analysis, historical reconstruction, and experimentation. This is not simply an issue of the positivist abolishment of religion from the sphere of truth. The reduction of the sense of truth to a particular method and its reality paradigm suppresses most of the spheres of human transaction with the world.

The Enduringness of Being

Having presented four theses on truth, I am ready to move to the climactic sections of this essay.

Reflection on truth in recent Continental philosophy has taken a certain direction. From Brentano to Derrida, there has developed an ever more radical understanding of human historicity and therefore of the historicity of truth itself. This we would expect once the primordial sense of truth is exposed. With this development is a sharpened sense of incompatibility between the historicity of truth and all concepts that would do violence to historicity; thus, presence, universals, structure, and even "philosophy" itself. For universals and structures name matters that float above time and history. "God," "human nature," essences, ontological features, and transcendental consciousness all occur in the sphere of the unhistorical. This direction of thinking about truth has an outcome that can be said to be "the problem of truth" on the forefront of Continental philosophy. Given a radical understanding of the historicity of truth—given an incompatibility between truth and presence, or truth and universals, or truth and structure—how can anything be manifest at all? Is manifestness destroyed instantaneously with its occurrence? Can manifestness and *difference* co-exist without slaughtering each other? Is there a *matter* of truth and, if so, what is it?

The question of truth appears in Heidegger in connection with the question of being (*Sein*); he proposes that what is manifest is the *being* of things. This does not mean that *being* in some unitary sense is revealed in each thing but that the *being* and *way-of-being* of each entity is manifest. But what is that? Presumably, it is neither mere identity nor difference, neither a timeless essence nor a destruction. I would suggest that it is the enduringness of things. I would also suggest that Heidegger's understanding of time is so dominated by his fundamental ontology of *Dasein* that the enduringness of beings, of what is manifest, remained hidden. And as long as this is so, the *matter* of truth will be caught in the incompatible split of the unhistorical and difference. I shall explore this in two steps: the surpassing of particularity in world transaction, and the problem of expression.

First, the surpassing of particularity. I argued previously that truth originates in the need (*erōs*) for a wisdom of enduring appropriate for the sphere of the interhuman. It originates, in other words, in a certain transcending of utter particularity. This surpassing is not an exception but a pervasive feature of all philosophies, histories, sciences, and everyday-world acts as they surpass particularity toward the past, toward the contexts of particulars, toward required conditions, toward repetitions, toward family groups or types, toward duration. The most vociferous critics of essences, universals, and ontology direct their criticisms not toward the utterly particular and ephemeral but toward states of affairs in the world (their opponents, represented views), which endure and have enduring features—that is, toward interpretations that have arisen in and persist in the world. Having relativized representation, Foucault represents whole epochs with enduring features and as ways of historical duration contrastable to other ways of historical duration. Wittgenstein's arguments against one view of language and for another have in view not just one specific ephemeral speaking event but language, something that occurs when speaking occurs.

These reflective and interpretive surpassings are instances of a more primordial surpassing of particularity that characterizes the human world transaction itself. Human beings occupy and survive in the everyday world only if they surpass focused attention on the particular toward insight and understanding of persisting conditions, characteristic behaviors, and features of types of things. In other words our transaction with facts, details, singulars, and even changes is always a surpassing transaction that posits resemblances, recurrences, and enduring features. When we cross a street, we do not grasp, interpret, and respond to a set of individual, ephemeral items of a microsecond duration, but a situation whose temporal duration must be taken into account and whose discerned types of entities enduring through time bear on us and on each other.[21]

When human beings make the reflective or cognitive move to understand world occurrences, they inevitably perpetrate various abstractions. One such abstraction is toward the particular itself. The particular can be anything from a discrete item of perception, an automobile for instance, to a large historical complex, Judaism or Western culture. But even those abstractions require a surpassing of particularity if it is grasped *as* automobile or *as* culture. And this surpassing involves a synthesis of meaning as to both type and enduring features. In fact, as one focuses on actual, existing particulars, one is drawn to the enduring entity and therefore to enduring features. Abstracting cognitive focusing on a particular can be ever more focused (as on an automobile carburetor or an amino acid in the human organism), but even that focus is on an enduring way-of-being with characteristic features or behaviors. Cognitive abstraction can and does go on in the other direction, from the particular to its type, its shared features with other types, even the shared features of all types. Whichever the direction, a paradoxicality and loss attends all these abstractions and therefore the human world transaction in its cognitive aspect. For abstraction is corrected by restoring the excluded items in such a way that the particular is grasped in its context, relationality, and complexity, but these moves toward totality involve a loss of the particular as particular, a loss of the focusing act in which the particular is present. A violence is perpetrated toward reality in whatever direction cognition moves. All knowledge then is a loss as well as a gain.

I conclude with the rather banal thesis that human beings experience and know actual things always in acts that synthesize the discerned particular with transparticular meanings, contexts, significances, and so on. That which renders this unavoidable is not something "in" the ego or created by the subject, but the complexity and enduringness of whatever is. The human world transaction is a surpassing of particularity toward enduring meanings, features of situations, and ways-of-being. Hence, *that which is manifest, the truth of things, is the enduringness of being.*[22]

Next, the problem of expression. The theme here is the role of the universal in manifestness or truth. Almost every contemporary philosophical movement has its version of the criticism of universals. The criticisms uncover that way of understanding universals which would place them above concreteness and change, or which would posit changeless features amid the historicity of human being or the "Heraclitean fire" (Hopkins). The criticisms themselves are made through a type of universal—that is, descriptive expressions that carry the surpassing of particularity. And in process philosophy, universals survive as eternal objects, pure possibilities prehended by actual entities. It seems clear that the human world transaction oriented toward the truth (manifestness) of things is conducted through expressions of the enduring of beings. Enduringness comes to expression in discourse about types, genres, features, syntheses, complexes, typical operations, identifiable behaviors, and the like. While it is the case that none of these expressions is a simple mirror of objectivity, brings the flow of things to a stop, or is a mere identity or repetition of something else, all of them in some sense express an enduring of a sort. *Even as there is no manifestness without enduring, neither is there a manifestness without the expression of enduring.* Even as manifestness is the primordial sense of truth, *the expression of enduring is the primordial sense of the universal.* Hence, all cognitive acts (apprehending the sense of something; perceiving; or grasping structural makeup, causal connections, and implications) presuppose the initial capacity to grasp the enduring (that is, the manifestness of things) and thus also depend on and make use of expressions of enduringness.

The Truth of Things in the Sphere of Faith

The sphere of religious truth is diminished virtually to a vanishing point as the result of being contested by natural and social sciences and by the rending of the body of truth. What survives is a sphere independent of science, history, and philosophy, and devoid of presence, manifestness, and concern with "the way things are." Faith appears to have gotten out of the truth business altogether. I shall explore the issues posed by this diminishment in three steps, drawing on the assessment of the disputes presented in the four theses above.

1. The Meaning of Truth

It is typical of some approaches to presuppose the correspondence theory when they assess the "truth" of religion or religious discourse. The result is the relatively easy task of showing that the sphere of faith has little or no facticity, nò verifiable reference. But the question cannot be posed that way if correspondence is itself always derivative of the primordial sense of truth as manifestness. Our question must rather be, Is there a truth of things in the sphere of faith in the primordial sense of truth? Even this question is undercut from the beginning if it asks for an immediate presence or manifestness of the sacred simply in itself. Such a question necessarily mundanizes the sacred by drawing it into the sphere of immediate (mundane) manifestness.

I argued previously that the primordial sense of truth as manifestness gives rise to multiple orders of truth. For what manifests itself is a vast variety of genres and types of reality. The sphere of faith is not simply the sphere of the sacred in some abstract sense but rather is itself a multidimensional sphere that combines a certain distinctive human erōs, redemption, traditioning, community, a symbol system, and so forth. The question of manifestness is the question whether in *this* gathering of genres a manifestation occurs. It is from and through this question that one poses the issue of the manifestness distinctive of the sacred. There seems, in other words, to be a manifestness occurring in connection with the sphere of faith as a sphere of freedom, of redemption. If correspondence is not destroyed by manifestness but is derivative from it, then truth in theology—faith's reflectivity—occurs in multiple orders because of the multiple dimensions of faith's context; thus it occurs in verifications, historical explorations, reflective and even speculative inquiries.

2. *The Genesis and Historicity of Truth*

The experience of truth and undertakings of truth are rooted in the sphere of the interhuman and the human need for a wisdom of enduring—that is, a wisdom concerning the conditions of the enduring of human being in various modes of well-being. This is why truth or manifestness is not simply a transcendent and unhistorical realm above the sphere of action. It seems apparent that the sphere of faith is not outside the sphere of the interhuman and action but a special way of interhuman and active existence.

Historical and empirical studies of religions and their symbolic contents all show that the mythos of faith centers in a wisdom of enduring. This is an enduring, individually and communally, in the situation of discerned tragic existence, evil, and redemptive hope. In other words, the wisdom of enduring is not limited to conditions of mere physical survival, bodily health, or how economic systems work, important as these things are. The human transaction with the world is characterized by self-conscious and experienced fragility, by the dynamics of evil, by social oppression, by relative freedom in relation to such things. It is just these kinds of matters that the communities and mythoi of religions thematize, ritualize, and institutionalize. They embody as well as articulate a distinctive wisdom of enduring. Hence, the wisdom of enduring in the sphere of faith is neither identical with nor cut off from the socio-political sphere. Particular paradigms of that wisdom effect reductions of that wisdom to the sphere of the individual or the sphere of the political.

I conclude from all this that faith and the sphere of faith is not an exception but an instance of the experience and task of truth as prompted by a need for a wisdom of enduring.

3. *Faith and the Enduringness of Being*

I have argued that the "matter" of truth is the enduringness of things and that the truthful discourse brings this enduringness to expression. All the attacks on "onto-theology" presuppose and make use of some form of manifestness, enduringness, and expressions of it. The focus and contribution of the attacks is the criticism of versions of enduringness (and its carriers) that posit timeless or immutable being-entities or linguistic entities in the midst of actuality.

It is apparent that the history of (Western, Christian) religion is dominated by a notion of truth incompatible with the historicity of truth. Christian theology (like philosophies, political and cultural systems, etc.) has often frozen into unrevisable doctrines and casuistries its cultural carriers of the wisdom of enduring. And this has made it vulnerable to the various erosions of the truth of the sphere of faith and to recent criticisms of all unhistorical versions of truth.

Yet the religious community, especially as it embodies the sphere of faith, exemplifies the historicity of truth. This is because the "matter" of its concern, the enduringness of being in matters of evil, redemption, and the sacred, is not identifiable with the generic categories descriptive of species, epochs, types of being, and so forth, but is an account that follows and adapts to the ever-changing human experience of evil and redemption.

The truth of religion is historical and universal at once. The wisdom with which a religious community is concerned *does* surpass utter particularity and *does* pertain beyond a specific day or week, a specific individual, or even a specific nation or epoch. The ground of this surpassing is the *enduringness* of these things.

But as long as human beings visit evil upon themselves, a wisdom about the dynamics of evil pertains even as it must at the same time always be reformulated. We have here an instance in which the historicity of truth and the matter of truth as the enduringness of being are not exclusive but interdependent.[23]

In conclusion, truth in the sphere of faith undergoes erosion when truth is reduced to its more derivative meanings, when the primordial sense of truth is forgotten, when the orders of truth are reduced to a single order and paradigm, when the genesis of truth in the human need for a wisdom of enduring is forgotten, and when the matter of truth as the enduringness of things is displaced by the utterly formal or the utterly momentary.

4

The Truth, The Nontruth, and the Untruth Proper to Religion

Daniel Guerrière

The truth proper to religion is at issue. How are religions true? An onto-phenomenology will allow an answer to this question. The phenomenological notion of truth as *alētheia* will be the key. Hence the question is: What "manifestness" is proper to religion? The answer—indeed the question itself—presupposes an articulation of the essence (*Wesen*) of religion, that is, of the necessary structures of an experience, whatever its modal variation be. But the question of the truth is also the question of the nontruth and of the untruth proper to religion. An investigation of them will help to exhibit religious truth. Accordingly, this chapter falls into four main parts: (1) essence of religion; (2) essence of religious truth; (3) truth and nontruth; and (4) truth and untruth. A brief conclusion follows.

Before the main parts, however, an orientation is necessary to clarify where the question of truth belongs in the wider task of a phenomenology of religion. Its locus is the second moment of phenomenology, as informed by several basic attainments of the third moment.[1]

Phenomenology has shown itself, generically, to be a progressively primordial reflection and, specifically, to be (1) the articulation of the structure of objectivity in correlation with the structure of subjectivity, (2) the envincement of fundamental objectivity and fundamental subjectivity, and (3) the circumscription of the primordial unity out of which objectivity and subjectivity arise.

In the first moment of a phenomenology of religion, the religious object or other appears as the ultimate, ambiguous, and invocative power, worth, and autonomy, while the subject appears as the prefocal, interpretive, and unique self-as-a-whole. In the second moment, the religious other appears as the sovereign power of salvation, while the subject appears as the quest-to-be who needs this other in order to be. In the third moment, the unity of the two poles in their purity—which unity phenomenology can only circumscribe but not know directly—is Love. This essay develops the second moment and appropriates from the third moment of phenomenology in general the ideas of Being and of truth (as *alētheia*). When phenomenology develops with explicit reference to Being, it may be called onto-phenomenology.

Here, then, is an onto-phenomenology of the truth proper to religion.

1. Essence of Religion

Religion is a fact. What is its way-of-Being (*Wesen*)? What distinguishes this phenomenon from all others? What is it in the ways-to-be of man and of world that makes factual religions precisely religious? Here an onto-phenomenology will articulate an answer; it will, with modal neutrality, exhibit the necessary structures of the religious subject and of his correlative religious object or other. This articulation has two stages: religion as remedy, and experience of salvational Power. The question of the truth proper to religion then has a basis and is the issue of the third section in this part: question(s) of truth(s).

Religion as Remedy

Why should religion ever arise? What makes it possible and universal? Religion is a response: but answers are intelligible only in reference to their questions. What, then, is the question to which religion is the answer? The question is both fundamental and existential.

The fundamental existential question is: Will we ever be able to achieve the self whom we have been given to be? Can we reach our selfhood, our Being? Or is our quest-to-be necessarily a failure? Is fulfillment or consummation possible? This is not a speculative question that we pose about an object susceptible of inspection: it is the question that we *exist*. For our every effort is an effort to *be*. The only reason to do anything, to only reason to be, is to *be*—that is, to be To-be, to be our Being. But this effort is made problematic in the extreme by the double fact of evil: the evil that we undergo and the evil that we undertake, evil suffered and evil done.

To suffer and then to die is the price of life. The first of the four noble truths of the Buddha is that living *is* suffering. The evil that we suffer culminates in death. If it were not the case that evil could kill us or, just as decisively, kill our desire to live, whatever we suffer would always be tolerable. Our endeavor and our desire is to *be*. For a self whose way-to-be is to-be-alive, to die is to be thrust into the possibility that one may no longer *be*. Evil is whatever militates against our possibility to *be*, to become, to grow; it is whatever would destroy our nature (*physis*: being, becoming, growing). And suffering militates against our possibility to grow, while death culminates suffering as the possibility of our impossibility.[2] That is why they are evil. They are evil also because they often represent aggression against our possibility to grow; much of the evil that we suffer is evil that we do to ourselves, each and other. But suffering, with its culmination death, is ambivalent. For suffering is also the test of our possibility to grow, and death may accordingly be its final test. That is why their evil may be made good.

But this transformation of evil to good is not peculiar to religion. Whatever the response to evil suffered be, it is not specific to religion. That is, religion does not constitute itself specifically as the human response to evil suffered. To be sure, religions often provide ways to interpret, to confront, to tolerate, and to transform it.[3] But since this series of possible responses may obtain outside religion (e.g., in psychotherapy, medicine, and politics), religion cannot be defined *as* it. Nonetheless, death does belong to the problem to which religion is the answer—when death be anticipated as the *acute form* of the problem of evil done.

The evil that we do is the specific problem to which religion arises as the response. For *this* evil is invincible by us: the condition into which man puts himself by the evil that he does is impossible for man to remedy. Religions have offered many symbols of this condition: man as prisoner, for example, or as deviating from the straight path, or as lost in the desert. A conceptualization of these symbols is possible. Moral evil is to undermine the effort to *be*, to become, to grow—in oneself and at once in others. To do evil is to act in such a way that the principle of one's own action is to make oneself or another not *be* (himself, his self, his Being). The problem is that once we fail to be, we can no longer, to that extent, *be*. To not be—that is, to do evil—is to not be there to *be*, to be our *Being*. Or again: once we do not do ourselves, we can no longer, to that extent, do ourselves; for our past is now beyond our power. We constitute ourselves—our selves, our Being—as incomplete, and this incompleteness is permanent; for as past it is no longer within our power to reconstitute. The human person puts himself into a condition that he cannot remedy; he renders impossible his own consummation. According to religious myth, this condition of iniquity is universal.[4]

The problem with death is that it is existentially the acute form of the problem of evil done. How is this? For a self who *lives*, death is the unsurpassable possibility of life. But it is not death as the culmination of evil suffered that would frustrate the effort to be. Suffering and death are inherent in life, which is a way to be and to try to be. Rather, the human self in his failure to *be*—that is, moral evil—frustrates the effort to be. Death would automatically be this frustration *only* if to be a self necessarily imports to be alive, only if personhood and life were mutually reducible, so that to be dead would import to no longer *be*. But it is impossible to prove that self-hood is reducible to organism.[5] What, then, is the problem with death? The problem is the possibility that the failure to be *necessarily* continues in death, that the condition of iniquity is made *definitive* by death, that in dying the self who has done evil will *never* reach his Being. The problem remains that of evil done.

It is here that religion arises. If human beings cannot remedy their own condition of iniquity, they can only hope that an other will do it for them. The therapy for the human project that frus-trates itself—a frustration that death may certify—is *the work of an other*. Religions name this work and this other in various ways.[6] Here the terms "salvation" and "the salvational Power" will be used. Philosophy can only project this event and this Power as the solution to the fundamental existential problem; it cannot say whether the solution actually takes place. Of course, the human person may make such a judgment or claim the competence to do so; the philosopher as such, however, is incompetent.

A minimal philosophic definition of religion is now possible. It would be: (1) to acknowledge our condition of iniquity, our need for an other to save us, our exigency for a salvational Power, and in-deed to hope for it; and (2) if, under certain conditions, it does ap-pear or does advent in experience, then to acknowledge it as what it is, to let it do its proper work, indeed to celebrate it. This definition aims to exclude everything that may be associated with historical religions but is not proper to religion, for example, a particular so-cial structure or even a particular moral code. The religious is the salvational. Of course this minimal religiosity may be concretized in many ways.

Philosophy can only project a salvational Power and the hu-man experience of it. But before any claim to an experience wherein it is present, philosophy can still, *given the fundamental existential problem*, elaborate the necessary structures of any possible salva-tional Power and of the experience of its work.

A salvational Power must have two characteristics. First, it must be personal and, basic to this, loving. For, to save man would be to let him *be*, to let him be himself, his Being. But to-let-be is the very definition of love. Whatever else it is, love is the promotion or the active affirmation of the person. To love is to will the person— myself and others—according to his proper Possibility; it is to allow him to be what he already-is-but-not-yet; it is to realize the person in his uniqueness and communality; it is to let him *be* his own destiny (*daimon*). But this is precisely what a salvational Power, to *be* a salvational Power, would do. Since love is proper to persons, it— henceforth *he*—would be a *personal* power.

Secondly, any possible salvational Power would be transcendent to time. For, if he is to undo the human past, if he is to reconstitute man, then he must be such that the past of mankind is presently available to him, is present for him. He must be such that past and present are *one* for his experience. But to be in *this* way is to be nontemporal. If there is to be a salvational Power, he must be *atemporal*.

Beyond this a priori determination of any possible salvational Power, can philosophy move to an affirmation of him? Not in an a priori way, according to some argument that begins with what is not him and concludes to him. Only prephilosophical experience can affirm a salvational Power; philosophy can recover in its reflection only what is there prior to it. The so-called proofs for the existence of God actually presuppose an experience of that Power. Their major premise is the affirmation of something supreme in its way, for example, an uncaused cause (but basically Being). Their minor is the identification of this with a salvational Power already discovered outside philosophy ("and this we call God"). Although philosophers have concentrated upon the major, the crux is the minor premise.[7] The identification is possible only if prephilosophical experience provides the God to be affirmed. This does not import, however, that philosophy cannot inform that experience with critical standards. Indeed, given the fundamental existential problem, philosophy can elaborate much that later investigation finds religious history to concretize; it begins with experience, finds its necessary structures, and thus anticipates further experience.

Experience of the Salvational Power

What could it mean, then, to experience a salvational Power? In what way does the human person here and now experience salvation and thus the other who would effect it? How does God enter into human experience?

Philosophy can project the critical standards for such an experience; it can a priori elaborate what it would minimally comprise. Since any salvational Power would have to be loving and atemporal, the human encounter therewith must be structured in certain ways. First, what atemporality implies; next, what personality implies.

The atemporal is not directly available in human experience; for anything temporal, everything concrete is temporal. "No man has seen God." If it is to appear in time at all, whatever transcends time must appear in it as not-itself.

But precisely that is the structure of a symbol: the indirect appearance of something, the ambiguous presence of a phenomenon, the ambiguous manifestation of that which presents itself in experience. As commonly understood, a symbol is a double-sense, the first (overt) of which both reveals and conceals a second (covert), which, for the immediate experience, is available only in this way. A sign, in contrast, is one sense that directs experience to another one. But a symbol is an inseparable double-sense. It is, in other words, *one* phenomenon that shows and hides itself at once. The overt sense *is* the covert sense—but ambiguously. The exemplary symbol seems to be *my body:* it is the person who I am, but ambiguously so; it is the revealment and at once the concealment of myself. A symbol, then, is a phenomenon that presents itself as *not* itself. However, this structure also defines a semblance (e.g., an illusion).[8] Hence a further precision is necessary. A semblance is a phenomenon that shows itself as *what it is not;* its appearance is, in turn, a positivity that exhausts the phenomenon; there is *no more* to the phenomenon than its "appearance." A symbol, by contrast, is a phenomenon that shows *itself* as not itself—that is, it remains itself and is not exhausted in what is not itself; it is not reducible to that *as* which it shows itself; it is *more* than its "appearance." A symbol is a phenomenon that posits a presence for itself that is less than itself; it is a phenomenon that shows itself as not itself insofar as what is not itself does not exhaust it; it is the ambiguous manifestation of a phenomenon that is more than this manifestation. For example, I myself am irreducible to, or am more than, my body; but my body is my self-presence in an ambiguous way. In this sense, the one phenomenon "announces" itself.

The atemporal would announce itself in time: a salvational Power would appear in experience only symbolically. (Later on we shall take up the symbols of the salvational Power as well as derivative religious symbols.[9])

That which enters human experience as a salvational Power would do so not only symbolically but also personally. What does this import? Despite appearances, a salvational Power would not appear as an object, as that-which-is-thrown-before(-me) (*ob-jactus*), as that-which-stands-over-against(-me) (*Gegen-stand*). The object is an other that is susceptible of possession, appropriation, incorporation; it may be located with respect to my body; hence it is definitely temporal. A salvational Power would announce himself as the person presents himself: the other par excellence, who freely disposes of himself and who can, while remaining unique and unpossessible, enter into communication and communion with another. The person is at once an ek-sistence (to-be-toward-others-and-oneself, to find an end in others and in oneself) and an in-sistence (to-be-in-oneself, to be original for oneself and for others). The person is an exteriority that remains interior to itself. Of course, the human person is *also* an object. But while the otherness of objects may undergo cancelation into the person, the otherness of the person remains definitive even though he may undertake communion with another. The object submits and resists; the person solicits and respects both the other and himself. The person is himself to the extent that he allows others to be themselves. His presence is a co-presence. Hence I experience other persons to the extent that their presence is evocative and affirmative of mine *and* to the extent that my presence is evocative and affirmative of theirs. What does this import for the experience of a salvational Power? There would be two poles in the experience: what is at his disposal and what is at mine.

First there is what is at his disposal—what he would be for me, or what his presence would mean for me. How does he "appear" in experience?

The experience of a salvational Power would be this: despite fault and its possible definitive form (death), I *can* become who I am. The experience would be: despite the condition of iniquity, my future will not be simply determined by my past, my future is not wholly vulnerable to my failure to be myself and thus to co-be. The experience of a salvational Power would be the realization that the process of my humanization need not end in failure.[10] It is the conviction that despite closure and autarky, human ek-sistence and in-sistence will come to fulfillment. The co-project that I am, flawed though it be, is not vain today, for the *novum*—that beyond anything that may be extrapolated from the past—is *already* here: the experience of *this* is the experience of salvational Power.

Hence an a priori experiential definition of the salvational Power is this: that-my-future-need-not-be-my-frustration. The Power cannot be defined as an object, expressible in a simple noun; this

Power can be defined only as a presence that evokes and respects me, expressible in a noun clause. God *is* that-my-tomorrow-can-ever-be-new: he is the power-of-Renewal, ever before me. God *is* that-my-past-will-not-destroy-me: he is the power-of-Regeneration, ever behind me. God *is* that-love-will-not-fail: he is the power-of-Love, ever beside me.

A salvational Power is nothing if he does not "appear" as the power-of-our-better-Future, the Power that conquers the condition of iniquity and the possible certification of it (death). It may well be that we lack such an experience. The lack, however, is not the counterexperience. *This* would be the persuasion that, despite love, we try in vain to be; that the condition of iniquity is invincible; that evil has the upper hand and that it shall lay us low. To announce that despair is a lie is what is at the disposal of the salvational Power.

Then there is what is at my disposal.

The experience of a salvational Power presupposes that I accept the need for such a Power. For one who does not acknowledge the exigence for a salvational Power, none can appear; only if I experience the question does the (possible) answer make sense. However, it may be that the need itself be not a matter of direct experience, that the need be available only symbolically. Indeed, this seems to be the common experience. For example, I may directly experience bitter regret or sad bewilderment about what I have done to myself or others. In that case, the experience of the need is conditional upon an interpretation of the regret or bewilderment.

Furthermore, the experience of a salvational Power is conditional upon interpretation. Correlative to symbol is interpretation or decipherment, which, for the mature person, is an option. Since a salvational Power appears symbolically, he is present for me only if I interpret one phenomenon or another *as* his (ambiguous) presence. For example, a radiant dawn may be a cosmic event; but it may also, for interpretation, be the concealed presence of the Dawn, the power-of-the-New. Or again: the saving grace and healing power of love among friends may be a human discovery and wonder; but it may also, for interpretation, be the ambiguous entrance of God into human experience.

What is at my disposal in the experience of a salvational Power is to admit my need, to freely interpret—and then to admit whatever interpretation unveils.

The experience of a salvational Power is a symbolic and personal experience. Since the two poles of the experience—the human person and the ambiguous presence of a personal Power—are temporal, the symbols will be historical. They arise, flourish, and decline. At any time, the symbols of the salvational Power are correlative to the forms that human freedom gives itself (which does not import that they are arbitrary). Hence they have been very extensive.

The symbols of the salvational Power—and (this means) the Power's presence, active presence, activity—will be called *the sacred*. Sometimes the sacred is definitively local, sometimes inherently universalizable. In fact, it can be and has been almost anything: objects and events, places and time-periods, personal acts and states, and, at the extreme, a person.[11] Among objects, the sky is a common symbol: we experience it as overarching, constant, incoercible; and, as such, it lends itself to the symbolization of a transcendent and sovereign power. The earth, too, as that from which human nourishment springs, is an apt symbol for a power-of-Regeneration. Oneiric symbols may themselves be experienced, to the second degree, as ambiguous manifestations of a salvational Power. The possibilities are indefinite.

In any case, the sacred always stands in a dialectical relationship with the profane (i.e., the two terms are related such that the meaning of the one depends upon the meaning of the other, like husband and wife).[12] The sacred is always a figure in the field of the profane. A recent Western phenomenon, the "secular" is the profane as autonomous. Secularization is not an antireligious experience; it rather represents the achievement of the autonomy of religious interpretation. The experience of the sacred is no longer automatic, a cultural involuntary; it must rather be achieved by each person in an explicit option. The "flight of the gods" is the autonomy of the religious option.

With the sacred as the primary religious symbol, philosophy may articulate the major derivative ones. Granted salvational action, the first derivative symbol would be the symbol of what this action effects: *the salvational condition of man* (e.g., a place in the heavens). This symbol could be complicated or explicated by various others (e.g., of the perfect community of salvation or of the termination of the cosmic process). In a dialectical relation to the salvational condition is *the present condition* of man, that is, the original condition with respect to the salvational; symbols for this (e.g., enslavement) would be second in derivation. Next are the origins of the present condition: on the one hand, *the origin of humankind* and of all things human and, on the other hand, *the origin of evil*. These symbols are expressive of the depth of the present condition but in a quasi-historical way. Behind them is *the origin of the cosmos* and of everything cosmic. The symbol of the origin of the cosmos as an event may at once be a symbol of *the Power* that effects it; for religion, this is the same as the Power of salvation.[13] However, the properly religious question is not that of the origin of the cosmos but is rather that of the end of man; and the reoriginative Power, the one that would effect human consummation beyond the present condition of iniquity, is also the originative Power, the one that brings the cosmos into its present.

The symbol of the salvational Power himself and the six derivative symbols constitute the a priori schema of religious symbols.

To differentiate the complete schema of symbols is the work of philosophic reflection. In terms of this schema, particular historical religions may be compact, or incomplete, or both. An example of compactness would be a symbolism that does not distinguish between the origin of evil and the origin of the cosmos; various other amalgamations may occur.[14] An example of incompleteness would be Buddhism as a religion, which has no symbol of a cosmogonic Power. In any case, what philosophy may a priori determine—the schema of primary and secondary symbols—may serve as a *criterion* in two kinds of judgment on religions: their position in the process of the differentiation of human experience, and their explicitness as religions. While the science of religions simply orders what it finds and finds what it orders, philosophy may explicate the criteria for judgment. Neither science as such nor philosophy as such may, however, institute a judgment.

But now it may be useful to show how the criterion could help to avoid sterile controversies. For example, is there such a phenomenon as an "atheistic religion," as some would characterize Confucianism? We may answer *no;* this religion is simply incomplete in its symbolic schema. Insofar as it is a religion, Confucianism is a way of salvation, which implies a salvational Power, whether or not this Power be explicitly symbolized. This is an example of a judgment, a critique of an historical religion, to which both philosophy and science must contribute.

Above, religion was defined as a double acknowledgment: of the human need for a salvational Power and of this Power's work. Now, it is possible to elaborate a more concrete definition. Religion is both (1) a tradition of a symbolic whole founded upon an experience of a salvational Power, and (2) a tradition of praxis that witnesses to the experience. Let us take each of these in turn.

First, we begin with the a priori schema of religious symbols. The salvational Power, the salvational condition, the present human condition, the origins of humankind and of evil, the origin of the cosmos, and the originative Power may all be symbolized; the first one is primary. The symbols themselves may be simple, or narrative (i.e., myths), or quasi-conceptual (e.g., "original sin").[15] Furthermore, the primary symbol—of the presence, action, or efficacy of the Power as salvational—may take on gestural as well as linguistic form; in that case it is a rite. A symbol may also take on artistic form; and of course the rite and the myth may themselves be works of art. In any case, the complex of myth, rite, and artwork is the focus of religiosity. This focus is the communal evocation of the salvational Power, whether periodic or occasional (like initiation into full membership in the community). Since it is historical, the complex may dissolve and the elements become dissociated. However this be, the symbols of a religion (simple, narrative, quasi-conceptual), in whatever form (linquistic, gestural, artistic), constitute a coherent whole. This is not a system, evenly developed throughout. Though it may contain the work of reflection, it is not a formal construct, deducible a priori from a few principles. Rather it is adventitious, dependent in its development as much on the profane as on its internal exigencies.

The symbolic whole is founded upon an experience of the effective presence of a salvational Power—an experience that elaborates itself according to the modes of possession (the economic dimension), the relations of power (the political dimension), and the possibilities of prestige (the social dimension) in a culture. Always cultural, a religion is *a tradition of a symbolic whole founded upon an experience of salvation.*

Secondly, as a tradition, a religion is a directive for comportment. The tradition is an expectation of a certain way of life; those who share it share an ideal of behavior. The "religious praxis" that the tradition of an experience of salvation defines is the "morality" of that religion.

But a critical reflection has to distinguish between ideals of religious praxis and moral codes. Although the two have, for the most part, been compact in the history of mankind, it has become clear in our day that they are not identical.[16] Moral codes are the guidelines that the human person gives himself in his quest for consummation, while religions are the human response to the evil (partly defined by moral codes) that renders this consummation impossible. What appear to be moral codes in religions are, if purified of their nonreligious elements, criteria of participation in a tradition. They define the comportment that follows a particular experience of salvation. For example, the first commandment of the Deuteronomic decalogue is: "I am Yahweh, your god . . . ; you shall have no other god(s) in defiance of me." Those who take Yahweh as their god are members of the community; those who do not, are not.

A religion, then, is a practical articulation of a specific experience of salvation, and thus of a salvational Power in effective presence. It is *a tradition of praxis that witnesses to the experience.*

Religion is, in brief, an experience of salvation and the implications of the experience.

We are ready, finally, to raise the question of truth. It is a question of the truth *proper* to religion.

Question(s) of Truth(s)

We may not ask any random question in any way that we please. To avoid arbitrariness, the above exposition of the *Wesen* of religion will provide the guideline for the questions to be raised and for their order. Their formulation proceeds from the exposition immediately and may therefore have to be revised later. Their content is various and therefore their unity is not immediately evident.

What about the salvational Power himself? Does the Power exist? Is any affirmation of him justifiable?

Does humankind experience a salvational Power? Does this Power appear in experience in a personal and symbolic way?

Is the experience genuine? Or reversely, is the nonexperience of the Power genuine?

What about the interpretation of symbols? Does it have a standard?

Are the symbols of the salvational Power genuine or illusory? Are they more or less so? In other words, are the primary symbols in religion true?

Are the derivative symbols true? How so? To what extent?

Is tradition true? How?

In general, how is religion true? What does it mean that a particular religion is true? Can one religion be more true than another? Is religion *tout court* true?

These questions have many variations and derivatives. How to approach them? A self-critical philosophy of religion worthy of the title will recognize that it can raise questions indefinitely, but it will also try to recognize their unity. The many questions of truth find their unity in the one question of *the truth proper to religion.* What could religious truth *be?* What is the essence (*Wesen*, way-to-be) of religious truth? How does religious truth arise? In what way is anything religious true at all? *Granted truth in general, what is proper to religious truth?*

To respond to this one question in a phenomenological way is the burden of this chapter.

2. Essence of Religious Truth

A phenomenology of religious truth will articulate the "essence" of it. How to explicate the truth proper to religion? Answer: as a mode of manifestation or manifestness.

Truth, for phenomenology, is not the coherence of a discourse or, before that, the adequation of discourse to its object. Rather, as Heidegger rediscovered, truth is manifestness (*alētheia*).

Within the correlation of subjectivity and objectivity, truth is the self-givenness of the object to the subject *and* the projection by the subject of the object. Within the unity of reciprocal implication, the object makes itself manifest and thereby makes the subject manifest in it *as at once* the subject makes the object manifest and thereby makes itself manifest in it.

For a phenomenological ontology, *truth is primarily* the process of beings coming to manifestness, *the process of* their *presencing*, their unconcealing, the Being-process itself. Whether subjective or objective, beings come to presence, they come into their own, they en-own (cf. *Er-eignis*); and this process from concealment to revealment is precisely truth or, perhaps better, truth*ing* (Husserl's *Bewahrheitung*).[17] For phenomenology, *truth is* secondarily *uncon-cealedness*, the stable acquisition of some moment of the process. This may have its subjective and its objective side. Presencing may congeal into a quasi-permanent stability, which is truth or, perhaps better, the truth*ed*. In brief, "truth" is to be understood primarily as the *process* and secondarily as the *stable acquisition* (both subjective and objective).

Granted "truth" so understood, it is possible to specify a priori what would be the fundamental truth proper to religion and then to elaborate its derivative senses.

Fundamental Truth

Religion is the experience of salvation and the implications of the experience.

But without a salvational Power—whether acknowledged or not—there is no salvation. Thus fundamental to religion is the ambiguous active presence of a salvational Power. The truth fundamental to religion would therefore be *the manifestation of the salvational Power*. However he appears in experience, if a salvational

Power makes himself manifest correlative to a human intention, then "truth" has taken place. If a religion is a tradition of the effective presence of a salvational Power, then, fundamentally, any religion is true to the extent that this Power is manifest in it. The greater the manifestation, the greater the truth. For example, if a salvational Power makes himself manifest as and through the sun, the religion founded thereon is less true than that founded upon the self-manifestation of the Power as and through a person (granted that the Power must be personal). The original and continuous manifestation that founds a religion is the fundamental truth of any religion. It may be the experience of Abraham and Moses, for example, or that of an anonymous tribal shaman, or that of the founder of a community of acceptance and mutual encouragement today. Truth is manifestation, and the fundamental religious truth is the manifestation of a Power that would resolve the fundamental existential problem.

However, it is not the case that the manifestation of a salvational Power occurs on the one side and a human observer on the other. To be sure, any objectivity is correlative to a certain subjective stance. But beyond this, philosophy must recognize the *unity* of these correlates. They are moments of a primordial oneness that differentiates itself into them. This prior unity may be approached in three ways.

First, it is not the case that experienc*ing* occurs on the one side and the experienc*ed* on the other. Rather, my-experiencing-of-it *is* its-being-experienced-by-me. There is only the experiencing-of-the-experienced: the one occurrence. In other words, *experience* is primordial. And it has two poles: (experiencing-)*experience* (-experienced). Religious *experience* is the human experiencing of a salvational Power experienced: one phenomenon that polarizes itself.

Secondly, this one phenomenon may be circumscribed as sense or meaning (Husserl's *Sinn*). A complete subjective act is a double act, an empty and a (partially) fulfilled intentionality. An act intends an object *through* a sense; it projects toward a referent through projecting a meaning; it refers to an object through a sense that would be filled by the presence of the object; it means a referent. The correlate of the complete act is the meant-object or the object-meant. The object, in turn, presents itself to the act as the sense that the act intends; as the meaning that fulfills the empty intention; as the fulfillment of sense that the act projects. Meaning is the mode of presentation of the object or referent. Meaning, then, is both the act projecting (itself) and the referent presenting (itself).

The acting "means" (toward) an object, and an object "means" (for) an acting. The sense, therefore, is the "synthesis" of act and object, of intuition and evidence, of sense-giving act and sense-presenting referent. In other words, sense is that in and as which subject and object are one; it is the unity of projection and referent. It is the unity that polarizes itself: (act-)*sense*(-object). (That is why the question of *Sinngenesis* has been called the basic phenomenological question.) Religious *sense* or *meaning* is the subjective projection of a salvational presence: one phenomenon with two poles.

Thirdly, this primordial phenomenon may be understood as temporality (the "living present" of Husserl, or the "authentic time" of Heidegger, or the *kairos* of St. Paul). To put it briefly: the subject is a temporal process, and the object is one as well. In other words, temporality polarizes itself into correlative processes: (subjectivity-)*time*(-objectivity). Concrete time, the temporal event, is not an objective event on the one side and a subjective event on the other; rather, it is a oneness that dualizes itself. The religious *event*, then, is the one personal process of man-and-God, the one time of the human acknowledgment of a salvational manifestation.

The threefold prior unity of subjectivity and objectivity is the "there" of religion, as it is of everything else. In brief, the religious experience, sense, and event are *one* phenomenon with two poles. The manifestation takes place within experience, sense, and time; there is no truth outside meaningful temporal experience.

The archaic manifestation—the original and continuous effective presence of a salvational Power—is the fundamental truth proper to (any) religion. In other words, religious "truth" happens fundamentally with the (temporal) *event* of salvation, by the irruption of salvational *sense* in the world, and in the salvational *experience*. Greater or lesser truth, a greater or lesser intensity of manifestness of salvation, is an a priori possibility. Philosophy, however, cannot make judgments of truth concerning historical religions.

This fundamental truth founds other religious truths.

Derivative Truths

Philosophy may a priori elaborate the major derivative truths proper to religion.

The first would be *the manifestive power of the original announcement or proclamation* of the salvational experience. The experience announces itself for the sake of its own reactivation. That this proclamation allows the archaic experience—"archaic" in the etymological sense—to itself become manifest is the "truth" of religious proclamation. The announcement may be more or less adequate to the experience, or manifestive of it—that is, more or less true. If it be such as to render possible a reactivation of the archaic experience of salvation, then it is true—to whatever degree.

Since experience is already linguistic but not reducible to language, the announcement is likewise. The proclamation is always also a praxis. The logos of the praxis may receive more emphasis than the praxis of the logos, or the opposite. In any case, the proclamation that makes the experience manifest is a way of life that gives itself words or, reversely, a discourse that communicates a way of life. Its manifestive power is its truth. (Hence to pose the question of religious truth as first of all a question of religious language is existentially naive.)

While it is a priori possible that the proclamatory words be either spoken *or* written, historically the relevant discourse is always speech before it is scripture. Here, scripture is to be understood as the *final* original announcement, as proclamatory speech that has edited itself for an audience beyond the immediate.[18] Hence scripture is not to be considered a separable derivative truth.

The next religious truth would be *the manifestive power of the tradition*. The archaic experience of salvation, proclaiming itself, continues to activate itself as a tradition. To the extent that the proclamation is effective, a tradition arises; and the experience, announcing itself, reactivates itself. Religion, as defined above, is both a tradition of a symbolic whole that communicates the archaic salvational experience, and a tradition of praxis that witnesses to it. That the tradition makes manifest the archaic experience is the "truth" of tradition. It may well have degrees.

Religious tradition may take the form of "sacraments"—of communal renewals of the archaic experience of salvation, of communal evocations of the effective presence of salvational Power. They are the congealments of tradition. Above, the sacraments of a religion were characterized as (artistic) mythic rites or (artistic) ritual myths. Insofar as they manifest the archaic experience and thus bring to manifestness the work of the salvational Power, they are true.

But tradition, in order to remain precisely tradition and to not become complete innovation, must have given itself a norm. This norm is basically the original symbols, whether in gestural, artistic, or linguistic form. If a religion has a scripture, this scripture serves as the norm. Scripture is the original announcement as it becomes

normative tradition or, reversely, tradition as it develops norma-
tively out of the original announcement. In this way, the truth
proper to tradition has a measure.

The last major derivative truth proper to religion would be *the
manifestive power of theological reflection*. Tradition clarifies itself and
gives itself new forms in the work of theology. It is important to
distinguish the archaic experience in its verbalization, the proclamation as linguistic, and the tradition as linguistic and even reflective,
from the theology of a religion; their truths are serial. Theological
reflection subserves the manifestations of salvational Power in the
tradition; its ultimate aim is to make salvational Power accessible, to
renew the archaic experience. That it allows the archaic experience
to itself become manifest—to become a meaningful temporal event
in experience—is the "truth" of theology. (Of course, within theological discourse, a proposition is true in a further derivative way.)
Theology finds its norm immediately in tradition but ultimately in
the archaic experience of salvation. While a theology can be no
more true than its norms, they can be more true than it. Theology
may appropriate each type of science (formal, natural, and human),
every kind of art criticism (literary, plastic, musical, and so on), and
philosophy. To the extent that it makes manifest the tradition and,
behind it, the original proclamation and the archaic experience, and
hence the effective presence of a salvational Power, theology is true.
It may well have degrees.

The major derivative truths proper to religion, then, are first,
the manifestive power of the original announcement, secondly that
of tradition, and finally that of theology.

In all this, how do we know that we are "in" the truth? What
is the criterion for truth? How can genuine be distinguished from
pseudo manifestness? Upon what is verification based in religion?

The criterion for truth can only be *experience*—in the case of
religion, the salvational experience. Since experience polarizes itself
into the experienc*ing* and the experienc*ed*, the *dialectic* or dialogue of
these poles *must continue or be able to continue* for the manifestation to
be genuine, that is, for the truth to be "there." If the subject acts
himself out in such a way as to destroy the objective presence or,
reversely, if the object presents itself in such a way as to frustrate
the subjective achievement; if, in other words, the dialectic becomes
impossible; then the experience shall not have been "truthful":

> True is that which is unconcealed, which is "seen," and not
> dreamt or fancied. For this reason, the true makes it possible

to continue the dialog, it "leads somewhere," opens a future, and eliminates frustrations and inconsistencies. Truth can be distinguished from untruth by its "fruitfulness."[19]

Hence if an alleged manifestation of a salvational Power were to constrict the person, if it were to encourage him to be less than his unique self and to undermine others, if it were to close off the future, that alleged manifestation shall have been outside the truth—that is, not fruitful, in other words, no manifestation at all. The archaic experience of salvation finds its criterion in fruitfulness.[20]

The major derivative truths proper to religion do likewise: since the truth of proclamation, tradition, and theology is their manifestive power for what is respectively more original than they, since they aim to make appropriable the archaic experience, their truth, too, finds its criterion in fruitfulness. The immediate criterion for each is fruitfulness with respect to the immediately more original form that religion respectively takes. The truth of announcement finds its measure in fruitfulness for a continuation of the original experiential dialectic; the truth of tradition, in fruitfulness for a continuation of the proclamatory dialectic; the truth of theology, in fruitfulness for a continuation of the traditional dialectic. The ultimate criterion is the *experience of salvation:* if human existence not be made new by a salvational presence, then there is no "truth" in religious experience.

If man were not to come into his own through religion; if the archaic experience, its proclamation, its tradition, and its theology were to lead a person to frustration; if, in other words, the dialectic of the religious subject and the religious other were to cease in the destruction of either; then the experience shall not have been religiously "truthful."

Beyond this, philosophy may clarify the truth proper to religion by articulating its opposite, nontruth, and its contrary, untruth. The former belongs to manifestness in its finitude and degree, while the latter is the uncritical way in which the human person belongs to the degrees of manifestness, to its limits, and to (possible) manifestness itself. To articulate the nontruth and the untruth proper to religion is the aim of the next two parts.

3. Truth and Nontruth

The question of nontruth in religion is the question of the limitations and the degrees of truth. Let us take each of them in turn.

The nontruth proper to religion is that in relation to which the *limitations* of manifestness appear; it is that opposite which the truth appears as finite. The original manifestation of the salvational Power—and a fortiori the derivative manifestations, mutatis mutandis—is finite in a threefold way.

First, every symbol (ambiguous manifestation) *is* such only in contrast to that which surrounds it. In other words, the sacred embeds itself in the profane: the finite truth de-fines itself within the nontruth.

Secondly, every symbol (ambiguous manifestation) *is* such only as the manifestation of a covert power in, as, and through the overt phenomenon; every symbol eventuates as the structure of original and image. In other words, the Power that discloses himself at once obscures himself in, as, and through his image; the one that appears as the power to effect human salvation appears in camouflage. For example, the cosmic sun is the nontruth that camouflages (even as it shines as) the reliable power-of-Regeneration.

Thirdly, every symbol (ambiguous manifestation) *is* such only as the manifestation of . . . , of a Power that hides himself. In other words, the Power remains the *Lēthē*—which makes himself *alēthēs*. The truth, the *alētheia*, remains the truth *of* the nontruth, the *Lēthē*. The truth for man is always determinate; but the *Lēthē*, precisely as concealed, is indeterminate. As determinate over against the *Lēthē*, the truth in finite; and the hiddenness of the Power is the nontruth of determinate truth.

The threefold nontruth proper to religion, then, is evident. The truth of religion happens *within* the nontruth, *as* the nontruth, and *out of* the nontruth. The finite *manifestness* of a salvational Power is the *finite* manifestness—always opposite its proper nontruth.

The threefold nontruth proper to religion—the profane, the overt, and the *Lēthē*—is the condition for the possibility of *degrees* of truth. Philosophy can a priori articulate three possible ways in which the truth proper to religion may take on degrees. Let us take them in reverse order.

First, the power that remains hidden or concealed is more powerful than any particular manifestation. The very fact that it remains covert imports that its fulness is never present in human experience. On that basis, one archaic manifestation may be more manifestive—more true—than another. Manifestness, then, may take on degrees of adequacy to the *Lēthē*. Of course, precisely because the salvational Power remains concealed, no human may claim to have exhausted the resources of this Power; but human beings may make judgments about comparative adequacy and about the nonfinality of the manifestation that serves as the standard for the comparison.

Secondly, the image, the overt phenomenon that presents the covert power, may be more or less appropriate to what is to be manifest. If the salvational Power be personal, then a nonpersonal image is less appropriate than a personal one. The manifestation, then, may be more or less powerful; the truth may be more or less true.

Thirdly, the image may stand out more or less from its background; what is to serve as the overt for the covert power, what is to be a sacred phenomenon, may be more or less distinctive. The sacred and the profane may differentiate themselves to a greater or lesser degree in experience. The more a figure differentiates itself from the profane field, the more truthful it is.

The finitude of truth makes possible the degrees of religious truth. While philosophy can explicate these possibilities, it remains for self-critical experience to investigate the concrete religions and to become the judgment of truth in its degrees.

Given the three genera of degree, philosophy may further project the highest degree of religious truth, the most intense degree of manifestation of power for salvation. First, the highest degree would be a manifestation that is *ecumenical*, that is, universal and inexhaustible; it would be one that in principle may subsume all others and at once remain open for an indefinite development in depth. Secondly, the highest degree would be a manifestation that is *personal* in some way, perhaps even a single person. Thirdly, it would be one that is *unique*, that is, that stands out most from its background. Has the highest sacred, the greatest degree of religious truth, ever become concrete in history? Philosophy as philosophy can only explicate the criteria for judgment; it cannot render that judgment.

Religious truth (manifestness) eventuates within limits and degrees: nontruth is proper to it. But what about untruth or falsity?

4. Truth and Untruth

Contrary to religious truth is religious falsity. The untruth proper to religion is complex. Given truth and nontruth, philosophy may a priori distinguish three kinds of untruth: falsity *for*, *in*, and *of* religion. The untruth or falsity *for* religion is a function of the degrees of truth (manifestness); that *in* religion is a function of the limitation or finitude of manifestness; that *of* religion is a function of the possibility of manifestness itself. In each case, falsity is a matter of *experience*. It lies in the human approach that is inadequate to its correlative objective presence. It lies in *uncritical* experience: experiencing that is unaware of its own limits correlative to the experienced. The untruth for, in, and of religion arises from an uncritical attitude in regard to, respectively, the degrees of manifestness, the finitude of manifestness, and the (possible) manifestness itself. The elaboration of the types of falsity proper to religion will show how precarious is religious truth.

Falsity for Religion

Falsity *for* religion arises in function of the degrees of truth. The threefold nontruth proper to religion—the profane, the overt, and the *Lēthē*— is the condition for the possibility of degrees of truth. And in the estimation that one religion has of another, untruth is a misapprehension of the degree of truth in experience; it arises when the human person adopts an uncritical response toward what is manifest in his experience.

One may be uncritical, first, in regard to the distinction of the sacred and the profane. In that case, falsity is, for a religion, *fetishism* when the response is uncritcal in that it takes the profane as if it were the relevant sacred; and it is *infidelity* or "paganism" when the response is uncritical in that it does not find the sacred at issue within the profane.

One may be uncritical, second, in regard to the appropriateness of the overt to the covert. In that case, falsity is, for a religion, either overinterpretation or underinterpretation. Overinterpretation occurs when the response is uncritical in that it takes the overt to be more revelatory than it is and to that extent substitutes the overt for the covert; religious experience then becomes *idolatry*. Underinterpretation occurs when the response is uncritical in that it takes the overt to be less revelatory than it is and to that extent ignores the covert in the overt; religious experience then becomes *impiety*.

One may be uncritical, third, in regard to the adequacy of the manifestation of the *Lēthē*. In that case, falsity is, for a religion, gnosticism or *presumption* if the response is uncritical in that it takes the manifestation to be more expressive of the *Lēthē* than it is; and it is meiosis or *laxity* if the response is uncritical in that it takes the manifestation to be less expressive.

With all these possibilities for falsity, it is easy to understand that for religion truth is not easy to secure. For the truth always lies between fetishism and infidelity, between idolatry and impiety, and between presumption and laxity.

Falsity in Religion

Falsity *in* religion arises in function of the finitude of truth. In the estimation that a particular religion has of itself, untruth is the failure to recognize the limits of truth. Since the archaic experience of the manifestness of a salvational Power extends itself into proclamation, tradition, and theology, falsity may lie in the archaic experience itself, in the proclamation of the experience, in the tradition of the proclamation, or in the theology of the tradition. In each case, falsity can be measured only over against the respective truth.

In religion, the falsity proper to the archaic experience is enthusiasm; that proper to proclamation is disloyalty; that proper to tradition is heterodoxy; and that proper to theology is ideology. *Enthusiasm* is experience that takes itself to be more full-of-God than is the case. It is archaic experience that does not recognize its own limitation and hence authenticity; it is truth forgetful of its finitude. *Disloyalty* is proclamation that makes itself to differ from experience-announcing-itself, from loyal or genuine proclamation. It is proclamation that does not recognize its source (the archaic experience) and thus its own limitation; it is truth defiant of its finitude. *Heterodoxy* is tradition that presents itself in one instance or another as more proclamatory than the rest of itself—that is to say, it does not fit right with the acceptances (*doxai*) that define the tradition as a whole. It is tradition that does not recognize the extent of orthodoxy and thus its own limitation; it is truth impatient of its finitude. *Ideology* is theology that presumes itself to be more comprehensive than is the case. It is theology that does not recognize the other theologies that show the limitation of its own truth; it is truth proud of its finitude.

With all these possibilities for falsity, it is easy to understand that in religion truth is not easy to secure. Truth in a particular religion would be authenticity in experience, loyality in proclamation, orthodoxy in tradition, and criticism in theology. It is always to be achieved, negatively, through suspicion about enthusiasm, denunciation of disloyalty, definition of orthodoxy, and vigilance against ideology. Positively, truth in religion is always to be achieved by total attention (meditation or even mysticism) in archaic experience, constant reversion to the source in proclamation, preventive patience in tradition, and modesty in theology.

Falsity of Religion

Besides falsity for and in religion, there is the possible falsity *of* religion. Beyond any particularity, religion in general may be untrue; the manifestness proper to religion may be a pseudo manifestness, a pure subjective projective.[21] In that case, the archaic experience of salvation would be illusion; proclamation would be fraud; tradition, superstition; and theology, mystification. *For* and *in* religion, of course, this judgment of falsity would be, respectively, unbelief, skepticism, secularism, and indifference. Philosophy recognizes the possibility of this judgment and poses the question of the truth *of* religion.

Is religion in general true or false? Fundamental to theology, tradition, and proclamation is the archaic experience itself; and the fundamental question is whether the experience of a salvational Power be illusory. In speculative terms: Does God exist? If the archaic experience be an illusion, then the announcement of it is fraud, the retrieve of it is superstition, and the reflection upon it is mystification. The originary experience—whether in the chronological or the existential sense—is the crux.

The truth or falsity of religion is a question of *experience*. It is *not* a question of argumentation that starts with non-God and concludes to God. After all, arguments are arguments *about* experience; they begin within it, clarify it, and end for the sake of it. That is to say, the speculative arguments for the existence of God *presuppose* religious experience and only subsequently clarify it (in terms of Being or some equivalent thereof). Experience alone counts.

How do the speculative arguments presuppose experience? Their structure makes it clear. Whatever the details, the arguments for the existence of God are a simple syllogism:

Major premise: Being.
Minor premise: Being $\equiv$ God.
Conclusion: God.

Consider first the major. In the history of philosophy, Being has received many titles—for example, the idea of the good, separate form, the one, the eternal, subsistent to-be itself, the infinite, and the end. In the proofs, it has commonly been articulated in ways that at first obscure it, for example, as the uncaused cause or as that which is necessarily necessary. What both proponents and antagonists of the argument take for the proof of God is actually the "proof" of the major premise, for example, in the five ways of St. Thomas. But this latter proof is only a mediate affirmation of what philosophy can in any case affirm immediately: Being. *This* is what philosophy brings to the "proof for God" before any question of God ever arises. The major premise is an affirmation of Being under one title or another.

But it is the minor premise that is the problematic one. It presupposes that "God" arises outside philosophic reflection and is *then* understood as identical to Being (as affirmed by philosophy). *Why* such an identity can be affirmed has hardly ever been the subject of clear investigation.[22] Here, a summary statement must suffice: Being and the salvational Power are identical in that they are both *eternal*, and eternality can only be one.

Basically the speculative "proof for God" is quite simple. What it presupposes, however, may be quite tenuous: religious experience. And *that* demands reflection. An argument that begins outside it can never conclude to its content. Only an experienc*ing* can reach, in a nonhypothetical or factual way, an experienc*ed*.

Experience alone counts. The fact that some human beings do indeed experience the effective presence of a salvational Power does, in principle, terminate the speculative argument. *However,* other persons challenge the experience. Hence the experience demands a reflection that defends it and even confirms it. This reflection may be called either fundamental theology or religious philosophy. In any case, the challenge is that the experience be illusory. And the relevant argument *begins* with the salvational Power in experience and concludes that the challenge is or is not decisive. The speculative juxtaposition of theism and atheism—suggesting that a decision between them is a matter of speculative argument— obscures the relevant argumentation. It is not relevant to begin with non-God and then try to prove or to disprove the existence of God. Rather, the experience of a salvational Power *announces itself,* the challenge *ensues,* and the attempt to defend or to confirm the experience *follows*. In this argumentation, theism (an affirmation of the salvational Power in experience) is the point of departure; the challenge to it progresses in explicitness, from nontheism, to agnosticism, to antitheism.

First, since "theism" imports the affirmation of an experiential God, *nontheism* imports the lack of an experience and hence the absence of an affirmation. Most of us are nontheists most of the time; even those highly conscious of their religious commitments do not usually experience salvational Power; after all, to interpret the sacred in the profane is an uncommon act. The lack of an experience is unobjectionable. Of course the lack of an experience is not the same as the experience of a lack. However, some nontheists go beyond simple nontheism and *interpret* their lack of an experience as either agnosticism or antitheism.

Secondly, *agnosticism* is the interpretive claim by one who lacks an experience of the salvational Power that *nobody can* experience what he does not. In colloquial and nonreligious terms, it is the claim that it is impossible to know whether or not "God exists." The critique and the refutation of agnosticism are simple. The critique is that it is the arbitrary universalization of *one lack* of experience. The refutation is the report that someone else *has* the experience or even *could* have it. In response to this critique and this refutation, the agnostic has two choices. He may acknowledge that his *one* lack of experience is not normative and hence revert to nontheism. In that case, his position is unexceptionable. Or he may deny the report; beyond religious judgments about truth *for* and *in* religion, he may institute a judgment *of* religion, affirming that nobody could have the salvational experience. In that case, his position advances to antitheism. Hence agnosticism is an inherently unstable position; under examination, it becomes either nontheism or antitheism.

Thirdly, *antitheism* is the interpretive claim by one who lacks an experience of the salvational Power that *everyone must* experience a lack. It is the categorical denial of any power for salvation and of any experiencing of it. In colloquial and nonreligious terms, it is the claim that "God does not exist." The critique is simple: antitheism is nontheism become militant for one reason or another. (The reasons fall into a few types, but cannot be taken up here.[23]) The refutation of antitheism is, in principle, also simple: some persons *do* experience salvational Power or at least *could* do so. However, the challenge to theism here becomes explicit and radical, for the antitheist argues that the theist has an *illusion*.

Hence the question becomes twofold: On what basis does the antitheist build his argument? And how does the theist defend his experience?

The antitheistic argument is just as simple as the so-called proof for the existence of God. One experiential content may be judged illusory *only* on the basis of another—whether logically immediate or not—that is taken to be incompatible with the first. Which content of experience, then, does the antitheist so take? Formally, *anything* could serve; but what is usually taken is either evil or human freedom.[24] How can a good God allow the suffering of the innocent? How can an omnipotent God give scope to my freedom? In syllogistic form:

> Evil/freedom is existent.
> But God is incompatible with evil/freedom.
> Therefore, God is nonexistent.

The various complications do not change the structure of this simple argument. It is based upon the experience of evil or of freedom.

The theist may defend his experience in at least two ways.

First, in order for the antitheistic argument to be cogent, it must deny *exactly* what the theist affirms. However, it does not. What it denies is some "God" who is incompatible with evil. But this is not what the theist affirms; indeed, he agrees that such a God does not exist (the argument, after all, is valid). But reversely, he does not claim that God is compatible with evil, either. Although the theist as a speculative theologian or religious philosopher may occasionally attempt a theodicy, as authentically religious he knows that no *system* of God and evil is possible. His salvational Power is neither compatible nor incompatible with evil; and he must maintain a modest silence on the question. The same holds mutatis mutandis for the speculative opposition of God and freedom.

Secondly, the antitheistic argument presupposes a complete knowledge of "God" and of evil. In order to know that they are definitively incompatible, the antitheist must know them completely. Once again, however, the "God" who is completely knowable is not the God—the *Lēthē*—whom the theist affirms. Furthermore, the claim to totally comprehend evil is presumptuous in the extreme: nobody understands evil completely. Ironically, in denying the divine, the antitheist must claim for himself a kind of "divine omniscience."

Hence the antitheistic argument fails.

What is left? There remains only experience. What about illusion? *That* is determined according to the criterion for truth—fruitfulness. If, correlative to interpretation, a salvational presence makes itself effective for a person who thereby deepens in personhood, then the religion founded upon and continued in this manifestation is, to that extent, true. It may well be that some alleged experience is empty—that the "experience" is not truthful. But this does not become evident by an a priori denial of any possible salvational Power. It becomes evident in a critical reflection on experience according to the criterion for the truth proper to religion. The untruth of a religious experience is not the conclusion of antitheistic speculation. But it may well be the conclusion of a rigorous examination of concrete experience. Nontheism neither affirms nor denies the truth of religion; it maintains a modest silence. Agnosticism, which imputes this modesty to itself, and antitheism, which would impose an aggressive silence, are uncritical and untenable. In the end, the only tenable positions are theism and nontheism: critical experience and the lack of it.

Given the possibilities of nontheism, agnosticism, and antitheism, it is easy to understand that the truth of religion is not easy to secure. Truth is the manifestness of salvational Power. Not everyone finds necessary the confrontation with these possibilities; but for those who do, falsity is a constant threat. For them, illusion first of all, then fraud, superstition, and mystification are serious matters.

Their experience requires the discipline of unbelief; their announcement, the discipline of skepticism; their tradition, that of secularism; and their theology, that of indifference. For what is at stake is the most serious matter: whether or not they will *be*. As a possibility for human decision, religion is the possibilization of man. That a salvational Power would advent to make the fulfilment of human beings possible beyond their condition of iniquity is the truth of religion.

But does the Power indeed become manifest? Is religion true? Philosophy, as such, cannot decide; phenomenology maintains a modal neutrality.

Conclusion

Philosophy, having articulated the essence of religion, may elaborate the truth, the nontruth, and the untruth proper to religion. The truth proper to religion is not easy to attain. It lies between the untruths *for* religion and *in* religion and beyond the untruths *of* religion. While more may be said in detail, this study has attempted to gauge the *scope* of the question of religious truth— to be complete in outline. It has taken up, in one way or another, all the questions posed earlier. Other approaches are certainly possible, but perhaps this one will bring some enlightenment where others do not.

A religion, it was said, is an experience of salvation and of the implications of it. At its simplest, religion is—given interpretation of the relevant symbols—the life lived as if love and not evil were invincible. That is why those who profess a religion may be falsely religious and those who do not may be truthfully religious. As always, the simplest is the most difficult.

Part II

Hermeneutic

5

Phenomenologies and Religious Truth

Merold Westphal

Religious Truth

Philosophy of religion since the seventeenth century has largely consisted of a debate between parties who share a crucial assumption—namely, that truth is to be understood in terms of mathematics and mathematical physics, and that religion must either produce truth of that kind or give up making truth-claims. Given the dogmatic character of this shared assumption, what is surprising is not that no clear winner has emerged, but that the debate has been neither uninteresting nor entirely unilluminating. Still, it would seem important to look for alternatives that do not begin with such an arbitrary a priori.

Phenomenology has sought to get to the things themselves, to be a nondogmatic mode of philosophical reflection. Can it better illuminate the question(s) of religious truth than those modes of reflection, friendly and unfriendly toward religion, which operate on objectivist, foundationalist, evidentialist assumptions? In exploring this possibility it would be ironical if, contrary to the spirit of phenomenology, we were dogmatically to assume an understanding of phenomenology at odds with the *Sache* that inspires the question, the truth of religion, or dogmatically to postulate an understanding of truth at odds with religion. Religious truth may turn out to be a chimera, but we should not set up the investigation so as to guarantee this conclusion in advance. So we shall have to proceed carefully, acknowledging with Kant that "the definition in all its precision and clarity ought, in philosophy, to come rather at the end than at the beginning of our enquiries."[1] We must not presume at the outset that either the nature of religious truth or the essence of phenomenology is at our disposal.

Yet we cannot start with nothing. Perhaps the best way to avoid a dogmatic starting point would be to draw our preunderstanding of religious truth from religious sources. In this way we can perhaps first hear what kind of truth-claims religion makes and seek to evaluate them by criteria appropriate to them. And, acknowledging with Ricoeur that we cannot see the world from nowhere but only from out of our own history,[2] let us turn to the Judeo-Christian traditions of biblical religion for a point of departure. We can ask in due course how reflection that orients itself in this way relates to that reflection whose access to the world is derived from other traditions.

We need not begin with a definitive and final statement about truth in biblical religion, for we are only looking for a point of departure. Two themes offer themselves quite readily, the finitude and the practicality of religious truth. So far as finitude is concerned, we find the contrast between divine and human knowledge eloquently expressed with reference to our knowledge of ourselves. After praising the detailed power of God's knowledge of him (or her), the Psalmist confesses:

> Such knowledge is too wonderful for me;
> It is too high, I cannot attain to it;

and eventually turns to God for self-understanding beyond human power:

> Search me, O God, and know my heart;
> Try me and know my anxious thoughts;
> And see if there be any hurtful way in me,
> And lead me in the everlasting way [Ps. 139:6, 23–24].[3]

If, contrary to Cartesian modernity, we are not transparent to ourselves, how much more will any knowledge of God we may have be limited. Thus, when the apostle exudes about "the light of the knowledge of the glory of God in the face of Christ," he does not allow the splendor of the object to obscure the finitude of the subject but reminds himself and his readers that "we have this treasure in earthen vessels, that the surpassing greatness of the power may be of God and not from ourselves" (2 Cor. 4:6–7).

That the image of the believing soul as an earthen vessel for the heavenly truth of the gospel has epistemic overtones is clear from an earlier epistle to the same church. In praising the supremacy of love over knowledge, the apostle insists: "We know in part. . . . For now we see in a mirror dimly, but then face to face;

now I know in part, but then I shall know fully just as I also have been fully known" (1 Cor. 13:9, 12).[4] Knowledge is presence, indeed, but all we have available to us at present is partial presence.

If we turn to the practicality of truth, biblically understood, we discover not just that to know is to know how, but also that to know is to do. Moreover, the doing in question is not at all practical in the most familiar senses of the term. It is not practical in the technological sense of using intelligence to discover and employ the most efficient means of achieving my (our) ends. The doing is rather a self-transformative activity intended to bring me (us) into conformity with God's ends. It resembles Aristotle's *phronēsis/praxis* more than it resembles his *technē/poiēsis*,[5] though the link to God's ends distinguishes biblical *praxis* from Aristotle's.

There is another familiar sense in which this doing is not practical. It is not realistic in the sense of being limited by what a given society expects and is used to getting from its members at any given time. From that point of view it may be shamelessly utopian, and in that sense, according to standard usage, unrealistic and impractical. To avoid the instrumental and realistic overtones of ordinary usage and to emphasize the link to *praxis*, I shall speak from now on of the praxicality of biblical truth, begging the reader's forgiveness.

What I have in mind can be readily grasped from three texts. The first is addressed by the unrealistic prophet to the all too practical king:

Woe to him who builds his house without righteousness
And his upper rooms without justice,
Who uses his neighbor's services without pay
And who does not give him his wages;
Who says, I will build myself a roomy house
With spacious upper rooms,
And cut out its windows,
Paneling it with cedar and painting it bright red.
Do you become a king because you are competing in cedar?
Did not your father eat and drink
And do justice and righteousness?
Then it was well with him.
He pled the cause of the afflicted and needy;
Then it was well.
Is not this what it means to know Me?
Declares the Lord [Jer. 22:13–16].

The second text is but a phrase that occurs at the beginning and end of the epistle to the Romans (1:5 and 16:26), "the obedience

of faith." This should be read as a genitive of apposition or definition, and thus as "the obedience which consists in faith."[6] Faith is a
form of obedience.

In biblical usage knowledge and faith are not opposed to each
other as knowledge and opinion in Platonic usage or as science and
superstition in Enlightenment usage. Knowledge, in the Bible, is no
pure scientific objectifying cognition, but an act whose meaning is
drawn in part from the usage that makes the sexual union of man
and woman a knowing. As such it retains the finitude already
mentioned.[7] On the other hand, faith is no second-class knowledge,
either because it is directed toward a second-class object or because
it possesses a second-class certainty. Like knowledge of God, it is
that act of the whole person in which God is apprehended, acknowledged, accepted, and affirmed (by earthen vessels who see in
a mirror dimly.)[8]

In biblical usage, then, knowledge and faith are two terms for
essentially one mode of relating to God. Because of the cognitive
component in each, both relate to the question of truth. Thus we
learn something about the praxicality of truth, biblically understood, when we learn from Jeremiah that to know Yahweh is to do
justice and righteousness (especially in relation to the poor) and
from Paul that faith is itself an act of obedience that commits one to
further obedience. The essential harmony of the two texts is indicated by Abraham Heschel's comment on the Jeremiah passage:
"Here knowledge is not the same as thought, comprehension, gnosis or mystical participation in the ultimate essence. Knowledge of
God is action toward man, sharing His concern for justice; sympathy in action."[9] J. A. Thompson makes the same point about the
same passage. "To *know* . . . God was to enter into a deep relationship of personal commitment, and this involved a concern to obey
the stipulations of the covenant."[10]

The understanding of religious truth implicit in the texts from
Jeremiah and Romans is overt in a Johannine usage: "But he who
practices the truth comes to the light, that his deeds may be manifested as having been wrought in God" (John 3:21).[11] This notion of
truth as something to be done is perhaps the fullest expression of
what I have called the praxicality of truth in biblical understanding.

Missing here are those features that so easily corrupt contemplative and instrumental views of truth—namely, the luxury or
superiority or power over the other that stems from having gotten
it right. Truth is neither a security blanket to be hugged, nor a
trophy to be displayed, nor a weapon to be wielded. It is less
something to possess than something to be possessed by. If it is a

task to find the truth, truth once found proves to be the ongoing task of a lifetime.[12]

This is the concept of religious truth that underlies Augustine's critique of those "philosophers," not further identified, whose ability accurately to predict eclipses made the Manichees look silly.[13] "Much that they say about what is created is true; but they do not seek religiously for the Truth which is the maker of creation, and therefore they do not find Him, or, if they do find Him and know Him to be God, they do not honor Him as God and give Him thanks."[14] The gap between these philosophers and religious truth is not just that they limit themselves to correct beliefs about nature. Even when they go on to correct beliefs about God, when "they do find Him and know Him to be God," they fail to do the truth, in this case to "honor Him as God and give Him thanks." And thus they fail to find the truth, in spite of their correct beliefs. Biblically understood, truth is not reducible to correct beliefs, even correct beliefs about God, because truth is something to be done.

Phenomenologies

My original question has now become more limited, but also more precise. What kind of light, if any, can phenomenology throw on the question(s) of religious truth, where religious truth is understood in terms of the biblical themes of finitude and praxicality? The answer would seem to depend on what is meant by phenomenology. My point of departure for sorting out the different kinds is a comment of Merleau-Ponty. In the Preface to *The Phenomenology of Perception* he tells us that Marx, Nietzsche, and Freud were practicing phenomenology long before that way of doing philosophy became self-conscious in Husserl.[15]

There is surely something strange about this. For these three, whom Ricoeur has called the "masters" of the "school of suspicion,"[16] would seem to represent precisely those tendencies against which Husserl directs his Cartesian dream of rigorous science. Impressed as they are by the ineluctable contingencies at work in human thought, their response would be highly skeptical at best to any talk about a human rationality with "complete and ultimate grounding on the basis of absolute insights, insights behind which one cannot go back any further."[17] They would not doubt that such a philosophy would embody such "freedom from prejudice" and "autonomy according to ultimate evidences" that it could rightly claim to be "absolutely self-responsible" and "absolutely justified."[18] But they would point, each in his own distinctive way, to the situated self-deceptions of human thought that generate suspicions about any such Cartesian/Husserlian claims. What hopes they have for human autonomy lie not in philosophy made scientific with the help of methodological rigor, but in social revolution, in the evolutionary quantum leap to a new (or post-) humanity, or in therapy and transference, all of which would well seem antiphilosophical from Husserl's perspective.

The first thesis of this essay is that in spite of the strangeness of Merleau-Ponty's claim, he is essentially, not merely historically, correct. For Marx, Nietzsche, and Freud not only belong to the prehistory of phenomenology; they represent its proper destiny as well. To follow Husserl's own argument to its end is to follow a path that makes not only the transcendental turn but also two posttranscendental turns, first to the hermeneutics of finitude and then—the "most unkindest" turn of all—to the hermeneutics of suspicion. Husserl does not follow this path to its end, and the steps he does take he takes kicking and screaming.[19] But others, such as Heidegger, Gadamer, Merleau-Ponty himself, and Ricoeur, being more tolerant of relativity and finitude, are able to show us where it leads.[20] In tracing the movement from transcendental phenomenology through the two post-transcendental turns to finitude and suspicion, I shall argue that phenomenology thereby fulfills itself by becoming fully realistic and honest about itself.

The second thesis of this essay is that it is along this path that phenomenology increasingly illuminates the question(s) of religious truth. The finitude of the hermeneutical circle and the situational epistemology that results from taking it seriously correspond to the finitude of religious truth, biblically understood. And suspicion can be a timely reminder of the praxicality of religious truth, biblically understood. Of course, it can degenerate into a cruel cynicism that knows only how to kill and destroy. But it need not limit itself to destructive sophistry. It has a negative thrust, to be sure. But this can function as an ascetic discipline by which the believing soul and the believing community seek to purify themselves from idolatry and ideology.

The Hermeneutic Phenomenologies

It may be argued that neither the hermeneutics of finitude nor the hermeneutics of suspicion come on the religious scene as utter foreigners, that both traditions have family trees with numerous religious and theological branches. Far from disputing such a claim, I would want to emphasize the importance of tracing such lineage as

fully as possible. For my claim is not that hermeneutical phenomenology brings something totally new to the discussion of religious
truth, but simply that its insights and techniques, whatever their
origins, can enrich that discussion. Theologians, including not only
the manufacturers (the creative writers), but also the wholesalers
(the teachers of theology) and the retailers (seminarians and pas-
tors), will be able to do their job better if they understand and appreciate the movement from the transcendental absolutism claimed
by Husserl to the transcendental finitism acknowledged by the
hermeneutics of finitude and on to the transcendental depravity un-
masked by the hermeneutics of suspicion.

While the designation of Husserl's Cartesian project as transcendental is familiar and fairly obvious, I am fully aware that my
designation of the move to hermeneutics as a post-transcendental
turn is neither familiar nor immediately obvious. So I shall first
sketch the move as I understand it and then indicate why it may
helpfully be called post-transcendental.

In spite of the clarity and forcefulness of Heidegger's claim
that understanding and interpretation have ontologically general
rather than epistemologically particular points of reference (as the
theory of, for example, biblical or legal interpretation), the impression is sometimes given that we turn to hermeneutics to deal with
special regions of experience. Sometimes the polysemy of language
takes center stage and hermeneutics appears as the theory of reading those texts, literary and especially religious, in which metaphor,
symbol, and myth are especially prominent. At other times it is the
objectifications of the human spirit, not just in texts, but in every
sort of cultural expression, that appear as the occasions for interpretation.

In either case we revert to traditions associated with Schleiermacher and Dilthey, which fall, in terms of scope, below the level
reached by Husserl. His project sought to encompass the whole of
human experience, and without the *Universalitätsanspruch* of hermeneutics, there would be no basis for the claim that hermeneutics is
Husserl's rightful heir.[21]

It is neither metaphor nor objective spirit but the as-structure
of experience that lies at the basis of hermeneutics. The crucial transition occurs in paragraph 32 of *Being and Time*. Even at the level of
ordinary sense perception and prior to any explicit assertion there is
no "mere seeing" but always the act that sees something *as* something. Long before we encounter symbols and social structures we
are engaged in understanding and interpretation. The hermeneutical situation is constitutive of *Dasein*'s being-in-the-world.

This discovery undermines the foundationalist project of Husserl in two ways. In the first place, even before we raise the question of the a priori element in interpretation, the fact that all experience has the structure of understanding something as something introduces an element of mediation into experience, which counters the claim to immediacy in Husserl's intuitionist account of evidence. That account requires something like what the philosophers of science call theory-free data, and the as-structure of experience precludes this possibility. Only that which is taken can be given—which is to say that nothing is given free of interpretation.

But in the second place, to make matters even worse, every interpretation presupposes an earlier interpretation. Contrary to Husserl's requirement, there are none that are "first in themselves and can support the whole storied edifice of universal knowledge," none that "are recognizable as preceding all other imaginable evidences."[22] Instead, "interpretation is never a presuppositionless apprehending of something given to us. . . . Any interpretation which is to contribute to understanding must already have understood what is to be interpreted."[23] The "as-structure of interpretation" leads directly to the "fore-structure of understanding," which Heidegger spells out in terms of *Vorhabe, Vorsicht*, and *Vorgriff*.[24] This hermeneutical circle cuts us off decisively from all foundational certainties. The move from Husserl to hermeneutical phenomenology rests on the acknowledgment, not simply that we find ourselves in this circle, but that no reflection, no matter how methodologically rigorous, enables us to outflank life and escape our entanglement with it.

Precisely such an escape is Husserl's project from at least 1911 ("Philosophy as Rigorous Science") right through the *Crisis*. It becomes especially urgent, if not yet quite desperate, as his own path in *Cartesian Meditations* leads to what might be called a co-discovery of the hermeneutical circle. For him the world is the world of nature and culture.[25] He has his own "already" in this connection, for he acknowledges that we always find ourselves in an already constituted world of nature and culture. "The beginning phenomenologist is bound involuntarily" by this fact, by "the restriction that a constituted world already exists for him." That makes it very difficult to discover any *"ultimate genesis."*[26]

Husserl returns to the problem in *Experience and Judgment*. There the *Verweisungsganzheit* of *Being and Time*, paragraph 15, appears as "the always already pregiven world." It is "always a world in which cognition in the most diverse ways has already done its work," and thus it is "always already pregiven to us as impregnated by the precipitate of logical operations. The world is never given to us as other than the world in which we or others, whose store of experience we take over by communication, education, and tradition, have already been logically active, in judgment and cognition." Because in all these ways "the world of our experience is from the beginning interpreted," we will "not so easily find [in it] that ultimately original self-evidence of experience which we seek," the ultimate genesis of *Cartesian Meditations*.[27]

Despite the acknowledged difficulty, it is precisely this task that is to be performed by the historical reduction of the *Crisis*. There the task of reflection is to shift the life-world from the subject side of experience to the object side. By making the subject's always already *operative and anonymous* intentionalities the theme of thought, Husserl hopes to neutralize their role as the thinking of another that thinks through us, as the ground of our *own* intentionalities that keeps them from being self-grounding. Whereas for Sartre freedom is possible only if I can objectify the gaze of the other who looks *at* me, for Husserl freedom depends on objectifying the intentionalities of those others who see the world *through* me.[28]

The Hermeneutics of Finitude

For hermeneutical phenomenology this transcendental freedom is neither possible nor necessary for mortal humans willing to accept their finitude. If Husserl sounds at times a bit like Empedocles, "I go about among you as an immortal god, no longer a mortal," Gadamer replies that "the ancient Greek, 'Know thyself!' still holds good for us as well, for it meant, 'Know that you are no god, but a human being.' What self-knowledge really is is not the perfect self-transparency of knowledge but the insight that we have to accept the limits posed for finite natures."[29] In biblical language, remember that you are but earthen vessels who see in a mirror dimly.

Many of the most striking and most familiar formulations by phenomenology of human finitude echo this theme in the analysis of the historicity and linguisticality of human experience. Thus for Heidegger, "hearing is constitutive for discourse," or, in other words, before I can speak, I must already have listened.[30]

For Gadamer this means that it is only as those upon whom tradition has already laid its claim and exerted its authority that we can make tradition an object of methodological investigation, deprived of its authority. For him, "Understanding is not to be thought of so much as an action of one's subjectivity, but as the placing of oneself within a process of tradition. . . . The anticipation of meaning that governs our understanding of a text is not an act of subjectivity, but proceeds from the communality that binds us to the tradition."[31] This is why Gadamer can say:

> It is not so much our judgments as it is our prejudices that constitute our being. . . . In fact, the historicity of our existence entails that prejudices, in the literal sense of the word [prejudgments], constitute the initial directedness of our whole ability to experience. Prejudices are biases of our openness to the world. They are simply conditions whereby we experience something—whereby what we encounter says something to us.[32]

Merleau-Ponty expresses the same theme when he affirms "the impossibility of a complete reduction" on the grounds "that radical reflection amounts to a consciousness of its own dependence on an unreflective life which is its initial situation." Thus, "even though consciousness is able to detach itself from things to see itself, human consciousness never possesses itself in complete detachment."[33]

Finally, Ricoeur reinforces this finitude not just of ordinary experience but even of philosophical reflection by saying:

> Because history precedes me and my reflection, because I belong to history before I belong to myself, prejudgment also precedes judgment, and submission to traditions precedes their examination. . . . If therefore we cannot extract ourselves from historical becoming, or place ourselves at a distance from it in such a way that the past becomes an object for us, then we must confess that we are always situated within history in such a fashion that our consciousness never has the freedom to bring itself face to face with the past by an act of sovereign independence. It is rather a question of becoming conscious of the action which affects us and of accepting that the past which is part of our experience keeps us from taking it totally in charge.[34]

In other words, subjectivity is always response, never origin.[35]

I call this move from the project of an absolute standpoint to the acknowledgment of inescapable finitude the move from transcendental to post-transcendental phenomenology, because it rests on the question that is the key to Hegel's *Phenomenology of Spirit:* Who is the transcendental subject?[36] This question takes us beyond the discovery of the constitutive role of transcendental subjectivity to its constituted nature, to its historical and cultural specificity and rootedness. It acknowledges that a transcendental ego wholly transcendent to the worlds of nature and of culture, residing in glorious freedom above the finitude of their determinacy, is a will-o'-the-wisp. It admits that some particular life-world inhabits and grounds all our intentionalities and that no act of reflection can deport it entirely to the object pole of our experience.

Thus, for example, for Heidegger the question, Who is *Dasein?*, presses beyond the essentially ahistorical analysis of the anonymity of average everydayness to the question of the meaning of modernity as the death of God and the will to power expressed in the scientific/technological project of unconditional dominion. That science is not primarily the addition of correct information to the body of human knowledge but a fundamental definition of what is and of truth, and that in its essence technology is not a mode of doing but a mode of revealing that transforms everything into an object at the disposal of the human (or possibly inhuman) subject—these analyses belong to post-transcendental phenomenology.[37] We analyze our life-world to understand our destiny, the givenness of our being, not to free ourselves from the "restriction" of our historicity. The freedom we could achieve is the freedom of honesty about the forces already at work within us, whether we like it or not, rather than the freedom of a (pretended) *causa sui*.

It begins to look, in keeping with the first thesis of this essay, as if a good Husserlian is a post-Husserlian, as if the Cartesian, transcendental project progresses toward fulfilling itself and attaining its proper destiny when it overcomes itself in the post-transcendental turn to the hermeneutics of finitude. The necessity of this turn has been thoroughly established by the work of Heidegger, Gadamer, Merleau-Ponty, Ricoeur, and others (including, incidentally, Wittgenstein). What especially concerns us here is the second thesis of this essay, the claim that in making this turn phenomenology not only follows its own immanent development but simultaneously gains in its ability to illuminate the question(s) of religious truth.

If we can say from a psychological point of view that Husserl's need for the absolute autonomy and total self-sufficiency of a self-grounding *causa sui* is neurotic, we can say from a religious point of view that it is self-defeating. It represents a methodological vaccine against religious truth that renders it immune from the contagion that any genuine contact might bring. It appears to be rooted in fear and pride, the pride that affirms itself as absolute and its truth as a trophy to be displayed, and the fear that turns truth into a security blanket to be hugged or a weapon to be wielded against the threats that actual human finitude pose to its pride. In short, it represents a posture toward truth systematically at odds with religious truth, biblically understood. It appears to be a method for those who would be God themselves, not the children of God.

There are religious traditions, in particular Hindu and Buddhist, that affirm that in reality, if not in appearance, the believing soul is not to be distinguished from the divine (Brahman, the Buddha nature). But Husserl's methodology is no better suited to these traditions, which teach the dissolution and absorption of the self, not its assertion in absolute autonomy.

By contrast, the hermeneutics of finitude is at home with the idea that the goal of the quest for religious truth is not that ascent above the world in which we become God or like God as self-grounded, but rather that opening of ourselves to God in which we receive God and become like God in self-giving love. The following prayer expresses what I have in mind here:

> Dear Lord, give me a growing desire to pray. It remains so hard for me to give my time generously to you. I am still greedy for time—time to be useful, effective, successful, time to perform, excel, produce. But you, O Lord, ask nothing else than my simple presence, my humble recognition of my nakedness, my defenseless confession of my sins, so that you can let the rays of your love enter my heart and give me the deep knowledge that I can love because you have loved me first, that I can offer acceptance because you have accepted me first, and that I can do good because you have shown me your goodness first.[38]

Phenomenology, which has taken the first post-transcendental turn, embodies the finitude appropriate to this posture of openness and receptivity. Two of its central themes illuminate the kind of religious truth appropriate to this mode of self-understanding. The first of these themes is plurality.[39] There is a twofold plurality to be noted. On the one hand, when understanding is understood as interpretation, attention is called to the plurality of texts, events, and practices (not obviously reducible to unity) to be interpreted. On the other hand, the nature of the hermeneutical circle calls attention to the plurality of traditions of interpretation by which the interpreter is already surrounded and makes it clear that it would be foolish (and arrogant) to think that one's own interpretation would somehow put an end to this plurality and become the definitive, final interpretation. Truth may be one in itself, but the mirror in which we see it dimly is also a prism that renders our grasp of it irreducibly manifold.

It does not follow that all interpretations are equally good or that one should eschew all desire for rigor in seeking to distinguish better from worse interpretations. But it is implied that the appropriate rigor is not that of the subject who seeks to master its object, but of the servant who seeks to be at the disposal of the truth that comes to light in what is being interpreted. And it is implied that any claim to give the best interpretation will have to be seriously qualified.

Clearly any truth that is so enmeshed in plurality is ill-suited to serve as a security blanket, a trophy, or a weapon. If we ask, then, what it may be good for, we are led to the second theme by which the hermeneutics of finitude illuminates religious truth. This is the theme of listening. Because hermeneutical phenomenology can be described as the art of good listening,[40] its posture is quite the opposite of the experimental sciences designed for "constraining nature to give answer to questions of reason's own determining."[41] The religious equivalent of this is Job, at the time when he issues daily subpoenas demanding that God appear and explain himself. Job's access to religious truth begins only when, in response to divine questioning, he abandons this posture and listens to the voice that puts him in question.

To interpret is to ask questions of texts, events, practices, and so forth. But it is also to listen, not just to the answers given to our own questions, but to the questions posed to us, questions it did not occur to us to ask, or questions that did occur to us, but that we would prefer to ignore. Here the finitude of understanding consists not just in irreducible plurality, but in the fact that we are not in charge, not the origin and ground of what emerges in the conversation. Far from achieving an absolute standpoint, we discover the questionability of our being-in-the-world.

If we are openly receptive to the truth that emerges from the text, event, or practice, we are interpreting; it is our practices as well as our beliefs that are put in question. This is powerfully expressed in Gadamer's notion that to interpret is to open oneself to the truth-claim in a text and to discover that this truth-claim involves application, not just assent.[42] In the hermeneutics of listening, finitude and praxicality are united.

In biblical religion truth is inextricably linked to the word of the Lord in the proclamation of the prophet or apostle, and the unending exhortation is to listen and obey. Theologians often call attention to this fact.[43] The hermeneutics of finitude calls attention both to the structure of this experience and to the wider horizon of experience in which it takes place. For this experience of truth is as fundamental to human life as is the experience in which some object is compelled by a subject, identifying his perspective with reason, to answer "questions of reason's own determining."

If the theme of plurality is the negative moment of the hermeneutics of finitude, denying all claims to absolute knowledge, the theme of listening is the positive moment, affirming our openness as interpreters to voices not our own, to texts, traditions, and speakers whose horizon is not ours. Thus from the post-transcendental perspective of the hermeneutics of finitude, the Cartesian *cogito* is radically changed. The ground of our intentionality is itself grounded in history and language. As such, subjectivity is both corporate or collective and culturally conditioned. Moreover, it finds itself response-able to claims on its belief and behavior that come to it from texts and traditions that put its own being-in-the-world in question. It belongs to a conversation it did not initiate and that it could terminate only by an arbitrary act of self-assertion. In respect to both identity and questionability, the subject fails to be an absolute origin. Subjectivity is finite.

The Hermeneutics of Suspicion

But suppose that subjectivity is devious as well. Suppose that "the ruses of self-consciousness are more subtle than those of things."[44] That will lead us beyond the hermeneutics of transcendental finitude to the hermeneutics of transcendental depravity.

The first step along this path is the recognition that the life from which reflection can never isolate itself is the life of desire. Hermeneutics must become the semantics of desire if Ricoeur is right when he claims:

> Representation obeys not only a law of intentionality, which makes it the expression of some object, but also another law, which makes it the manifestation of life, of an effort or desire. It is because of the interference of the latter expressive function that representation can be distorted. Thus representation may be investigated in two ways: on the one hand, by a gnoseology (or criteriology) according to which representation is viewed as an intentional relation ruled by the objects that manifest themselves in that intentionality, and on the other

hand by an exegesis of the desires that lie *hidden* in that intentionality.[45]

The hermeneutics of finitude represents the first of these projects under conditions of historical finitude. The hermeneutics of suspicion represents the second, the exegesis of *hidden* desires and the self-deceptions by which we distort what we see in a mirror dimly. It reminds us of a "rootedness in existence" more radical than that of the hermeneutical circle. For it keeps before us "not only the unsurpassable nature of life, but the interference of desire with intentionality, upon which desire inflicts an invincible obscurity, an ineluctable partiality."[46]

It is not the mere presence of desire that leads to suspicion, but the presence of *hidden* desire. Desire as such can be handled without much difficulty by the hermeneutics of finitude. It is simply a dimension of that life (life-world) that turns up on the subjective side of experience. Thus, for example, the desire for purity plays a central and illuminating role in *The Symbolism of Evil*, in which suspicion plays no significant role. Hidden desire enters the scene when the transcendental subject is fundamentally ambivalent. It cannot acknowledge its desires, even or rather especially to itself, because they are in conflict with values or norms that it espouses. Neither saint nor demon, the transcendental ego of hidden desire is, as it were, too good not to have a conscience but not good enough to have its desires in conformity with that conscience.

The suspicion that responds to the role of hidden desire gives a new meaning to the concept of distance in hermeneutics. The dialectic of belonging and distance has a double meaning for the hermeneutics of finitude. Though I find myself at a distance from texts, events, and practices that belong to a life-world other than my own, a fusion of horizons is possible that makes it possible for me to belong to those worlds at least in comprehending conversation. On the other hand, I find myself belonging so essentially to my own world of tradition that I can never completely distance myself from it, as Husserl had hoped, though I can distance myself sufficiently for reflection and thus for phenomenology to remain a possibility. It is just that my reflection can never be absolute nor my phenomenology a rigorous science.

The distance required by suspicion is like this second mode of distance in that the task is not the overcoming of the distance between self and other but the establishing of some distance from myself.[47] In both cases I must distance myself from myself in order to notice something about myself previously unnoticed. But there is a crucial difference. In the case of suspicion my failure to notice does not stem from casual, accidental inattention but from motivated, intentional inattention.

In other words, suspicion is unlike ordinary skepticism. Instead of being aimed directly at propositions believed or practices performed in order to challenge their truth or value, suspicion is aimed at the individual or community who believes and performs in order to challenge their integrity. It looks for that discrepancy between professed meaning and actual use which renders life ironical; for it is the essence of the ironical (speech) act that it performs a function quite at odds with its surface meaning. Thus an ironical compliment functions to express a criticism. For this reason suspicion is less interested in the official meaning of beliefs and practices than in their operative meaning, the clue to which is the life-world from which they arise and which, in turn, they legitimize. Where the operative meaning differs from the official meaning, as when the God of love becomes the architect of apartheid or of "revolutionary justice," it will be because the desires that shape the life-world are hidden from a transcendental subjectivity that cannot acknowledge them without shame.

Where that transcendental subjectivity is individual we can speak with Freud of illusion; where it is corporate we can speak with Marx of ideology; and in both cases we can speak with Nietzsche of the dishonesty in which the will to power seeks to hide itself from moral values that would place constraints upon it.

Because hidden desires do shape the intentionalities that give shape to human existence, the phenomenological project completes itself only when it incorporates into itself the kind of suspicion that carries the task of interpretation to this level. The move from the original Husserlian project to the hermeneutics of finitude needs to be followed by the move on to the hermeneutics of suspicion. Merleau-Ponty's comments about Marx, Nietzsche, and Freud as phenomenologists are essentially correct. They represent the proper destiny of the phenomenological project.

This second post-transcendental turn, which uncovers the devious self-deceptiveness of transcendental subjectivity, gives us a third mode of phenomenological reflection. What light, if any, can it throw on the question(s) of religious truth?

In the first place, the hermeneutics of suspicion provides a constant reminder that the parties to debates about religious truth are not disinterested spectators. Whether the disputes are between believers and unbelievers, between adherents of different religious faiths, or between members of different traditions/denominations within one religious faith, we are reminded that the disputants are not just finite but liable to self-deception, not just situated but situated sinners whose (perceived) self-interests enter (quite unperceived, to themselves at least) into their judgments about what is reasonable. Between the parties and the truth in itself (the truth face to face) stands not only the hermeneutical circle in which each is caught up, but also the resistance to which each has been given over. The blindness that comes from perspective is compounded by the blindness that comes from perversity.

This reminder that there are none so blind as those who will not see is no magic wand for restoring sight to those with motivated blindness. But the light it shines into otherwise conveniently darkened corners provides a powerful counterforce to our tendencies to self-deception. No doubt it would be foolish to hope that we can be rescued from our sinfulness by any method. But where the self becomes a set of techniques for self-deception, the will to honesty needs a countertechnique of exposure. This is the role of suspicion.[48] It provides tools, for those willing to use them, for unmasking the false pursuit of truth.

The religious concern for orthodoxy is often such a false pursuit of truth. Orthodoxy is right belief. The religious concern for religious truth is often focused on validating the correctness of belief (and practice). Post-transcendental phenomenology challenges that concept of truth which often underlies this project. The hermeneutics of finitude requires of every orthodoxy the humble (but often reluctant) confession that it can never definitively attain its goal, can never have the truth naked and complete. The hermeneutics of suspicion goes further by noting the dialectical unity of insecurity (lack of trust) and self-assertion, already noted in Husserl's project, which motivates this demand for validated truth. The need for total certainty and certain totality in my system of beliefs corresponds to an understanding of truth as a security blanket, as a trophy, and as a weapon. As the possessor of such truth I can save myself, and when my enemies prevail in the world, I can comfort myself with the superior knowledge that I am right and they are wrong. Even if, mirabile dictu, I were to possess the complete system of correct beliefs, suspicion would ask whether my motivations have not shut me off from the truth.

Suspicion is not the claim that correctness is unimportant. It only insists that there are other crucial questions when it comes to religious truth. In addition to the question about motivation, there is the question about function. What role do my beliefs (and practices) play in my life? What work do they do for me? What life-world do they sanctify and thus legitimize? Does my God-talk, for example, legitimize racism and economic injustice by remaining silent about them, making it possible for me to participate in them while remaining an exemplary believer? Does it sanctify militaristic nationalism by restricting the religious life to metaphysical doctrine and liturgical cult, leaving politics to define its own truth? Or, conversely, does my God-talk sanctify my social, economic, and political views, pretending that theology can define all truth and not allowing social evolution, for example, or economic innovation, or political prudence their own place? Do my religious beliefs function to legitimize opinions about public policy reached on other grounds? Since in some cases beliefs legitimize by their silence, it is clear that no measure of correctness could keep them from having this function. Even if religious metaphysics could escape the hermeneutic circle and have "the good fortune to enter upon the secure path of a science,"[49] that would not keep it from ironically having a function quite at odds with its professed norms.

It is questions like these about motivation and function that lead Kierkegaard to refuse simply to identify correctness with truth, and to talk about truth as subjectivity. In a notorious passage he writes:

> If one who lives in the midst of Christendom goes up to the house of God, the house of the true God, with the true conception of God in his knowledge, and prays, but prays in a false spirit; and one who lives in an idolatrous community prays with the entire passion of the infinite, although his eyes rest upon the image of an idol: where is there the most truth? The one prays in truth to God though he worships an idol; the other prays falsely to the true God, and hence worships in fact an idol.[50]

It is the praxicality of truth that makes it impossible to identify correct belief (or even correct belief with a Cartesian certificate of certainty) with truth.

The conjunction of orthodoxy and idolatry would seem impossible, were it not historical. For history has shown how ready religion is to prostitute itself to the sinful interests of its patrons. Idolatrous theology is the expression of instrumental religion, the attempt on the part of human will-to-power to domesticate the divine power and make it serve as the instrument of human purposes. Human projects are the end; God is the means. This relationship between human and divine power is overt in magic, where the sacred invites manipulation by its impersonal character. But where the God of the Bible is concerned, manipulation would be violation most foul. This does not mean that the project is abandoned, only that it cannot publicly acknowledge itself.

The most useful device for domesticating God and changing biblical religion into instrumental religion is that of selective reading. The biblical texts stubbornly insist on including bad news along with the good. For Israel the covenant included the solemn promises of the entirely faithful God to bless and prosper His people if it were faithful, but to curse and punish it if it were not. When John the Baptist and Jesus introduced what Christians have come to understand as the new covenant, they did so with the words, "Repent, for the kingdom of God is at hand." The good news of the kingdom begins with the bad news of a call to repentance. The bad news (the hard sayings) of the covenant and the kingdom render implausible the interpretations most favorable to instrumental religion. Thus the pious path to illusion, ideology, and idolatry is not so much the path of disbelief as the path of selective reading. Theology, perhaps with the help of the hermeneutics of finitude, seeks to recover or recollect the deepest meaning of its sacred texts and traditions. But its customers, who after all pay its bills, would often prefer that it filter out the bad news, leaving an adulterated residue of unadulterated good news. The hermeneutics of suspicion stands as a deliberate methodological check against this tendency. It is an indispensable complement to the hermeneutics of receptive recovery and to any theology more concerned with truth than with popularity.[51]

The discussion of suspicion's contribution to the question(s) of religious truth began, above, with the reminder that none of the parties to disputes about religious truth is a disinterested spectator. Then attention narrowed to focus on the project of orthodoxy. What needs to be noted now is that a similar analysis is appropriate for other participants. The militant unbeliever, who is as eager to establish the falsehood of religion as the orthodox apologist is to prove its truth, is susceptible to the same kinds of self-deception and needs to be asked the same questions about motivation and function. The same is true for those (believers and unbelievers) who, unlike the antagonists just mentioned, are more or less indifferent to questions of religious truth. For denial or indifference in the face of religious truth-claims may also be motivated by desires less honorable than the love of truth, such as the desire to avoid having those desires which define my life put in question by anything or anybody. Thus the absence of significant religious truth-claims from my life may function as effectively in the service of my own will-to-power as religious beliefs do for the instrumentally religious. Suspicion is no respecter of persons.

Conclusion

Nothing in this essay implies that it would be inappropriate for one religious interpretation of life to claim superiority, with respect to truth as correct belief, to other interpretations, religious and nonreligious. But to whose for whom the validating of such claims is the primary issue relating to religious truth, the results may be disappointing. For, while declining simply to dismiss the question of correct belief as somehow inappropriate (as noncognitivists and some postmodernists would like to do), these reflections (1) insist that no claim to be the best available interpretation in terms of correct belief can rest upon the claim to be a final and definitive interpretation, (2) provide no help, at least in any direct way, in discovering which (finite) interpretation of life, if any, can best claim truthful superiority, and (3) tend to displace or decenter the question of correct belief by pointing to the praxicality of truth as something to be done. Those for whom the Enlightenment project is an absolute will either have to abandon phenomenology as useless or first rescue Husserl from his most faithful followers by realizing his dream of rigorous science and then find a way to make that rigorous science an effective umpire in disputes about religious beliefs.

For those willing to let the phenomenological project deconstruct the Enlightenment project that gave it birth, the gains are twofold—the reminders of *the finitude* and *the praxicality* of religious truth, which together bring philosophical reflection into talking distance with biblical religion. Here another objection may be raised—namely, that the closeness of hermeneutical phenomenology and religious truth, biblically understood, is due to the religious origins of the hermeneutics of finitude and the hermeneutics of suspicion.

Two replies seem to be in order. First, to the degree that this is the case, it only reflects the fact that all thought is caught up in some hermeneutical circle and that the best we can do is to practice something like what Rawls calls reflective equilibrium. Secondly, to an important degree hermeneutical phenomenology does not have a Judeo-Christian point of departure. Heidegger, Gadamer, and Merleau-Ponty on the one hand, and Marx, Nietzsche, and Freud on the other, can hardly be said to be Christian thinkers, like Kierkegaard, or even listeners to the Christian message, like Ricoeur. The case for hermeneutical phenomenology does not rest on theological premises. Together its two modes of reflection represent the self-overcoming of the Cartesian-Husserlian project, which (1) opens the door to détente or even dialogue between philosophical reflection and biblical religion, and (2) in the process produces great discomfort among some of the most zealous apologists and antagonists of these religious traditions. Whether this opening will continue to prove fruitful will depend on whether these apologists and antagonists can overcome their discomfort and renew their debate under new auspices, and whether the philosophical community can overcome the smug assurance that hermeneutical phenomenology is a fashion now several decades out of date.

6

Ideology and Religion:
A Hermeneutic Conflict

Richard Kearney

An indispensable element in any contemporary discussion of religious "truth" is the question of ideology. Much of modern critical theory—from Marx to Althusser and Barthes—sees religion as the paradigm case of ideology understood as "false consciousness." In order to describe the truth of man it is considered necessary to expose the untruth of God. And an essential step in this direction is the demystification of the ways in which religious ideology *alienates* human consciousness by attributing the real source of meaning to some absolute power *outside* of man. In order for man to return to himself, and discover his own truth, the pseudo truth of religion must be debunked.

The standard equation of ideology with false consciousness, and of false consciousness with religion (in the primary instance), was not always the case, however. The first recorded use of the term *idéologie* was by Destutt de Tracy at the end of the eighteenth century—and he defined it as the "science of the genesis of ideas." But the initial claim of ideology to provide a scientific foundation to social law was soon subjected to ridicule. *Idéologue* became a word of abuse for those who engaged in lofty abstractions rather than facing up to the truths of reality. Napoleon set his seal on this derogatory connotation when he denounced as ideologues all who opposed his imperial ambitions by letting idealist principles take priority over the exigencies of *la politique réelle*.[1]

It was this negative sense of ideology as a system of abstract untruth or illusion which was later taken up by the philosophers. Hegel invoked it summarily in his *Philosophy of History*; and Marx went on to analyze its workings and implications in a now famous passage of *The German Ideology* where he speaks of a *camera obscura* that reverses the proper rapport between reality and ideas. We shall return to this analysis below. The main point to be made at this stage is that it was the negative definition of ideology as falsehood that dominated most subsequent theories. Lenin, it is true, used it in the more positive sense of a propaganda weapon; but, so defined, the question of its truth was considered irrelevant. What mattered was its efficacity as an instrument of class warfare. Most other modern critics of ideology—Mannheim, Aron, Althusser, Geertz, and Ricoeur—tend to take it for granted that scientific truth is alien to ideology. To describe something as ideological is to describe it as false, or at least as epistemologically neutral.

Of course, once the epistemological question is bracketed, it is possible to conceive of ideology as serving a *symbolic* function in a society. It may be analyzed, for example, as illustrating the *social imaginary* of a given culture. It may be investigated to explain how certain images, myths, ideals, or rhetorics motivate a society. But it is no longer considered as a science of social truth in the sense originally proposed by Destutt.

On the contrary, ideology has come to mean the very opposite of science. And, not surprisingly, the modern opposition between science and ideology has often been superimposed—especially since Marx—on the related Enlightenment opposition between reason and religion. Whereas scientific reason dealt with truth, religious faith was frequently dismissed as an ideological exercise in mystification and illusion. Indeed, religion was considered the most damaging form of ideology, since it represented the highest degree of human alienation. Marx and his disciples, following Feuerbach, believed that God was the image of human perfection projected into a transcendental realm. God was man alienated from himself. The task of science was to unmask this ideological distortion and return man to himself. Science, in short, promised to convert false consciousness into true consciousness, to transform religion into reason.

In this essay, I wish to examine (1) the way in which the critique of religion evolved as a critique of ideology in the modern period; and (2) the way in which a new movement in contemporary hermeneutics, most cogently represented by Paul Ricoeur, has challenged the reduction of religion to ideological distortion and argued for an affirmation of its eschatological truth potential.

The Hermeneutics of Suspicion

The most sustained contemporary critiques of religion have tended, as mentioned above, to focus on its ideological role as a purveyor of false consciousness. This method of critique has been labeled a *hermeneutics of suspicion* by Paul Ricoeur. By this is meant a practice of interpreting (Gr., *hermeneuin*) discourse as a masked consciousness so as to expose the hidden sense under the apparent sense.

The hermeneutic strategy of removing the mask in order to uncover repressed meanings was developed in the nineteenth century by the "three masters of suspicion"—Marx, Nietzsche, and (later) Freud. Nietzsche advanced a *genealogical hermeneutics of the will*, which interpreted religious values as distortions whose intention it is to replace a strong will to power with passivity, resentment, and self-abnegation. Dismissing religion as "Platonism for the people," Nietzsche endeavored to expose religious cults of otherworldly transcendence as no more than disguised negations of life. Freud, for his part, championed a *genetic hermeneutics of desire*. Religion, he held, is an imaginary substitute for lost primitive or infantile objects. As such it represents an "obsessional neurosis," whereby human desire is repressed through a complex of unconscious, self-concealing mechanisms. Thus in *Moses and Monotheism* and *Totem and Taboo*, Freud explained the origin of religion as a symbolic compensation for prohibited pleasures. And thirdly, there is Marx who developed a *hermeneutics of "false consciousness,"* which discerned the hidden connection between ideology—of which religion is the ultimate and most fundamental expression for Marx— and the historical phenomenon of class domination. Marx interpreted religion as a coded language of submission, where the myth of a supernatural paradise becomes the opium of the people totally concealing its own socio-economic motivation. In this respect, Marx's denuciation of the religious character of the great money fetish in the first book of the *Capital* constitutes one of the central planks of his critique of ideology.

Marx shares with Nietzsche and Freud the suspicion that religion is a mythological structure that remains ignorant of itself as a creation of false values. It is a "myth" in the sense that it inverts the real and the imaginary, compensating for historical injustice with some ahistorical and otherworldly justice—which, according to Marx, is no more than a fantasy projection. "The *critique* of religion," Marx affirmed accordingly, expresses "the categorical refusal of all relations where man finds himself degraded, imprisoned or abandoned."[2]

I would readily acknowledge the legitimacy of such a negative *hermeneutics of suspicion*. There is always need to unmask the ideological content of religion. Indeed, it is arguable that this critique is an indispensable component of modern culture in general and of modern theology in particular. As Ricoeur accurately observes in a study entitled "The Critique of Religion" (1973):

> The reading of ideology as a symptom of the phenomenon of domination will be the durable contribution of Marxism beyond its political applications. From this point of view Marx does not belong solely to the Communists. Marxism, let it not be forgotten, appeared in Germany in the middle of the last century at the heart of the departments of Protestant theology. It is, therefore, an event of Western culture, and I would even say, of Western theology.[3]

In this connection, it is also appropriate to recall that one of the most influential attempts to "demythologize" religion was in fact sponsored by a Protestant theologian, Rudolph Bultmann (in the *Theology of the New Testament*[4] and elsewhere). Bultmann held that Christianity must be emancipated from those "mythic" accretions whereby Christ became idolized as the sacrificial *Kyrios* of a savior cult—a cult modeled on the pagan heroes of Hellenic, Gnostic, or Babylonian mystery-rites. Bultmann's demythologizing is leveled against the mystification of authentic Christian spirituality. His critique casts a suspecting glance at all efforts to reduce the genuine scandal of Cross and Resurrection to an ideological system wherein the newness of the Christian message is ignored or betrayed. Bultmann systematically exposes the manner in which the Living Word of the Gospels has frequently degenerated into cultic rites—for example, the attempt to express the eschatological promise of the Kingdom as a cosmological cult of heaven and hell; or the attempt to reduce the historical working of the Spirit through the church to a cult of triumphalistic temporal power. To "demythologize" Christianity is, for Bultmann, to dissolve these false scandals so as to let the true scandal of the Word made flesh speak to us anew.[5]

The common task of such critical hermeneutics, atheistic or theistic, is to debunk ideological inversions of the original relationship between the real and the imaginary; it aims to unmask the true meaning behind the "mythologized" meaning. Such a critique is clearly necessary. But we would go further than the masters of suspicion in arguing that this critique must *itself* be subject to critique. And this extension of the hermeneutic critique makes it possible to recognize, in the symbolizing activity of myth and ideology, the possibility of another, more positive content obscured by the negative falsifying content. The hermeneutics of suspicion may in this way be preserved and also supplemented by a *hermeneutics of affirmation*. But before exploring such a hermeneutics of affirmation, I propose to examine in more detail the ways in which ideology works.

The Critique of Ideology

There are three principal features of ideology: (1) integration, (2) dissimulation, and (3) domination.[6]

Integration

Ideology expresses a social group's need for a communal set of images whereby it can represent itself to itself and to others. Each society creates or invokes a tradition of mythic idealizations whereby it may be aligned with a stable, predictable, and repeatable order of meanings. This process of ideological self-representation frequently assumes the form of a mythic reiteration of the founding act of the community. It seeks to redeem society from the crises of the present by justifying its actions in terms of some sanctified past, some sacred Beginning.[7] One could cite here the role played by the Aeneas myth in Roman society or the cosmogony myths in Greek society, or indeed the Celtic myths of Cuchulain and the Fianna in Irish society. And where an ancient past is lacking, a more recent past will suffice—the Declaration of Independence for the U.S.A., the October Revolution for the U.S.S.R., and so on.

Ideology thus serves to relate the social memory of a historical community to some inaugural act that founded it and can be repeated over time in order to preserve a sense of social integration. The role of ideology, writes Ricoeur, "is not only to diffuse the conviction beyond the circle of founding fathers, so as to make it the creed of the entire group; its role is also to perpetuate the initial energy beyond the period of effervescence. It is into this gap, characteristic of all situations *après coup*, that the images and interpretations intervene. A founding act can be revived and reactualized only in an *interpretation* which models it retroactively, through a representation of itself." It is arguable, moreover, that no social group could exist without this indirect relation to its own inaugural event. "The ideological phenomenon thus begins very early; for domestication by memory is accompanied not only by consensus, but also by convention and rationalization (in the Freudian sense). . . . At this point, ideology . . . continues to be mobilizing only insofar as it is justificatory."[8]

The ideological recollection of sacred foundational acts has the purpose therefore of both integrating and justifying a social order. While this can accompany a cultural or national revival, it can also give rise to a "stagnation of politics," a situation where each power rehearses an anterior power: "every prince wants to be Caesar, every Caesar wants to be Alexander, every Alexander wants to Hellenise an Oriental despot."[9] Either way, ideology entails a process of schematization and ritualization that stereotypes social action and permits a social group to recollect itself in terms of rhetorical maxims and idealized self-images. In this sense, ideology is identified by Durkheim as the inner mechanism of the "national spirit." [10]

Dissimulation

If the schematic "rationalizations" of ideology bring about social integration, they do so, paradoxically, at a "prerational" level. The ideology of foundational myths operates behind our backs, as it were, rather than appearing as a transparent theme before our eyes. We think *from* ideology rather than *about* it. And it is precisely because the codes of ideology function in this oblique manner that the practice of distortion and dissimulation can occur. This is the epistemological reason for Marx's denouncing ideology as the falsifying projection of "an inverted image of our own position in society." Ideology is by its very nature an "uncritical instance" and thus easily susceptible to deceit, alienation—and by extension, intolerance. All too frequently, ideology functions in a reactionary or at least socially conservative fashion. "It signifies that what is new can only be accommodated in terms of the typical, itself stemming from the sedimentation of social experience."[11] Consequently, the future—as opening up that which is unassimilable and unprecedented vis-à-vis the pre-existing codes of experience—is often translated back into the orthodox stereotypes of the past. This accounts for the fact that many social groups display traits of ideological orthodoxy that render them intolerant toward what is marginal, different, or alien. Pluralism and permissiveness are the bêtes noires of such social orthodoxy. They represent the intolerable. This phenomenon of the intolerable arises when the experience of radical novelty threatens the possibility of the social group recognizing itself in a retrospective reference to its hallowed traditions and pieties.

But ideology can also function in a dissimulating capacity to the extent that it conceals the gap between what *is* and what *ought* to be—that is, between our presently lived *reality* and the *ideal* world of our traditional self-representations.[12] By masking the gulf that separates our contemporary historical experience from mythic memory, ideology often justifies the status quo by presuming that nothing has really changed. This self-dissimulation expresses itself as a resistance to change—as a closure to new possibilities of self-understanding. While it is virtually impossible for a social consciousness to endure otherwise than through *some kind of interpretive detour* via ideological codes and traditions, there is always the danger of reducing the challenge of the new to the acceptable limits of an established heritage of meaning. With this in mind, I proceed to analyze how the ideological functions of *integration* and *dissimulation* may become the joint allies of *domination*.

Domination

This property of ideology raises the vexed question of the hierarchical organization of society—the question of authority. As Max Weber and later Jürgen Habermas observed, social systems tend to *legitimate* themselves by means of an ideology that justifies their right to secure and retain power. This process of legitimation is inherently problematic, however, insofar as there exists a disparity between the nation-state's ideological *claim* to authority and the answering belief of the public. Ideology thus entails a surplus-value of claim over response, of power over freedom. Put in another way, if a system's claim to authority were fully and reciprocally consented to by those whom it governs, there would be no urgent need for the persuasive or coercive strategies of ideology. Ideology operates accordingly as a "surplus-value" symptomatic of a discrepancy between the legitimizing "ought" of our normative codes on the one hand, and the "is" of our lived social existence on the other. It is because there is no transparent coincidence between the claim to authority and the response to this claim that ideology is deemed necessary to preserve the *semblance* of a united social consensus. Ideology thus assures what Weber termed the "charismatic" function of the social order. As such, it is a direct consequence of modernity, for it seeks to fill the gap left by the disappearance of tradition. Ideology attempts to compensate for the modern "disenchantment" of society.

This analysis of domination is comparable to Marx's celebrated critique of ideology.[13] Marx identified the ideological function of domination as a distorting inversion of the true relation of things. In *The German Ideology* he wrote that "if in all ideology men and their circumstances appear upside down as in a *camera obscura*, this phenomenon arises just as much from their historical life-process as the inversion of objects on the retina does from their physical life-process." Marx developed Feuerbach's suggestion that religion is ideology par excellence. By projecting a heavenly other-world beyond our historical world, religion inverts the true relation between the ideal and the real—superstructure and infrastucture—and thus makes man stand on his head. This religious inversion represents, for Marx, the fundamental form and content of all ideological systems ranging from the ancient mythological comogonies to the metaphysical idealisms of Plato, Descartes, and even Hegel. Ideology is thus considered the agency of "false consciousness" insofar as it gives priority to the imaginary over the material, superstructural theory over infrastructural praxis. Marx's critique of ideology is a hermeneutic of suspicion that proposes to invert the inversion—to liberate man from his false idealizations so that he may repossess himself as he is in *reality*. In this respect it is an "archeological" interpretation that relocates the origin (*archē*) of meaning in the material forces and relations of production.

This Marxist critique serves the useful purpose of negating the negative function of ideology. It unmasks illusory representations and fantasies that serve the interests of the dominant class by keeping the dominated class servile. Any genuine commitment to religion must be prepared to expose itself to the risk of this purgative critique. A critique of religion nourished by Feuerbach, Marx, and the masters of suspicion, as Ricoeur suggests, "pertains to the mature faith of modern man."[14] A genuine theistic hermeneutic would do well, therefore, to appropriate to itself the demystification of religion as a "mask of fear, a mask of domination, a mask of hate." A Marxist critique of ideology could thus be endorsed as "a view through which any kind of mediation of faith must pass. . . . To smash the idols is also to let [authentic] symbols speak."[15]

But Ricoeur also takes issue with the Marxist critique of religion. Marx's equation of the form of ideology with a specifically religious content, and his equation of the latter with the sole function of inversion and domination, lead to a reductive understanding of both ideology and religion. Religion and ideology can indeed serve the interests of class domination by propagating a false consciousness of historical reality. But they can also serve other interests—for example the interest in emancipation. (I shall return to this point in my discussion of the hermeneutics of affirmation.) But even within the critical perspective of a hermeneutics of suspicion, Marx's exclusive equation of ideology with the distorting practice of religious inversion is too limited. Ideology is a broader and more extensive phenomenon than Marx realized. With the demise of religion as the dominant superstructure of society, other discourses can come to serve as the ideological means of justifying and integrating new orders of domination. In the modern era, science (be it in a liberal or conservative guise) frequently fulfills the role of ideological legitimation and dominatiion even though it was, ironically, science that claimed to overcome ideology.

While we remain indebted to Marx, therefore, for exposing a specifically religious functioning of ideological inversion, we should be prepared to supplement this critique with a further critique of the claim of scientific reason itself to have discovered some preideological vantage point of *total* knowledge. The positivist claim to nonideological understanding is both naive and deceptive. In fact, one could argue, taking a cue from the Frankfurt School, that such a claim itself constitutes a new form of ideology, for it justifies a new social order dominated by principles of disinterested objectivism that mask a system of technological rationality and manipulation. Even Marxist societies, founded in large part on the critique of ideology, often lay claim to a scientific materialism that assumes the function of an ideology of domination in its own right.

The critique of ideology must itself be exposed to critique. Otherwise the unchallenged rule of anti-ideological reason can become an uncritical dogmatism that conceals its own ideological practices of legitimation. In short, the positivist cult of science can also become an opium of the people in the modern technological era (insofar as it justifies the dominating interests of a particular social system).

To the extent, therefore, that Marxism after Marx dogmatically invokes the model of scientific materialism to legitimate the official doctrine of the party and, by extension, of the ruling group within the party, it performs the role of ideological domination denounced by Marx himself. Whence it follows that the truly critical potential of Marxism can be liberated and realized anew only if the use of Marx's work is "completely dissassociated from the exercise of power and authority, and from judgments of orthodoxy."[16] And this can occur only when Marxism extends its critique of the *religious* ideology of domination to its own tendency to replace this with a *scientific* ideology of domination.

Ricoeur sums up his critique of Marx's critique: "That religion . . . reverses the relation of heaven and earth, signifies that it is no longer religion, that is, the insertion of the Word in the world, but rather the *inverted image of life*. Then it is nothing more than the (narrow) ideology denounced by Marx. But the same thing can happen, and undoubtedly does happen, to science and technology, as soon as their claim to scientificity masks their justificatory function with regard to the military-industrial system"[17]—that is, the system practiced by both advanced capitalism and bureaucratic communism.

Ideology, understood in the broad sense of social self-representation, is an unsurpassable phenomenon of human sociohistorical existence. Social reality, as recent writings by Lévi-Strauss and Castoriadis have shown, always presupposes some sort of symbolic constitution, and it frequently includes an "interpretation in images and representations of the social bond itself." [18] It is impossible therefore to discover some ideologically free zone from which it would be possible to speak in any absolute scientific manner about ideology. Ideology is an indispensable dimension of the hermeneutic circle in which our historically situated understanding is obliged to operate. Hence while reaffirming the need for a perpetual critique of the deforming function of ideology, we must reject the presumption that we can totally abolish ideology—understood in the general sense of a symbolic constitution and interpretation of the social bond.[19]

Toward a Hermeneutics of Affirmation

Ideology is indeed a function of false consciousness. But it is not *only* that. And the same goes for the mythico-religious expressions of ideology. These expressions require the vigilant scrutiny of a hermeneutics of suspicion in order to deconstruct their negative alienating content. However, once this work of suspicion has taken place, once the *archeological* unveiling of the concealed meaning behind the apparent meaning has removed the masks of falsehood, there still remains *another* interpretive task. This second or supplementary practice is what Ricoeur terms a "hermeneutics of affirmation." Such a hermeneutics seeks to discriminate between falsifying and emancipating modes of symbolization. Having smashed the idols of false consciousness, it labors to identify genuine symbols of liberation.

Symbolizations of utopia or the Kingdom pertain to the futural dimension of our ideological representations. The hermeneutics of affirmation focuses not on the origin (*arché*) behind such symbols but on the end (*eschaton*) *in front of* them—that is, on the horizon of aspiration opened up by these symbols. In this way, it is possible to rescue mythic or religious symbolizations from the distorting strategies of reactionary domination. Ideology can thus be purified of its mystifying function and *reinterpreted* in terms of a genuine symbolic anticipation of liberty, truth, and justice. By extending an archeological hermeneutics of suspicion into such an *eschatological* hermeneutics of hope, Ricoeur offers the possibility of redeeming symbols from the ideological abuses of doctrinal prejudice, racist nationalism, class oppression, or totalitarian domination; and he does so in the name of a universal project of freedom from which no creed, nation, class, community, or individual is excluded. Eschatological myths differ from most archeological myths in that they tend to be inclusive rather than exclusive modes of representation; they open human consciousness to the possibility of a common goal of liberation rather than closing it off in the narrow security of reactionary conservatism.[20]

This distinction between archeological and eschatological interpretations of symbols, between the regressive movement toward an archaic past and the progressive movement toward the emergence of new meanings, has important epistemological implications. The former (i.e., the archeological) tends to treat symbolic expressions simply as illusory representations of some reality that pre-exists symbolic representation and is concealed by it. Hence Freud argued that dream symbols should be deciphered in order to disclose the *anterior* reality of infantile desire or trauma. Nietzsche denounced metaphysical metaphors of the suprasensible as resentful deformations of an *anterior* will to power. And Marx criticized the religious phenomena of ideology and fetishism as strategic inversions of the *anteriority* of the material conditions of production over the superstructural interpretation of these conditions. According to these three masters of suspicion, symbolization operates as an effacement of some original reality. Consequently, their respective programs of critique aimed to demystify symbolic representations in order to uncover the original cause (*arché*) of the representation. In short, *archeological hermeneutics* interprets the symbol in terms of a causal reference to some predetermining reality hidden *behind* the symbol.

Eschatological hermeneutics also recognizes that symbols operate according to a double intentionality—that the ostensible reference of the symbol contains within itself a hidden reference to some meaning that is not immediately given.[21] But the eschatological interpretation discerns in symbols a reference that is not exhaustively or exclusively determined by anterior causes. This eschatological reference is a "second order" signification wherein a symbol can refer not just to some pre-existing reality, which resides *before* the representation, but to some future horizon of meaning: some "possible world" that the symbol *opens* up. Here meaning is *in front of* the symbol, not behind it; it is disclosed as a posterior horizon of future possibilities. This is what Ricoeur means when he refers to the "symbol giving rise to thought." In a dialogue entitled "The Symbol as Bearer of Possible Worlds" (1978), Ricoeur elaborates on this eschatological reference opened up by the projection of symbols:

> Hermeneutics is concerned with the permanent spirit of language . . . not as some decorative excess or effusion of subjectivity, but as the creative capacity of language to open up new worlds. Poetic and mythic symbols (for example) do not just express nostalgia for some forgotten world. They constitute a disclosure of unprecedented worlds, an opening onto other possible meanings which transcend the established limits of our actual world . . . and (function as) a recreation of language.[22]

However, a hermeneutic analysis of symbolizing expressions involves not just epistemological considerations but also ethical ones. And this is where phenomenological hermeneutics, as practiced by Heidegger and Gadamer, needs to be complemented by the critique of ideology advanced by Marx and, in a more advanced form, by Habermas and the Frankfurt School.[23] Symbols are not innocent or neutral, as romantic ethnology would have us believe. They are authentic or inauthentic, according to the human "interests" that they express. These interests, as Habermas recognized in *Knowledge and Human Interests* (1968), can be those of domination or those of emancipation. The symbols of myth, religion, and social communication can be used as ideological weapons of reaction or of liberation. The Christian metaphor of the Kingdom, for example, can be interpreted either as an opiate of the oppressed (as Marx realized) or as an antidote to their oppression (as the theology of liberation in Latin America today reminds us). Similarly, it could be argued that the myths of Irish republicanism can be used to liberate a community or to incarcerate that community in tribal bigotry. And the same would apply to a hermeneutic critique of the Protestant-Loyalist mythology of "civil and religious liberties." Indeed, this critical question of authentic and inauthentic ideological representations can be applied to the founding and utopian projects of most nation-states.

When I speak therefore of the need for a critical hermeneutics, I do not mean that we should simply deconstruct figurative symbols into literal facts. I mean rather that we should unravel the concealed intentions and interests that operate in symbolic projects so as to discriminate between their authentic and inauthentic uses. And this requires a critical distinction between what Ricoeur refers to as the *explicatory* function of ideological symbols, which justifies the status quo in a dogmatic or irrational manner, and the genuinely *exploratory* function that puts the status quo into question and opens us to a new project, to a possible world of justice, equality, and peace.[24]

What is required is a hermeneutic dialectic between the claims of a critical *logos* and a symbolic *mythos*. Without the constant vigilance of critical evaluation, *mythos* remains susceptible to all kinds of perversion and abuse. (One need only consider, for instance, the way in which fascist movements in our own century unscrupulously exploited Germanic or Roman myths.) The hermeneutic critique of *mythos* is indispensable, for ideological symbolizations are neither good nor bad by virtue of their ongoing *reinterpretation* by each historical generation of each social community. As Ricoeur makes plain, hermeneutics cannot afford to approach mythic symbols in a naive or uncritical manner:

> We are no longer primitive beings living at the immediate level of myth. Myth for us is always mediated and opaque and . . . several of its recurrent forms have become deviant and dangerous, e.g. the myth of the absolute power (fascism) or the myth of the sacrificial scapegoat (anti-semitism and racism). We are no longer justified in speaking of "myth in general." We must critically assess the content of each myth and the basic intentions which animate it. Modern man can neither get rid of myth nor take it at its face value. Myth will always be with us, but we must always approach it critically.[25]

The movement from the epistemological to the ethical critique of symbolization signals a convergence between the claims of myth and reason. It is only when *mythos* and *logos* conjoin in a common project of universal liberation that we can properly speak of authentic symbols. For when a religious or ideological myth is considered as the founding act of one community to the total exclusion of all others, the possibility of perversion inevitably arises. Ricoeur argues therefore:

> The potential of any authentic myth goes beyond the limits of any single community. The *mythos* of a community is the bearer of a meaning which extends beyond its own particular frontiers; it is the bearer of *other possible worlds*. . . . Nothing travels or circulates as widely and effectively as myth. Whence

it follows that even though myths originate in particular cultures, they are also capable of emigrating and developing in new cultural parameters. . . . Only those myths are genuine which can be reinterpreted in terms of liberation, as both a personal and collective phenomenon. We should perhaps sharpen this critical criterion to include only those myths which have as their horizon the liberation of mankind *as a whole*. Liberation cannot be exclusive. . . . In genuine reason (*logos*) as well as in genuine myth (*mythos*), we find a concern for the *universal* emancipation of man.[26]

Toward a Critical Hermeneutics

The critical moment of demythologization is not to be confused with a reductive practice of *desymbolization*. Instead of simply reducing symbols to some putatively "literal" content, a critical hermeneutic of affirmation exposes the inauthentic perversions of symbols in order to recover their genuinely eschatological project. To the extent, therefore, that mythic or religious symbols play the role of an ideological justification of the status quo, they have already abandoned their "exploratory" role as disclosures of possible worlds. One could even say that this abuse of symbols usually occurs when they are interpreted as *literal facts* rather than *figurative intentions*—for example, when a particular state or church argues that it and it alone possesses absolute truth. This leads to sectarian triumphalism in religion and to totalitarian domination in politics. Here we witness ideology at its worst—ideology that misrepresents a symbolic project as a literal *possession*. It occurs when a church declares that it *is* the Kingdom; or when a state—capitalist or communist—declares that it *is* Utopia (i.e., the sole possessor of freedom or equality). This is the language of religious wars and cold wars: the language of ideological closure.

The hermeneutic function of critical reason is not to suppose that we can, or even should, dispense with the symbolic *mythos*, but rather that we can and should debunk the alienations of symbolic meaning in order to restore its eschatological project of liberty for all.

Insofar as religion is based on a divine revelation that can be transmitted only through history, it too belongs to a cultural and mythologizing heritage that requires critical interpretation. Because religious traditions involve historical mediation and distantiation, they participate to greater or lesser degrees in the ideological process. I have already noted how ideology expresses a disparity between symbolic representations and present reality. But this disparity need not always entail an alienating inversion of the true relations of things. It may also express a fundamental aspiration toward utopian images of universal justice, peace, and beauty—images that, as Herbert Marcuse and Ernst Bloch have pointed out, endorse the categorical imperative: *things as they are must change*. We would cite here the eschatological image of the last days when the prophetic promise of justice will be fulfilled in the coming of the Kingdom on earth.

Not all utopian imaginings are, of course, liberating. All too often they have served the millennial ambitions of megalomaniacs. But abuses do not make for good law. And here again the question of ethical critique is all-important. Such critique would enable us to show, for example, that religious representations of the eschatological project are authentic whenever they serve to explode not only the present reality of injustice but also the alienating ideologies that dissimulate and justify this reality. Otherwise stated, religious ideologies are authentically utopian to the degree that their eschatological *forward look* critically reappropriates their archeological *backward look* in such a way that history itself may be positively transformed.[27]

We may consider here Ricoeur's hermeneutic attempt to overcome the opposition between Gadamer's hermeneutics of tradition (which privileges the "backward look" of inherited preunderstanding) and Habermas's critique of ideology (which sponsors a "forward look" of utopian emancipation based on undistorted communicative action). Ricoeur succeeds in introducing Habermas's critique into the heart of the hermeneutics of tradition, thereby opening up the latter to a utopian project; but he insists that such a project requires a fundamental respect for tradition if it is to safeguard itself against the danger of arbitrary or ahistorical voluntarism—that is, a future project completely divorced from the historical heritage of the past. Ricoeur's conclusion to his assessment of the Gadamer-Habermas debate in "Hermeneutics and the Critique of Ideology" (1973) is most instructive in this regard:

> How can [Habermas's] interest in emancipation remain anything other than a pious vow, save by embodying it in the reawakening of communicative action itself? And upon what will you concretely support the reawakening of communicative action, if not the creative renewal of cultural heritage?

Here we are compelled to acknowledge an intimate link between the reawakening of political responsibility and the reactivation of traditional sources of communicative action. The apparently insurmountable opposition between a *hermeneutic* and a *critical* consciousness is thus overcome. Where the hermeneutic consciousness (in Gadamer's sense) invokes a common understanding that precedes us, the critical consciousness projects a future meaning in the form of a regulative idea—the ideal of unrestricted and unconstrained communication. But this antithesis disappears if one espouses a critical hermeneutics that realizes that critical theory cannot "speak from" the basis of a transcendental subject (which it has denounced) and so must presuppose some kind of tradition. For critical theory such a historical tradition would not be that of romanticism (as it was for Gadamer) but rather that of the Enlightenment understood as a project of emancipation. In this way, critique as a project of freedom nourishes itself from a historical tradition that finds its modern impetus in the *Aufklärung* but that actually dates back much further to include the religious tradition of liberty and truth. As Ricoeur puts it:

> Critique is also a tradition. I would even say that it plunges into the most impressive tradition, that of liberating acts, of the Exodus and the Resurrection. Perhaps there would be no more interest in emancipation, no more anticipation of freedom, if the Exodus and the Resurrection where effaced from the memory of mankind. . . . If this is so then nothing is more deceptive than the alleged antinomy between a [hermeneutic] ontology of prior understanding and a [critical] eschatology of freedom. . . . As if it were necessary to choose between reminiscence and hope! In theological terms, eschatology is nothing without the recitation of acts of deliverance from the past. . . . It is the task of philosophical reflection to eliminate deceptive antinomies which would oppose the interest in the reinterpretation of cultural heritages received from the past, and the interest in the futuristic projections of a liberated humanity.[28]

Conclusion

Ideology inhabits the gap between the real and the ideal. It vacillates between representations of pre-existing traditions and projected utopias. And insofar as we remain critically aware of this vacillation, it can serve to remind us that history—like its social representations—is an open-ended process of transformation. If, however, the gap between the real and the ideal becomes absolute or rigid, ideology in turn becomes either a sterile conservatism that dogmatically upholds the status quo, or else an equally sterile escapism that denies present or past reality altogether. In both instances, ideology functions as alienation and precludes the possibility of authentic historical praxis. Ideology can be considered genuine, therefore, (1) only when it knows itself to be ideology—to be a figurative-symbolic representation rather than a literal fact; and (2) only when it ensures that the ideal is kept in close and creative relationship with the real, thereby motivating historical action. Such action is possible only when the disparity between the real and the ideal does not preclude the continuous adaptation of man to a historical reality constantly in flux.

But to suggest that *no* disparity exists between the real and the ideal is absurd:

> Ideologies are gaps or discordances in relation to the real course of things, but the death of ideologies would be the most sterile of lucidities; for a social group without ideology and utopia would be without a plan, without a distance from itself, without a self-representation. It would be a society without a global project, consigned to a history fragmented into events which are all equal and insignificant.[29]

In the final analysis, a critical hermeneutics of historical understanding is the most satisfactory basis for a dialectical rapport between ideology and reason. The model of the hermeneutic circle provided by phenomenological hermeneutics can be extended to include both our *belonging* to the traditional representations of history and our critical *distance* from them. The phenomenon of *belonging* (i.e., the recognition that our understanding always presupposes a historically situated preunderstanding) rules out the possibility of reaching some nonideological vantage point where scientific reason could assume an absolute knowledge beyond the limits of historical understanding. All objective knowledge about our position in a social class, historical epoch, or cultural tradition presupposes a relation of prior *belonging* from which we can never totally extricate ourselves. The claim to total knowledge is no more than an illusion—another example of inauthentic ideology. "Before any critical distance, we belong to a history, to a class, to a nation, to a culture, to one or several traditions. In accepting this belonging, which precedes and supports us, we accept the very first role of ideology— the mediating function of the image or self-representation."[30] Of course, it is precisely because of this same phenomenon of belonging that we are also subject to the alienating possibilities of ideology—dissimulation and domination. Hence the need for the second hermeneutic function of critical "distantiation."

But the phenomenon of critical distance is itself an integral dimension of the hermeneutic circle of understanding. This is so because the gap between the present, which is real, and the future or past, which are ideal, provides the possibility of historical distantiation. This historical distancing implies a self-distancing, a distancing of the subject from itself, which allows for a critical reinterpretation of our self-understanding. This historical phenomenon of critical self-understanding may be compared with the textual model of interpretation. In both instances we are concerned with a mediation of the subject through the distancing detour of signs and images:

> The mediation by texts has an exemplary value. To understand a saying is firstly to confront it as something said, to receive it in its textual form detached from its author; this distancing is intimately part of any reading whereby the matter of the text is rendered near only in and through a distance. This hermeneutics of the text . . . contains crucial indications for a just reception of the critique of ideology. . . . Distanciation, dialectically opposed to belonging, is the condition of possibility of the critique of ideology, not outside or against hermeneutics, but within hermeneutics.[31]

This hermeneutic dialectic of belonging and distancing allows for the possibility of ideology passing from prejudice to critical self-reappraisal. In this dialectic passage from *mythos* to *logos*, the understanding of ideology can free itself partially from its original anchorage in historical preunderstanding (e.g., the representations of tradition). But it cannot do so in any absolute sense. The positivistic notion of a disinterested, unattached, free-floating reason is a fallacy. Scientific reason, to which critique often aspires, is obliged to remain partial and incomplete. For reason is always hermeneutically founded in the unsurpassable condition of historical preunderstanding, which maintains *distantiation* in a dialectical rapport with *belonging*. A positive feature of this historical limitation of understanding is the refutation of the claim to totalitarian knowledge. In this manner, I would advance a *hermeneutics of nontotalization*, which disabuses us of the twin errors of dogmatic idealism and dogmatic materialism. (And I would add that even the "hermeneutics of affirmation" requires to be mediated by a "hermeneutics of suspicion.")

We may thus conclude that the critique of ideology must always be sustained by an authentic interest in emancipation. Philosophical examples of this would be Habermas's reinterpretation of the Marxist critique as motivated by a utopian goal of unrestricted communication; or Ricoeur's reinterpretation of the Judeo-Christian promise of the Kingdom as an eschatological project of universal liberty. Either way, both of these readings involve a critique of ideology that *distances* us from historical prejudice while acknowledging that we continue to *belong* to a specific historical interest—the interest in liberation. To completely renounce this hermeneutic bond to the historical horizons of our symbolizing *mythos* is to relapse into the illusion of a *logos* elevated to the rank of absolute knowledge. There is no short cut out of ideology that does not lead back into another ideology. When reason pretends to surmount *all* ideological mediation—religious or otherwise—it simply becomes a new ideological function in its own function in its own right. The critique of ideology is a task that "must always be begun, but which in principle can never be completed."[32]

There has been much written in recent times about the "end of ideology." Curiously enough, this sense of an ending has been registered by intellectuals of both the left and the right. While Daniel Bell and other neoconservatives have hailed the "end of ideology" as a victory for the universalist values of liberal Western humanism,[33] one also finds neo-Marxists like Louis Althusser in France or Frederic Jameson in the U.S.A. equating the demise of ideology with the disintegration of bourgeois humanism. Althusser advocates the "science of socialism" insofar as it represents an "epistemological rupture" with the "ideological prehistory" of bourgeois thought.[34] And Jameson develops this argument when he states that in the present postmodern context a new "map of knowledge" will have to replace the old humanist-inspired critique of ideology. "The luxury of the old fashioned ideological critique," he notes, "the indignant moral denunciation of the other, becomes unavailable."[35]

What these and other "prophets of extremity" also remark is that the *end of ideology* and the *end of man* have as invitable concomitant *the end of truth*. An era "after truth" would, of course, be one in which ideology would be irrelevant. But such a postepistemological culture would, by the same token, signal the collapse of the very opposition between science and ideology, between legitimate knowledge and imaginary untruths—an opposition that the proponents of the "end of ideology" actually presuppose! The distinction between science and ideology dissolves as soon as one voids the question of truth. For as truth disappears, so too does untruth.

From the point of view of religion, such a situation would preclude the possibility of a hermeneutic discrimination between authentic and inauthentic expressions of religion, between true and false prophets, between fanaticism and genuine religious expressions of tolerance and transcendence. In other words, the end of ideology would spell the end of the very distinction between the true uses of religion and its ideological abuses. Quite obviously, religious truth is not the same as scientific truth (particularly in the modern sense of an empirical science). But however tentatively one may wish to define religious truth, some definition is necessary if one is to sustain the hermeneutic task of critically differentiating religion as a perversion of justice, liberty, and love from religion as a promotion of justice, liberty, and love.[36]

7

Radical Hermeneutics and Religious Truth: The Case of Sheehan and Schillebeeckx

John D. Caputo

Hermeneutics has gotten to be something of a troublemaker. In the place of facts, it insists that there are only interpretations; in the place of objectivity, that there is only what Gadamer unabashedly calls prejudices. In general it has a way of saying that the canons of "truth" have a good deal more give in them than we would like to think. What we today call hermeneutics, the theories of interpretation that have emerged in the wake of Heidegger's *Being and Time*, are to no small degree a relentless critique of objectivistic conceptions of truth, in particular, of historical objectivism. Humanists everywhere are worried that the advent of hermeneutics means the subjectivizing of literature and history, of philosophy and religion. In a word, hermeneutics seems to spell the end of truth.

In the pages that follow I intend to pursue a case in point, and quite a pointed case indeed, of the sort of upheaval that hermeneutics has brought about in our understanding of religious truth in particular. I am concerned here with the way hermeneutic theory is affecting contemporary research into the historical Jesus, or at least one part of it. Specifically, I want to take up the recent work of Thomas Sheehan, who has everyone buzzing with a—to say the least—provocative interpretation of the historical Jesus. I want to pursue the implications of hermeneutics for this debate, and in particular to explore what sort of "truth" remains once the hermeneutic claim is taken to heart, to see what conception we require to accommodate the demands of hermeneutics.

Sheehan is arguing that the historical-critical method has uncovered the cold historical truth about Jesus:

In Roman Catholic seminaries, for example, it is common teaching that Jesus of Nazareth did not assert any of the divine or messianic claims the Gospels attribute to him and that he died without believing he was Christ or the Son of God, not to mention the founder of a new religion. . . The Gospel accounts of the claims Jesus supposedly made to be Christ and God did not come from his own mouth but were interpretations his followers created in the decades after his death.[1]

That the Christ of faith, the eternally begotten Son, true God of true God, come down to earth to save us from our sins, is the product of a *hermeneusis*, a construal of the historical Jesus. New Testament scholars will readily concede that this hermeneutic is *already* at work in the New Testament itself, which thus is not to be treated as a simple transcription of the ipsissima verba of Jesus, taken down directly from his lips by eyewitnesses. For Sheehan that means the word is out on the gospel truth, and the news is not good. The good news is being undone by the historico-critical method, which shows that the rock upon which Christianity is built is not a fact, but an interpretation. On Sheehan's rendering, the message of Jesus is that God has descended "without remainder" into mankind. Jesus himself is a case of a messenger trying to get out of the way of the message. The historical church that issues from his life and death is a misinterpretation that arises from divinizing the messenger whom the Romans killed. The good news, according to Sheehan, is that God disappears into man, and Jesus just plain disappears. The death of Jesus is the end of God and of religion generally.

Sheehan, who has sifted through a staggering and complex literature, seems in particular to draw most heavily upon the writings of Edward Schillebeeckx, a Catholic biblical scholar who also places the hermeneutic method at the center of Christological research. But Schillebeeckx thinks hermeneutics leads us down quite a different path than that staked out by Sheehan. *And it is just this conflict of interpretations and its implications for the problematic of truth that I want to pursue in this study.* In Schillebeeckx's hands the hermeneutic method yields the traditional faith—albeit without what he sometimes calls all the "hocus-pocus" (J, 649).[2] In his view, if the historico-critical method has removed the magic, hermeneutics retains the mystery, and his "experiment in Christology" is a call to a considerable, indeed I would say a classical faith (even if Kierkegaard would object that he has removed some of the scandal). The case of Schillebeeckx and Sheehan provides us with a good example of John Meier's observation, "In the end there is a hermeneutics of belief and a hermeneutics of unbelief."[3]

At the heart of Schillebeeckx's approach to Christology lies the disciples', particularly Peter's, "conversion experience": that God stood by Jesus to the end, which is what they meant when they said that God had raised him up, and that they were forgiven for abandoning him.[4] In such an approach a lot depends upon a phenomenological sensitivity to the texture of experience and a hermeneutic acuity in rendering it in words. A great deal depends on what we think happened to Peter in the days and weeks immediately following the crucifixion. Indeed there is almost existential ardor in Schillebeeckx's attempt to put us in the disciples' shoes, urging us to make a decision quite like the one the disciples faced.

My own interest in this debate lies in pursuing the implications of adopting the hermeneutic strategy to which both Schillebeeckx and Sheehan are committed. Sheehan puts it best, in my view, when he writes:

> The point is to see the *inevitability of interpretation*, that is, to see that what makes us be human is our inexorable finitude, which condemns us to being acts of indirection and mediation, where all is "hints and guesses / Hints followed by guesses" (T. S. Eliot). If . . . living the kingdom means maintaining undecidability (the impossibility of distinguishing the worldly from the divine), then human existence itself, as an act of interpretation, is the *enactment* of undecidability [FC, 226; cf. FC, 120].

Instead of the hard rock of objective truth, we have only interpretation to fall back upon. But the case I will press against Sheehan is he has closed down the mystery of undecidability and let God disappear into man in a gesture, not of undecidability, but of reduction—so that the kingdom of God comes out with a very left-wing Hegelian twist.

Still, I have an inverse complaint about Schillebeeckx. He, too, pays homage to hermeneutics and the inescapability of interpretation; there is no raw, uninterpreted experience that is not always already infiltrated by language and history. But if *that* is so, then there is a much more "radical" rendering of the disciples' experience than Schillebeeckx is prepared to admit. Schillebeeckx thinks that without the resurrection faith the disciples, and the rest of us, would be driven into the ground by the hopelessness and futility of

life, that history would have no purpose. But that is *just* what Sheehan means by hoping Jesus out of the grave (FC, 162); it is just a
complaint about the meanness of the cosmos, not a way around it.
So if Sheehan has closed down undecidability in the direction of an
atheistic humanism, Schillebeeckx closes it down in the direction of
a trust in things for which hermeneutics gives no warrant.

All of this comes out once you see that *both* Schillebeeckx and
Sheehan have a *common* commitment to a peace and justice program—in the one case theistically conceived, in the other atheisti-
cally—which gives the world an onto-theo-logical centering and
establishes a "moral order." But such ethical good news has to be
put into question if you are going to take hermeneutic undecidability seriously (as do the later Heidegger and the deconstructionists).
Sheehan and Schillebeeckx are commonly committed to *a metaphysics of morals*, which functions like an Archimedean point for them,
enabling one to turn toward faith, the other against it. But there is
no place for Archimedean centers and onto-theo-logical levers once
one has started down the hermeneutic path. Hermeneutics spells
the end of metaphysics.

But if that is so, then what of left of truth? What more is there
to do than to invoke the Nietzschean saying, and the touchstone of
a good deal of postmodernism, that truth is a fiction that we have
forgotten is a fiction? Is the end of metaphysics not also the end of
truth? It is at that point, I will argue, that we need to turn to
Heidegger's notion of the mystery that withdraws, to his postmeta-
physical experience of truth as *a-létheia*.

So in what follows I will do three things: (1) I will start out by
playing off Sheehan against Schillebeeckx—any responsible reader
can tell they are worlds removed from each other—and that will
open up the interesting hermeneutic question of the disciples' experience of Jesus. (2) I will then offer a criticism, first, of Sheehan's
left-wing Hegelian hermeneutic, which attempts to cut off the historical Jesus from the Christ of faith, and then of Schillebeeckx's
attempt to link them. (3) Finally, making use of what I call "radical
hermeneutics,"[5] I will move beyond this confessional dispute
within Christian scriptural scholarship and show how, from a
hermeneutic standpoint, the question of the disciples' experience
points to a conception of religious truth as *a-létheia*.

Sheehan, Schillebeeckx, and the Kingdom of God

Sheehan and Schillebeeckx draw on the results of the "new
questers," the post-Bultmannian quest for the historical Jesus
launched after World War II, which unlike the first quest does not

reduce Jesus to a humanitarian liberal, and unlike Bultmann does not reduce Jesus to an unknown X separated by an abyss from the Christ of faith. The new questers concede the gap—Jesus probably did not call himself the Son of Man, did not take himself to be the coming messiah, the Son of God, or much less God the Son. But they also find a basis, a *fundamentum in re*, in the historical Jesus for the later claims of faith—namely, the extraordinary authority with which Jesus conducted himself (he was not a mild-mannered liberal) and the great freedom he felt with respect to the Law, thus suggesting an exceptional, unprecedented, even mystical (J, 657) intimacy with the one he called his father (*Abba*). While Schillebeeckx is painfully scrupulous in maintaining the continuity, the *fundamentum in re*, Sheehan thinks the best work of the new questers is to no avail, that a leak has been sprung that there is no way to plug.

Who, then, was the historical Jesus, according to the new questers? He was born of Joseph and Mary, in Nazareth not Bethlehem—the virgin birth and the Bethlehem nativity stories are a later "theological reflection" (J, 554)—into a politically beleaguered Jewish world with rising "eschatological" expectations of the end of the world. In the midst of confusing, competing expectations of a messiah king or messiah prophet, there also arose the idea of an "eschatological prophet," sometimes taken to be a new Elijah, who would come on the scene at the beginning of the end and announce that the rule of God was at hand; that was the context for Jesus' preaching.

Jesus may well have started out as a disciple of John the Baptist. The synoptic version of his baptism—with the voice from heaven—that he let himself be baptized as a show of humility is what Schillebeeckx calls a later "updating" or "secondary reflection." Sheehan describes such differences as putting words into Jesus' mouth, colored memories, inventions, and so forth. But that just raises the question as to whether Sheehan thinks, in flat defiance of the basics of the hermeneutics he professes, that there is an uncolored, unprejudiced memory. Jesus starts out under the spell of John's grim version of the eschatological message that calls for conversion, a change of heart (*metanoia*—Schillebeeckx translates this as "about turn"—J, 174), because the day of God's judgment is at hand. But John's is an eschatology—the end is at hand—without apocalypse, no wild vision of cosmic fireworks; an existential, not a cosmic, reckoning, which asked persons to change their lives. John was a renegade religious figure. He leveled his critique at Israel itself, not its enemies; and he told Israel it would not be saved by a casuistic adherence to the Law, but by a change of heart (FC, 54).

"Jesus," Sheehan thinks, "was pierced to the heart. He repented and was baptized" (FC, 53; cf. J, 136–39). Maybe Jesus became an intimate of John's inner circle and was delegated by John to carry on the work of baptizing.

In any case, the message that Jesus himself delivered was clearly a variant of John's, and after John's beheading John's enemies became Jesus' enemies. In the place of John's grim dirge, Jesus put a lyric that "preached the joy of God's immediate and liberating presence" (FC, 57). He replaced John's mercilessly judging God with a loving father. "Change your heart. God's reign is at hand!" (Mark 1:15)—the loving forgiveness of the father is at hand, and it begins right here and now, in Jesus himself. Instead of a life in the desert and meals of locust and honey, Jesus scandalized the Pharisees by his indiscriminate companionability and his taste for a good meal. The Pharisees were nonplussed at the way Jesus put the kingdom into practice: dining with sinners and tax collectors, befriending a prostitute, violating the multiple prescriptions that had turned man into the slave of the Sabbath, instead of letting the Sabbath serve man (as a time of rest and revivification). As Schillebeeckx points out again and again, the God of Jesus stands solidly on the side of man. He takes man's side, espouses the cause of the outcast and the excluded, the sinner and the despised, the poor and the disenfranchised, the "crippled and the lame, all who are cold-shouldered" (J, 145). Jesus came to say that this coming kingdom was already underway, in him and in the easy familiarity he felt with the father. The future is up ahead, but it is also now. The kingdom of God is at hand, starting with Jesus. The Pharisees were stupified by all this.

Now for the most dazzling disjunction between Sheehan and Schillebeeckx: Sheehan thinks—this is *his* updating, his secondary reflection or, let us say, a-theologoumenon (J, 752)—that the "kingdom of God" of which Jesus speaks means that God has dissolved into man:

It meant God's act of reigning, and this meant—here lay the revolutionary force of Jesus' message—that God, as God, had *identified himself without remainder with his people*. The reign of God meant the *incarnation* of God [FC, 60].

We will be pardoned if we are reminded of Feuerbach's *Essence of Christianity* (or maybe even Marx's *Theses on Feuerbach*). If we put this passage alongside a parallel text in Schillebeeckx, we will see where the hyposthesis originates:

What we have here cannot be other than a message and style of conduct that proclaim God's universal love, the true God's lordship, *without* reservation or *remainder* [J, 145, italics added].

The kingdom of God means that something happens "without remainder"—but what? For Schillebeeckx, God's reign means that the father *loves us* without remainder. The measure of the father's love is love without measure. There is no stopping it, and there is no one who is excluded from it, so that Jesus makes a special point of shocking the Pharisees (*perishayya*, "separation") by keeping company with the very persons from whom they wish to keep themselves separate.

But for Sheehan the kingdom of God means God just *disappears into man* without remainder, in his very being, ontologically, in a kind of ontological hominization. The kingdom of God, then, is an ontological declaration that God (in Himself) is dead but the God-for-man, the God who *is* man, is alive and well in good works and orthopraxis, peace and justice. For Sheehan the kingdom of God becomes an onto-atheology along with a metaphysics of morals. Jesus is the eschatological prophet, announcing the beginning of the end—not of the world, but of Old Testament religion and of religion generally insofar as it is centered on a transcendent God.

For Schillebeeckx the father commits himself to the human cause, without remainder; for Sheehan the father just slips into human shoes, without remainder.

For Sheehan the post-Easter period represents a peculiarly perverse turn of events. The new questers agree that Jesus is a messenger who was trying to get out of the way of his message. He was trying to remain invisible himself so that the father's forgiveness would be visible to all. He did not speak of himself, but of his father. He came proclaiming not himself, but his father's loving rule. The one time he spoke of the coming Son of Man, he very likely did not have himself in mind. But what happened is that after the Romans killed the messenger, the disciples divinized him. In a matter of a few decades the message that Jesus had delivered was displaced by the person of Jesus himself. The preaching of the kingdom gave way to the preaching of the preacher; the proclaimer became the proclaimed.

Like Schillebeeckx, Sheehan attaches a lot of importance to the fact that Jesus' message was rejected, not just by the establishment, who had everything to fear from him, but by the people, whose side he was taking. Jesus' fatal journey into Jerusalem appears to be a last-ditch stand to put the movement back on its feet. But as

Schillebeeckx points out, Jesus would have been a fool not to know that by going up to Jerusalem, to the center of power of the religious orthodoxy of the day, he was putting his life in mortal peril. He had held no punches, calling the powers that be "hypocrites" and a "generation of vipers." A cloud of lurking danger, of impending doom, hung over his final meal with the disciples—"I shall not drink again of the fruit of the vine" (Mark 14:25)—in which he enjoyed for the last time his fellowship with the disciples.

The point is that Jesus had taken his stand on the kingdom of God absolutely, and he was willing to see it through to the bitter end. They could kill him, but they could not refute him. Even if they killed him, they could not silence his father. The father would be with him, and he would trust the father, even if the worst happened. The father's loving hand is everywhere, even in the killing of his messenger, even if that messenger be a son—that is, someone with a special intimacy with him.

This was lost on the disciples. They were devastated by the crucifixion and they scattered to the four winds when it happened. But Schillebeeckx (and Rudolph Pesch)—and this goes to the heart of the hermeneutic issue—imagine Simon/Peter back in Galilee, back at his fishing trade, mulling these matters over, fishing and thinking, and crushed by his own desertion of the master. And then it hit him: God did not abandon Jesus.[6] Sheehan puts it well: everything, even Jesus' merciless death, is in the hands of the loving father. Jesus trusted God, but the disciples fled; they abandoned him after he shared with them "the cup of a fellowship that was supposed to be stronger than death" (FC, 103).

If the disciples had expected that Jesus' faith in the father's loving care would be validated by his being safeguarded from the sword of his enemies, that was a misunderstanding on their part that painted the kingdom of God in too earthly a tone. The point of Jesus' unfathomable confidence in his father was to trust the father no matter what, no matter even if they put the messenger to death, no matter even if the disciples themselves abandon him. The father's loving care was with Jesus up to the end, even in letting him fall victim to his enemies; and it is here, with them *now*, extended to them in Jesus' *forgiveness* of them, even now, after they deserted him and fled as he was put to death. Jesus is the suffering servant, the martyred prophet, who trusted God up to his last breath of life and he will come again on the last day, and his father is a God of forgiveness. His faith in Jesus thus restored, Simon set about reassembling the disciples.

So Simon's "conversion experience," his "Easter experience," is the pivot around which the disciples regroup shortly after the crucifixion. Simon is the *kēphas*, the hard rock, of the regrouping, and that is the basis of the knickname he got—*kēphas, petrus*, Peter. The synoptics later on put this knickname into the mouth of Jesus and have him founding a new church. A later "theological reflection"? Or just plain revisionary history? It depends on whether you use a hermeneutics of belief or a hermeneutics of unbelief.

On the one hand, Schillebeeckx has incurred a good deal of wrath because of his confidence in the historico-critical method at this point. The disciples' retreat to the upper room awaiting the Spirit, Jesus' appearance to them—coming right through a bolted door—doubting Thomas sticking his hand in Jesus' side, eating food in the risen body, his appearances to the disciples on the road to Emmaus and elsewhere, the angel at the empty tomb with the rock rolled back: in short, all the miraculous Easter and post-Easter stories, everything that the mainstream faithful has taken to be the gospel truth, is taken nowadays to be later updating, secondary reflection, added on at a later date by the synoptics. Even the Gospel of Mark, the earliest, shortest, simplest, and above all the starkest of the synoptics, had been altered. Mark starts with Jesus' baptism, skipping all the nativity stories (of which he seems to know nothing), and ends with the women fleeing from an empty tomb on Easter morning—afraid, with no visions, and consigned to silence (Mark 16:1–8). Later on a new and more reassuring ending is tacked on (Mark 16:9–20).

But for Schillebeeckx the historico-critical method has removed the magic but not the mystery. The stories of the appearances and the empty tomb are a historically conditioned way of "expressing" in terms that made sense to themselves and to others the very profound "experience" they had undergone and the faith they already had. Now here is where we require some phenomenological and hermeneutic acuity, in short, a phenomenological theory of truth. Schillebeeckx thinks in effect that to understand the appearances, you have to bracket natural reality—nothing happened that a video tape would pick up—in favor of the experienced reality. You cannot get the point of these stories without a religious version of the phenomenological *epochē*. Faith in the resurrection is not *based* on the appearance stories but *presupposed* by them. These stories do not serve the apologetic purpose of justifying or legitimating belief in the resurrection, which antedates and does not depend upon stories of the appearances. Rather they give a hermeneutic rendering or expression to an experience that transpired (J, 329–97). The appearance meant: they had "seen the point" that Jesus was making.

But Schillebeeckx thinks that these experiences, to use a little more Husserl, are "motivated" on the "noematic side" by the movement of Jesus' spirit, which is also the father's spirit. He thinks these experiences have an intentional correlate, that they are not just an arbitrary flow of *Erlebnisse*, even if they do not have a natural object for their correlate. The appearances are not perceptual objects, but they do have their reality. Schillebeeckx believes that Jesus has somehow been lifted up into the father's power, and that he exerts his influence upon the reassembling disciples. " 'Where two or three are gathered together in his name, Jesus is in the midst of them'; this New Testament text is in my view perhaps the purest, most adequate reflection of the Easter experience" (J, 646).

Sheehan, on the other hand, thinks that the historico-critical cat is out of the bag, that there is no closing this historico-critical gap. For Sheehan, whatever "experience" Peter underwent after the death of Jesus, it is available neither to us, *nor to Simon*, since all experience is mediated by the available language one has to articulate it. Whatever happened, it is *merely Simon's interpretation* that Jesus has been taken into God's eschatological future, has been vindicated by God, and will come again at the last day. Thus back at the founding moment of Christianity, we find not a fact but a hermeneusis, not historical evidence but Simon's hermeneutics.

That leads Sheehan into an interesting rereading of Simon's "denial," which lay not in abandoning Jesus—that under the circumstances was only prudent, or the whole movement would have gone under—but in following him. Simon was attaching importance to Jesus personally, just when Jesus himself had always taught that the father was all and had tried to get out of the way of his own message. But Simon turned him into "a hero and an idol, an obstacle to God-with-man" (FC, 124). Thus Simon's interpretation of his Easter experience *perpetuated the denial of Jesus*, of what Jesus was really getting at, institutionalized that denial, and makes of the standing church a heresy (FC, 223–24).

Starting out with Simon's misinterpretation of Jesus, and his self-interpretation of his Easter experience, a whole series of progressively more divinizing interpretations evolves, which finally culminates in the formulas that the Councils attempt to write in stone, and thus as it were to pluck out of the flow of history, just at the point that the "established" church finds convenient. The Councils reduce the plurality of interpretations that are to be found among the early Christians and establish (enforce) a single, normative, canonical version. After a while that produces the illusion of an uninterpreted fact of the matter, an objective event, which finally *erases* the hermeneusis (FC, 160). The origin of Christianity starts looking like the origin of geometry according to Derrida: they both come down to erasing the trace. But by *retracing* the "genealogy" of the orthodox belief that has been worked out by Schillebeeckx and others, Sheehan thinks that the contingency, not to say capriciousness, of the orthodox view has been exposed. Presumably, the longevity of orthodoxy is in no small part due to the institutional power that backed it up and closed off alternative readings, which is a good example of what Foucault means by power/knowledge. But the historico-critical method has put an end to that cover-up. The truth is out.

According to Schillebeeckx and Pesch, Peter's "Easter experience" in Galilee transpired without his knowing anything about the empty tomb stories that were beginning to form among the Jerusalem community. The earliest disciples, starting out with Simon Peter, became convinced that God had vindicated Jesus and had taken him into his heavenly power, so that Jesus still lives—in heaven, with the father, and will come again, probably soon, as the appointed Son of Man to act as God's judge. And they put all this simply by saying that "God has raised him from the dead" (1 Thess. 1:10). It was within the context of a preexisting belief that the father had stood by Jesus and (somehow) raised him up to be with him that the stories of the appearances and the empty tomb, that the whole Easter chronology regularly celebrated in the liturgy and spelled out in the New Testament, were to evolve.

But according to Sheehan that is a gross misinterpretation. Sheehan accepts the notion of the empty tomb, and that the body of Jesus just disappeared, but he attaches quite a different significance to it: that we have to learn how to live with the "absence of Jesus" and love it. The women's futile journey to the empty tomb is emblematic of humankind's futile search for transcendence, its longing for what it cannot have. At the other end of the human project upon infinity lies nothing at all. Man is a projection upon nothing, upon absolute absence. The human condition is absurd, and so the point of the story is being missed. We should do what the women do: leave the scene and lay off the search. The point is: to get on with establishing the rule of earthly justice and stop malingering over the person of Jesus himself (FC, 163–73). Under Sheehan's hands, the stone rolled back from the tomb looks a lot like Sisyphus's rock, and the angelic messenger sounds like a French existentialist. You have to wonder at this point how someone committed to hermeneusis can be so sure that there is nothing on the other end, and how someone who talks a good line about undecidability (which throws all presence/absence systems into confusion) can let "absolute absence" slip from his lips. What Sheehan is serving up is not hermeneutics but an *ontotheologia negativa*, with a-theistic humanism at the center. But more about that later.

Once again one finds the correlate of this absence-of-Jesus theme back in Schillebeeckx—to wit in his presentation of the Gospel of Mark (J, 417–23). In the original version—already an updating, composed around 70 A.D., and probably drawn from the liturgy that was celebrated around Jesus' tomb on the anniversary of his death (FC, 138)—the women find the empty tomb, are told by an angel that Jesus is raised and is not there, and finally that they should tell the disciples, especially Peter, that Jesus will meet them ahead in Galilee. Instead, the frightened women flee and say nothing to anyone. The Gospel ends with this mute fear: no appearances of Jesus, no ascension—just silence and fear. Later on, this austere and disconcerting ending is updated—that is, brought into conformity with the more reassuring accounts in the still later Gospels of Matthew and Luke (85 A.D.) and John (90 A.D.).

Needless to say the "absense of Jesus" sounds a lot different coming from Schillebeeckx. Mark's account evolved from a pre-Marcan oral tradition that gives us an insight into the earliest version of belief in Jesus, centered in the Aramaic-speaking Jewish converts in the Jerusalem church. The story was meant to enjoin the point that Jesus lives with his father in heaven and so it is fruitless to come to his tomb in search of him. In its earliest version it did not include a reference to a future appearance in Galilee; and its "angel" (*angelos*, messenger) is a standard narrative vehicle of the day to communicate a message, a biblical message-bearing Hermes.

Mark thinks that Jesus died and that was the last that was seen of him. He thinks that Jesus lives with his father in heaven but, for the present at least, in a kind of suspension or *epoché*, "absent in the brief period of the eschatological community" but "soon to come" (J, 417). Marcan theology moves entirely between the memory of the earthly Jesus and the hope in the second coming, so that "Mark does not see the celestial Jesus as presently operative, but affirms the complete absence of Jesus from his sorrowing and suffering Church" (J, 418). For the present, Jesus is dead—between the two comings of Jesus there is only the empty tomb—and we are summoned to faith that he will come again. Come, lord Jesus! *Maran atha*. Mark's is a *maranatha* Christology, a *Christologia negativa*, where Jesus is presently absent but coming in the future. The church is an orphan, and Jesus is the Lord of the future, so that

Mark is wary of present pneumatic experiences of the risen Lord. As for Paul's theology of the church as the mystical body of Jesus in which the celestial Jesus is continuously effective, Schillebeeckx says that "in the Marcan Gospel there is not the slightest opening for it" (J, 422). In Mark the emphasis falls on the Parousia, not on the resurrection or presently reigning, risen Jesus.

Mark is not a skeptic; he is just faithful to the earthly Jesus' preaching. The kingdom of God is near; it has begun in Jesus' first coming, and the death of Jesus is the beginning of the eschatological woes. Now we await in "a drab but necessary interim period" (J, 422) the second coming, the fulfillment of Jesus' prayer that his father's kingdom may come, when Jesus himself will return.

But with the *delay* of the Parousia—the Christological deferral of presence—a supplement is required (542–43). Thus over and beyond *maranatha* Christology a divine miracle-man Christology (*theios anèr*) is evolved among Greek-speaking Jews, which demonstrates Jesus' divine character by telling tales of marvelous miracles and acts of power and stories of the risen Jesus (J, 424–29; FC, 192–205). Now the disciples claim that, far from having to wait for the Parousia (which is starting to look far off), believers have *already* received salvation. Jesus is exalted as reigning Lord, called in Greek the *christos*; his personal status is enhanced; the futural, eschatological dimension begins to weaken. Lastly, Greek-speaking Gentile converts, who were steeped in wisdom literature, identify Jesus with a hypostasized wisdom who cooperates with God in the creation of the world, of which the Johannine prologue is the best example (J, 431). The wisdom Christologies pave the way for the now normative Christologies of John and Paul in which God's eternal Son became man, died for our sins, and rose again to reign with God, whence he shall come to judge the living and the dead.

Thus the earthly Jesus undergoes a series of "theological reflections" (Schillebeeckx) or "enhancements" (Sheehan): from eschatological prophet (the historical Jesus), to the coming Son of Man (*maranatha* Christologies), to the reigning Lord (divine-man Christology), to the eternal Son of God. Only in the last version does Jesus acquire flat-out divinity, which gives the Councils the opening to "define" the status of Jesus unequivocally as God the Son and to work out the doctrine of the Trinity of persons.

Beyond the Hermeneutics of Belief and Unbelief

I want now to argue that the hermeneutic consequences of this debate cut deeper than either Sheehan or Schillebeeckx allow, and that, properly pursued, they force out a more radical conception of religious truth as *a-létheia*.

In Sheehan's hermeneutics of unbelief, the historico-critical method has irreparably severed the Jesus of history from the Christ of faith, and exposed the kingdom of God as the death of God. Schillebeeckx, on the other hand, deploys a hermeneutical move that would bridge the gap and preserve the continuity; his faith unshaken, he is willing to let the historico-critical chips fall where they may, as John P. Meier says.[7] I, on the other hand, do not think that either move succeeds hermeneutically—I really do think *there is something to undecidability*. My aim in the present section is make trouble for both these versions of hermeneutics. Then, in the next section, I will address the question as to where this all leads us, *whether and in what sense we can any longer speak of religious truth* within a hermeneutics more radically conceived.

Let us return to the truth status of the resurrection, given the results of the new questers. Both Schillebeeckx and Sheehan identify three ways of interpreting the resurrection, which I will follow Sheehan in calling the traditional, the moderate, and the liberal views (J, 644–46; FC, 164–65).

1. The traditional version takes the gospel at its face value, as the *literal gospel truth*, which records a series of miraculous contraventions of natural law. The resurrection is conceived in physicalistic terms, as an empirical, perceptual event that would have been picked up by a video camera, were one available. Resurrection means resuscitation. Now it is this traditional view—which really is the mainstream belief and the one commonly preached to the faithful—that has been washed out by the historico-critical method and reduced to the status of biblical fundamentalism. Neither Sheehan nor Schillebeeckx, nor any higher criticism, accepts this.

2. In the moderate view, the resurrection is conceived as an ontological event, *a parte objecti*, but not a physical one, in which God has somehow assumed Jesus into his power. It is not literally but *ontologically true*. That is the prevailing view among informed Catholic New Testament scholars. In Schillebeeckx's version in particular, the resurrection stories are taken as "expressions" of a "faith-experience" that actually antedates the stories themselves; but the stories nonetheless have a real, though not perceptual, correlate.

3. Finally, there is the liberal view found in authors like Bultmann and Marxsen, which treats "Easter" as a *symbolic truth*, inasmuch as it signifies something that took place, *a parte subjecti*, strictly in the subjective life of the disciples. If in the traditional ver-

sion the body of Jesus is physically risen, and in the moderate view, his spirit continues to guide us, in the liberal view it is but his "meaning" or "cause" that lives on.

But Sheehan, as we have seen, is to the left of everybody else, because he thinks that all three interpretations are a misinterpretation covering up the fact that God makes a Feuerbachian descent into humanity never to surface or ascend again. The disciples rescued just what should have gone under and they ended up divinizing Jesus himself. Now that seems to me just perverse—not just perverse, but brilliantly perverse, and very anachronistic. For if Sheehan wants to play historico-critical hardball and to work the church over for not abiding by Jesus' own historically limited self-interpretation, then to put in the mouth of this devout Jewish man of Galilee the main argument of left-wing Hegelianism is to dwarf any of the later "updatings" in the synoptics, which he is so fond of criticizing.

The historico-critical picture of Jesus that is emerging does not portray him as a death-of-God theologian, but a devoutly monotheistic, slightly mystical Jew. Contra Sheehan, the *Abba* experience does not mean that the father has just disappeared *into* his children, but that he stands unequivocally *with* them, takes their side in thick and thin, like a faithful and loving father. The whole point of this is *religious* in just the sense that Sheehan denies—namely, to give every assurance to the poor and the despised, the outcast and excluded, that they have infinite resources to draw upon, that they are nourished by a higher power, that they are in a special way the ones whom the father supports. Even if from a strictly worldly point of view they have drawn the short straw, Jesus assures them that the father is with them no matter what. Jesus was not just trying to boost their morale. He was telling them that there was something on their side, which the philosophers would call "ontological." So his special calling, the reason he came into the world, was to deliver this message—he was carrying out a prophetic-hermeneutic role—that they had an infinite support behind them and that the kingdom was theirs for the seeking.

It is true that he spoke with shocking authority and freedom, but this arises not from his *own* authority, but from his scandalous sense of intimacy with the father. His authority was delegated; he was a special emissary empowered to speak on his father's behalf. He does not speak in his own proper name, but in the name of his father. In the historico-critical picture Jesus always defers to the father, speaks on behalf of the father. He is always delivering the message of the one who sent him and for his own part tries continually to get out of the way of the message itself.

According to the historico-critical view, Jesus attached no importance to himself, and that is why he walked right into the teeth of death: he had an unfathomable confidence in the father and a sense that the father would prevail even if he personally were erased. He called Simon a satan when Simon suggested to him that he should look for a way around this mortal peril, for it is only the father that matters and he, Jesus, has come only to spread his word. He is not himself the word, but the one who has come to deliver the word; he is not the message but the messenger; not the proclaimed but the proclaimer.

There is nothing in the historico-critical picture to sustain Sheehan's hypothesis that God has dissolved into human solidarity, nothing to suggest a proleptic version of left-wing Hegelianism. What it does suggest is a profoundly Jewish monotheism, and a sense of human solidarity rooted in the fatherhood of God. As brilliant as he is, Sheehan seems to me headed out to sea.

This is not to say that I find nothing to quarrel with in Schillebeeckx's use of hermeneutics. I do not think Sheehan can cut Christianity off by arguing that Jesus taught the death of God. But the fact that Jesus was not a left-wing Hegelian does not imply, on the other hand, that he had anything like Christianity in mind, not if he is a devout Jew who does not speak in his own name but in the name of the father, not if he means to be the messenger and not the message. Christianity looks like a mistake, like the child who looks at the finger instead of what the finger is pointing toward, not because, as Sheehan makes out, Jesus was an atheist but because he was so devoted to the true spirit of the Torah.

On this account Christianity is not what Jesus had in mind. He did not mean to displace Judaism but to say that its eschaton was at hand, here and now, that what it was about had come about. He intended to be the end of Judaism, not in the sense of its demise, but of its fulfillment. He meant to announce the beginning of the end, that the father's loving rule had begun. He thus recalls Judaism to its most profound intuitions, revivifies its deepest insight into God's loving care for Israel, and blows the whistle on the legalism and hierarchical hypocrisy that was obscuring the genuine meaning of the Torah.

If this is right, the traditionalists are dead in the water and their claims to absolute fidelity to what really and truly happened back in the first century are hopelessly discredited.

But the moderates see this objection coming and they are ready with a hermeneutical comeback—namely, that they are not governed by the intentions of the author. Schillebeeckx writes:

> Unintentionally, therefore, though Jesus preached not himself but the rule and lordship of God, it was "himself" that he had proclaimed: the Proclaimer is the One proclaimed [J, 543].

That is, at this point Schillebeeckx and the moderates invoke the hermeneutics of Gadamer and Ricoeur, which is descended from Heidegger, and they claim that the meaning of a text, an event or— in this case—a life, is not governed by the author's or the agent's self-understanding, that a text or an event has a sense and significance, repercussions and implications, that "exceed" the original intention, which far outstrip it, which continuously unfold in, through, and as a "tradition." The ability of a tradition to "appropriate" its founding act is what keeps it afloat; that enables the moderates to establish the much needed link or continuity, and to justify the talk about updating and secondary theological reflections. So it is not necessary for the historical Jesus to have understood all that much about the "Christ of faith." In an ironic turn of events, then, the moderates should start throwing Heidegger and Gadamer up *against* Sheehan—who should know better and who should have addressed this issue in *The First Coming*. Given the inroads the historico-critical method is making, establishing apostolic continuity is not enough. The problem is the gap between Jesus *and the apostles*, and the only way to bridge that gap is with a hermeneutic theory that puts the author in his place and allows a thing really to get going only after the death of the author.

While this is a classic hermeneutical gesture, and while Gadamer's theory works very nicely with Shakespeare and the American constitution, there are rather special complications involved in the claims that the moderates make. I see three such complications.

1. To begin with, the moderates have a very peculiar version of the argument, indeed an inverted one. The argument against privileging the intentions of the author says that you should ignore the person of the author and pay heed to the intentional content, the *Sache*, of his message. But the moderates are doing exactly the opposite—namely, overriding the message of the author and exalting his person. Jesus seems clearly to disavow his own importance as an author and to make himself a vehicle of the message. He attaches no importance to his empirical reality—that he is willing to offer up in the name of the father—and every importance to the

message, the *intentum*, the intentional object of his utterances and actions. But the church absolutizes, divinizes Jesus, personally, makes something out of the personal life and death of the author of the message, while altering the message. On the death-of-the-author schema, that is like making a cult out of the person of Shakespeare or Thomas Jefferson and ignoring what they said or wrote.

2. If the historico-critical portrait is uncovering hard truths— and nobody except the traditionalists denies that it is—mainstream Christianity is in the delicate, not to say contradictory, position of wanting to *divinize* the author but also to override his intentions. Jesus was divine, but he himself did not quite appreciate it; that was the work of the disciples—and it is the work of their disciples in turn, right up to the present day. The church declares his person sacred and holy, attributes divinity to his life and death, words and deeds, says that he could just look at somebody and drive the devil out of him, but also claims to have a *different* (and maybe even a *better*, more thematic, reflective) understanding of what he was do-ing than he himself had.

Furthermore, it may even be the case that the disciples' inter-pretation of Jesus is actually inconsistent with and opposed to Jesus' self-interpretation. If Jesus himself was thoroughly turned toward the father, he may well have *objected* to these later developments. If—as a purely counterfactual conditional—someone had projected the subsequent course of events in Christian theology after the cru-cifixion and submitted it to Jesus' consideration, we may well imag-ine that he would have been scandalized by it and said that the suggestion came of Satan. Would the moderates still persist, even if the historical Jesus would have rejected the later interpretation that was put on him? How far can you go in disregarding the intention of the author if you also claim the author was divine?

3. Finally, suppose Jesus's message was roundly accepted by everyone, that he lived a long life, and died as an honored prophet who had revivified Judaism with his *Abba* spirituality, having sensi-tized it to its legalism and hypocrisy. Then Christianity would have never gotten off the ground, because everybody would have be-lieved Jesus and not Christianity, believed that the father was all and Jesus was nothing. Jesus's own message would have prevailed and he would have cut off in advance the idea that he himself was personally important. His message would have been abundantly clear and it would have been perfectly obvious that he had no inter-est in transcending Judaism or in attaching a divine status to him-self. In other words, Christianity could not get going unless Jesus is

rejected and killed, and is no longer around to explain himself. If he succeeded in doing what he wanted to do, there would be no Christianity.

So if I do not agree with Sheehan's use of hermeneutics, that the kingdom of God spells the end of religion, neither do I agree with Schillebeeckx and the moderates' version of death-of-the-author hermeneutics. I do not think that Jesus was a left-wing Hegelian, but I do not think that invoking the "tradition," and "letting the historical chips fall where they may," answers all the questions that adopting a hermeneutical method lets out of the box.

Radical Hermeneutics and *A-létheia*

I do not think that either Sheehan or Schillebeeckx has come to grips with the full and, as I like to say, "radical" implications of hermeneutics. Sheehan and Schillebeeckx are in agreement about the inescapability of *hermeneusis: we are always already interpreting; nothing escapes a hermeneutic fashioning.* There is nothing outside textuality, outside the interpretive web, no way around language and history, no secret passage that gives us access to a privileged, unreformable insight into what is happening. *That is what I mean by "radical hermeneutics."*

Faith itself is a kind of hermeneutics, a way we have of reading the traces in the sand of human existence. That is true not only of faith, but a good many philosophers today are agreed that it is true of reason, too. Both faith and reason are ways of reading and construing, and both have no other recourse than to invoke historically conditioned models and linguistic artifacts. Faith is a read we have on the human condition; it is not a supervenient gift coming from on high (FC, 6). That explains the difficulties that believers of all sorts get into with the rest of the human race. They seem to think, and everybody else thinks they think, that they have obtained privileged access to a "truth" that the rest of humankind has not. But in radical hermeneutics this clean line between believer and infidel begins to smear.

The question is whether anything at all remains, whether we can still speak of *religious truth*.

"Radical hermeneutics" proceeds from a vivid, disturbing sense of the historicality and linguisticality of what phenomenologists once too naively called "experience." There is nothing called experience, or perception, or the things themselves, outside the textuality of language and history. So the radical hermeneutic situation leaves us without solid footing. My complaint with Sheehan and

Schillebeeckx is that both bail out on the flux, and in the end cast anchor in a rock solid metaphysics—of morals. They have recourse to an indestructible ethics of mercy—but what they have both forgotten is that ethics, too, is an interpretation, which explains why Sheehan is so eager to decode the kingdom of God into its definitive meaning and why Schillebeeckx thinks life *must* have meaning, it just must!

Let us return to Simon Peter's experience, only this time with a hermeneutic more radically conceived—that means, keeping the undecidability and the slippage, the "through a glass darkly," in mind. Fishing and thinking, Simon is trying to bring to words what had *happened* to him in the short space of a year or two. Simon was trying to unfold, explicate, lay out (*aus-legen*), the implicit horizons and content of an experience, to reach an *Auslegung*, an interpretation. This man, he thought, had knocked him off his pins. What to make of that? Who was he? Where did he come from? "Rabbi, where do you dwell?" (John 1:38–39), he remembered asking him. "Who do you, Simon, say that I am?" he remembered Jesus asking him. What Simon came up with and began to run by the other disciples—that Jesus *was* the coming Son of Man, not just the forecaster of him, and that God had vindicated his death—is a formulation of a man working within an inherited tradition and its handed-down vocabulary (it is unlikely that he would have used that formulation today); so it came from a history. Moreover, as everybody admits, it also had a subsequent history, which was to lead all the way up to the Nicene Creed.

From Sheehan's point of view, this subsequent history is a scandal that makes a mockery of the historico-critical method. From Schillebeeckx's point of view it means that Simon hit on something that captured the imagination of its hearers, formulated their experience for them, and generally gave them an *Auslegung* to hang on to. What it means from my point of view is that Simon had a brush with *a-létheia*, had a chance not afforded to everyone to meet someone who just brought him up short and left an unforgettable impression on him, who just would not go away even after they killed him.

But what does that mean? Let us bracket Sheehan's God-is-dead atheology, and bracket likewise Schillebeeckx's doctrinal concerns, and do a little old-fashioned phenomenology. I will, I trust, be permitted to usher a Jewish phenomenologist—Emmanuel Levinas—onto the premises. I would say that there is a deep phenomenological base to what happened to Simon, and to the other disciples, and that it has to do with what Levinas would call "the impossibility of murder."[8] You can of course kill somebody physically; that is a tragically well-known fact. But you cannot, as they say in the gangster movies, "erase" that person. Levinas explains this by attributing a certain "infinity" and hence inextinguishability to the other person. The arm of the murderer is not long enough to reach the other, not in the other's true otherness, which is infinite, which thus exceeds everything empirical, and is thus an excess, an irreducible transcendence. In Levinas himself this analysis is focused on the murderer who is always haunted by his deed, by the "ghost" of his victim, and Levinas had the holocaust on his mind. I want to shift this focus to the impact of the murder on the survivors, the intimates, the disciples of the victim; and I want to say that they, too, experience the ghost of the victim, his *Geist, spiritus*, especially when they assemble together.

By deploying this Levinasian theme we can say that Simon and the other disciples had a remarkably profound experience of the stamp of infinity upon Jesus, the transcendence, the infinite depths, the mysterious sources and resources of Jesus. "Rabbi, where do you dwell?" Where do you come from? What landed on Simon one day was the inextinguishability and inexhaustibility of Jesus, and the best way he could find of expressing that inextinguishability was to use the best language at his disposal—the coming Son of Man.

We can imagine that Simon had been penetrated by the look of Jesus, pierced by those eyes, that he was sometimes just paralyzed by the face of Jesus. When Jesus "turned and looked straight at Simon" the night of his arrest, Simon ran out and wept bitterly (Luke 22:61–62). Sheehan does a remarkable analysis of that look (FC, 121–22). Face to face, Jesus had power. When he would talk to those who were described in his day as "possessed by devils" (we would not describe them that way anymore), he could calm them down. Sometimes Jesus would just enter a room, Simon might have remembered, sit down with a disturbed man, perhaps take the man's hand in his, look him straight in the eye, and the poor fellow would calm down. Jesus could do things like that.

Now I want to push this Levinasian analysis one step further. The Jewishness of Levinas is not an obstacle here but crucially important. He helps us to see how Jesus would be turned so essentially to the "father." But more importantly Levinas has this strong Jewish sense that we cannot see the face of God, that no one can see the face of God—even Moses only caught the back of God—except in the face of our fellow human beings. *So what Simon experienced when he experienced the infinity of Jesus, the depths of that*

extraordinary man, was a glimpse of the face of God. Not directly, unam-
biguously, in a naked experience outside history and unaffected by
language. Not without textuality. But with a reality and liveliness
that when he ran this by the other disciples they agreed. Something
very extraordinary had just happened to them.

So one side of Simon's undecidable experience is coming into
view. This is not meant to be a phenomenological proof for the divinity of Jesus, but a phenomenological—specifically, a Levinasian—"explication" (*Auslegung*) of one side of Simon's experience—
namely, the kind of power that came crashing in upon the disciples,
and which can come crashing in upon all of us, the kind of "infinity" that a depth encounter with another person harbors. Now for
Levinas the experiential contact we make with the life of God in this
experience of the face of the other is strictly *ethical*; it consists in
justice, in a life of service to others. That deep Jewish spirituality
goes to the heart of Jesus' message about the father's loving care for
human beings. That is why Schillebeeckx cites Levinas to make a
point about Jesus:

> Even when dying, Jesus has no desperate concern with his
> own identity . . . but is taken up with the matter of God's
> rule. . . . God has man's interest at heart, but in a world
> which itself does not always appear to do so. . . . It says some-
> thing that it was a Jewish thinker and philosopher, E. Levinas,
> who could speak of the irresistible power of the "defenceless
> other one" who goes on trusting [J, 638].

It is always the "widow and the orphan"—that is, the innocent and
the defenseless one—who evokes our responsibility, according to
Levinas. Jesus's life was given over to the message that the father
loves us and has already forgiven us, and he kept that faith in the
face of death. For that he was brutally punished and murdered.
What lies at the basis of Simon's experience, I submit, is this experience of the *impossibility of murder*, of the inextinguishability of innocence, of the triumph of love over death, which Simon expressed
by saying that Jesus lives, that God has raised him up. The impossibility of murder is the phenomenological counterpart to the theology of resurrection.

Now what I, with Levinas, am describing here is *an experience
that is in principle available anywhere*, and is not localized in Jesus of
Nazareth. I am making quite a universal claim, which exceeds what
one does or does not think of Jesus, which is not localized to Christianity or even Judeo-Christianity. What I am saying does not at all

support Schillebeeckx's claim that there is something exclusive or definitive about Jesus. It is a more philosophical, universal claim, more like Heidegger's reference to the coming to presence of the divine "in the world of the Greeks, in prophetic Judaism, in the preaching of Jesus"—as if there were multiple occasions for this manifestation.[9]

From a phenomenological point of view, the infinity that Levinas describes is present in us all. These innocents are everywhere, from Jerusalem to Auschwitz and beyond. Everyone reveals the face of God. Jesus would not be the exclusive locus of our experience of the divine. There is an infinity that inhabits us all; *we are all of us*, each for the other, *a possible locus of the divine*, a potential launching point for transcendence. That means that the extraordinariness of Jesus, his difference, would lie in being an extraordinarily good example of a universal human possibility, an exemplary occasion for human transcendence. *In Jesus something would happen with an explosiveness and white-hot intensity that in principle can happen elsewhere.* In Jesus we would be brought up against the divine, hear its echoes, catch a glimpse of the back of God as He passes us by. Jesus would be a particular place of divine advent, of God's coming, maybe the best case a lot of Greco-Europeans can remember, but not the only possible one.

In this phenomenological rendering, Jesus is an occasion for the experience of *religious truth*. In the Jesus described in the historico-critical method—the friend of the outcast and the enemy of hierarchical hypocrisy, with a faith in the father stronger than death—we come crashing up against something that confounds us, that brings us up short and opens up the mystery of the *léthé*. We start to hear divine voices, feel touched by transcendent power and love, and in general are torn out of our average everydayness in a way that Heidegger has described better than most by calling it "openness to the mystery."

The problem with Sheehan is that he has closed off the mystery and proferred us a definitive hermeneutic key, a perfectly transparent *Erklärung* of what happened in Jesus of Nazareth. Derrida has put that sort of thing on the skids; he called it onto-hermeneutics and he shows how it keeps popping up—when Heidegger tries to reduce *Ereignis* to some unique meaning of Being, when Freud tries to reduce the unconscious to male sexuality, when Marx tries to reduce historical profusion to "historical materialism," and the like.[10] So when Sheehan describes what he does as "deconstruction" (FC, 142) and speaks of "undecidability" (FC, 225), I would say: Beware of them who wear hermeneutic robes. He is *not*

serving up deconstruction but a reductionist hermeneutics of suspicion—and deconstruction is neither reductionistic nor hermeneutical key-making—with a strongly left-wing Hegelian *Vorurteil*. If
Jesus is an undecidable, then he is a place where the bottom drops
out, a place of opening to the mystery of *léthé*, and he may have
been right about his *Abba*.

I insist—and this is the whole point of the present essay—that
we stay with the notion of *a-létheia*, that we adhere rigorously to its
element, that we do not break off too quickly and reach a resolution
of this hermeneutic conflict. For Simon's experience may be understood in another way.

According to both Sheehan and Schillebeeckx, the kingdom of
God means universal shalom (J, 594), the rule of peace and justice
—for Sheehan in such a way that God *reduces* to peace and justice
without remainder, and for Schillebeeckx in such a way as to give a
transcendent *warranty* or backup for the human order of peace and
justice. Schillebeeckx thinks that Jesus gives us a promise that history has a meaning, that suffering has an opponent (J, 615–16),
while Sheehan thinks that this promise should be translated "without remainder" into orthopraxis. In the face of innocent suffering,
Schillebeeckx says, philosophy and theology are bereft of counsel.
History has a demonic strain; evil eludes our explanatory devices (J,
62D); and the only answer is given in Jesus' message of faith and
trust that the father is with us, no matter what:

> Despite the historical failure of this message, Jesus bore wit-
> ness to the indestructible certainty he felt regarding the salva-
> tion given by God, to a certainty which in his case was
> grounded in an exceptional *Abba* experience. For us it entails a
> promise from God that the salvation and "making whole" of
> man is possible and there is ultimately a point, a meaning to
> human life [J, 625].

It is through Jesus that "limitation and alienation, impotence and
even death, are finally overcome: the finite itself—for that is what
we are—is redeemed" (J, 666). For Schillebeeckx everything turns
on the notion that death and suffering must be overcome, defeated.
The world must be redeemed. Sheehan agrees, and he thinks that
if "Jesus" moves you in that direction, then fine, but you do not
need Jesus, for an ethics of mercy *sans* Jesus will do just as well
(FC, 222–23).

In short, both Sheehan and Schillebeeckx are out to still the
hermeneutic flux, to arrest the play that is set in motion once you

concede the inescapability of *hermeneusis*. There is for both a *fundamentum inconcussum*, a bedrock layer, from which neither will budge—namely, an ethics of mercy, peace and justice, shalom. This means that for them shalom is not an interpretation, but that in the name of which all interpretations are made. Their main disagreement from this point of view is whether God can be reduced to the moral order or whether by retaining His transcendence God backs up the moral order. Sheehan is not serving up the end of religion but its flip side, the secularized version of universal shalom. He still has an onto-theo-logical center—social justice—which retains all the theological momentum of religion, but with just this difference: that God has become Man (cum capitalization). This is the end of religion in the sense of its completion and translation into an orthopraxis that is out to redeem a fallen world but that is bereft (*kenosis*) of the divine, transcendent backup.

But the implications of the "undecidability" of it all, of the radical hermeneutical fix we are in, cut deeper than this. *For it just may be that the world is innocent and does not need saving*, whether by Jesus (Schillebeeckx) or Marx (Sheehan). Suppose with Nietzsche that the world was never guilty, that nothing needs to be redeemed, that everything is innocent, suffering included. When Nietzsche spoke of the "innocence of becoming," he meant that transience and history, change and travail, are not a fall from *ousia*, not depraved, evil, unjust, or sinful. The world just plays itself out, the quanta of energy just discharge, and *it*—the world, *das Spiel, das "Es"*—just does not know that we are here.

It is no objection to say that if this were so, history would have no goal, life would have no meaning, and we would have nothing to hope for or in. That is a complaint, not an objection, and the cosmos is under no obligation to answer our complaints. Put another way, the ability of an idea to answer our complaints, to give us meaning and comfort, is little guarantee of its truth.

Nietzsche was making a case for a tragic, irreligious view of life. I know that there are strongly religious and prophetic streaks in Nietzsche, but on this point I take him to be deeply irreligious. Nietzsche had a "merciless" way of viewing things; he saw the cosmos, not in the religious terms of universal shalom, of an ethics of mercy, but in a pre-Socratic vision of war where the only justice is the sort that one finds in Anaximander and Heraclitus, where the endless strife of things, the incessant going-over and going-under, strikes an overall balance. Now *that* is a hard saying. Nietzsche had a merciless view of truth, a truth without mercy:

How much truth can a spirit *endure*, how much truth does a spirit *dare*? . . . This does not mean that [his philosophy] must halt at a negation, a No, a will to negation. It wants to cross over to the opposite of this—to a Dionysian affirmation of the world as it is, *without subtraction, exception, or selection.*[11]

In another place Nietzsche says that "his" philosophers do not want the truth sweetened, softened, blunted, attenuated. All things are caught up in an eternal wheel that binds happiness with suffering, birth with death, pleasure with pain, joy with sorrow. There is no suppressing of one side in favor of the other, no subtraction of one part from the whole to which it belongs. All things are wedded to each other so that to affirm life is to affirm the whole wheel of becoming, the going-over and the going-under. We cannot accept life with mental reservations, for better but not for worse, like a bridegroom with his fingers crossed when he makes his vows. In the place of "redemption"—whether by God or by revolutionary social movements (for Nietzsche it is a matter of indifference how you prop up "morals")— he puts *amor fati*, love of the earth as it is, without allowance for line-item vetoes. And it is not the Lord Jesus that he prays would come again, but the eternal circulation of life itself, with its endless wheel of joy and sorrow.

Now we can see the full dimension of facing up to the inescapability of hermeneusis and the radical concept of *a-létheia* with which we are faced. *A radically hermeneutic reading of Simon's experience has to concede the possibility of this reading of it.* I do not see that Schillebeeckx seriously considers in *Jesus*—perhaps it is not the place—that history has no point at all, that suffering has no meaning, that the cosmos does not know that we are here. Yet surely *the believer must concede this possibility.* Everything in *Jesus* is premised on the assumption that Jesus makes a good fit for someone looking for a rebuttal to evil. Sheehan just gives us the secularized counterpart to this, that Jesus can be translated into socio-political orthopraxis with pretty much the same results—but without the trappings of transcendence.

I want to say that things are worse than that, that *undecidability puts us in a position where the abyss opens out on us*, where *léthé* stretches out before us, and where the best move that we can make is (what Heidegger calls) *openness to the mystery.*

The one point where Schillebeeckx comes closest to recognizing what I am insisting upon here is found in his occasional references to "God's silence" (J, 651). That silence—read *léthé*—I think is intrinsic to any talk about God's saving word. The prototypical case of the silence of God in the Christian tradition is God's silence at the crucifixion.

The historico-critical method paints a different picture of it: none of the (male) disciples at his feet, no heavens opening up at the crack of 3:00 P.M., no centurion confessing that this was the Son of God in truth. Just abandonment, death, and maybe even burial in a common grave. "My God, my God, why have you forsaken me?" The seven last words may be a later adornment, but that one has the ring of truth to it—Nietzsche's cold, merciless truth. That historico-critical portrait is sobering and as filled with religious import as the later "updatings."

In the Jewish tradition the holocaust is the most painful evidence of the silence of God, and about that I have no right to say anything more than has already been said, by Elie Wiesel and by countless others who have heard this silence and have lived to tell it. Where is the father's loving care then? How does one continue to push an *Abba* spirituality then? Who can imagine a human father like that? Here's where we need negative theology lest we throw the whole thing over.

This silence is the concealed heart of *léthé* in any religious truth, any *a-létheia* to which the believer lays claim (or by which the believer is claimed), and it takes raw courage to weather it out.

Let me close with a final rendering of Simon back at the Sea of Galilee—only this time with *a-létheia* and the silence of God in mind. Who is this man, Simon asks himself, and where does he dwell? What voice speaks to us here? Heidegger once put a similar question: "Is it the soul which is speaking? Is it the world? Is it God?"[12] Who do you say I am? Jesus asked Simon. Contra Sheehan and Schillebeeckx, I would let a radical hermeneutical thought cross Simon's mind, that Jesus' cruel murder was just part of the way the cosmos discharges its energy, that the universe knows no mercy, that the cosmos does not know or care about Jesus, and that the taking of Jesus' life belonged as much to the cosmic economy as does Simon's own work as a fisherman, which spelled death for the fish but life for Simon. Simon would had to have shuddered with that thought, too, before he started to round up the disciples; and even after he had gotten the whole thing going and they started to call him the rock, he would continue to worry about that.

Part III

Ethical

8

The Face of Truth in Rosenzweig, Levinas, and Jewish Mysticism

Richard A. Cohen

In all faces is seen the Face of faces,
veiled, and in a riddle.

Nicolas of Cusa
The Vision of God

For both Franz Rosenzweig and Emmanuel Levinas, the human face is the site of truth. The face is where truth *happens* in its *absoluteness*—that is to say, in its divinity. "Truth is from God," says Rosenzweig in his great work, *The Star of Redemption*.[1] Truth is "to God" (à-Dieu), says Levinas in many of his later texts. Clearly, neither Rosenzweig nor Levinas thinks truth here simply as the coherence of a set of propositions or their correspondence to a state of affairs. Neither, of course, do they simply exclude or ignore these forms that truth takes, as if they did not exist. For both thinkers, however, the "truthfulness" of coherence truth and correspondence truth is based on *revelatory truth—truth as expression, sincerity, and moral force*. It is truth in this social and ethical sense that is *ultimate*. It is truth in this sense that "appears" *in and as the face*, in the face-to-face relation to the alterity of the other person. Truth is thus *an excessive proximity*, a proximity whose alterity is absolute, exceeding being, closer than being, the call of a moral force. Thus an always utterly unique relation—the face-to-face relation—becomes the source of universality.

To legitimize this peculiar combination of ethics, religion, and epistemology, Rosenzweig and Levinas have much to say about the face. They have much to say, and there is much for expositors to explain about what these two thinkers say about the interpersonal orientation of truth. The aim of this study, however, is limited to illuminating the faces in Rosenzweig and Levinas in the light cast by the many faces found in the Jewish mystical tradition.[2] Such a line of inquiry would be of interest under any number of circumstances, especially given the general neglect of Jewish studies in mainstream philosophical discussions. That it is specifically called for to illuminate the philosophies of Rosenzweig and Levinas, however, is justified by what and how the face appears on the penultimate page of Rosenzweig's *The Star of Redemption*, and by the profound influence that the whole of this book exerted on the whole of Levinas's thought.[3] The face that appears at the end of *The Star* manifestly resonates with the Jewish mystical tradition. In this chapter I intend to trace this resonance.[4]

Over and beyond the particular interests of Rosenzweig, Levinas and the Jewish mystical tradition, *the image of the human face* has for millennia served the entire West—indeed, the entire world[5]— not merely as the place of this or that truth, but as a primary and primordial opening between the human and the divine, as *the place and test of truth*, as *the very "truth" of truth*.

Before entering into the faces of Rosenzweig, Levinas, and Jewish mysticism, then, I am going to begin with a brief look at the face in the broader spiritual heritage of the West. I am going to begin by giving three general reasons why the human face plays a middle role between the divine and the human. In attending to these reasons one must not forget that the Western tradition, even when it is most reasonable, has at least two beginnings; or rather, the Western tradition has an origin and a beginning: an origin in Greece and a beginning in the Holy Land.

The Preeminence of the Face

Perhaps the most obvious reason for the preeminence of the face, for its quasi-divine stature, is its natural verticality, the "above and below" it orients in conjunction with the natural verticality of the standing human body. Erwin Straus's famous study of the body's upright posture has made us familiar with the phenomenological significance of this aspect of human physiology.[6] The human body and the human face are upright, both literally and ethically. One is oriented toward the uppermost part of the other's body; one is oriented upward to God. The face looks out from atop the body; God looks out from above creation. A spirituality articulated in terms of the dimensions of height, of the above and the below, *axis mundi*, joins the experience of verticality encountered in the human face and body. This verticality is at play when in *The Star* Rosenzweig writes: "There is an Above and a Below, inexchangeable and irreversible. . . . And just because there is an Above and a Below in the truth, therefore we may, nay we must call it, God's countenance. . . . Man has an above and a below in his own corporeality."[7]

A second reason for recognizing the juncture of man and God in the image of the face is that the human face is not only upright, literally and morally, but it is also the locus of more openings than any other place on the surface of the human body. Furthermore, all the senses are at play there. The face is alive with expressions and impressions. As the place of so many openings, as the place of extreme sensitivity, it is *the place*; as the center of a multitude of exchanges and passages, it is *the center*. No other comparably compact area of the body is open to a greater range of give and take. The face is by nature intense, a zone of intensity, of exchanges—the true omphalos is the face.

A third reason to recognize the face as the place where divine and human meet is its very life. That the face is alive does not mean solely that it is active, fluid, moving and moved, but more importantly that it is irreversible, that it is oriented by a past, a present, and a future. After writing of the uprightness of the face, which joins the human and the divine, Rosenzweig writes of its life: "We speak in images. But the images are not arbitrary. There are essential images and coincidental ones. The irreversibility of the truth can only be enunciated in the image of a living being."[8] Living beings grow, their life travels one way from birth to death, passing through infancy, youth, maturity, and old age, never returning the same or to the same like reflection. The face of the other, Levinas has taught since 1946,[9] is precisely the excessive dimensionality of time, "diachrony," irreversibility, the irruption of an immemorial past and an always surprising future. At the same time, without contradiction, the face crystalizes a whole life; it gives evidence of accumulated and accumulating vulnerabilities and powers, characteristics etched in lines and wrinkles. Whole and part at once, presence and passage, it is a fitting image of the divine.

These three reasons alone would suffice to "explain" the biblical *panim el panim*,[10] the excessive rectitude, openness, and directness of the *face-to-face* between God and the human. Because they are both cognizant of these three reasons, it is obvious that additional factors must account for the differences in the faces found in Rosenzweig and Levinas.

The Difference of the Face in Rosenzweig and the Face in Levinas

One of the most striking moments at the end of Rosenzweig's *The Star*, even more striking than the transcending intention dramatized by the triangulation of the book's final sentences,[11] is the appearance of the human face (*Gesicht, Antlitz*) described on its penultimate page. In an altogether brilliant and astonishing book, this epiphany stands out as one of the most astonishing moments. What makes for the amazement it inspires is both the surprise of its appearance and the detail of its description.

With regard to its surprise, upon reflection we realize that it is no accident that Rosenzweig describes the human face just before making the final and ultimate gesture of *The Star*—that is, just before launching out from text into life, from conceptual or imaginary truth into *eternal* truth, truth lived as love for the neighbor within a revealed religious community. Eternal truth, as Rosenzweig understands it, is found in a return from concepts and images to the face, to a face both human and divine.

With regard to the graphic detail of Rosenzweig's description of the face, it stands out especially for readers familiar with the face in Levinas. It goes without saying that the face plays a central role in Levinas's thought. The face is more essential, if this be possible, to Levinas than to Rosenzweig. Even apart from Rosenzweig's influence, the entirety of Levinas's thought is easily and correctly characterized as a long and profound meditation on the significance of the face. When the influence of Rosenzweig on Levinas is taken into account, what becomes conspicuous is the contrast between their faces. Rosenzweig's description of the face on barely one page of *The Star* presents a face far more graphic and symbolic than anything found anywhere in the entire work of Levinas. There are, indeed, no comparable descriptions of the face in Levinas, not even in *Totality and Infinity*, to take the prime example, where one-quarter of the text is devoted to the face (*le visage*).[12] In contrast to the face in Levinas, Rosenzweig's face is both *graphic*, meaning that it details concrete features, eyes, ears, cheeks, mouth, and the like, and *symbolic*, meaning that the *Mogen David*, the star of *The Star*, and all of the fundamental elements and structures developed in *The Star*, are superimposed upon it.

The differences between the faces in Rosenzweig and Levinas are, in addition, at first sight all the more difficult to explain inasmuch as it is Levinas who is trained in the *descriptive* phenomenology of Husserl, and Rosenzweig who is trained in the *conceptual* phenomenology of Hegel. That is to say, one would quite naturally have expected concepts from Rosenzweig and descriptions from Levinas. But this expectation is not met. It is not met, to give the most obvious reason, because Rosenzweig finally rejects the Hegelian mode of philosophizing just as much as Levinas finally rejects the Husserlian mode of philosophizing. While their mutual rejection of their mentors helps to explain why the face is central to both thinkers—for the face is ultimately neither a concept nor an essence but lies beyond both[13]—it is not sufficient, even taking into account Levinas's chronological position relative to Rosenzweig, that is to say, even taking into account Levinas's appropriation of Rosenzweig's criticism of Hegel, and Levinas's reading of *The Star*, and Levinas's proximity to Husserlian and Heideggerian phenomenology. None of these additional factors, even taken together, are sufficient to explain the differences in the faces that appear so importantly in Rosenzweig and Levinas.

How, then, do we account for the differences that clearly distinguish the faces in Rosenzweig and in Levinas? Why does Levinas attend exclusively to the ethical claim of the face, apparently disregarding the facial graphics and symbolism so important to Rosenzweig? Why does Rosenzweig delineate a facial graphics and symbolism? To answer these two interrelated questions, let us begin by looking first at the face in Rosenzweig.

Rosenzweig's Face

I will begin by quoting the entire paragraph of *The Star* where "The Face of Man" appears. This paragraph occurs in the final section of *The Star*—in a section entitled "Gate," a gate which leads into real life, beyond the book.

Just as the Star mirrors its elements and the combination of the elements into one route in its two superimposed triangles, so too the organs of the countenance divide into two levels. For the life-points of the countenance are, after all, the points where the countenance comes into contact with the world above, be it in passive or active contact. The basic level is ordered according to the receptive organs; they are the building blocks, as it were, which together compose the face, the mask, namely forehead and cheeks, to which belong respectively nose and ears. Nose and ears are the organs of pure receptivity. The nose belongs to the forehead; in the sacred [Hebrew] tongue it veritably stand for the face as a whole. The scent of offerings turns to it as the motion of the lips to the ears. This first triangle is thus formed by the midpoint of the forehead, as the dominant point of the entire face, and the midpoints of the cheeks. Over it is now imposed a second triangle, composed of the organs whose activity quickens the rigid mask of the first: eyes and mouth. Not that the eyes are mutually equivalent in a mimic sense, for while the left one views more receptively and evenly, the right one "flashes"—a division of labor which frequently leaves its mark deep in the soft neighborhood of the eye-sockets of a hoary head; this asymmetric facial formation, which otherwise is generally conspicuous only in the familiar difference between the two profiles, then becomes perceptible also en face. Just as the structure of the face is dominated by the forehead, so its life, all that surrounds the eyes and shines forth from the eyes, is gathered in the mouth. The mouth is consummator and fulfiller of all expression of which the countenance is capable, both in speech, as, at last, in the silence beyond which speech retreats: in the kiss. It is in the eyes that the eternal countenance shines for man; it is the mouth by whose words man lives. But for our teacher Moses, who in his lifetime was privileged only to see the land of his desire, not to enter it, God sealed this completed life with a kiss of his mouth. Thus does God seal and so too does man.[14]

The following figures may be helpful in visualizing what Rosenzweig is describing.[15]

Rosenzweig does not belabor the geometrical correspondances he establishes between the primary elements, structures, and religions elaborated in *The Star* and "The Face of Man." It is as if he wants his readers to turn from *The Star* to real faces, faces "beyond the book," and not get bogged down in "The Face of Man." Nonetheless the stunning description of "The Face of Man" does reveal a new register of meaning for the entire *Star*.

When Rosenzweig writes that "the Star must once more mirror itself in that which, within the corporeality, is again the Upper: the countenance [so that] it is not human illusion if Scripture speaks of God's countenance and even of his separate bodily parts," or when he writes that "the life-points of the [human] countenance are, after all, those points where the countenance comes into contact with the world above"[16] (emphasizing the absoluteness and unity of the divine above and the human below, a unity found precisely in the human face as a mirror of God's face), these words are clearly echoes coming from a long mystical tradition in Judaism. As

THE FACE OF MAN

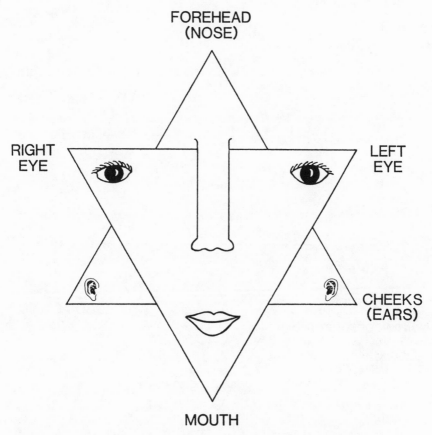

FOREHEAD
(NOSE)

RIGHT
EYE

LEFT
EYE

CHEEKS
(EARS)

MOUTH

Figure A shows Rosenzweig's face in relation to the Mogen David.

his text and the above figures show, Rosenzweig brings this tradition into too great an evidence to ignore.

The Jewish Mystical Tradition

In attending to the Jewish mystical tradition, I must begin with several disclaimers. First, I do not claim to read the minds of Rosenzweig or Levinas, or reveal their hidden intentions. Secondly, I

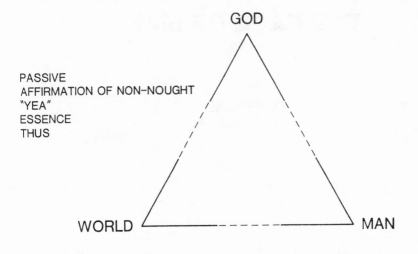

GOD

PASSIVE
AFFIRMATION OF NON-NOUGHT
"YEA"
ESSENCE
THUS

WORLD   MAN

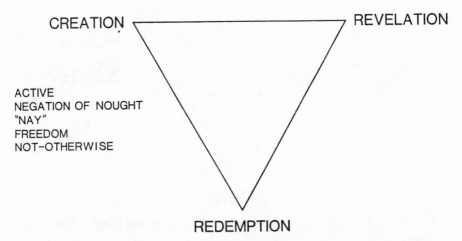

CREATION   REVELATION

ACTIVE
NEGATION OF NOUGHT
"NAY"
FREEDOM
NOT-OTHERWISE

REDEMPTION

Figure B shows some of the significations correlated to the two triangles of the Mogen David as elaborated in the first part of *The Star*.

make no claims about how much or in some instances even whether Rosenzweig or Levinas knew about particular mystical texts. Thirdly, my object is not to label Rosenzweig or Levinas "mystics."[17] Fourthly, my aim is not to show that Rosenzweig or Levinas tapped Jewish mystical sources to prove their philosophies.

THE STAR OF REDEMPTION

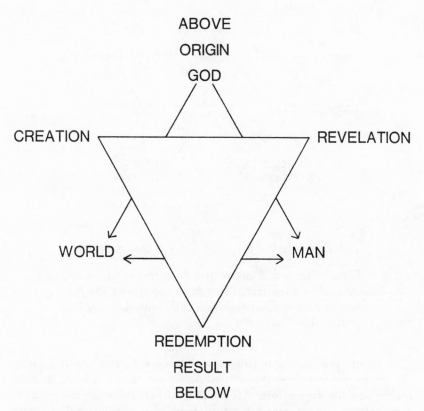

Figure C shows the Mogen David as the symbol of the primary elements and structures of *The Star*. This star is *the* star.

Though their written words show beyond a shadow of doubt that both Rosenzweig and Levinas are not merely aware in some vague way of a Jewish mystical tradition, but directly refer and allude to Jewish mystical sources, I would argue that their philosophies do not in any essential way rely on these references and allusions for their truth. Despite or in view of these four disclaimers, an examination of the Jewish mystical sources, an attunement to their subtle resonances, will cast light on the faces that appear in Rosenzweig and Levinas.

JUDAISM: THE FIRE

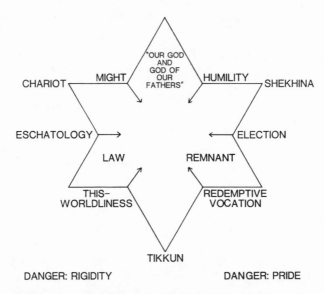

DANGER: RIGIDITY   DANGER: PRIDE

Figures D and E show the Mogen David as the symbol of the eternal fire of Judaism and the historical rays of Christianity as elaborated in the last part of *The Star*.

Before proceeding to this topic, however, I must briefly take up the more general question of method in mysticism. I have deliberately used the vague term "resonance" to characterize the connection between the various faces of Jewish mysticism and the face Rosenzweig presents at the end of *The Star*. I have done this because to the philosophically trained mind—that is, the mind trained in reason, in giving reasons—all the connections whose meanings are legitimized by Jewish mysticism are highly unregulated. Within certain boundaries, almost anything goes, almost any association of meaning is legitimate.

The restriction of meaning, or the meaning of restriction, in Jewish mysticism is primarily of two sorts: first, mystical claims are bounded to the extent that they cannot ultimately contradict the higher authority accorded to the claims of halakah or haggadah. A mystical claim may deepen the meaning of a halakic regulation, but it will never contradict or overturn it. The same holds for the inci-

CHRISTIANITY: THE RAYS

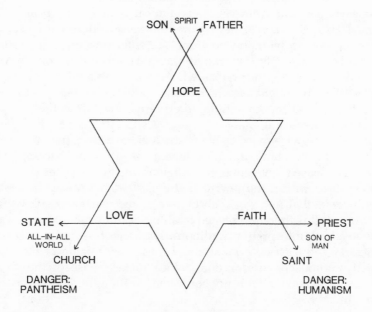

DANGER: SPIRITUALISM

SON ──SPIRIT── FATHER

HOPE

STATE ← LOVE ──── FAITH → PRIEST

ALL–IN–ALL
WORLD

CHURCH

SON OF
MAN

SAINT

DANGER:
PANTHEISM

DANGER:
HUMANISM

DANGER: HARDNESS

dents and ethical truths of haggadah. Secondly, the connections made in Jewish mysticism are bounded by the connections *already* made within the Jewish mystical tradition. That is to say, mystical claims are bounded by the authority of transmitted tradition. It is only within these strictures—halakah, haggadah, and tradition—that anything is possible in Jewish mysticism.

Given these restrictions one may question the aptness of the term "anything," but the latitude left to mystical interpretation, having actually been taken up in wildly imaginative glosses on prophetic visions (especially of God's chariot, throne, and palace[18]), in exotic correlations of meaning established through *gematria* and in manipulations of Hebrew letters and parts of Hebrew letters, which border on the stunning, seems adequate to justify this characterization. However irregular these "methods" may appear to the standards of philosophy—to Greek standards, that is to say—themeanings established through such "artifices" of connection have often proven to be quite suggestive and illuminating.

But Jewish mysticism is not just poetry. Jewish mysticism is what one makes of the divinity of the created universe over and beyond the authority of halakic and haggadic significations.

The wide-ranging freedom of the mystical reading is one of its prime virtues, and with equal certainty it is one of its prime dangers. That it is a danger, Jewish tradition has underlined by setting restrictions onto who and how one can enter into mystical studies. That it is a danger, Jewish tradition emphasized further by the well-known story of the four rabbis who entered the garden of mystical knowledge, from out of which only one emerged sane and with faith intact.[19] At the same time, interpretive freedom is the virtue of mysticism because it enables its devotees to mine a wealth of significations otherwise inaccessible to the logic of affirmation and negation, or to the limitations of human poetical production. This mining is based on genuinely religious insight—expressed in its fullest force within the Jewish tradition by Rabbi Moses ben Jacob Cordovera—that in a world absolutely sacred, each and every thing contains and is therefore related to all other things in all ways. Thus the mystical interpretive tradition—sod, secret—is within certain strictures the least determinate and most unregulated of the traditional methods of interpretion, which makes sense of the sacred universe.[20] The symbol is not equivalent to thought; it "gives rise to thought."[21]

A final disclaimer is required: my aim in the following is not to enter as an esoteric agent into the infinite terrain of infinite possible interpretations. My aim is not to "do" mysticism in this sense. I do not know if I would emerge alive or sane. My overall purpose is to better understand the significance of the faces in Rosenzweig and Levinas.

The initial motivation for this voyage into Jewish mysticism is the manifest link between this tradition and the face that appears at the conclusion of Rosenzweig's The Star. The face in Levinas is at first sight far less evidently connected to the Jewish mystical tradition, but excluding other fairly compelling reasons that I have not mentioned,[22] its close association with the face in Rosenzweig is reason enough to pursue its link to this tradition.

The entire Jewish mystical tradition is an attempt on the symbolic plane to solve a central religious-metaphysical problem—namely, the problem of making sense in a finite world of God's absolute transcendence. The key here is the term "God." What is at stake in the Jewish tradition is determining the singular relationship between a perfect and good God (who as one is the totality) and the imperfection or evil of His creation. Metaphysics for the Jew is not the abstract science of the Greeks but an always specific ontology regulated by God's goodness. It is not only knowledge but worship.

Within Jewish mysticism there are many sets of symbols designed to show or manifest the link between the infinite and the finite, the perfect and the imperfect, between the perfect God and His imperfect creation. All these symbolisms by necessity can only utilize elements of the finite world. Elements of the finite world are, when given mystical significance, taken to be signs or metaphors or ciphers or mirrors, which when appropriately manipulated, through praxis or intellect or both, manifest the infinite or bring it near. It is no accident that the precise term or movement of this juncture cannot be fully articulated. One must have recourse to symbols. In the course of its long history,[23] Jewish tradition has already articulated many sets of symbols, of which the most outstanding are: names of God, the letters of the aleph-bet, parts of letters, letters of particular words, personal pronouns, the human body, biblical personages, celestial spheres, lovers, nations, colors, days of the week, and numbers. In this tradition one finds the human face within the set of symbols that utilizes the figure of the finite human body. Within this set of symbols there are innumerable faces and interfaces of faces.

I will now examine four types of corporeal symbolism: one from the *ancient* period, two from the *medieval* period, and one from the *modern* period. The first comes from a very early Jewish mystical text devoted entirely to the body of God, the *Shi'ur Qomah*,[24] a title that can be translated either as *Measurement of Body* or *Measurement of Height*. The two sets of medieval symbolisms come, first, from three relatively early portions of the *Zohar*, which are attributed to Moses de Leon (b. 1240), of Catalonia, and second from kabbalah texts written by Moses ben Jacob Cordovera (1522–1570) and Elijah de Vida (d. ca. 1593), of Safed in Upper Galilee. In the modern period, finally, we will examine the corporeal symbolism found in a book dear to Emmanuel Levinas, *The Soul of Life* (*Nefesh Hahayim*),[25] by Rabbi Hayim of Volozhim, Lithuania (1759–1821).

It goes without saying that throughout any examination of Jewish mystical sources one must keep in mind what the authors of these sources certainly had in mind—namely, the Jewish prohibition against idolatry. The symbols used in the Jewish mystical tradition are not meant as independently divine agents or intermediaries between God and humankind. Rather they are meant as openings, openings from God to the human and from the human to God.[26] "World and man," says Rosenzweig, "are deified without being idolized."[27]

The point of this examination is to find and explain the particular symbolic-sets that are important for Rosenzweig and Levinas, respectively.

The Ancient Period

The content of the *Shi'ur Qomah* is basically quite simple. It provides the exact numerical dimensions of a gigantic humanlike body—millions and millions of miles high and wide—which is meant to be God's body. The size of this divine figure is so large, so huge—it is vast—as to defy the capacities of human visualization and imagination. It thus solves the religious-metaphysical problem of uniting divine and human by means of giganticism—that is to say, by an excessive amplification of finite spatiality that overloads, overwhelms, and thus transcends the finite powers of human visualization and imagination. It explodes visions and images.[28]

The *Shi'ur Qomah* presents an image that opens up a passage between God and humanity precisely because it destroys images. It short-circuits perceptual intentionality, breaks the correlation of perceiving and perceived, by means of the simple, even childish,[29] mechanism of hyperbolic enlargement. Space is abused to create the inability to reduce the divine to the finite dimensions of space. Thus in an almost ironic rejoinder to Maimonides's reservations about mysticism, the divine body of the *Shi'ur Qomah* precisely prevents the idolization of space.

Both Rosenzweig and Levinas, though they do not themselves utilize gross resemblance or giganticism as a technique, are in agreement with the *Shi'ur Qomah* that the alterity of God is not a spatial exteriority. The exteriority of God is an exteriority that explodes spatial exteriority.

The Medieval Period and Rosenzweig

The method of exaggeration utilized in giganticism is a technique too simple and too specifically focused on visual perception and imagination to be long satisfactory as a conduit between humanity and God. It does little more with the finite organs, shape, and posture of the human body than give them huge dimensions.

Moving beyond giganticism, two developments occur in the medieval period that are of successively increasing significance in the interpretation of the human body as a mystical symbol.

The earlier of the two developments is the supplementation of the *Shi'ur Qomah's* exclusively quantitative account with a plurality of qualitative glosses. The symbolism of God's body is overlaid with many other sets of symbols, symbols loosely attached to the facial organs, their functions, and relative positions within the facial and corporeal schema. This loose attachment is at best legitimized (to the mind looking for reasons, for justifications) by resemblance, but as often as not its connections are merely a matter of *juxtaposition*.

The second development in the medieval period occurs three centuries later. It radically alters the significance of the entire mystical enterprise. All the quantititative and qualitative correspondences of the earlier mystical texts, which operate within the assumptions of a contemplative framework, are now shifted to an active and ethical model of *imitation*.

The magnitude of this latter shift, from the contemplation of symbolic correspondences to the ethical imitation of God, appears forcefully when one compares the thirteenth-century Catalonian texts of the early *Zohar* to the sixteenth-century Safed texts of the *kabbalah*. The thirteenth-century texts that have most to say about the divine body and face are three by Moses de Leon.[30] The sixteenth-century text that has most to say—and is most original—about the divine body and face is without question *The Palm Tree of Devorah* (*Tomer Devorah*) by Moses ben Jacob Cordovera.

The Earlier Medieval Period of the Zohar

Early portions of the *Zohar* are attributed to Moses de Leon. In the three texts in question, great size is no longer the primary metaphor. The features of the face—skull, forehead, hair, eyes, ears, nose, mouth, and especially the beard—are associated with divine attributes (such as will, judgment, and mercy), with biblical words and passages, with names of God, with colors, with natural phenomena (such as dew, snow, and smoke), with numbers, and to a lesser degree with other sets of symbols. Associations are made in ways that seem haphazard, at least to the uninitiated or to the philosopher seeking reasons. Certain patterns do recur throughout the three texts, yet except for their consistency they seem no more "legitimate" than other correspondences that do not recur.

The correspondences of the *Zohar* are correspondences of juxtaposition; never are any reasons or explanations given.[31] We never find out, for example, why the ears hear only of good and evil, rather than hearing tales of brave Ulysses, or the names of insects, or jokes. It is not even the case that what is attributed to the divine head is limited to what at that historical time was thought to be "empirically" known about the human head. Rather, almost anything that can be said about the human head and its features—or about almost any entity, for that matter—is here also said about the divine head. It is as if these relations between the human body and the divine body were established by their very assertion, by the authority of fiat, by a sort of impressive display. Meaning here is a way of reverence. No significations are intended as "invented."

The connections, we could say, are not only curious and suggestive but arbitrary. Precisely because they are arbitrary they disturb the universality and necessity that together constitute the logic of conceptual thought. By the end of the thirteenth century, then, Jewish mysticism conceives itself in terms of a dual negative task: clearing a channel between God and humankind *otherwise than by images and otherwise than by logic*. In their mystical usage, images and concepts are violated. They are undermined, subverted and shattered by their contact with the divine. In another context, but regarding the same distance between the above and the below, Levinas writes: "The relationship with alterity is neither spatial nor conceptual."[32] Rosenzweig would say the same. Despite their agreement on these two negative points, however, it is clear that the face does not serve Rosenzweig and Levinas as it serves Moses de Leon, as a magnet attracting symbols arbitrarily brought close to it.

There is one exception to the distance Rosenzweig takes from the mysticism of Moses de Leon. It is an exception that joins *The Star* to the *Zohar*. Rosenzweig links the face to the geometrical shape of the Mogen David. This linkage is precisely the sort sanctioned by the *Zohar*.

Excluding this one instance, however, we must turn to the second development in medieval Jewish mysticism, to the *kabbalah* of Moses ben Jacob Cordovera, to grasp the profound affinity that joins this tradition to the face in Rosenzweig.

The Later Medieval Period of the Kabbalah

The change in the meaning of Jewish mystical symbolism that occurs in the sixteenth-century *kabbalah* texts of Safed has with good reason been characterized by a scholar of this period as "one of the most significant and remarkable chapters in the history of Judaism."[33] The change is indeed radical and its consequences are far-reaching. What occurs is *the unification of what was until then an exclusively contemplative and personal mysticism with the positivity and sociality of Jewish ethics*. In this new union the entire sense of the mystical body and face changes.

In the mysticism of the man whom Scholem has called "the greatest theoretician of Jewish mysticism,"[34] Moses ben Jacob Cordovero, this new union is inaugurated and established. Indeed, the call to shift from contemplation to ethics is made in the very first paragraph of Cordovero's great work, *The Palm Tree of Devorah*, as follows:

> It is proper for man to imitate his Creator, resembling Him in both likeness and image according to the secret of the Supernal Form. Because the chief Supernal image and likeness is in deeds, a human resemblance merely in bodily appearance, and not in deeds, abases that Form. Of the man who resembles the Form in body alone it is said: "A handsome form whose deeds are ugly." For what value can there be in man's resemblance to the Supernal Form in bodily limbs if his deeds have not resemblance to those of his Creator? Consequently, it is proper for man to imitate the acts of the Supernal Crown, which are the thirteen highest attributes of mercy.[35]

From these sentences onward, Jewish mysticism turns from solitary spiritual exercise, contemplation and meditation, to the refined and regulated behavior of social ethics and moral piety.

As a result, too, for the first time mystical texts are widely read in the Jewish community and take their place in the mainstream of Jewish tradition. Elijah de Vida's ethical-mystical treatise, *Beginning of Wisdom*—which follows directly from Cordovera's *The Palm Tree of Devorah*—becomes (along with Bahya ibn Paquda's twelfth-century *Duties of the Heart*) one of "the several most influential Jewish ethical works ever written."[36] Elijah de Vida's treatise and Jacob Poyetto's abbreviated version of it together will go through fifty-five editions, from 1579 to 1937, published all over Western and Eastern Europe.

In place of the contemplative epistemology of association through resemblance and juxtaposition, *the mystical tradition now presents an ethical model of behavioral imitation.* The divine face (and body) is no longer either an exaggerated spatial image or the relatively arbitrary site of various qualities, but also and more importantly *the moral exemplar par excellence*, the divine paradigm, the absolute model from which human expressions and behaviors take on their fundamentally ethical-religious significance. It is precisely this development, we can now say, that attracts Rosenzweig. With Cordovera and de Vida not only are perceptual images and abstract conceptualizations of the divine broken, they are broken through and positively exceeded by ethics.

The ethical-mystical account of the divine head and face in Cordovera's *The Palm Tree of Devorah* and in de Vida's *Beginning of*

Wisdom (and in Poyetto's *The Abbreviated Beginning of Wisdom*) are almost identical. Both texts devote about four pages to the divine head and face, treating them under the category or *sepharah* of divine humility (*keter*).[37] In order, Cordovera writes of the mind, forehead, ears, eyes, nose, face, and mouth.[38] De Vida follows the same order, with the sole exception that he treats of the ears before the eyes.[39] Both texts bridge the gap between divine and human by moving from a perfect pattern above to the human below, aligning the above and below across terms such as "resemble," "imitate," and "just as." They teach that *human expressions and deeds should resemble or imitate or be just as the divine head and face in order for the human to be ethical.* A sample from Poyetto will make this movement and its divine standard clear:

> It is good for an individual to regard himself as nought in comparison to the exaltedness of God. . . . Just as the supernal Forehead is known as "gracious," . . . so too a person should not engage in strife and contention. . . . When it comes to the eyes, one should be certain that his eyes are ever vigilant to show compassion to the poor and to care for them, just as the supernal Eye does. One's eyes ought to be downcast as is the supernal Eye for the purpose of nourishing the lower world. . . . With regard to one's ears, they must be alert in order to hearken to the sound of Torah and prayer, as well as to the voice of the poor so as to show them compassion. But the ears should pay no attention to the sounds of evil gossip and other such things which blemish an individual . . . for even the Holy One, blessed be He, pays no attention to the [moral] debts which men incur. . . . As for his nose, a person should imitate the quality of patience as it manifests itself in the supernal Nose. . . . With respect to the face, one should imitate those supernal qualities which are called Countenance. . . . As for his mouth, a person ought to resemble the supernal Mouth, uttering neither a curse nor words of ostracism, condemnation, impudence, or harshness. . . . An individual who avoids speaking much about worldly matters prolongs his days, inasmuch as his mouth thereby resembles the Supernal Mouth.[40]

With an eye to the influence of these *kabbalah* texts on Rosenzweig, I would highlight two points. First, there is the general shift from contemplation to ethics. Shifting from contemplation to ethics means, negatively, that both images and concepts are inadequate to bridge the gap between the finite and the infinite. Positively, it means that moral behavior is demanded. Torah means Torah-life, life according to Torah. Secondly, then, the ethical aspect of behavior—the true life—comes from a movement that begins with the infinite, as perfect model, and comes to the finite. Ethics is now a movement from top down, from above to below, the perfection of the divine head and face coming first and serving as the stable model, pattern, or paradigm to be imitated through the imperfect strivings of human ethical behavior. The ought ought to be what truly is, God.

It is this movement of imitation—*imitatio dei*[41]—that constitutes the *mystical* side of the ethics that Cordovera joins with mysticism. It must be noted that nothing about the ethical behavior recommended by Cordovera or de Vida is new, qua behavior, within the Jewish ethical tradition. The moral behavior and piety these kabbalists propose were normative to the Jewish community well before and will remain normative well after the sixteenth-century. Indeed, they are still normative for Rosenzweig, Levinas, and the contemporary Jewish community. It is the significance of ethics, its meaning, its contextualization, that Cordovera and de Vida alter. *By joining the Jewish ethical tradition to the Jewish mystical tradition they elevate the status of ethics.* It is precisely *this elevation of status* that attracts Rosenzweig to Cordovera's *Kabbalah.* Henceforth the cosmic, or, if the term "cosmic" is too Greek, the divine status of ethics becomes the issue in Jewish mysticism, up to and including Rabbi Hayim of Volozhin. Once Cordovera elevates ethics by uniting it with mysticism, the essential role of mysticism within the Jewish tradition is never again seriously challenged—despite occasional recidivism—and the level of ethics is never again lowered.

Professor Joseph Dan—one of Gershom Scholem's preeminent students and the successor to Scholem's chair at the Hebrew University in Jerusalem—in his fine book, *Jewish Mysticism and Jewish Ethics*, sums up the significance of Cordovera's *The Palm Tree of Devorah* for Jewish ethics and mysticism:

> Jewish ethics in the Middle Ages and modern times is not concerned so much with the problem of what should be done in a certain set of circumstances, as with the question of why should one follow the ethical demands. To this question Cordovera presents the first clear and unambiguous mystical answer: ethical behavior should be adopted and followed not only because God says so, but because God is so; one should conform not only to the divine laws, but to the divine nature. The righteous, thus, is not only an obedient servant of God,

but an imitator of His essence, and therefore a part of the divine system as a whole. Mystical ascent and everyday ethics are fused into one, and the highest achievement of communion with God is attained by following the most mundane and elementary demands of social ethics. This is a revolution not in the behavior of the righteous, but in the meaning of this behavior. . . . The distinction between an ethical work and a mystical one was erased, and a whole literature came into being, the literature of mystical ethics, which dominated Jewish thought during the next three centuries. [42]

With Cordovera, in other words, there begins a tradition within which *ethics takes on a mystical dimension and mysticism takes on an ethical dimension.* It is this tradition that continues right up to *The Star of Redemption* and beyond. Thus, in the tradition of Jewish mysticism Rosenzweig's face must be located alongside the face of Cordovera. Of course, there is one aspect of Rosenzweig's face, as we have remarked, its geometry, that comes from an earlier mysticism. But with this one exception, the central point of Rosenzweig's face—its truth or life—is drawn from the deep well of Cordovera's mysticism.

Without invoking proper names, Rosenzweig labels the Cordoverian structure of his thought "theomorphism." While this term does not appear in *The Star*, it is the central topic of a course entitled "The Science of God," which Rosenzweig gave at the Free House of Jewish Studies in the autumn of 1921—that is, shortly after the publication of *The Star*. [43] The problem the term "theomorphism" is introduced to solve is a problem central to contemporary thought and central to the whole of *The Star*. It is the problem of how to criticize idealist philosophy and remain a philosopher; or, in another register, it is the problem of how to criticize the orthodoxy of traditional revealed religion and remain genuinely religious. After having criticized the old philosophical "All" and the old theological God, Rosenzweig does not want to fall into the subjectivisms of Kierkegaard, Schopenhauer, and Nietzsche, on the side of the philosophers, or into the anthropomorphism of Schleiermacher and the theological historicists, on the side of the theologians.

Rosenzweig realizes that after criticizing the old thinking for its neglect of the living individual, religion and philosophy would not be whole or healthy if they were also to eliminate the subjectivity of the individual. But, on the other hand, he also realizes that neither will the individual be in the truth if the objectivity or necessity of philosophy and religion are entirely abandoned. It is precisely to escape this latter danger, while maintaining his radical criticism of the old thinking, that Rosenzweig takes up what he calls a "theomorphic" orientation, an orientation that is at the same time precisely the orientation of Cordovera's ethical-mysticism.

What is theomorphism? Rosenzweig's theomorphism appears most clearly with his central notion of revelation. "The bridge from maximum subjectivity to maximum objectivity," Rosenzweig writes, "is formed by theology's concept of revelation."[44] What Rosenzweig means by "theology's concept of revelation"—which he puts at the heart of *The Star*—is not literally the ten commandments given to Moses at Mount Sinai, but the command that each man must love his neighbor *because* God loves man. To avoid subjectivism, to avoid anthropomorphism, to avoid historicism, while also avoiding the old conceptualized thinking and the old orthodox theology, Rosenzweig appropriates the Cordoverean model: man must love his neighbor *just as* God loves man. To be good, man must *imitate* or *resemble* God. By means of this theomorphic move, Rosenzweig overcomes the sterility of the *old* thinking while insisting on the thoughtfulness of the new *thinking*. According to Rivka Horwitz's summary of Rosenzweig's 1921 lecture course:

> Rosenzweig asserts that the only reason that man is capable of love at all is because God loves. All human action, speech, and thought are in the image of God. A God who is a reality has, according to Rosenzweig, of necessity to be integrally involved in corporeality. Man can speak because God speaks. . . . The Kabbalist, in saying that God's "hand" stands for a higher form of reality, is evincing a similar tendency. As in Platonism at its extreme, God is the archetype of all existence.[45]

The face of Rosenzweig is the face of Cordovera: the imitation of God.

The Modern Period and Levinas

Levinas, in contrast, is not a "theomorph" in Rosenzweig's sense. The face in Rosenzweig—bringing God's law down to earth, embodying God's commandments in the command to love the neighbor just as God loves man—is less like the face in Levinas than like the *mezuzah* on the doorway of the traditional Jewish household, containing God's word while welcoming the neighbor in love. To understand the face in Levinas we must move beyond the medieval mysticism of sixteenth-century Safed to the celebrated Yeshiva Judaism of nineteenth-century Lithuania.

Rabbi Hayim of Volozhin's *The Soul of Life* (*Nefesh Hahayim*) was published in 1824, posthumously. As Scholem has noted, it is a text that reveals "a manifest indebtedness to kabbalistic sources on every page."[46] But *The Soul of Life* is not another version of Cordovera's kabbalah. Two important and intimately connected developments make this text an original contribution to Jewish mysticism—and a decisive influence on Levinas's thought.

The Reversal: From Human to Divine

The first development is a reversal, a reversal that because it is fundamental is nonetheless more than a simple reversal. While *The Soul of Life* takes up and continues the central contribution initiated by Moses Cordovera, *the union of ethics and mysticism, its originality lies in reversing the direction of that union.* For Cordovera and de Vida—and, as we have seen, for Rosenzweig—human ethical behavior is modeled on divine ethical behavior: what is done above, because it is done above, should be done below. For Rabbi Hayim of Volozhin, in contrast, *the divine realm itself depends on human ethical behavior.* What is done below establishes what is done above. Instead of man imitating God, the divinely created realm is determined *by* the actions of humankind. Thus immoral behavior on the part of humans produces immorality or disorder in creation; moral behavior on the part of humans produces a "healing" or "repairing" (*Tikkun*) of the created realm.

These astonishing claims are made in the first chapter of *The Soul of Life*, where Rabbi Hayim comments on the three celebrated passages of Genesis having to do with the creation of man in God's image (*zelem*), and with his likeness (*d'muth*) to God—namely, Genesis 1:27: "And Elokim created man in His own image; in the image of Elokim created He him"; Genesis 9:6: "For in the image of Elokim made He man"; and Genesis 1:26: "Let us make man in our image, after our likeness." To be sure, the words "image" and "likeness" do not refer to a geometrical or spatial congruence. To understand the meaning of human likeness to God, Rabbi Hayim instead focuses on the Bible's use of the name "Elokim" for God in His capacity as creator of man in His own image and likeness. This name, Hayim reminds us, signifies "master of all powers." It is as master of all powers that Elokim "created man and gave *him* dominion over myriads of powers and over numberless worlds."[47] In other words, creating man in the image of Elokim means giving to man the absolute mastery that is Elokim's mastery, the power over all worlds.

By transferring divine power to man, *the perfection of the divine realm now depends on the perfection of human behavior*. This is the key to Rabbi Hayim's reorientation of Cordovera's kabbalah. Human behavior, bodily movements directed by the soul, now have cosmic repercussions:

> Just as each of his individual bodily acts is directed by the force of the soul within him, so is man himself the force and living soul of unlimited numbers of upper and lower worlds which are dominated by his actions.[48]

> From the point of view of the position of his body man is at the latter end of creation [the tenth *sephirah* (*malkhut*, "kingdom") of the fourth and bottom realm (*olam ha-asiyyah*, "the material world")], but with respect to the upper root of his living soul he rates before the works of the Chariot—even before the world of the Throne.[49]

To elaborate and justify this doctrine of human ethical-cosmic centrality, Rabbi Hayim invokes the entire Jewish mystical tradition: the *Zohar*, the *Idra Zutra*, the *kabbalah* of Cordovera and Isaac Luria, the Divine Palaces (*Hekhalot*), Ezekiel's Throne of Glory and Holy Chariot (*Merkabah*), and so forth. He invokes these texts to reorient them.

The point is not simply that the *Nefesh Hahayim* is strewn with mystical references, but, to repeat, that it takes up these references in order to reverse their orientation. *The Soul of Life* moves not from God's power and goodness to human power and goodness, as do all prior sources, but from God's power and goodness to human power and goodness *back to* God's power and goodness. Human ethical behavior determines the orderliness of the cosmic order, its divinity:

> In the measure that we present to Him a smiling and happy face, in that measure there appears to us below His smiling and happy Face.[50]

> Thus God says to Israel . . . My connection with the worlds is entirely dependent, as it were, on the direction to which your

deeds point. . . . The Sages had this in mind when they said that "human worship is a necessity for the One Above."[51]

The real truth is . . . that the World to Come is actually identical with Man's own deeds; it is that portion which he expanded, added, and prepared by his own efforts.[52]

This orientation from man to God, we know, is precisely the orientation of Levinas's "face-to-face," where the movement of the one toward the other, of the subject subjected to the other who commands, an upright movement because an upward orientation, is nothing other than the movement "to-God."

The Correction: Reversal of the Reversal

It is clear, however, that an unchecked or simple reversal of the medieval orientation would tread dangerously close to the secular humanism of Ludwig Feuerbach, and to the subjectivisms and anthropomorphisms that so troubled Rosenzweig. This danger brings us to the second development of *The Soul of Life*.

An anthropological or subjectivist reading is obviated—in Hayim of Volozhin and later also in Levinas—by a subtle, even paradoxical, but all-important nuance: Elokim does *not* give up His mastery of all worlds in giving up mastery of all worlds to man. We must be very careful here. Elokim neither does nor does not give up mastery. Either alternative, either affirmation or denial, either "yea" or "nay", would by itself paralyze reason. Rabbi Hayim is reminding us of what reason cannot remember, but what the flesh-and-blood individual can somehow remember: Elokim does not *posit* man, He *created* man. Humankind begins, but does not have its origin in itself. Elokim *created* man, according to Rabbi Hayim, "*as though* he were actually master of the energy of those worlds." This *as though* or *as if* makes for all the difference.

Against—or "otherwise than"—the exclusions of traditional logic's "either . . . or," its excluded middle, God *both* retains for Himself *and* gives to man *all* His powers. Faithful to this overcharged "logic," to this ethical-religious dimension, Rabbi Hayim distinguishes—on quite a different plane than Kant—"God as he is for-Himself" and "God as he is for-man." The excess of one over the other is another reason, beyond the "borrowing" that Levinas so often acknowledges in relation to Descartes, for calling God "Infinite." Only infinite being can give away an infinity of being without in the least diminishing its own original infinity.[53]

The Levinasian Appropriation of the Subjunctive

What is crucial in Rabbi Hayim's distinction, as in all mysticism, and, we can now add, as in all ethics, is not simply the logical distinction between God-for-Himself and God-for-man, but the way the unity (*echod*) of God so distinguished is maintained. And this unity is maintained precisely through the ethical force of the "as though"—which is precisely the force Levinas understands *as* ethical force and names the "to-God." Man is created by God and at the same time man is an autonomous ethical agent insofar as he acts *as though* he himself, by his acts, were the irreplaceable—nonsubstitutable—center of the universe that his own acts create. It is precisely the subjunctive case that Levinas learns from Rabbi Hayim. The subject is the one who supports everything, including the insupportable. Here we can recall the words of Dostoyevsky that Levinas is so fond of quoting: "We are all guilty of all and for all men before all, and I more than the others."

Levinas and Rosenzweig can both agree with Rabbi Hayim when he writes: "At the time of Creation God fixed all the rules by which the worlds are regulated, in such a manner that they should depend upon the good or evil deed of man."[54] But for Rosenzweig this means that *to be good*, man should *imitate* God, while for Levinas it means that *in being good* man is making sacred history, service to God, *mitzot*.

The Levinasian sense in which the face is language,[55] then, is precisely its subjunctive sense. Face to face with the other person, the command of the other person comes "as though" the I were commanded by God. The I itself is through this same face-to-face relation *ordained* as a responsible I, just as through another face-to-face relation, in love, the Rosenzweigian individual moves from his character to his soul. The I is obligated to the other person infinitely, "as though" it were obligated to God. It is precisely the *as though* structure, joined to the orientation or movement from man to God, as in Rabbi Hayim of Volozhin, that is the face in Levinas. The "as though" (*comme si*) appears on almost every page of *Totality and Infinity*. It is perhaps the fundamental gesture of this demanding text, the "essence" of the ethics it proposes, the "saying of its said," even if *Totality and Infinity* never makes the grammar of this gesture explicit.

Many years later, in *De Dieu qui vient à l'idée*, Levinas takes up this topic explicitly. He writes: "We understand in the 'as though' the equivocation or the enigma of the non-phenomenal, the nonrepresentable: the testimony prior to thematization, testifying to a *'more' awakening-a-'less'-which-it-disturbs-or-inspires*, the 'idea of the infinite,' the 'God in me.' "[56] Such an "as though" derives, Levinas continues, not from the "uncertainty or simple resemblance of the philosophies of the *als ob*,"[57] nor, we can add, does it derive from any logic or metaphorics of Greco-Christian hermeneutics.[58]

The structure of the "as though" is also found, as Rabbi Hayim and Levinas are both well aware, in the peculiar hermeneutics of the rabbis of the Talmud. It is found, for instance, in the "method" of *kal ve-chomer* ("from the light in weight to the heavy"). Without sacrificing difference to identity or identity to difference, without submitting to the constraints of affirmation and denial, the "as though" (*kee lu*) maintains difference in identity. On this topic, in *The Slayers of Moses* Susan Handelman writes that the "as though" used in *kal ve-chomer* effects a "perception of resemblance despite difference (not a collapse of difference)," and "leads not to statements of predication . . . but to inclusion without identity. . . . Here resemblance never effaces difference, *as if* never becomes *is*."[59]

Just as man neither is God nor is not God, but is created in the image and likeness of God, and just as man neither is nor is not the creator of the universe, but acts *as though* he had divine creative power, the face of the other person neither is nor is not God's face—for God has no real face, no spatial or conceptual face. *Still*—a rejoinder that can only be effaced by will power, by the will to power—the face of the other person *nonetheless, enigmatically, paradoxically, disturbingly* "appears" *as though* it were God's face. It obligates infinitely, making the subject responsible, Levinas will say, for the very responsibility of the other person, even beyond the death of the subject, whether that death be my own mortality or the death of the other to whom I am bound.

Conclusion

What Rosenzweig means by "eternal *truth*" is the face in its relation to the divine, the human face that imitates the divine face. "To do justice and to love mercy," he writes on the last page of *The Star*[60] (using a phrase from Micah 6:8) one must come "to walk humbly with thy God." Justice and mercy follow from God. Rosenzweig's orientation is quite close to that of Levinas, but it is an all-important nuance away. For Levinas "to do justice and to love mercy" is also "to walk humbly with thy God," for walking humbly with God arises in the doing of justice and the loving of mercy. God is where there is justice and mercy. Or, to express this in a formula dear to Levinas and close to Rabbi Hayim of Volozhin, and close too to the transcending intention at the conclusion of *The Star*, to be face-to-face with the alterity of the other person, to be for-the-other-before-oneself, is to be for God, *à-Dieu*.

Part IV

Deconstructive

9

Freud, Husserl, Derrida:
An Experiment

Walter Lowe

In one provocative remark among many, Jacques Derrida classifies Husserlian phenomenology as an example of Western "metaphysics." But, he goes on to specify, it is a "metaphysics in its most modern, critical, and vigilant form."[1] We may characterize metaphysics as that mode of thinking which conceives of reality on the model of the object, entity or thing. Husserl, the arch-rationalist, rejected this "natural attitude" as naive—but so too does Derrida, the seeming irrationalist. Thus there arises the possibility of a certain convergence between these two thinkers regarding what it means to be truly vigilant and critical.

But there is about Derrida's procedures an irreducible strangeness. To deal with this, let us consider another figure who is more familiar, but who also tends to stick in the craw of common sense: Freud. Indeed, there is a certain affinity between these two. For Derrida's work may be read as a recent addition to the unsettling tradition, which Paul Ricoeur has termed "the hermeneutic of suspicion."[2] The challenges of the masters of suspicion like Freud and Nietzsche focused most particularly upon the "truth-claims" of religion. But here everything depends upon the understanding of "truth."

A certain continuity of Husserl and Derrida, a certain affinity of Derrida and Freud, and the issue of truth—these are the elements that I propose to bring together. It will be the wager of this chapter that such an experiment will contribute something to a new way to understand "the truth proper to religion." Accordingly, my procedure will be to move from a consideration of Freud (part 1), through an exploration of Husserl (part 2) and a critique of Husserl by Derrida (part 3), to a conclusion on the issue of truth (part 4).

Freudian Psychoanalysis and the Logic of Suspicion

Half the problem with psychoanalysis has always been getting clear on the exact extent of the truth-claims made in its name. In brief, schematic fashion, there are four possibilities. It may be said that (1) psychoanalysis claims to say everything about everything; (2) more modestly, it claims to say everything about something; (3) more modestly still, it claims to say something about something; and (4) finally and most intriguingly, it claims to say something about everything.

"Everything about everything" is the classic formulation of reductionism. Freud says that everything is sex, everything is phallic symbol or vaginal symbol—*tertium non datur*—and if you voice reservations, that is a sure sign of your own resistance. Freudianism thus appears as a closed, self-referencing system, a sort of metaphysic. Either one buys the whole program, at the price of intellectual capitulation, or one retains one's common sense and dismisses it altogether.

In contrast, the "everything about something" reading sees psychoanalysis as more circumspect. Every science has its proper object; Freud's achievement was to have brought to light a hitherto unrecognized object—namely, the unconscious. Obviously the unconscious is not everything, but it *is* something, and we in the twentieth century would be foolish to deny it altogether. Often this second approach is cast in the language of hierarchy: what Freud says holds true for certain lower aspects of human experience, but there are other, higher aspects as well, which cannot be explained away.

The third approach, "something about something," is an extension of the second. Once again the unconscious is acknowledged as a legitimate object or area of study, but now questions are raised as to the founder's adequacy even there. Freud is regarded as a sort of Columbus, for having set foot upon a new world, but also for having misnamed and misconstrued it. He was led astray, it is often said, by the Helmholtzian physics of his day. The antidote is an alternative hermeneutic, such as the existentialist or the Jungian.

What is striking in our account of the three approaches is how closely linked are the ways of defining Freud and the ways of responding to him. The moment you cast psychoanalysis in any one of these ways, the rest of the discussion seems to be foreordained. In the first case, it is simply a matter of dismissing the entire enterprise, perhaps by humor and irony, perhaps by turning it upon itself. In the second and third cases, it is a matter of exploiting the fact that psychoanalysis has been defined, in the root sense of the word: limits have been set to its validity. Attention quickly shifts to other matters.

The very predictability of these critiques of Freud may be enough to pique one's interest in something new. Certainly the fourth alternative, "something about everything," is remarkable in the extent to which it avoids a number of the moves observable in the other three. It does not portray psychoanalysis as seeking total control of the conceptual terrain; yet neither does it delimit a priori the conceptual space within which or about which psychoanalysis is allowed to speak. And this very fact, were the fourth alternative to prove valid, would help to explain the peculiar reception that has been accorded psychoanalysis. It would explain how, without its making the sort of truth-claim characteristic of an absolute reductionism, psychoanalysis could nevertheless seem to be reductionistic. After all, for the person on the receiving end, a psychoanalysis that proposed to say "something about everything" could very well *feel as if* it were claiming to say "everything about everything." For there would still be that peculiar insistence: it would always be there, it would presume to speak about even the most trivial matter. There would be no way of de-fining, no way of setting limits to it—no way of securing for oneself a safe and privileged space.

This, I want to suggest, is what it is like to be on the receiving end not simply of psychoanalysis, but of *any form of the hermeneutic of suspicion.* The interpretation is only an interpretation: *it claims only to say something about everything.* It is not a metaphysic; it only voices a suspicion. But the suspicion is insidious, it continually insinuates itself, it leaves no place to hide. Here, in the received impact of psychoanalysis, we have an important clue to the distinctive character of what Freud was about, a clue to what distinguishes the hermeneutic of suspicion from the apparent predecessors, such as mechanistic metaphysics, with which it is too freely confused.[3]

Having fashioned a minimal terminology with which to talk about Freud, we now need to do something similar with Husserl. Undoubtedly this effort, which will occupy the next two sections, will entail considerable simplification; and for the reader versed in phenomenology, it will mean going over familiar ground. But the very generality of the account may serve a purpose, in that it will provide a common language that can then be applied, as well, to Derrida.

Husserlian Phenomenology and Objectivity

It is a truism that the thought of Immanuel Kant represents a watershed for the modern discussion of religious belief and truth.

As to the exact nature of the Kantian influence, however, there is a good deal less agreement. Responses range from celebration to lament, and the voices of lamentation are often to the fore. It is commonly asserted that the new development that we find in Kant is a turn to the subject, a heightened awareness of the role that the subject plays in constituting human knowledge. The gain in such a turn is heightened self-awareness. But that gain has brought with it a grievous loss or misdirection, which is portrayed as one or more of the following: an obsession with questions of epistemology, an entrapment within the subject, and a disabling skepticism about the knowability of the object.

The castigation of Kant breathes a reassuring air of common sense. Certainly we know that there are things that actually exist and that, in the end, we should not let ourselves be bamboozled by hyperreflective introspection. But this common sense is utterly reliant upon the natural standpoint; it is shot through with unexamined assumptions. To set the framework for our argument, it is useful to state these assumptions as clearly as possible.

Reviewing in reverse order the points of a moment ago, the common assessment of Kant aims to reaffirm the reality and knowability of the object. Here it is important to state explicitly what would seem to require no comment: namely, that the critique focuses on an *entity*, the object. Indeed, its reaction against Kant's alleged overemphasis upon the subject leads it to focus upon that entity which is most clearly an entity. (The character of the subject, after all, is somewhat more ambiguous.) But once this focus and apparent clarity are assumed, the subject, too, is apt to be regarded as an entity—simply an entity of another sort. This is an altogether crucial move; yet it readily escapes notice because it is underwritten by an ostensibly self-evident framework assumed in the critique of Kant. When Kant is taxed with having skewed the subject/object balance, the very notion of such a balance implies some common structure, some common conceptual framework embracing both subject and object. The moment this has been assumed, only the greatest vigilance can prevent the subject from sharing the status of the object, viz. that of a thing among things.

However, should this be pointed out and should one seek to approach the subject in some alternative manner, the proposal will inevitably appear to the eyes of common sense and its metaphysics as an exaltation of the subject. The metaphysical framework of the dichotomy and then interrelationship of subject and object is tacitly regarded as a way, indeed the only way, of keeping subject and object in balance.

Thus it is appropriate to say that what is happening in the critique of Kant is that metaphysics is being allowed to preempt the entire discussion. The move seems from the natural standpoint so obvious as hardly to require mention, much less defense. But it dictates a priori that questions shall not be posed about the "interrelation-realm," the medial moment, and pursued in their own right. Indeed, it is difficult in metaphysics even to conceive what it would *mean* to pursue such an intermediate realm in its own right.[4]

The achievement of Husserlian phenomenology—contra the metaphysical critique of Kant—may be summarized in formulaic terms as a shift of focus from object to *objectivity*. For the natural standpoint a certain notion of the object predetermines what "objectivity" is. *The natural standpoint begins with the notion of an object existing independently "out there," and proceeds to define objectivity as just such a condition of out-there-ness.* Objectivity, understood as independence of the subject, becomes defined, in terms of a presupposed metaphysical framework, as existence "outside" the subject. The Husserlian strategy, faced with these assumptions, is not one of denying the reality of the object, nor even of denying the reality of the object conceived as existing independently "out there." Such a denial would still be metaphysics, albeit in a negative mode. Rather the strategy is simply to hold the entire question of "outside" existence in abeyance.

It is in one sense a very modest act, this Husserlian bracketing. It does not prejudge; it is in fact the very essence of *not* prejudging. It simply disengages from the metaphysical framework. Yet in its very modesty it is a resistance and a refusal—a refusal that elicits a shudder within the natural standpoint. For viewed from within that standpoint, the Husserlian abstention is an incursion of strangeness and a removal of security. It must seem, from within that standpoint, that Husserl, in displacing from its defining position the "independent" status of the object, has removed the one sure guarantor of objectivity. And the natural misgivings can only be heightened when he proceeds to relocate objectivity in the closest correlation with the activity of the subject. It must seem, then, that he is headed ineluctably in the direction of idealist self-enclosure.

I dwell upon this strangeness and shuddering, this apprehension before a position that may well prove arbitrary and enclosed, because it suggests how the impact of Husserl—the rationalist, the champion of the scientific spirit—can be like that of Derrida. It suggests the possibility of engaging the two thinkers not at the point of their obvious dissimilarities, but at the point of their received impact, which is the point where each is most "critical and vigilant." In effect, Husserl proposes a wager: it is that *objectivity could have a breadth beyond the metaphysical notion of out-there-ness, a breadth yet to be explored.*[5] It is that possibility which guides and justifies the considerable labor of phenomenology.

How, then, does Husserl propose to bring forward an alternative understanding of objectivity? His solution is to observe, in effect, that when one sets aside the notion of objectivity defined in quasi-spatial terms, as existence "out there," it is still quite possible to understand objectivity by reference to time—namely, as invariance across time and, more specifically, as invariance across a series of "imaginative variations." A classic example is the geometric figure of the circle. In and through various imperfect and transitory representations, one grasps a single concept, which is that of the circle. Something analogous may be said of the word: we write "circle" and we speak it; we find it in a variety of accents and scripts, and may imagine a greater variety still. And yet in and through those particularities, we understand a single meaning. The compelling character of this sense—here the geometric example is especially apt—cannot be reduced to mere convention. "A meaning can be treated *as* self-identical only because it *is* self-identical."[6]

This *invariance of sense*, this transcendence of contingent fact, constitutes Husserl's first and fundamental understanding of *objectivity*; as such, it informs and determines his other, derivative understandings. Its importance cannot be stressed too much. Certainly in proposing such a notion Husserl went against common sense, exposing himself to the charge of Platonism. But it was Husserl's firm conviction that without such invariance, common sense and the European sciences along with it made no sense: both stood powerless in the face of cultural crisis. Only through a robust reappropriation of the original Greek vision, for which Platonism is by rights a proud title, could European culture rebound from its failure of nerve. Thus it is that *in Husserl invariance of sense provides a foundational notion of objectivity*, which allows one to speak derivatively of the objectivity of the noema. Then, based upon the objectivity of the noema, one proceeds to certain specific cases, cases in which "what is experienced has the sense *'transcendent' being. . . . "*[7] And it is this latter sense that prompts one to speak more derivatively of the object as existing "out there."

This, then, is the process by which the object "out there" is dethroned, relieved of the perogative of dictating the meaning of objectivity. Instead, *object "out there" appears as a tertiary, derivative subset within a larger, more inclusive, "objectivity."* Skeptics will object, however, that the Husserlian strategy is only a conjurer's trick and that, far from resolving the issue, it has made matters worse. For this inclusive objectivity, it will be charged, is paradoxically no more than something "within" consciousness. The endless examination of the contents of consciousness and the continual postponement of the lifting of the phenomenological brackets amount to solipsism of a more subtle and seductive form.

The response to this objection must be twofold. The first point is to acknowledge, indeed to affirm, that it was never a part of Husserl's purpose to demonstrate the existence of an "outside world." Rather, assuming such an objectivity, he asked, "How are we to understand the fact that the intrinsic being of objectivity becomes 'presented,' 'apprehended' in knowledge, and so ends up by becoming subjective?"[8] In short, "the point is not to secure objectivity but to understand it."[9]

But beyond this, the second response must be to call into question the terms of the objection. For we misconstrue the Husserlian project—or at least fail to take it on its own terms—the moment we say "within consciousness" in such a way as to suggest that consciousness itself is an entity lying alongside other entities. And we only elaborate the misconstruction when we speak of consciousness itself as containing a series of entities, called "mental objects," which stand in uncertain relationship to other things outside. This is not so much an objection as an unreflective return to metaphysics. Yet it is a distortion that can readily take hold within phenomenology itself. To forestall it, one must energetically affirm that the act of phenomenological bracketing does not give us a new set of objects as such; rather it enables us to inquire into objects' "subjective manners of givenness, i.e. into *how* an object . . . exhibits itself."[10] We attend to *the way in which* the whole range of already familiar objects appears or is presented. And similarly it must be stressed that the *whole* range of objects is so inspected; there is not some *other* range, set apart somewhere beyond.

These points are quite obviously crucial if phenomenology is to be accorded the courtesy of being understood, at least initially, on its own terms. What is remarkable is how similar they are to the points I made earlier, when I sought to understand psychoanalysis on *its* own terms. To recast the present discussion in the earlier terminology: phenomenology does not purport to say everything about everything—that is, to reduce all of reality to (a function of) consciousness. But neither does phenomenology confine itself to saying something (or everything) about a restricted region—that is, about those things that are within consciousness as opposed to other things without. Rather it undertakes precisely to say something, having to do with the mode of presentation, about everything (that is presented).

We thus have an intriguing formal similarity between two modes of investigation, which are in many ways antithetical: between phenomenology, which seeks to save the phenomena, and psychoanalysis, which receives all phenomena with suspicion and seeks to look behind. I wish to argue that this similarity is by no means accidental, but that it signals the possibility of a more meaningful encounter between the two perspectives.

For assistance toward that goal we now turn to Derrida, from whom we may anticipate a critique of Husserl as well as clarification of the logic of suspicion.

Derrida's Critique of Husserl

We have seen how invariance of sense constitutes the foundational level of Husserl's understanding of objectivity. Husserl is of course aware that, in point of fact, this invariant sense is commonly conveyed by a material mark or sound. But for Husserl the principal implication of this fact is that the sense must therefore be clearly distinguished from the variable and per se inchoate matter, which is its vehicle. "When we normally express something, we do not, *qua* expressing it, live in the acts constituting the expression as a physical object . . . but we live in the acts which give it sense."[11]

These Husserlian premises already provide the necessary foothold for an abbreviated form of Derridian deconstruction. For the position invites two conceptual moves, both of which have become hallmarks of deconstructive criticism. The first is *a distrust of emphatic distinctions or oppositions*, which the deconstructionist suspects are born of a desire to protect the purity of one member of the distinction from being compromised by the other. Such a distinction so maintained is well on the way to becoming a hierarchy. The second deconstructive move is indeed *a distrust of hierarchy*: a determination to show in a case-by-case manner how the "higher" element in various purported hierarchies not only depends upon, but in the proponent's textual practice actually becomes confused with, the "lower" element from which it pretends to insulate itself.[12] A good deal of deconstruction can indeed be accounted for in these terms.

What would a deconstructive critique of Husserl look like? It is remarkable that, contrary to the irrationalist image often applied to deconstruction, Derrida's critique is one that *sides with the significance of sense*—witness his starting point, which is not unlike that of Paul Ricoeur. The latter observes: "consciousness is doubly intentional, in the first instance by virtue of being a signification and in the second instance by virtue of being an intuitive fulfilling."[13] Derrida makes a similar distinction, noting a *"formalist"* and an *"intuitionist"* moment in Husserl's phenomenology. And so far from lamenting the former, Derrida is intensely concerned to keep it from being lost within the embrace of the latter:

> We know that the act of meaning, the act that confers *Bedeutung* (*Bedeutungsintention*), is always the aim of a relation with an object. But it is enough that this intention animates the body of a signifier for speech to take place. The fulfillment of the aim by an intuition is not indispensable. It belongs to the original structure of expression to be able to dispense with the full presence of the object aimed at by intuition.[14]

In simplest terms, the implication of the *formalist* aspect of Husserl's thought is that "one can speak without knowing."[15] Speak—*and make sense*—without knowing! So put, the notion is contrary to common sense; and it is quickly covered over by the other, intuitionist aspect of Husserl's thought. Yet it is precisely in the contra-intuitive insight that Derrida locates *the distinctive achievement of Husserl the logician* "against the whole philosophical tradition."[16]

To understand how this is so, we must look to Husserl's First Investigation, which Derrida credits with having surmounted the "aporias or absurdities" of "all the classical theories of language" by dint of its clear, insistent delination of the difference between intention (of sense or meaning) and intuitive fulfillment (of that intention) by the presence of an object. Derrida observes that this delineation involves another foundational distinction.

> [Husserl made] the distinction between *Widersinnigkeit* and *Sinnlosigkeit*. If it obeys certain rules, an expression may be *widersinnig* (contradictory, false, absurd according to a certain kind of absurdity) without ceasing to have an intelligible sense that permits normal speech to occur, without becoming nonsense (*Unsinn*). It may have no possible object for empirical reasons (a golden mountain) or for *a priori* reasons (a square circle) without ceasing to have an intelligible sense, without being *sinnlos*.

In other words, "the absence of an object (*Gegenstandlosigkeit*)"—that is, the absence of an object given to intuition—"is hence not the absence of meaning (*Bedeutungslosigkeit*)."[17] To have brought this forth is Husserl's distinctive accomplishment.

Yet the entire effect of Husserl's theory of truth is to cover over this very point. For his understanding of truth is steadfastly oriented toward a *telos* of intuition, fulfillment. Thus Husserl writes:

> If "possibility [of intuition]" or "truth" is lacking, an assertion's intention can only be carried out symbolically: it cannot derive any "fulness" from intuition or from the categorial functions performed on the latter, in which "fulness" its value for knowledge consists. It then lacks, as one says, a "true," a "genuine" meaning (*Bedeutung*).[18]

In short, in Husserl's own work the ground that is gained by Husserl's logic—"the purification of the formal"—is surrendered forthwith to "a concept of *sense* which is itself determined on the basis of *a relation with an object.*"[19]

Earlier we experienced some of the shudder Husserl evoked within the natural standpoint. Now we may be observing something similar within the Husserlian phenomenology, a tremor occasioned in part by strangeness and in part by recognition of one's own distinctive yet only half-acknowledged commitments.[20] Henry Staten observes that, like Husserl's bracketing of the existence of the object, *Derrida's crucial move* of thinking representation *as such*, apart from fulfillment by the object, *constitutes a sort of wager*. Its fruitfulness and legitimacy can be judged only in the trying:

> [The proposal] to think representation *as such*, the essence of standing-for short of what is stood-for, performs a conceptual operation that is, considered in isolation, a new way of looking at things, comparable in a way to the new operation by which Husserl attained the phenomenological standpoint, and the question "Is it valid?" must be suspended while we consider the full scope of the possibilities it opens.[21]

It is, moreover, *a considered wager*, arising from a close reading of Husserlian texts and *seeking to secure the gain, the extension of the realm of sense*, effected by the text.

Specifically, Derrida's proposal may be regarded as a cogent clarification of Husserl's seminal liberation of sense or meaning from dependence upon, and confusion with, the presence of the *object*. This is the gist of the Derridean critique of "presence," where presence is anything—sense datum, spirit, whatever—that asks to be considered self-explanatory, a final recourse, having meaning in and of itself. The role of final recourse is commonly assigned to the "simply given," the object. It thus becomes possible to argue that, so far from being arbitrary, Derrida's move away from the supporting entity or object reaches toward a deeper truth, a deeper objectivity.

The Question of Truth

It is understandable that one would wish for some combination of Husserl and Derrida; after all, Derrida himself affirms that deconstruction is not self-sufficient but always "parasitic" upon another text. If we are to take either of the two thinkers seriously, however, it is altogether crucial that we avoid the temptation of a comfortable eclecticism. In the end I too will suggest a combination of sorts. But I hope to do so in such a way as to honor the mandate with which we began—that one be ever vigilant and critical regarding the covert metaphysics of the natural attitude or common sense.

What seems to me decisive is the time-honored criterion for resolving philosophical disputes—the criterion of comprehensiveness. Put simply, Derrida can include more of Husserl's truth than Husserl can of Derrida's.

Husserlian phenomenology is convinced that all sense, to be sense, must be coherent, must finally be one. Hence what is not conceivable on Husserlian premises is the notion of an irreducibly *other* sense. Yet this is what Derrida proposes. He proposes an extension of sense; thus his position may be regarded as not irrational and as the more comprehensive. But the extension goes so far as to propose a sense which is irreducibly other, a sense inseparable from the variable, inchoate matter which is its "vehicle." This Derridean inclusion—the finding of sense in puns, free associations and chance juxtapositions—must seem from a Husserlian perspective to be arbitrary, perverse, a pursuit of literary effect for its own sake.

But *if* one shifts perspective, it is possible to share Derrida's incredulity before a phenomenology that acts "as though literature, theatre, deceit, infidelity, hypocrisy, infelicity, parasitism, and the simulation of real life were not part of real life."[22] For Derrida, these things are, one must emphasize, a part of *real* life: they are not just secondary matters that could finally, by a methodology, be discounted. This is the basis, I am suggesting, for deconstruction's greater comprehensiveness. While Husserl cannot make sense of the Derridean proposal, Derrida *can* make sense of the Husserlian refusal.

Alongside this relative endorsement of Derrida, however, I wish to set a further affirmation. It seems to me that Derrida's own approach finally makes sense only within the context of *a fundamental struggle about "truth"*—and specifically within the area of debate opened up by Kant's transcendental turn, more recently represented by Husserl's phenomenology. Given limitations of space here, I will argue this thesis only briefly.

Lately a certain rejection of "foundationalist" thought has become widespread in the field of religious studies: so much so that it would be difficult nowadays to find any mainstream figure who would *want* to be called foundationalist. Now these rejections of foundationalism invariably present themselves as a more sophisticated, more critical awareness. But it must be said that many such rejections are not truly "vigilant," and thus not truly critical. For they regard the foundationalist project as readily identifiable and patently absurd; an illusion to be broken, there is little need for vigilance against it, once it has been disavowed.

This giving up on the foundationalist project, this simple letting go, is worthy neither of the transcendental tradition nor of deconstructionism. It is not worthy of the former because it fails to comprehend that for Kant and Husserl—what virtually defines their common effort—is that philosophy could be foundational *because* it is truly critical; its being critical is inseparable from its effort after foundations. Husserl cautioned in a moving passage that "Europe's greatest danger is weariness."[23] One senses in disavowals of the foundationalist effort the complaint that it is just too difficult.

Nor is the disavowal worthy of the best of deconstruction, which is exemplary in its determination to be vigilant. A Derridean approach realizes that what is disavowed cannot be simply disavowed; that it reappears in subtle and unexpected guises; and that it is therefore essential to exercise a certain suspicion.

The greatest obstacle to a careful consideration of Derrida is the reading of him, common among advocates and detractors alike, which understands him as saying that, in the end, all we have is language. Language in this instance is understood as a series of conventions and constructs, a succession of more or less useful metaphors. Once we realize this is all there is, it is said, we are no longer held captive by the chimera of some objective truth; we are free to enter unreservedly into the realm of metaphor.

There are indeed passages in Derrida that seem to encourage

such an interpretation. In the essay on "Structure, Sign, and Play in the Discourse of the Human Sciences," he distinguishes "two interpretations of interpretation." The first, represented in that essay by structuralism, "has dreamed of full presence, the reassuring foundation, the origin and the end of play." The second has entered unreservedly into "the Nietzschean *affirmation*, that is the joyous affirmation of the play of the world, . . . the affirmation of a world of signs without fault, without truth and without origin which is offered to an active interpretation."[24]

In terminology that has become widespread, the first interpretation is still merely "modern," still tied to the Enlightenment; only the second position moves beyond that, to the "postmodern."[25] The lines just quoted may well seem to invite one to the latter.

But on the following page Derrida makes his intent quite clear: "I do not believe that today there is any question of *choosing*." Rather, given the difference and the irreducibility of the two positions, "we must first try to conceive of the common ground, and the *différance* of this irreducible difference."[26]

This neglected statement can serve us, I believe, as *a point of reference for an understanding of truth*. For the statement has two salient characteristics: it refuses to choose, and it seeks for "the common ground." The refusal to choose is not a simple entry into free play; there remains the quest for common ground.

The situation may be illumined by reference to the typology with which we considered psychoanalysis. The first three positions were variously efforts to define, and thus to delimit, the spheres in which psychoanalysis would and would not apply. But there was something about psychoanalysis that resisted this setting of boundaries and was thus unsettling to the Enlightenment mind. Yet this elusive quality is not one that would be explained by the alternative, "postmodern" view. Certainly it is tempting to suppose that psychoanalysis says "something about everything" because it constitutes a hermeneutical framework, a way of looking at things, a series of powerful metaphors. But that leaves unaddressed the question of why this particular set of "metaphors" should be so powerful, so unsettling.[27]

The reason, in simplest terms, is that psychoanalysis has hit on a fundamental *truth*—that there is an irreducible elusiveness and tension at the heart of finite reality; that the sought-for foundation of all things is not univocal. This is the truth of "undecidability." It holds true for all texts, for all language, for all existence. This is why psychoanalysis says "something about everything." Undecidability is reflected in that between Husserl's truth and the (distinctively) Derridean truth there is no question of choosing. *Glas*, with its bell-like movement, swinging between two columns of text, aims to convey and confirm this undecidability.

But this also means that if one resists choosing, it is because undecidability is not just a choice but *an objective condition*, a state of affairs. In *Positions* Derrida speaks of "writing" in the radical sense as "the common root of writing and speech," and of "différance" as "the common root of all the oppositional concepts."[28] The notion of that sort of common root is not impossible, it is merely difficult: difficult in the sense suggested by Heidegger—not the Heidegger of the philosophy of presence, but the Heidegger of "equiprimordiality." It is this way of envisioning the common ground that makes Derrida's position the more comprehensive. Thus Derrida need not exclude Husserl's quest for a univocal sense. After all, Derrida himself is questing for the common ground, which is in some sense a quest for the univocal. All he needs to exclude (or undermine) is Husserl's own a priori exclusion of the possibility of an other sense.

For all that may be said about Derrida's Jewishness, there is still about his thought something profoundly Western and Greek. He partakes of the tradition of truth as "unveiledness"—when that tradition is coupled with the affirmation that the revealing is at the same time a concealing, and that truth loves to hide itself.

These too are Heideggerian themes; and a great deal of Derrida's thought may be understood as a series of tactics for taking the concealing with radical seriousness, as Heidegger did not, while never giving up on the quest for unconcealment. There is more than a suggestion of the Greek conception of Fate in Derrida's understanding of discourse as an event in which sense and "nonsense," "chance and necessity, arbitrary and motivated, converge"— witness the way in which he sees a person's life as encrypted in the proper name the person happens to have been given. His thought breathes as much of tragedy as of bacchanale.

What could this import for the question of "the truth proper to religion"? The postmodernist position realized that truth, as hidden, is not something that can be grasped. It concluded that the question of truth must therefore *be let go*. But what it failed to realize is that the *question* of truth is more than a question: it is a reality. And it is a reality which has hold of *us*.

Part V

Transcendental

10

Divine Truth in Husserl and Kant:
Some Issues in Phenomenological Theology

James G. Hart

This paper is a dialogue between Kant and Husserl with the interest weighted, perilously perhaps, more in the clarification of some matters in Husserl. It can also be seen as a footnote to Iso Kern's monumental and pioneering *Husserl und Kant*, and to Steven Laycock's rich essay in this volume as well as his fine new book, *Foundations for a Phenomenological Theology.*[1]

1. Introduction: the Divine Entelechy

All absolute being is a stream of teleologically concordant becoming directed toward ideal goals. (This, of course, is not becoming in an empirical sense.) This is the one stream of "divine" being; and God is the entelechy, or the pure form, toward which the ontological development strives in the drive of its *eros.* But this form is an idea but still the all present effective power in all being [B I 4, pp. 52ff.]

Husserl's philosophical theology may perhaps be said to center on his concept of "the divine entelechy." Although this notion was never an explicit theme in the published writings or the enormous *Nachlass*—here it is referred to about fifteen times—there is perhaps reason to promote it to the status of an "operative" notion (to borrow Eugen Fink's term)—that is, one that functions unthematically in many basic discussions.

The issue of the divine entelechy in Husserl recalls most obviously Aristotle, who first coined the term. Indeed, the multivalence of the term in Aristotle recurs in Husserl. Let me very briefly point to some of the issues here with no pretense of doing full justice to them.

It would seem that there are at least two basic senses in Aristotle. The first has to do with what Aristotle means by "actuality"— the usual English translation of *entelecheia*. This gives expression to Aristotle's view that being in the most proper sense is a complete unity (cf. *De Anima*, 412b 8ff.). The completion and unification are related to one another in accord with the kind of being under consideration. The more perfect the being, the more its completion (*telos*) and unity are essential to it and inseparable from it. Here the end or completion (*telos*) is not the termination or cessation but rather its purpose or goal; the completion is the culminating perfection of the thing.

Thus the three words that the neologism brings together— *hechein* (having), *telos* (end), and *en* (within)—may be initially rendered as "having the goal immanently." In Aristotle's primary sense "entelechy" derives from the consideration of the action accomplished or brought to its term in contrast to an action that is in the course of being realized. Thus entelechy (actuality) is *the perfection characteristic of the achievement* or the actual complete unity.

Yet there is a second but not disconnected sense of entelechy: the form (*eidos*), or *the inherent principle of structure* or specific intelligibility that *enables a determinate actualization of a power.* Here entelechy refers to a formal-essential actuality that functions as the actuation of *hylē* and is therefore in regard to this functioning not yet complete or fully actual. Toward that end it works immanently in the realization of that *telos* or perfection. Entelechy in this sense is like actually possessed knowledge that precedes new acts of knowing.

Husserl's writings contain at least these two senses of entelechy—that is, perfect being as actuality and the formal-essential principle of actuation (of a potentiality). On the one hand, the divine entelechy is infinite perfection in the ideal teleological realm; in this sense it is all that it can be. Here, it is comparable to the "regulative idea" in Kant. But on the other hand, it also has a "constitutive" function as the formal principle of actuation in the monadic realm. Thus the topic of the divine entelechy emerges in Husserl in two interconnected meditations. One concerns the regulative idea (see #2 ff. below). The other concerns the constitutive function (see #3). What is at issue here is the conditions of reason as they emerge at the foundations of so-called inner-time consciousness and passive synthesis. The issue of "divine truth" (#4) is a further development of entelechial causality, granting the assumption that the divine entelechy is a kind of personal consciousness.

2. The Regulative Idea and Divinity

In order initially to get a handle on how the concept of "entelechy"—and eventually the topic of "divine truth"—emerges in a Husserlian context, it seems best that we begin with the Kantian notion of the regulative idea.

The regulative idea for Kant is to be contrasted with the constitutive idea. The latter, as a principle of the understanding, determines the object directly given in experience. Thus substance, cause, accident, and so forth, as principles of the understanding are constitutive ideas of what we experience. The regulative idea, on the other hand, does not create concepts of objects given in experience, but rather generates an ordering and ideal unification of the concepts that understanding has generated. The regulative idea thus determines the systematic unity of all experience, and therefore does not enjoy the determinateness of constitutive ideas but rather a measure of indefiniteness. As regulative, it gives us rules to go further on unto infinity and thereby provides us with endless tasks for conceptual and practical determination of the field of experience. As neo-Kantians put it, the regulative idea presents us with a task to be done and is not something already present (*ist uns aufgegeben, nicht gegeben*).

Kant anticipates Husserl's integration of the regulative idea into the co-meant, co-given, but not directly meant and given, *horizon of experience* when he discusses how reason provides understanding its field through principles, which integrate the manifold of experienced objects with higher-order conceptual unities and which, in turn, integrate the individuals, species, and regions in higher order genera and eventually in one same logical field suffused with affinity and continuity (*Critique of Pure Reason* [CPR], B686ff.).

Kant here uses the notion of horizon to illustrate how an infinite number of things can be surveyed from a given standpoint. This then provides a model for how a unifying higher-order concept can form a common horizon or logical space that unites and systematizes an endless number of subordinate concepts/logical spaces, which, in turn, themselves arrange an endless number of concepts subordinate to them. Thereby:

> As from a common centre, they can all be surveyed; and from this higher genus we can proceed until we arrive at the highest of all genera, and so at the universal and true horizon, which is determined from the standpoint of the highest con-

224 PHENOMENOLOGY OF THE TRUTH PROPER TO RELIGION

cept and which comprehends under itself all manifoldness—
genera, species, and subspecies [B687].

For Kant, the self as a systematic unity of all experience, nature or
world, and God were examples of such highest ideas.

For Husserl—at least in the central case of "world"—Kant
made a mistake, one that he should have seen if he attended to his
example of horizon:

> Now Kant teaches in an insistent manner that the world is no
> object of possible experience—whereas we, on the other hand,
> are always speaking with complete earnestness of the world
> precisely as the universal object of an experience which is uni-
> versally extended and one which is to be universally encom-
> passing (*universal gespannten und zu spannenden Erfahrung*).[2]

Hursserl insists that *things are always experienced from out of the world;*
world and things are inseparable inasmuch as each same thing is a
member of the universal identity-synthesis of all validly experienced
samenesses.[3]

But things (i.e., spatial-temporal realities) themselves are given
to us *as regulative ideas:* they are the apperceived identical same,
which, though not adequately given, are manifest through a possibly endless flux of profiling perspectives (*Ideas*, I, #149). And although there is no single experience in which the particular thing—
for example, my Ford—is given adequately in its fulness, yet it may
be said to be co-given and co-meant as that of which the profiles are
aspects. Each perspective contains within it a rule or an indication
for further advancement toward the realization of the ideal (full, adequate) revelation of that of which it is a perspective. Each perspective is at once an incremental fulfillment of an infinite task as well
as an indication of the possible perspectives still outstanding.[4]
Things thus are rules of possible appearances—that is, they are a
unity of a manifold of appearings, which come together in a regulated way:

> Were we to deny that the world as world were able to be ex-
> perienced then we would have to deny the same for each indi-
> vidual thing. For, on the one hand, it is at each time perceived
> but, disregarding its worldly surrounding, it itself is only
> present with horizons of unknown aspects. Each experience
> leaves it open that of the same real thing there might still be
> able to be experienced novelty.[5]

Clearly for Husserl the world is no more *an* object of experience than the profiles of things are objects of experience; but this comparison misses something crucial: *the world as horizon is that of which one is always aware when one is aware of something.* Thus the world is not one object among others. Rather, because it is the absolutely unique horizon of all objects, it admits of no plurality—as profiles and objects do.[6] There is only one world; and all efforts to show a manifold of worlds, radical contextual shifts, and the like, can make sense to us only by finding a place within the total unique horizon of our understanding.

May we say that the infinitely determinable fringe or horizon is *the same as* "the idea?" Experiencing world is experiencing the fringe or horizon of perception as determinable, as a field of possible acts of determination. But appreciating world as "idea" is experiencing this horizon as having been already determined by oneself and beckoning endlessly and inexhaustibly to further determinations.

The world as an infinite idea is also occasionally referred to as a pole. As the correlate of the I-pole, the world-pole is the ultimate referent, center of cohesion, founding base of assertions, and invariant context of what is present.

In one of many discussions in which "world" is fused with the "infinite idea," Husserl once noted that the experience of the world involves structures without which this experience would be senseless. That is, "the world has sense only as a filled meaning and it itself is the idea of filled meaning, the idea of the all-comprehensive system of constitutive self-givenness."[7] This does not mean that the world is given in a filled intention; rather, the world, as the emptily intended horizon, is the idea of filled meaning as the correlate of the systematic intention of the world.

Idea and the Two Types of Essence

As is well known, Kant placed the necessities of the structures of the world in the categories of understanding. Especially problematic is what status Kant gave to his presentation of these categories and transcendental criticism. Before I turn to this matter I wish immediately to attend to some Husserlian distinctions, some of which (as we shall see), because of their necessity, will hold for all kinds of knowing, even the divine—a view, of course, that Kant, as we shall also see, could not accept.

For Husserl, as for Kant, concepts are the way we organize a manifold of presentations into a unity that is not a mere aggregate but a rule-giving unity. For Husserl these concepts themselves may be considered as ways of taking these presentations. Depending on whether they enjoy a kind of necessity, they may be promoted to the status of essence or *eidos*. Although essences come to light in the ways humans in community organize the experience of the world, *empirical* essences are occasional to a particular historical society's experience. Indeed, we grasp the distinctive identity of a people when we grasp those empirical essences without which we cannot imagine the particular people to be or have been. Consider, for example, how particular cultures have been or are distinguished by having pervading types as nun and monk, wage-laborer, commodity, virus, religious mendicant, presidential primary, ether, bull markets, *polis*, pogrom, police, black humor, Madison Avenue hype, dragon, shaman, soothsayer, witch, wizard, dream time, shunning, toxic waste, and the like. Although we might find universal and necessary categories to handle some of these examples, at least in part—for example work, society, rhetoric, anomalies, natural causes—still these historical specifications of these alleged universal genera, in terms of the "world as such" or in terms of the essentials of the human organization of the world, are not universal and necessary.

In contrast to these empirical essences Husserl contrasts pure or strict morphological essences. These would not be occasional to a people and would be invariants of all subjectivities and all organizations of "world." The necessity and universality of such pure "morphological essences" is most evident when they are tied to those regional concepts that delineate the ultimate framework for intersubjectivity's world-constitution.[8] This mode of "being in the world" is always either a perceiving, an apperceiving, or an appresenting: an agency toward and experience of nature as the all of bodies, an agency toward and experience of living-sentiment beings and toward persons or centers of I-acts, an agency toward and experience of the cultural world of idealities as humanized nature. Each of these fundamental modes of intentionality is characterized by guiding rules for the course of involvement with bodies, animate-sentient things, personal-rational consciousnesses, and the founded idealities that these consciousnesses have produced with their higher-order rules—that is, "culture." These regional rules are consitutive of the way humans are in the world. Ultimately the rule-structure of every object as an instance of an essence is an index for the rule-structure of transcendental subjectivity.[9]

In apperceiving, the flux of profiles follows the rule of a spatial-temporal same-whole wherein the relation of the profiled parts to the whole are determined by the kind (contiguous or continuous, gaseous or solid) of spatial-temporal body-thing in a causal nexus.

In the appresenting (of sentient beings and persons) the flux of profiles follows the rule of a spatial-temporal same whole within a causal nexus for which the milieu and the other percipients are "there" within a field of cognition and agency. Thus the profiles are not mere parts of an apperceived spatial-temporal whole of a certain kind, but what is manifest is a *lived* body as the "there" of manifestation and in which the profiles are also *expressions* of a percipient center. And, in the case of the founded idealities (humanized nature or objective spirit), the profiles follow the rule of being embodiments of already achieved performances of absent persons who, in spite of the nonappresentable presence of these performances, have the power to *indicate* the appropriate modes of apperceiving and agency, and so forth, for the one coming into contact with them.

The encounter with the unfamiliar and anomalous species—like black holes, quasars, slugs, angels, gods, and Stonehenge—is always prepared for by the predelineation or rulelike guidelines tied to the ultimate regions that define the basic situation in which transcendental subjectivity must act and the basic frames for experiencing the world.

If we determine "essence" of any kind whatsoever as an invariant type in the flux of experience, and if we further maintain that the invariant type is established in passive association constituting a horizon of familiarity—that is, sameness, similarity, likeness, and so on—we might be inclined to deny a distinction between empirical and morphological essences. But free imaginative variation—the thought experiments by which we press the essences to see what variation of properties they will tolerate (e.g., are *promises* such that robots or squirrels can make them?)—enables a distinction between types that are invariant to a people and types without which there would be no experienced human world at all.

The latter generic types are spatial-temporal thing, sentient or living thing, person, and cultural ideality. The pure essence is evident not only in the analysis of the invariant regions of the world, and the world as the invariant context of these invariants, but also in the analysis of the kinds of experiencing that the passive-associative typifying itself is or presupposes— that is, perception, apperception, empathic appresentation (of others), and the founded apperception (apperception of apperceptions mediated by appresentations) that cultural things are.

It is in the reflective attitude of the reduction that there is disclosed the a priori correlation between these generic types, which Husserl calls the regional concept and on occasion "idea," and the

basic kinds of experience or attitudes (*Stellungnahmen*). These encompassing genera, not the specific morphological essences, are the
focus of material ontological analyses that found the basic sciences
of physics, biology, psychology, sociology, and history.

Change or constancy is always within the framing regional
concept, which is the fundamental kind of world-relating. Regardless of the content of perception there is always a "thing" as a
spatial-temporal sameness with spatial-temporal perspectival differences. We cannot learn that there are "things" from experience, because all learning as a bringing of differents under a spatial-
temporal same, or as recognizing amid the same spatial-temporal
differents, presupposes a prior acquaintance with "things." All content of perception is incidental to this framing "idea." Persons, in
this sense, are encompassed under the regional concept of things.
(Yet Husserl also speculates on an a priori presence of others which
presumably would have to be presupposed in all human kinds of
learning.[10]) When we take the thing as a person, however, we are
within a new (founded) way of experiencing, a new kind of intentionality. Here all individual and types of persons are incidental to
this framing idea. And the anomalies are experienced as such in
relation to the frame constituted by appresentation. If the "person"
turns out to be a robot, a mannequin, or a plant, we do not make
adjustments within the appresentational intending but rather we
abandon this kind intentionality—that is, move to apperception of
things or to the unique apperception of a cultural ideality, as in the
case of a product of technology.

We may now recall Husserl's distinction between *exact* and
morphological essences.[11] Exact essences are the ideal formations
that preoccupy the mathematical and natural sciences. Their genesis
is the world of perceptual experience wherein emerge forms,
shapes, and features that we idealize by projecting to an ideal limit.
Thus, for example, a surface with its share of knots, waves, and
bumps is imaginatively smoothed out to an ever-greater flatness, to
an unimaginable conceptualization, which results in "the plane" of
geometry. Although imagination does not presence the ideal limit
but only the approximations, we can define the ideal limit conceptually and thereby entertain it as free and independent of the approximations. Now we have a perfect exact identity (a plane, a
point, a line), which has perfect ideality. As such its objectivity, or
the kind of public meaning it has (as the same for all), is free from
contrasting points of view of situated humans. When we study exact essences we are taken up with these "absolute" objectivities and
are unmindful of either their genesis or the achievement of the ide-

alizing imagination that holds them in being. The exact essences and their components with which geometers and natural scientists deal—a parallelogram, a cone, a vortex, a hypotenuse, an ideal gas, a frictionless state, a Newtonian ray of light, an ideally efficient steam engine, a perfect vacuum—are what they are and there is nothing we can do to change them.

Further, as ideal limits they do not admit of more or less or better or worse states. To such invariant ideal entities, as Aristotle noted, the good, as the principle that is the "wherefore" of change and movement, is of no relevance.[12] These exact essences, however, are not found in the flux of experience, whether self-reflective experience or experience of the world. Rather, they emerge in the observation of the world as having features approximating ideals. We cannot make present the exact essences except through the idealizing of these approximations into absolute idealities. Thus the entertaining of the ideal unimaginable objectivities is not separable from the imagined approximations that serve as the basis of the idealizing to the unimagined *focus imaginarius*.[13]

The exact essence in one respect is a kind of Kantian idea. For our purposes here we can distinguish the essentially adequately given idea from the essentially inadequately given idea or the essentially closed and perfect ideas from the essentially open ones. The first is the *result* of an infinite imaginative intentionality, which achieves a complete ideality with its unimaginable but determinate, conceived, and definable evidence. This is the exact ideal essence of the natural sciences and geometry. It is an infinite idea in the Kantian sense only in relation to the objects of the world of experience and the imagined objects, which may be taken as finite approximations of it. In its conclusive, fully determinate, conceptual end-state it "conquers the infinity of the experiential world."[14]

However, as an exact irrelative essence—that is, not in relation to perceptual experience—it is not properly what Kant has in mind as an infinite *idea* and is not correlated to an infinite intending. Rather in contrast with the exact essence we have the ideas that are essentially inadequately given and have a necessary indeterminateness and endless determinability. Here there is an infinite intending and an original infinite presumptiveness, which is not conquered or conquerable.[15]

Regional (or eidetic) phenomenological as well as transcendental phenomenological description is of types, styles, and forms evident in the flux of experience. Thus community, virtue, color, animal, empathic perception, memory, and the like, are the sorts of matters upon which it dwells. It seeks through "free imaginative variation" the necessary and possible features of these sorts of things. Within the pregrasped adumbrated meaning-determining frame of the theme under consideration, the imagination presences the invariant features of—for example, promise—by entertaining possibilities absent in the familiar instances or types, like the promise to one who is comatose, the promise to oneself, the promise never expressed, and so forth. Thereby the specific differences within the common genus, the invariant features of the essence, and the essential incompatibilities, are teased out.

Here we have to do with the famous "synthetic a priori"—that is, the necessities that are not merely analytic (or tied to the definitions of terms or concepts) or a result of empirical inference. Like the latter these essences or necessary states of affairs are manifest in the indeterminacy of the flux of experience. Furthermore they are not a result of an idealizing that achieves perfect idealities, which, like exact essences, are indifferent to the experienced forms and types as well as to the human point of view. (The concept of a plane or ideal steam engine or frictionless state does not have individuating profiles tied to space-time or historical perspectives.) Thus *Husserl distinguishes the exact essence* (which for the perceptual perspective is a Kantian idea) *from the morphological essence* or what he also calls *eidos* (in the Introduction to *Ideas*, I) because the latter are immersed in the flux of perceptual experience and have their application there. There is necessarily a measure of vagueness and indefiniteness in the presencing of the *eidē*. The exact essences, on the other hand, are not descriptions of what is in the flux of experience. Rather they stand to the realm of experience as Kantian ideals, ideal limits, which experience can more or less approximate— even though in their perfect irreal conceptual presence they are closed, complete, and not regulative ideals. Thus the presencing of morphological essences and regional concepts will necessarily involve the tension and interplay of dialogue and competing perspectives, which, nevertheless, can yield amid the flux constant generic identities and clear distinctions; but these must not be confused with the exact formalities of the exact essences whose scope and element is one that is exclusively ideal (*Ideas*, I, #74).

The Divine Idea as Regulative

A theological connection between world and the divine is found in the rich passages in sections 51 and 58 of Husserl's *Ideas*, I. Here Husserl claims that *the divine is transcendent in a totally different sense than is the world* (#58). Here it is clear that the transcendence of the world is comparable to that of things: as things are identically the same throughout a manifold of perspectival profiles, so the world is profiled through the manifold of things; the profiles of things and the things are both immanent with respect to the transcendent world. For Husserl as well as Kant the idea of world is the ideal of the unity of all categories and concepts (morphological essences and regional ideas.) Every judgment about aspects of things as well as things themselves is a judgment about the world; every negation of aspects and things is a modification of the world as the ideal synthesis of these judgments.[16] The thread that knits the world together is a total intention and a general will at both passive and active synthetic levels—themes that recur ceteris paribus throughout the writings of both Kant and Husserl.

Before adding the constitutive function to our considerations, a significant claim in one of the most important of Husserl's theological manuscripts may be addressed. This text (E III 4) asserts that the ideal pole-idea is "the ultimate total meaning-giving principle . . . even for the absolute subject and totality of subjects"— which I take to refer to a constitutive function. It further refers to the divine idea (p. 62):

> [as] an essence (*Wesen*) that is not an *eidos*, but rather as essence in absolute truth, as essence in no relativity of situations, as essence without horizontality. This idea is to be thought of as essence, which, bearing all true being in itself in absolute necessity is unique and is actual reality (*Wirklichkeit*); actual reality in the sense of being the universal actual reality founding everything and making everything possible.

Husserl does not elaborate any further. Permit me to wager a brief commentary. First, *I take this to deny that the divine is a morphological essence.* A morphological essence is always one among many: person, promise, contract, oath, resolve, infidelity, lie. But *the divine idea is the essence that both encompasses all other essential-formal meanings* (morphological essences) *and is absolutely unique.*

Furthermore, the morphological essence is immersed in the flux of experience and we conceive it by thematizing the features of constancy and distinctiveness that are indeterminately present in the flux. The divine idea in this respect is comparable to "world": *it is the invariant horizon or frame* of the flux and the features of the flux. Yet it is not *in* the flux. As the invariant unique same that unifies, implies, and relativizes the ingredients of the flux, it transcends the flux and is beyond the relativity of situations.

Another possible consideration is that *Wesen* as essence is always the essence of something. *Eidē* on the other hand, considered in themselves (redness as such, promising as such, horseness as such) may be thematized as ultimate *topoi* or meaning spaces. Considered in this way *eidē* enjoy an ideal existence quite apart from any essence that expresses them and is the formal or morphological feature of some actual being. The divine ideal pole-idea or divine entelechy is clearly the formal *and* final cause, in Aristotle's terms, and may not be characterized as existing merely in the manner of *eidē* as ingredients of the *kosmos noētos*, or pure meaning *topoi*. The divine *Wesen* indeed has the ideal formal perfection of all the *eidē*, but it has the concretion of entelechy as the formal-final cause of the all of monads.

Further, in this text (E III 4, 61ff.) the divine is referred to as an ideal pole-idea. And to this idea is ascribed the prefix *über-* so that the divine is super- or trans-being, super-real. This suggests that the divine is essentially *an infinity*, not merely what cannot adequately be made present *to us*. But more basically it is infinity as *the idea of the all of monads, the divine entelechy*, the form that determines the actualization of the monadic *protē-hylē*. In contrast to Aristotle's divine entelechy as always already pure act, the divine entelechy for Husserl is essentially entelechy enabling the development of monadic *hylē*. It thus resembles more an Aristotelian than a (world-)soul as "first grade of actuality," "a kind of continuous and enduring motion" (Cicero, *Tucs. Disp.*, I, 10).

Therefore, infinite development is connected with the divine entelechy. How is it connected? Is there a sense in which the divine becomes ever more divine through the divine's actuation of the monadic *hylē*? I think that Husserl was inclined to an affirmative answer. But in very few texts does this issue become an explicit theme. One text (F I 14 10b and 11) asks (but does not explicitly answer):

> whether and to what extent the absolute being can be regarded and recognized as an existing God or as the self-development of the idea of God in factual existence . . . whether there can be an absolute point, an absolute goal in the sense of a being at rest, or of an always abiding flow amidst formations which remain always the same; or whether it belongs to the essence of the existing Godhood, that it be the development of levels in such a manner that an ultimate level of value is inconceivable? In such a case the highest value which is thinkable is such only in the progression of an endless development of levels.

Would we not then come to the Aristotelian metaphysics, therefore to the *poioun*, as an animating goal-idea, which at the same time, would have to be grasped as a Platonic Idea? But still it would not be this metaphysics in so far as it would not posit, properly speaking, an ideal goal (in the sense of the schema of the completed tree as the limiting goal of development).

Husserl does not decide the matter explicitly. What is clear here as in most of the other passages is that the divine entelechy is essentially tied to the monadic *hylē* and that this *hylē* provides an infinite field of entelechial agency for the divine.

3. The Divine as Constitutive

God is analogously the pole of the world as the world is the pole of things and as things are the pole of aspects/perspectives and as these are the pole of the "flow" of inner-time consciousness. And yet this transcendence is said to be one which is totally different from the transcendence of the world. It is totally different because the divine is also absolutely immanent to consciousness; Husserl calls it a transcendence in immanence of the I-pole. But the divine is not given as is the I-pole but comes to evidence in a mediate way—as the pervading idea of rationality which holds sway over the facticity of the primordial flow. The divine is not two principles but one which holds sway over the absolute life in its immanent and transcendent aspects.[17]

Hence the divine is both absolute *telos*, infinite regulative idea, horizon of horizons, *and* immanent prevailing, guiding, besouling norm within awakening and "regulating" the unbegun and undying monadic *hylē*. (These latter themes of "immortality" I merely mention in this essay; cf. Husserliana XI, 377ff.):

There is thus occasioned by the appropriation of Aristotle's doctrine of entelechy by transcendental phenomenology, the thought which Leibniz pursued under the title of confusedness (*Verworrenheit*). [For us] that would mean: each of our hyletic data is already a "developmental product," and therefore it has a hidden intentionality which refers back to synthesis. Everything refers back to a *prote hyle* which is a completely undifferentiated material (*Stoff*) and to primal-constitutive processes with intentional motivations which belong therein [F I 24, 41b].

If we think of *the constitutive idea as providing determination immanent to what is experienced,* then *the divine may be considered also a constitutive principle.* The transcendental (I-pole) determination, however, is not properly something to be experienced nor how something is experienced. Rather, the determination is that the foundation of this "how" (or these appearings) bears witness to a protorationality, i.e., elementary identity synthesis and teleology.

As the principle that is the regulative idea of the pole of the world and that holds sway over the facticity of the primal stream of presencings and endowing it with rationality and teleology, *the divine is a unity of a dipolarity, transcendent to worldly transcendence and transcendent to the immanence of the I-pole, regulative and constitutive—* that is, entelechy in senses that recall Aristotle but would be alien to his theology.

Kant's Rejection of the Divine as Constitutive Idea

As is well known, for Kant, only lazy reason (*faule Vernunft, ignava ratio,* B 717), would want to make of the regulative idea of God also a constitutive idea because it would make reason's true object—the synthetic unity of the concepts of the understanding—the object of understanding, i.e., of what appears in sensibility. Thus although it is, if not logically necessary, at least more commodious for logic and for understanding's possibility of totally organizing the world in a systematic unity to envisage the world as having originated from out of the intention of a divine mind (B 714 ff.; cf. Einstein in reference to Bohr's indeterminacy/chaos theory: "God does not play dice with the universe"), this most real being is itself an idea and the idea is not a most real being. And similarly as it is best to envisage the world as if it had sprung forth from the idea of a supreme mind, the causality of this supreme mind is an idea and this idea itself is not a cause. "Most real being" and "cause" are categories of the understanding and have to do with the objects of experience; the realm of reason in its generation of regulative ideas has to do with the context that ultimately makes possible the validity of the experience of substances and causal connections.

Yet, as is well known, there is a tension in Kant's discussion of the regulative ideals. They are often regarded as *mere* ideals, and in this sense it sounds as if they are merely our heuristic, even pragmatic, postulates (see B 698ff.). But, at the same time, they seem to be enjoined by a form of logical necessity if science and moral action are to be possible—that is, meaningful. Here too there lurks a kind of shiftiness that Hegel noted in Kant's ethics: the ideal, *A,* as most real being and cause, seems, on the one hand, as the highest development of theory and commitment, that for the sake of which we undertake *B*, research and action; yet there is a shiftiness by which *B* is regarded as the only thing really worthy of our devotion, so that *A* is for the sake of *B*.[18]

There seems to be another possible sense of Kant's meditations—namely, that the most real being and causality of the ultimate idea must be found in the ontological meaning of the idea's ideality. This is Bruno Bauch's position (also ceteris paribus that of Maurice Blondel and some neo-Thomists influenced by Kant, Hegel, and Blondel), that the causality of the idea is that of the logical condition for a systematic ordering of the world. In this case it is not simply true that the idea is thus only a heuristic concept (B699) which does not show us how the object is constituted but rather "how, under its guidance, we should *seek* to determine the constitution and connection of the objects of experience." If this posited highest intelligence is the condition for reasearch and action, and if we cannot enjoy the objects as intelligibly constituted without this ultimate idea, then, although the idea is indeed not an ostensive concept (B 699), it nonetheless in its functioning determines the constitution and connection of objects—and is therefore *constitutive*. In this sense, the causality of nature is founded on the causality of the idea and the sense of things on the sense-bestowing of the idea; and insofar as the idea of the highest understanding must include "form and content" in itself (see below), the world, understood not merely as an idea but as the object of (divine) understanding, must be envisaged as having originated in an idea. Again, in this sense the idea is not merely regulative but also constitutive.[19]

Transcendental Reflection and Faith in Reason

The result of transcendental reflection for Kant aspires but does not presume to achieve the transcendental structures that characterize the divine vision. The sense of the idea as regulative is thus also that the determinations we give the mind and world may be thought of *as if* they were actually or approximately the achievement of the divine wherein, through an intellectual intuition, form and content are one. This is the profound theological sense of the belief in reason and in reason's capacity to generate regulative ideas (Findlay, 160 and 102 ff.).

In Kant there is a tension, however, in the status he gives to transcendental philosophical descriptions and deductions. On the one hand, Kant envisaged his critical philosophicy as reason's disclosure of its productive agency in regard to the world of experience, and therefore it approached, at least in this realm, a godly knowing because

> nothing in the systematic inventory of all our possessions through pure reason can escape us, for what reason brings forth entirely from itself, cannot be hidden from reason, but must itself be brought to light by reason [A xx; cf. B 23].

Yet we may wonder, with J. N. Findlay, whether here Kant

> has forgotten the fact that, in his view, we know as little of ourselves in ourselves as the ultimate dynamic sources of all our mortal workings, as we know of the Things-in-themselves which underlie all external manifestations [p. 129].

Indeed, it remains for Kant that transcendental philosophical reflection must face the possibility that it is profoundly in error and that it is immersed in "misleading appearances of misleading appearances," as Findlay puts it (p. 107). The basic issue is that for Kant, even in the realm of transcendental reflection, the mind grasps only the appearings of things. And the appearings have to do only with the relations of things, foremostly their relations in regard to us. This says nothing about the things in themselves. This holds for self-reflection because self-reflection is not pure self-generated activity but also receptive of the affections of its prior experiences. Therefore, even self-reflection does not grasp things in themselves (cf. B 67 ff.).

For Husserl, of course, there is not this gap between being and appearings. Therefore appearings are not essentially mere appearances, because even the establishment of such a position is dependent on the appearings. While it is true that there is an analogous *poesis* in the mind's presencing of the world and the things of the world, transcendental reflection on constitution is not simply a constitution of *poesis* of the transcendental realm. At least at the foundations of the world's appearing in the foundations of inner-time consciousness, there is a being-in-itself through a self-appearing in which that which appears necessarily is.[20] It is this which secures the hope in the idea of philosophy as a rigorous science.

Of special interest here is a theme in the transcendental aesthetics of Kant which points to the proper sense of *metaphysics* for Husserl: the issue of the conditions for reason as this theme emerges in the ultimate sphere of transcendental phenomenological reflection. In Kant a well-known text reads: "There are two stems of human knowledge, namely, *sensibility* and *understanding*, which perhaps spring from a common, but to us unknown root" (A 15, B 29). In the first edition of the *Critique of Pure Reason* Kant entertained the view that the productive imagination was perhaps the common root; or even (in A 94) that the imagination was itself one of the original sources along with sense and appreciation (understanding). And the major achievement of imagination, synthesis, is named a blind but indispensable function of the soul (A 78).

The basic issue, of course, is relation between understanding and its conditions in sensibility. Typically Kant keeps these as distinct realms that somehow work together in harmony. Indeed, in one case (B 79), the primal achievements of the productive imagination are considered, as Findlay puts it (p. 139), an alias of the achievements of the understanding.

But for Kant there is no way for us to know the primal founding strata of phenomena upon which sensibility and understanding build. Kant must assume that the phenomena we actually enjoy are the harmonious conformity of the objects to the forms of sensibility and that they lend themselves to the determinations of understanding. This achievement, assigned by Kant to the productive or transcendental imagination, lies wholly beyond the realm of experience and beyond the grasp of transcendental reflection. Indeed it is a noumenal achievement of the transcendental noumenal self. Not only do we not know these foundations of the appearings (that is, the things in themselves giving rise to the phenomena), not only do we not know how these phenomena (or things) are geared into one another (that is, there must be something which gives them their associability and affinity if they are to be associated in such a way as to found nature [A 102]), we further do not know how they correspond with our achievements. (See, e.g., A 114, 121–22.) What Husserl names the primary associations and passive synthesis are for Kant unconscious or pre-conscious noumenal achievements. These achievements "have to be thought of, believed in, not known or seen."[21]

For Husserl, on the other hand, perhaps *the crowning achievement of transcendental phenomenology*, upon which perhaps its entire edifice stands or falls, *is the disclosure of the protoreason in the realm of the awareness of inner-time consciousness and passive synthesis*—the realms that loosely parallel Kant's transcendental esthetic and the noumenal achievements of the transcendental imagination. This is not a postulated harmony of intuition and understanding, but an original unity of *hyle/Empfindung* and (proto-)intentionality. Here, at the basement of sensibility and wakefulness and prior to intellectual agency and the egological informing of the stuff (hyletic materials, *Empfindungen*, etc.) of knowledge, there is a primal rationality interwoven in the very stuff of the flux.

Although for Husserl *appearings are the way being is manifest* and there is no issue of the fit between the noumenon and phenomenon, still there is the problem of bringing to light the foundations of the appearing of what appears and of how these provide the basis for the higher-order achievements of the I and the entire teleological edifice of action, science, and culture. The issue is that of *Ideas* I, how the fact of the primal flow may be considered a source for rationality and the teleology that characterizes "world" (see *Ideas*, I, sections 51 and 58).

There is much to be said here.[22]

Initially we may note that occasionally Husserl's mediations on this protoreason are in an "agnostic" vein—that is, he does not introduce theological themes (in contrast to *Ideas* I and elsewhere) to account for how it is that the nonbeing (the surds, anomalies, irrationalities, etc.) is subordinated to being and reason. In some passages—for example, in Husserliana XVI, pp. 285–93, and Husserliana XIII, pp. 346–57—Husserl is content to call attention to the *fact* of reason and being in the midst of a contingent flux and to show how the *propter hoc* is ineluctably founded in a *post hoc*. But other texts make it clear that we are here in the realm of the foundation of the conditions of reason—that is, in the proper transcendental phenomenological sense, "metaphysics." Husserl, indeed, once referred to the systematic phenomenology of the constitution of world as "showing from below how God creates the world in a perpetual creating."[23] And in contrast to Kant the disclosure of the achievements of the transcendental *esthesis* is not merely a disclosure of how the world affects us as subjects, but also of how being is in itself and how we are in ourselves (see Findlay, p. 99).

We here deal with the foundations of reason and the basis of belief in reason; indeed, I elsewhere propose that there is here a "transcendental self-trust" at the heart of the matter. Whereas for Kant the fit between understanding and sensibility and the reliability of the constituted primal phenomena *must* be believed in and cannot be known, for Husserl there is a unique form of evidence for this protorationality. And this elemental "verification" is ineluctable and to be accounted for only by a kind of theological meditation—in which the divine idea plays a constitutive function.

The upshot of Husserl's wrestle with the "protorationality" in passive synthesis and its foundation in so-called inner-time consciousness is the metaphysical position that *the divine "regulates" the* elemental) *materials of consciousness*—that is, the primal *hylē*, which ire the stuff of protoidentity syntheses and teleology—not as cre- itor from nothing or demiurgic efficient cause, *but as idea:* "We thus igain run into the riddle of the Platonic and Aristotelian material, nto the 'rational' *hylē*. But this does not mean the same thing for \ristotle as it does for us" (F I 14, 10b/11):

> Things refer back to regulations of absolute consciousness and these regulations are eternal. Similarly the personality is eternal but as a regulation of the formation of capacity. And God, the effecting idea of the Good, the *unum, verum, bonum*, is eternal as entelechy and as idea of development: as that urging, filling, and ever-higher filling *telos*. The *natura naturans, natura naturata*. God does not create the world as magician but as existing idea which as such presupposes a not-existing (*nicht seienden*) underground, the more or less dark consciousness. God's creating is untemporal (not objectively temporal)— but it is clear that the actual occuring sensations, phantasms, and their associations which stand under the form of a regulation, exist in "dependence on the body" [B IV 6, 105].[24]

This elemental achievement ("regulation"), which transcends ind founds individual egological achievements, we have also called ranscendental self-trust. It is a most improper sense of "faith" and 'trust," even though it may be said to found the more proper ienses of belief in reason. The originating ineluctable improperly 1amed "trust" or "faith" is not sufficient to hold open the horizons)f hope necessary for the pursuit of research and action. Further, <ant developed a theory of "pragmatic beliefs," i.e., those beliefs hat must come into play regarding goals of theory and practice (A i24 ff.). These beliefs were intrinsically connected with the projects)pened up by the infinite regulative ideals of theory and practice, .e., the "infinite tasks." Husserl once put it this way:

> As long as I have an open horizon for which no termination is definitely predelineated, and so long as I have given to me a recognized realizable value—even if it be merely in a vague presumptive mode of givenness—which presumably can lead to new practical values in the direction of the best possible or the absolutely binding, I have the duty of acting. . . . When I believe [in the practical realizability of the goal of history] and perform self-consciously this belief, when I freely perform this belief out of this practical source, there is given meaning to the world and my life; there is given also a joyful confidence that

nothing is in vain and that all is to the good [Husserliana VIII, Beilage V, p. 351].

When I believe that through our living toward the apprehended ideal it can be approximated unto infinity, thereby is a corresponding ethical-practical life rationally required [ibid., p 355].

Postulation of "God" and Utopian Poetics

As is well known, Kant holds that "God" was not a strictly pragmatic belief for theoretical reason, i.e., one that was tied to a necessary condition for a goal that itself is necessary. The theoretical postulate of God was, however, more convenient and suitable than its opposite. On the other hand, God was a necessary postulate or pragmatic belief of moral action (A 824–31).

Kant's pragmatic postulates or beliefs may be seen to be a "utopian poetics." On the one hand, theory and action are pushed to their theoretical limits; on the other hand, the affirmation of the actuality of the non-given, not-evident conditions of theory and action are not only posited but furthermore humanity is exhorted to create ever more fruitful versions of these postulated conditions in order that both action and theory may flourish. Postulation and "poetics" in theory is more stringent than in the realm of action; "God," understood as an expression of the pursuit of the infinite ideal of the theoretical understanding of nature, is a matter of convenience but not necessity. In theory "God" is a "doctrinal belief," not a pragmatic one, because it is not necessary and is inherently unstable and fraught with theoretical difficulties. However, in the order of action, Kant claims, God is a necessary postulate.

In utopian thought this theme takes wings as a poetic edification that nurtures hope in the realization of conditions of action. In William James it becomes the will to believe. Husserl is at home with this development. Husserl argues that in the absence of evidence, any attempt at ameliorization is bound to fail, and so long as a case can be made that the pursuit of what is great and beautiful can be successful, a creative self-displacing into a horizon nurturing hope is in order:

> I will do best to overestimate the probabilities and to act as if I was certain that fate was not essentially hostile to humanity and as if I could be certain that through perservering I could ultimately attain something so good that I could be satisfied with my perseverance. What is theoretically reprehensible, i.e., the overestimation of probabilities or of what is only

slightly likely at the expense of empirical certainty, is practically good and required in the practical situation [F I 24, 88b].

In Kant's *Critique of Judgment* utopian poetics has some especially good formulations. Here we see that the function of assigning specific attribution to God, who remains essentially unknown to us, is the edifying determination of our self and our wills.[25] (For Kant this is also the function of prayer.[26]) Thus we posit certain attributes of God not knowing what God is, with the prospect in mind that "God" being so conceived will determine us and our will in accord with this (infinitely edifying) idea of "God." Thus we conceive God on our thought and action—not for the sake of theoretical determination (prediction) in regard to (the noumenal) God.

It is of special interest that "God" here, as a matter of belief in reason and postulation—that is, as an effect generated by reason's transcendental regulative ideal—also has some measure, Kant maintains, of a *constitutive* principle. What the regulative principle devises for us as alone conceivable functions, accordingly, as constitutive (not in the theoretical determination but) in the production of goals.[27]

It is noteworthy that such a poetics for Husserl is never merely a postulate founded in a regulative idea, but also on the divine as constitutive—that is, God as the "quickening and besouling principle of perfection," which "holds sway" over that which, for transcendental phenomenology, is the source of the world's appearing, the uniquely contingent fact of the primal presencing or the foundations of inner-time consciousness.[28]

Divine Knowledge in Husserl and Kant

The recognition of this divine foundation probably requires what Kant denies and Fichte defends, an "intellectual intuition."[29] Such an intuition is ruled out by Kant because it is appropriate only to the divine as an *intellectus archetypus*. For such a mind, which, in Aquinas's terms is absolutely standard-making (measuring: *mensurans*) and in no way measured (*non mensurata*), there is no difference between what appears and its appearings, because this mind authorizes and is the author of both the appearings and what appears. Things are not true because the divine mind corresponds to them, but they are true because they are generated products of the divine mind.

According to Kant (B 71 ff.), we may assume that the divine mode of knowing is intuitive and not a mere conceptual thinking because this latter always involves limitation. This poses a problem in regard to the status of space and time as forms of possible sensible intuition. Either these are objective forms belonging to things in themselves, or they would seem to be part of the conditions of God's existence (a consideration which, for Kant, is unacceptable). Kant proposes that the very concept of God as an intuition in which the existence of things originates (*intuitus originarius*)—and not an *intuitus derivatus* or one deriving from the causality of things working on sensibility (which is essentially soaked with space and time)—resolves the matter. Of the divine mind alone may it be said that there is an intellectual intuition, i.e., an intuitive intellection free of sensibility, which is not empty.

Kant freely admits that there is something theological in his theory of sensibility; that is to say, it is a negative doctrine of the noumenon and points to a knowledge of things in themselves without appearings, or—what amounts to the same thing—without relation to our sensible mode of intuition. And because the categories build on the unities in manifolds in space and time, this postulated divine knowing would be essentially free of our categorial system. Thus what this intellectual intuition would be which grasps the things free of both sensibility and the categories of our understanding is beyond our ken (B 307–308).

Husserl's responses to these questions of Kant are among the most important clues to what his full philosophical theology might look like. (In what follows I am much indebted to Iso Kern's pioneering work on this matter in his *Husserl und Kant*, pp. 119–34.)

Kant's skepticism (or modesty) regarding transcendental philosophical reflection leads him to posit a divine mode of knowing in which all apperception, receptivity, and development are excluded. Husserl's hopeful (or sanguine) convictions concerning phenomenology as a strict science lead him to entertain a divine mode of knowing looking very much like the human form. If there is transcendental phenomenological essential intuition, then the realms uncovered by this reflection as necessary apply also to the divine.

For Kant there is an essential dualism in regard to being and manifestation. Being is always other than its manifestation; manifestation is tied to appearings, which are tied to sensibility, which is always only the way being affects and is perhaps effected and contaminated by humans. Yet if we are in a position to know this, then we do not need the postulated unknowable noumenon.

For Husserl, being is inseparable from its appearing; being-in-itself is always tied to a being for consciousness. What appears, the appearing of . . . (the genitive of appearing), is inseparable from that *to which* it appears. The ultimate "dative of manifestation" (to use Thomas Prufer's rich term) or so-called transcendental I cannot be eliminated in any version of being or nature.

For both Husserl and Kant there is room for the (e.g., monadological) reconstruction of realms or modes of knowing to which philosophers have no access in the first person. Thus slugs and starfish may be considered to have analogous modes of sensibility and apperception deficient in comparison with the human. The divine, on the other hand, is going to be different by reason of exceeding the human. Thus we may imagine "star spirits" to be such who have completely new modes of knowing and incredible insights into the world.

But Husserl insists that if these insights are to be appreciated as novel and incredible, if they are to be characterized by higher layers of cognitive contexts, they still must stand in essential connections with our own. Similarly these insights must be in a basic unity with the world, which we so feebly uncover. As to the supposition of *das ganz Anders* in the realm of knowledge:

> The general talk of possible modes of knowledge which have nothing in common at all with ours is meaningless and is actually nonsense (*widersinnig*) because there is nothing which sustains the unity of the concept of knowledge. If such possibilities are to be discussed meaningfully it must involve modes of knowledge which are intuitively identical in essence in their generic features.[30]

Husserl's view does not exclude an analogy of knowledge between the divine and human if this means that the differences are specific ones within the phenomenological genus. If analogy means exceeding the generic conception and still remaining meaningful and not equivocal, then, as Iso Kern points out, Husserl does not admit of an analogy of knowledge. Thus, whereas for Kant the *intellectus archetypus* is not an absolute impossibility but a problematic possibility into which we cannot have the least insight, for Husserl such an intellect is rejected because it spurns the discoveries of phenomenology as only phenomena for us or it sets up a two-world metaphysics: the synthetic a priori truths of phenomenology are not true for the divine but only for human minds.

Furthermore Kern is also right that Husserl's philosophizing makes little or no room for theories founded on formal logical possibility or noncontradiction. Transcendental phenomenological reflection moves within the real-possible spaces of the genera of eidetic analysis. The horizons of intentional implications predelineate the possibilities of being; it is not as if it were an open and wholly accidental matter as to what can count for being. Theological doctrines, like Kant's *archetypus intellectus* and the Thomist *creatio ex nihilo,* are not within the parameters of necessity and possibility as held open by the legislating spaces of phenomenological reflection. For Kant and Aquinas (and a Husserlian who is also a Thomist, Robert Sokolowski[31]), it is not contradictory to suppose that these very necessities and possibilities themselves are created. Therefore a problematic possibility is opened, which radically relativizes the necessities uncovered by philosophy and science.

Kern proposes (p. 134) that Husserl diminishes the richness of the meaning of to-be (*Sein*) in his enhancement of human knowing to encompass the divine itself. This claim might be true on the basis of formal-logical reasoning—that is, on the basis of a conception of the divine that is not formally contradictory. But, again, it might not be true. The concept of God as *archetypus intellectus* or even *ipsum esse subsistens* must meet somewhere along the line the test not only of the noncontradictory but also of available senses of things, especially of the good. That is, a question of great importance is whether the parameters of experience that serve as the base of transcendental reflection may be simply left behind if we are going to continue to use "good" and "bad" meaningfully. Notions such as greater, better, and the like, will eventually have to meet the larger tests of full human experience as it faces tragedy and irrationality. As is well known, Plato's receptacle is introduced not only for cosmological reasons but also for the seemingly ineluctable experience of *ananke,* fate, the surds of life—to account for the universe being reasonable *for the most part.*

The most basic consideration that governs Husserl's view is that the transcendental primal presencing is, indeed, a contingency, a fact, but such that is evident and meaningful only within transcendental reduction. That is, there is indeed facticity in the primordial "streaming," yet it is one that founds all proper senses of essence, necessity, and contingency. The "facticity" of primal streaming is not one of the possibilities among which others might just as well occur. Rather it is the absolute source of the proper meanings of necessity and contingency, and it has the peculiarity that with its essence its existence is necessarily given.[32]

A problem of interpretation, to which Kern (p. 128) calls attention, must be here noted. Husserl, in a letter to Erich Przywara (dated July 15, 1932), holds that his discussions of God often involve an epistemological limit notion of human knowing and that this "idea" of an infinite increase of human knowing toward an unlimited mode of understanding (cf. "exact essence," in #2, above) is not to be understood as an anticipation of the proper and genuine phenomenological sense of "God."

Thus some texts may perhaps be said to be improper because they make use of the classical notion of a timeless God encompassing all retentions in an actual present (as in Husserliana X, p. 175). But it is not only in such "thought experiments" that Husserl conceives of God as human knowing raised to an endlessly higher power. It is also in metaphysical contexts (e.g., B II 2, 42ff.). Part of his argument here is that phenomenology as strict eidetic science does not grasp merely "our" knowing but knowing as such. In which case, it seems to this student, why this conception of God as endlessly higher power is not the "genuine" phenomenological one is because it is incomplete: its making use of classical notions of the divine as the actuality of all possible perfections portrays only one of the poles of the divine and does not deal with God as the divine entelechy that awakens the hyletic monadic dimension into a wakeful medium of the divine self-realization. When, as we shall see, Husserl has occasion to speak of the divine principle, it is within the parameters of both God as constitutive entelechy as well as the regulative idea as an infinite enhancement of consciousness—indeed, of the community of consciousnesses—which transcendental phenomenology uncovers.

In order to get acquainted with Husserl's view on the divine-human analogy of knowing, we may begin with facts. For Kant's God, facts are true because God made them to be so; they are not true for God because they are that to which the divine mind must conform if God is to know them. For Kant's God, the knowledge of the world cannot be a posteriori, because this would tie the divine to sensibility and receptivity. Thus presumably for Kant's God there is no distinction between the a priori and a posteriori.

But, holds Husserl, God is bound by the essential laws and the a posteriori facts. Consider that God in advance knows a fact or state of affairs, which God wants to create. This knowledge does not, properly speaking, make this fact a priori. A judgment does not become a priori, even when it is correct, when I know that the judged state of affairs surely will be the case. Consider the case wherein I have chosen to realize a state of affairs. Here I am certain that it will be the case before it is really so. But this judgement is not strictly a priori. It expresses facts that rest on one's power and, in God's case, on God's all-power. But this is not a judgment about the actual state of affairs eventually effected.[33]

Perhaps most scandalous is Husserl's claim that divine intuition is just as sensible as ours.[34] It holds also for God that "intuitions without concepts are blind." If the divine intuition were infinite but without concepts it would be infinite stupidity (*Dumm-*

heit), because it would see everything but grasp nothing.[35] Similarly, because it is an essential state of affairs that the evident value of things is correlated with feeling and will presupposes and builds on this correlation, the divine will presupposes the divine feeling of the world's value.

In *Ideas*, I, #43 we find the famous correction regarding a basic mistake—that is, the one that Kant makes—that it is essentially possible that there be a divine mode of intuition or perception that would grasp adequately the spatial-temporal thing without any mediation through "appearings." On the contrary, God cannot make it so that a thing is absolutely adequately given. Things and world remain transcendent and presumptive *in infinitum* also for the divine knowledge.[36]

Furthermore, this Kantian view, in an effort to give to the divine a radically heterogeneous and transcendent mode of being, in fact effects the opposite. It destroys the essential distinction between the transcendent and the immanent modes of presentation. Thereby it holds that for the postulated divine intuition the spatial-temporal thing becomes an essential ingredient constitutive of the divine mode of consciousness and part of the stream of consciousness (*Ideas*, I, #43).

Of course, for the Kantian or medieval philosopher this mode of argument is a *petitio principii* inasmuch as it assumes that Husserl is correct in holding that transcendental phenomenology uncovers the generic parameters in which discourse about all forms of knowledge may take place. And, of course, Husserl must hold this view if transcendental phenomenology is to be considered an achievement of the phenomenology of mind as such.

Of special interest is the implication that if the divine mode of knowing faces necessarily "things" given adequately *in infinitum*, then the divine too faces infinite ideals and infinite tasks. In which case the divine ideal and divine truth would stand equally as regulative for all modes of consciousness—including the divine. But if there is no sense in which the divine is actually what the regulative idea indicates, must not the divine be essentially constituted and in no way constituting? Clearly Husserl's view of divine knowing excludes the view that the divine is actually infinite perfection in every respect.

Furthermore, Husserl consistently pursued his theory of the generic sameness of human and divine knowing when he held that if there is to be an understanding between God and humans, somewhat like that between different humans, and if humans are able to see the same as God and God as us, God must see with sensible experiences and be bound to a *Leib*.[37] But this is another story.[38]

11

God as the Ideal: The All-of-Monads and the All-Consciousness

Steven W. Laycock

Plato's enigmatic dialogue, *The Parmenides*, presents a philosophical perplexity of insistent relevance to the discipline of Husserlian phenomenology, and, by extension, to phenomenological theology as well. Parmenides establishes a systematic analogy that seems to have devastating consequences for the theory of forms espoused by the "young Socrates." A particular master exercises mastery over a particular slave. And, borrowing Socrates' assumptions, we may even say that the Form *Mastery* masters the Form *Slavery*, or at least that *Mastery* is intrinsically Mastery *of Slavery*:

> Mastership itself is what it is [mastership] of slavery itself, and slavery itself is slavery to mastership itself. . . . The things in that world are what they are with reference to one another and toward one another [133e–134a].[1]

But the logic of Socrates' theory of Forms will not permit the Form of *Slavery* to be mastered by a particular master:

> Suppose . . . one of us is master or slave of another; he is not, of course, the slave of master itself, the essential master, nor, if he is a master, is he master of slave itself, the essential slave, but being a man, is master or slave, but being a man, is master or slave of another man [133e].[2]

What seems, to Socrates, an uncontroversial set of relationships forms the basis of bewilderment when transposed into an alternative key. A particular act of knowing can be said to grasp a particular object of knowledge. Indeed, *Knowledge* itself can be said to apprehend *Reality* itself.[3] But if all the relationships are to survive transposition, it must also follow—given the separation of Forms and particulars—that a particular act of knowing, on the part of a particular knowing subject, cannot apprehend *Reality:*

> None of the forms is known by us, since we have no part in knowledge itself. . . . So beauty itself or goodness itself and all the things we take as forms in themselves are unknowable to us [134b–c].[4]

And this result can hardly prove sanguine for the unfortunate Socrates, a particular philosopher, particularly eager to grasp *Reality* itself, and particularly indisposed to consider the particular objects of experience as anything but distant, and perhaps distorted, reflections of *Reality.*

Phenomenology is not, of course, obliged to preserve all the Platonic assumptions in confronting this conundrum. But one desideratum, at least, remains common: the transcendental-phenomenological reduction discloses not merely the welter of contingently occurrent particular acts of consciousness, but the very eidetic structure, or "form," of the act: *intentionality.* Transcendental subjectivity, eidetically embracing intentionality, is the full "reality" of phenomenology. And the "dative" of this disclosure is precisely the particular practitioner of phenomenological reflection. Even the mighty Caesar could not master *Slavery.* How, then, can transcendental subjectivity (or even intentionality) be disclosed to the humble phenomenologist?

Phenomenology would plunge into the same puzzlement as that which engulfed the young Socrates, were it to remain speechless before the query. And the response, once voiced, will be seen to rest upon the *internal complexity* of the most fundamental of phenomenological concepts: intentionality. Intentionality is not, however, or not for its own sake, the locus of our present concern. Nor is its complexity. A philosophical theology achieved through the reflective, epochetic, and eidetic-intuitive methods of phenomenology is confronted with *two interconnected problems* of utmost gravity: the problem of *divine constitutive dependence,* and the problem of *the formal congruence of human and divine mentality.* Intentionality is indispensable to the resolution of both.

Epoché

Phenomenology gives voice to phenomena, first through reflection, then through language, articulating the *logos* inscribed within the domain of experienced objectivity. Having little in common with the abstract conceptual architecture of speculative metaphysics, *theoria*, for phenomenology, as for the Greeks, is intuitive "seeing." And *logos* (the "saying" of the "seeing") is the articulation of the "seen" *precisely as and only as* it is "seen." Phenomenology is thus the *logos* of the "seen qua seen" (the "phenomenon"). And "reason" (Latin: *ratio*) is the constant "ratio" of the "seen" and its manifold manner of being "seen." Reason, then, is the immanent and eidetically registrable structure of experience whereby the single and selfsame "seen" is multiply "seen," the form of unity within multiplicity.

What makes of phenomenology a "discipline" is its methodological aversion to the betrayal of experience, its adamant insistence upon "saying" no more than it "sees," and its consequent purgation from articulate theory of any premethodological assumptions (any "presuppositions") that could enter into a distorting commentary upon experience. Phenomenology aspires thus to be "presuppositionless."

The *epochē* is the indispensable "first step" of phenomenological loyalty to experience. Understood as a deliberate "act," it can only be a "privative" act, an "omission," rather than a commission. The *epochē* is neither affirmation nor negation in the face of experienced reality, but the withholding of both. It is a peculiarly self-reflexive act, a second-order act inhibiting our natural first-order tendency to posit the objects of our experience, and thus the world itself, *as existing*. The *epochē*, once again, does not act *upon* experienced objectivity. It imposes neither affirmative nor negative judgments of existence. As the act par excellence whereby reflective consciousness is made receptive to first-order experience, it rather allows experience to "speak" for itself. And it is only within the permissiveness created by this deliberate and reflective self-inhibition that the *logos* of *phainomena* can be voiced. We, as agents of reflection, must be silent in order that experience may "speak."

It is tempting to suppose that the suspension of our "natural" positing of the world amounts to a qualitative "loss"—that the *epochē*, in unnaturally depriving experienced objectivity of our obligatory tribute of existential commitment, has thereby plundered experience of some crucial feature, leaving it impoverished, reduced, depleted. But precisely the reverse is the case. The discipline of the *epochē* may exact from me a covenant not, qua phenomenologist, to make pronouncements such as "the Koolau range rising majestically before me exists." But the asceticism is merely apparent, and my phenomenological efforts redeemed, by the concurrent necessity to surround all such forbidden utterances with "*it appears that. . . .*"

Undeniably, and in complete consonance with the requirements of the epochē, it appears that the Koolau range rising majestically before me exists. "Exists" does have a "home" in phenomenological discourse. It is sheltered from the cruel contingencies of extraphenomenal parlance by the "appearance operator." Thus, experience, as given within the epochē, is not left qualitatively bland, deprived of the salt of existence.

If "the Koolau range exists" is mute, while "it appears that the Koolau range exists" is, through the epochē, given voice, what does the latter "say" that the former does not? What is made evident by the latter and not by the former? Precisely, the very appearing itself of the Koolaus qua existing: the manifestation (phenomenon) of their being. What is made evident by the epochē is manifest being: Bewusst-sein. The epochē is, in the sense etymologically implicit in the German, the revelation of consciousness.

Phenomenological theology is the systematic reflective disclosure of God-as-experienced (the "God-phenomenon"). Phenomenological theology takes, not God, but "God" (God-in-brackets) as its theme, and concerns itself, not with the being of God, but with the "being" of "God." It thus concerns itself with the "known" (bewusst), or manifest, being (sein) of God. And all Bewusst-sein is in principle open to the "silent," receptive, and nonintrusive apprehension of assertorically self-inhibiting reflection. Yet God-as-manifest is a phenomenon. It is only through our own reflective silence that the manifest-being (our "consciousness") of God is given voice. Bowing to the epochē, phenomenological theology makes no extraphenomenal assertions regarding the divine being, nature, or modes of relatedness to the world. "God exists" is not (at least at the inception) a phenomenological utterance. "It appears (to me) that God exists" does, however, accord with the epochē, and "speaks" the revelation of the divine being.[5]

The Problems of Divine Dependence and of Formal Congruence

In the fullness of its sense, a phenomenon is inseparable from a given intentional act, a given episode of Bewusst-sein. If, in turn, God is inseparable from God-as-manifest, and if, as clearly follows from a Husserlian understanding of the reduction, what falls before the reflective gaze are necessarily one's own intentional acts, deity would assuredly be a unity of meaning entirely constituted by entirely human acts of meaning-bestowal. We are faced with three equally untoward responses to this perplexity. (1) We can simply face and accept the apparent implication: God is a constituted and dependent "meaning," a constitutive construct. Alternatively (2) we can sever the divine from the divine-as-manifest, asserting that, at least in the unique theological case, the intentional "object" is not integrally and internally united to its "mode of givenness." Both have serious ramifications with regard to divine transcendence. Finally (3) we can abandon the assumption that reflection is the reflexive self-discovery of a unitary consciousness, allowing, instead, that, in reflection, we may have access to *another* mind.

The first, the "Feuerbachean," alternative—making of God a projection, "the sigh of the human heart," the locus of an entirely human constitutive process—would seem to exclude the very possibility of a genuinely phenomenological theology. A constituted "projection," even a projection of the deepest and noblest elements of the human soul, simply cannot answer to the demands placed upon theology by the very conception of God. The gravity of this concern is underscored by Ricoeur's claim that "the transcendental idealism of Husserl contains implicitly the same atheistic consequences as does the idealism . . . of Feuerbach. If consciousness posits itself, it must be the 'subject' for whom the human being becomes 'predicate.' "[6] A certain "ontological independence" is inscribed in our very notion of God.

Divine "transcendence" may, however, import more than the logical and theological infelicity of envisioning God as contingent upon humanity. As our second response suggests, may not the divine, as being wholly immersed in the noumenal realm, "transcend" even the region of appearance accessible to human consciousness? To respond in the affirmative is to dissociate "object" from "object-as-manifest"—and to lapse into a Kantian noumenology inimical to phenomenological insight concerning objectivity. A "phenomenon," in the Husserlian acceptation, is precisely an object *as it appears*. The "thing-in-itself" is inseparable from the thing qua appearing, the "noumenon" being an integral aspect of the "phenomenon." The supposition that God is noumenal, in the Kantian sense, casts the divine beyond the veil of appearance. It is not *God* who appears at all, but only, at best, the "appearance" *of* God—the "of" signifying an extrinsic and phenomenonlogically indemonstrable relatedness to an ineluctably "mysterious" extraphenomenal being. As German Idealism was quick to point out, relatedness to the utterly noumenal is logically (and we shall add, phenomenologically) incapable of proof. Thus, the ill-fated Kantian *Ding-an-sich* forms no element of a rationally ordered system of concepts (or a phenomenologically derived vision of reality). A putatively noumenal God is no God *for us*.

252 PHENOMENOLOGY OF THE TRUTH PROPER TO RELIGION

The third alternative would introduce the most pernicious and destructive aporia into the method of phenomenology. For only if the egological source of empirical and reflective activity retains its integrity can the self-insights of phenomenology preserve any warrant.

Were it even abstractly possible that the theme of reflection differ internally from the reflecting consciousness itself, self-knowledge could be no more than a contingent accomplishment, a deliverance of empirical psychology, perhaps, but falling immediately through the eidetic net of phenomenological insight. But of equal seriousness is the opposite possibility. Should we be assured of the identity-in-interiority of reflecting and reflected consciousness, we are nonetheless left to wonder what possible bearing eidetic insight gained through the reflective techniques of phenomenology could have upon theology. While the formal constraints and permissions articulated through the eidetic phase of the phenomenological reduction may well govern distinctively *human* (i.e., *our own*) cognitive possibilities, God is not, and cannot be conceived as, a *human* mind. The necessities and allowances that rule our understanding of the divine mind may have little, if anything, to do with the human mind. Nothing, perhaps, could be more damaging to the project of phenomenological theology than the consequence that, indeed, divinity is not "formally" accessible to consciousness in the attitude of phenomenological reflection.

No phenomenologically achieved theology can be adequate that fails to preserve (1) the ontological independence of God, (2) the disclosure of divinity itself within its manners of appearing, and (3) the internal integrity of reflecting and reflected consciousness. Before offering a solution to the problems of constitutive dependence and formal congruence that accords with these desiderata, let us return, briefly, to the "worst difficulty" encountered by Socrates, and our phenomenological resolution of it.

A Single Unitary Complex: the Subject/Object

The Platonic Forms are (perhaps to the detriment of the theory) "monadic," incapable of exemplification by pairs or n-tuples of particulars. And this would seem to cohere well with certain of our intuitions regarding *Mastery*. *Mastery* is not exemplified by the pair, Epaphroditus and Epictetus, but, of course, by Epaphroditus alone. And analogously, Parmenides argues, *Knowledge* is exemplified by particular acts of knowing, not by ordered pairs of knowing acts and objects known.

There are, as McPherran points out, several courses of response open to Socrates:

The more plausible of these are: (1) eliminate immanent characters from the ontology of the theory of Forms, (2) contend that [the "law of factual separation"[7]] is somehow illegitimately applied to the case of knowledge, and/or (3) deny . . . that Forms may not possess immanent characters.[8]

McPherran urges (3) on Socrates' behalf. We, in circumventing certain difficulties of the Platonic scheme, are free to urge (2) on behalf of transcendental phenomenology. Suppose that the Forms were, while remaining strictly "monadic" (singly exemplified), nonetheless internally structured. If *Mastery* were, for example, upon eidetic inspection, seen to be intrinsically *Mastery-over-Slavery*, then a single particular exemplification of *Mastery* would thereby be an exemplification of *Mastery-over-Slavery*, and the particular master, unlike Epaphroditus, or even the mighty Caesar, would, indeed, exercise mastery over *Slavery* itself. If Caesar is not thus fortunately endowed, it is because *Mastery* and *Slavery* are not thus internally related.

While Parmenides may have been right with regard to *Mastery*, the phenomenological rejoinder turns upon rejecting the analogy. Intentionality, while monadic (i.e., exemplified singly by particular episodes of consciousness), is nonetheless internally complex—analyzable into discriminable but inseparable determinations ("moments"). At the most superficial level of analysis, intentionality is articulated as the formal complex: *Subject/Object*. Husserl is very clear that the internal relatedness of formal determinations is not to be explicated in virtue of a purported "relation" (even an "internal relation") that spans them. *Subject* and *Object* are united without the mediation of some ontological *tertium quid*. Thus, intentionality cannot be conceived as a "bolt" or a "rivet" locking together otherwise separate formal determinations, a "bridge" yawning between them. Intentionality is rather the complex structure comprised of the immediate unity of reciprocally dependent "forms": *Subject* and *Object*. And just as the immediate unity of *Pitch* and *Volume* presents either through the other (volume is apprehended precisely "in" or "through" pitch; and pitch "through" volume), so too *Subject* and *Object*, as "aspects" of *a single unitary complex*, reciprocally reveal one another.

Both "natural" prereflective consciousness and the eidetically "purified" reflective consciousness of the transcendental reduction exemplify the internally integral *Subject/Object* structure of intentionality. But the "object" of transcendental reflection is precisely intentionality itself. Only transcendental reflection exhibits the peculiarly self-reflexive *eidos, Subject/(Subject/Object)*, in virtue of which the act of reflection exemplifies the very structure that serves as its object. In this way, then, a tack not sanctioned by Platonic metaphysics, the "worst difficulty" is, for our purposes, resolved. "Reality" (the full _"truth" of phenomenology: transcendental subjectivity) is an immediate moment of the complex and self-reflexive "transcendental" *eidos, Subject/Transcendental Subjectivity*, a formal structure exemplified by particular performances of transcendental reflection, and one that ensures the enjoyment of "Reality" by a particular instance of "Knowledge."

God, Subject/Object

With the "worst difficulty" resolved (for phenomenological purposes), we are now prepared to confront our own conundrum with borrowed insight. Again, the very possibility of a coherent phenomenologically derived theological vision hinges upon satisfaction of the following fundamental conditions:

The constitutive requirement: Insofar as the divine serves as an "object" of human awareness, God must appear "in some way." And a consistent phenomenology requires both that God be inseparable from the divine mode of revelation, and that the latter be, in turn, inseparable from the entirely human intentional activity whereby the divine is disclosed. This requirement appears, however, to hold the unwanted consequence that God is constitutively dependent upon human consciousness (a mere "projection").

The reflective requirement: Phenomenology concerns itself *exclusively* with that field of experience (transcendental subjectivity) disclosed to the transcendentally reflecting consciousness of the individual (human) phenomenological practitioner. Eidetically "purified," phenomenology is, then, quite simply an examination of the intentional structure of *one's own* mind. And it follows inescapably that the divine "essence" (the *eidos, God*) must be formally identical with intentionality or one of its substructures. Yet—by the constitutive requirement—the divine appears to be dependent upon human consciousness for its manifestation in a way that renders questionable the very enterprise of phenomenological theology.

In apparent conflict with the constitutive requirement with its purportedly atheistic shackling of the divine to the human, and also in conflict with the reflective requirement (leaving us to ponder the legitimacy of making pronouncements concerning the divine nature on the basis of an *entirely human* articulation of a form that in-forms *entirely human* consciousness), stands an equally trenchant demand—a demand, so to speak, on the part of the very concept of God, that deity *not* be rendered as a Feuerbachean projection. *How, then, do we preserve divine independence?*

The solution I wish to commend for consideration is, I believe, Husserl's own. Let us begin by owning up to what could seem an altogether too costly entailment of strict phenomenological method. God, conceived as the "object" of human intentional reference is, and must be, a constituted "meaning," hopelessly chained to human constitutive activity. But this is merely the first chapter of our story.

Jacobi's unsubtle disjunction has at least the virtue of articulating a key assumption, acceptance of which would render the Husserlian position problematic: "Either God exists and exists outside of me, a living being subsisting apart; or else I am God. There is no third way."[9] While Jacobi was insensitive to any theological possibility aside from traditional theism or Feuerbachean atheism, Hegel was not. Husserl's theological vision, though not Hegelian in significant detail, coheres with the general outlines of Hegelian "third force" theology. Robert Williams writes of the ontological argument, central to the Hegelian theological project:

> It dispels the illusion of subjective-psychological immanence, to which transcendental philosophy is prone, and resurrects objectivity, as the self-objectivating concreteness of thought itself.[10]

Should it turn out that our constitution of the divine is indistinguishable from divine self-constitution, or should it turn out, minimally, that the divine constitutes itself through the deific constitution of the intersubjectivity community, our problem will have been solved. None of the functions of human constitutive activity would then need to be sacrificed at the altar of divine ontological independence. Indeed, divine constitutive *dependence* upon the human would be a necessary condition for divine ontological *independence*.

For Husserl, immanence is not "illusory." But neither is it merely "subjective" or "psychological." And, though "absolute" in a determinate sense, it is not ultimate. Divine transcendence is precisely the inverse of that characterizing our God-object—"a transcendency standing, as it were, in polar contrast to the transcendency pertaining to the world."[11] God is conceived as "an extra-worldly 'divine' being," which transcends "not merely the world but 'absolute' consciousness."[12] The divine would thus be "an *'absolute' in the sense totally different from that in which consciousness is* an absolute, just as it would be *something transcendent in a sense totally different* from that in which the world is something transcendent."[13]

While "God-as-object" cannot escape the iron logic of constitution, the "God" liberated from constitutive dependence is precisely "God-as-subject." The "liberated" God stands, not *before* the human constitutive gaze, but, as it were, "behind" our eyes, looking "through" them. That this is Husserl's intent is seen in his explicit insistence that "God . . . sees the thing from one side (with *my* consciousness) and 'at the same time' from the other side (with the consciousness of the *Other*)."[14] God sees "with" (or "through") our consciousness. Our consciousness serves as the "medium" of divine conscious revelation.

Inasmuch as the intersubjective community *as a whole* comprises a single, comprehensive "way of seeing," the divine subject sees in this "way." And inasmuch as God-as-object serves as an invariant intentional locus, thematically or horizonally given, for every possible mind comprising the "intersubjective college," God-as-subject intends God-as-object through the mediation of finite subjectivity so that *divine self-constitution* (or "self-realization") *is effected through human constitution of the divine.*

But, of course, this resolves the issue *only if* (1) the intersubjective community can indeed be said to comprise a single comprehensive "way of seeing," and *only if* (2) God-as-object does indeed serve as an intentional locus for every possible mind. These claims deserve a few words of clarification.

The Intersubjective Community and Apperception

As Husserl avers, where a number of minds collectively regard a single object, each from its own unique standpoint, "God would not have . . . *one* visual field but as many as there were consciousnesses."[15] Yet this assertion is immediately problematic. For a visual field is essentially the ensemble of visual objects present to *a single* observer at a time. Crucially, fields are individuated by agents of perception (as well as times). Thus, it seems, God could have a multiplicity of visual fields only on pain of a particularly virulent variety of ontological schizophrenia. How, then, can we purchase Husserl's assertion without paying for it in the coin of divine integrity?

The only course available, and the one that makes consistent and useful sense of Husserl's pronouncement, is to interpret the "having" of a visual field as *apperceptual* (rather than *perceptual*) having. God thus "has" a plurality of visual fields in a way no different from the way we "have" them (even though God might be *better* at it). Apperception is our "counterfactual" mode of intentionality. Through apperception we enjoy intentional access to the *other* profiles of the sugar cube, even though the cube is perceptually present to us only in *this* profile. And through apperception, we likewise enjoy intentional access to the other *viewings* of the cube, even though we are neither performing those acts of viewing nor reflectively thematizing our own viewing. We cannot, of course, perceive the object in ways not given, nor perform the intentional acts of others. But we can *apperceive* the sugar cube in a plurality of profiles, as if a plurality of viewers. We do so in virtue of our eidetic apprehension of the *eidos: cube.*

It is sometimes complained that Husserl, in violation of his own covenant of doxastic neutrality, surreptitiously imports an ontology of Platonic *eidē*. If Husserl can speak of "eidetic intuition" (*Wesensschau*), and can borrow without comment even the expression (*eidos*) from Plato—for whom it bears the crucial ontological commitment—is not phenomenology sullied by metaphysical reification? The short response, and the only one permitted by the scope of this present discussion, is simply that, unlike the Platonic, the Husserlian *eidē* function within epochetic "brackets."

Eidos is Husserl's technical idiom replacing the richer and less formal *Wesen*, the latter replete with etymological suggestions not conveyed by "essence." *Wesen*, of course, in the humus of its archaic sense, signifies "being," and would thus be uncomfortable in the role of the Scholastic counterpart of designated matter. But neither can *Wesen* simply stand in for our word "being." Its sense—and that which clings to *eidos*—is rather that of an overall "style" of being pertaining not to a particular object but to a particular *kind* of object.

An *eidos*, in the Husserlian acceptation, is not a timeless abstraction impassively awaiting penetration by an act of intuition. The objects of our experience present themselves in light of certain expectable patterns, certain overall "modes" of manifestation. A solid that displays a curvilinear edge is no cube. To see the object before me *as a cube* is to expect that no possible view of it will display a curvilinear edge. Nothing, or course, excludes error, and I may certainly be *wrong* in seeing the object as a cube. Only further perceptual exploration will tell. But independently of the merely contingent question of factuality, I may wish to consider the manners in which any cube *would* present itself from different angles or under various conditions. To so consider is to be in the presence of the *eidos*.

We are enabled to apperceive the cube in alternative profiles on the basis of the *eidos, cube*, precisely because, on analysis, the *eidos, cube*, can be analytically decomposed into a system of relativized profiles, each approximately of the form: "Under condition *A*, a cube will appear as . . . " (where the blank holds a description of the cube *as it appears*). The *eidos* is the system of typical "ways"—the "Way" of such "ways"—in which a certain kind of object presents itself. It is explicated by considering the "how" of presentation. And every "how?" has an adverbial response. Accordingly, *eidé* signify "adverbial," not "adjectival," universals, "ways," not properties.

I may attempt to make plain to myself what lies within the *eidos*. In the attempt, I will discover a hierarchy of generality. "Confronted front-on, the cube presents four angles and four edges" occupies a lower rung. The more general deliverance, "regardless of perspective, the cube will never display a curvilinear edge," occupies a higher. Whatever its level of generality, each such articulation will be intuitively registered as "valid": *true*, not in virtue of its logical form, nor in virtue of the contingent rules of the "language-game" in which its terms function, but in virtue of the eidetically registrable relationships among its component determinations. In general, an *eidos* is far too rich in content to be thoroughly apprehended in a casual eidetic glance. But it can be progressively articulated. And if the "existence" of an *eidos* simply is (as, it seems, it must be) its *validity*, we can become progressively assured of its "existence."

Unlike Platonic Forms, *eidé* are "constituted." They can be enriched, augmented, and their analytic content expanded by fresh insight. Like transcendent particulars, *eidé* are "identities-in-manifold," invariant *kinds* constituted across variant conceptual contents. Contemporary qualms (notably represented by Quine) over the legitimacy of the "analytic"/"synthetic" distinction are here *à propos*. The precise content of a judgment's "subject-concept" is relativized to standpoint. The Greeks did not see water as H_2O. We do. Influenced by Newtonian mechanics, eighteenth-century science regarded space as "absolute." Today, after Einstein, we commonly experience space as "relative." It is not that one conception has been supplanted by another one. Both are conceptions *of space*. It is the *eidos, space*, that underlines such dramatic conceptual revisions.

Thus, to entertain the *eidos, cube,* does not import the ability to anticipate the way a cube would look from *every possible* angle, or under *every possible* condition. Instead, eidetically grounded apperception is typically indeterminate, lacunary, and general. To *apperceive* the cube as you perceive it strictly entails within the *eidos* only sufficient complexity to ground *two* ways of seeing: cubes appear *this* way from *this* angle, *that* way from *that.*

But this is all we require to explicate the apperceptual "having" enjoyed by the divine. It is a "having" of a plurality of profiles and fields—a field simply being a *single* whole of a *multiplicity* of objects. God entertains the *eidos,* and apperceives a plurality of profiles in its light. And the content of the *eidos* entertained by divine consciousness is enriched by human constitutive insight.

Human Intentional Activity and World-Horizon

The thesis of divine self-constitution through human constitution of the divine still requires, however, that God-as-object be the constant and invariant object of all human intentional activity.

This requirement appears, upon surface inspection, flatly false. Surely, human consciousness is not incessantly occupied by God. We perceive flowers and sunsets, imagine winged horses and unicorns, and conceive of mathematical theorems and possible worlds, none of which can be straightforwardly identified with God. Indeed, it seems possible that we could spend our entire conscious life without the least intentional reference to God. Although God has, as a matter of contingent historical fact, occupied the intentional life of humanity in some measure, it seems conceivable that the intersubjective community as a whole might never have adverted in thought, in faith, or in reverence, to the divine. And were this admittedly abstract possibility actual, there would be no human constitution of the divine, and consequently no divine self-constitution through human constitutive activity. Moreover, were this possibility actual, the human constitution of the divine would be a merely contingent occurrence, not an essential structural feature of human consciousness as such.

It is insufficient simply to demonstrate that universal failure of constitutive reference to God is a possibility contingently unactualized. We must show, radically, that there simply *is* no such possibility.

Granting that the divine does not necessarily occupy our focal attention, we shall nonetheless see that God is an essential and invariant horizonal structure of consciousness. Toulemont accurately expresses Husserl's view in his declaration that "la perfection absolue que visent tous les êtres à travers et par delà les réalizations relatives, c'est Dieu."[16] God is, for Husserl, the *telos* of conscious life. The life of the mind has a certain vector, flows in a certain direction. Mind flows toward God as water toward the sea. Yet it must be possible for human consciousness to maintain its teleological orientation while being thematically occupied with the cups and saucers of the world.

That this is indeed possible is revealed in two stages: *first*, the chairs and tables of the world are to be understood as the modes of presentation whereby *the world itself is brought to conscious givenness;* and *secondly, the world*, as the ultimate pole of conscious reference, *is to be identified with God-as-object*.

First, it is a mistake of great phenomenological consequence to suppose that the intentional act brings to presence *merely* its object, as if the object could simply be disclosed contextless, filling the mind so completely that no reference to background presence were even conceivable. Intentionality, of course, is not the presentation of objects, but the presentation of *objects-in-context*. And since contexts themselves may be contextualized, the sense of any intentional experience leads concentrically outward in the direction of the ultimate "fringe," the context of all contexts: the *world-horizon*. Every intentional object is, in language borrowed from contemporary physics, the particulate "condensation" of the universal "field," a field of conscious givenness bounded ineluctably by the world-horizon. And very much as the entities of modern particle physics can be viewed indifferently as particulate or as field-like, so also intentional objects can be ambiguously "looked at" or "looked through," functioning *opaquely* as "objects" or *transparently* as revelations of the world-horizon.

In the naivety of "natural" consciousness, apperceptual reference to the world-horizon remains prethematic. It is only in phenomenological reflection that the filaments of sense forming the framework of "natural" experience come to light. Reflection discloses the natal bond indissolubly uniting *every* generated experience with its world-matrix. The world thus appears, within the phenomenological posture, not merely as horizon but as "pole"— the ultimate intentional terminus tethering all its modes of presentation, all intramundane objects.[17]

But, secondly, in what sense can the "world-pole" be appreciated as "divine"? While with the world-pole we may well have struck the deepest vein, we seem also to have encountered the most rarified abstraction. How can such a hollow specter answer to our concrete descriptions of God? Only part of the answer lies in a requisite shift from an Aristotelian logic of subsumption—a logic that would make of "world" the highest, and thus emptiest, of genera— to a logic of synthesis.

More vital, however, is the appreciation of God as *summum bonum*,[18] not merely that principle whereby the valuable is granted its value but, self-reflexively, that which is itself of preeminent value. Thus, Husserl conceives of God

> as idea, as the idea of the most perfect being, as idea of the most perfect life, which constitutes itself a perfect world, [of a life] which creatively develops from itself a universe of perfect spiritual beings in relation to a nature perfect in the highest degree.[19]

To say that God is, in the Anselmian formula, "that than which no greater [and thus, no more valuable] can be conceived" is not, of course, to make of God merely a being of maximal conceivable value, the "cap" on the scale. For suppose that, for any "conceivable" (and thus, *constituted*) object of value, there is a better. It is nonsense to suppose that deity is the constituted product of the regress of "betters," found at the end of the series defined by determining, for each "good," a "better still," for *ex hypothesi* there *is* no "end." On this hypothesis, if nothing is better than God, then God cannot be (completely) constituted. The constituted objects of value of our series may eventually be shown to be "moments" of the divine. But divinity itself remains prearticulate, preconstituted.

What draws these insights together is the recognition of the innately *teleological* character of transcendence. The transcendent object *is* a *telos*, an "ideal." This is a claim secured by understanding both the axiological and the infinitary quality of transcendence. Husserl is lucid in his recognition that active recurrence to unity— the explicit consideration of the "selfsame" in different ways manifesting "the disposition to bring the intuitively given object to givenness from all sides"[20]—is motivated by *interest*, both "existential" and "cognitive." Existential interest is, of course, "an *interest* in the object of perception as existent,"[21] while in genuine cognitive interest:

> A voluntary participation of the ego is in play in an entirely different way: the ego wishes to know the object, to pin it

down once and for all. Every step of cognition is guided by an active impulse of the will to hold onto the known as the same and as the substrate of its determining characteristics. . . . The goal of the will is the apprehension of the object in the identity of its determinations, the fixing of the result of contemplative perception "once and for all."[22]

And we need not follow Perry in the details of his axiology to find wisdom in his identification of value as an object of interest.[23] An object could not be transcendent *for us* without serving, thematically or prethematically, as a locus of interest and thus as a value.[24] The investment of intramundane transcendencies with interest-value is, of course, a purely contingent matter. The world-pole, being the ineluctable terminal referent of all intentional activity, is not of merely relative worth.[25] Here we encounter a transcendency of ultimate and absolute value. God is not, in Toulemont's words, merely "la perfection absolue," but is, moreover, absolutely and unsurpassably perfect. The identification of God-as-object with the world-pole is irresistible.

But an ideal, like a star, is out of reach. Unlike a star, however, the ideal of *infinite* perfection is *infinitely* out of reach and, by the logic of infinity, unreachable. Even the intramundane transcendencies of our everyday world are thus "unreachable." Our cube is an inexhaustible reservoir of possibilities. The object can be seen in this way or that, from far and from near, and under various conditions of lighting, atmosphere, mood, and so forth. Its modes of givenness are potentially endless. It is not that this bottomless well of potentiality is thoroughly actualized, the object radiating its effulgence of views into empty space for the fortunate few who may happen to be illuminated by a ray or two of its appearance. Phenomenal potentiality is not fully actualized for potential viewers, but partially actualized by actual viewers. The actualization of phenomenal potentiality is the work of consciousness. Of course, the object as presented under its various aspects *is* the object. But the object is always and necessarily incompletely constituted. A fortiori, while the world-pole is, through human endeavor, partially constituted, its majestic magnitude lies submerged in preconstitutive potentiality, infinitely exceeding the insignificant shred that we have managed to articulate. In Strasser's reading, "the idea of God does not correspond to the highest axiological degree we could imagine, it corresponds to an *infinite and unlimited augmentation* of values."[26] In its infinitary character, the world-pole is, again, divine, the locus not merely of *absolute* value, but of *infinite* value.

The Subject/Object, the Absolute Ideal, and God

Husserl offers an intriguing commentary on his vision of the teleological directedness of consciousness:

> When I called teleology the form of all forms, how is that to be understood? Is it a most general form which can be made manifest in experience as belonging to all beings? And, as the most general is it that which first of all can be made manifest? Of course not. It is what for us is posterior, although in itself it is what is prior. All forms in their full universality must first be manifested. The totality as totality in its complete system of special forms (inclusive of the world and the world-form) must first be disclosed in order that the teleology can be manifested as that form-principle which constitutes, most ultimately enables, and thereby realizes all being in its concrete and individual totality.[27]

This, quite clearly, is no passing thought penned in the heat of more urgent reflections, but a careful statement of the fundamental relationship of formal and final *aitia*. The final awaits the formal. *In the ideal*, the world-pole would be exhaustively manifest, its potentiality for presentation perfectly and completely actualized. Yet this supreme and absolute *telos* could be achieved (*per impossibile*) only through the serial manifestation of every possible "world-stage," every possible constitutively in-formed disclosure of the world. The series exhibits a vector, a direction toward the "absolute presence" of the world-pole. But, of course the teleology pervading the series is, and must ever remain, indeterminate without the consummatory realization of its *telos*. Teleology is the "form of all forms," not in the sense of *subsuming* all world-stages—for it is not the genus, *world-stage*— but in the sense of *uniting* them as their vector.

Phenomenology is primarily a theory of *experiencing*, not of "experience," a theory of intentional *activity*, not of abstract and lifeless "acts," and at its most profound, a theory of *primal presencing* (*lebendige Gegenwärtigung*), not (as the deconstructive prejudice would cast it) a metaphysical speculation on "presence."

While a race is in progress, it cannot be depicted as long or short, breathtaking or trivially expectable. Nor is the winner yet determined. Of course, even in progress, the race can abstractly be broken into segments subject to such judgments. And, of course, the *direction* of the finish line becomes increasingly evident throughout.

Analogously, "epistemological" questions concerning the existence or nature of the intentional "object" can be raised only upon completion or segmentation of intentional activity. We could ask of the completed and thematized "act" whether it successfully attained its epistemological "finish line." But while the activity is occurrent, this question is out of order. We can only inquire concerning its "direction" and the manner of its "running." Similarly, it is senseless to trouble ourselves with puzzlement over the issue of whether world-intending attains an actually existent world-pole. That issue—the issue of whether God-as-object *exists*—is strictly and of necessity "bracketed." The question could be raised only upon termination of world-intending, a fatal consummation that would spell the extinction of consciousness. It is enough to know that consciousness is directed *toward* the world-pole, and to describe its manners of functioning in being thus teleologically oriented.

Finality, derivatively manifest, is of primary phenomenological concern. Yet formality, immediately manifest, is of foundational importance. Without the "world-forms," their serial manifestation indicates no leaning toward the world-pole. Thus, it devolves upon the phenomenologist to examine the skeletal remains of once-living acts. Somewhat like the anthropologist who "sees" the evolution of the species in the series of remains, the phenomenologist "sees" teleology in the eidetic enrichment illustrated by successive "world-forms." Formal eidetic analysis of world-*noemata* and their correlate world-*noeses* thus becomes crucial.

If, in practicing the reduction, I have before me merely the structure of *my own* (empirical) consciousness, what assurance do I have that the allowances and exclusions sponsored by my eidetic insights have any purchase upon the divine? Could it not turn out that where human mentality meets eidetic impossibility the divine is not thus confined? And is it not tantamount to the most flagrant impiety to arrogate to the human mind the Protagorean prerogative, making the human the "measure" of the divine? Of course, were the divine confined where the human is permitted, we could simply say that there is more eidetic "freedom" in the genus than in the species. "The isosceles" is limited where "the triangle" retains its possibilities. This would make of God the (presumably unique) exemplar of the species: *divine mind.* If "divine" serves as *differentium*, the mystery is solved—but only by substituting for it another. If not simply a solecism, "dead cow" does not denote a species of cow, but rather a cow of any species insofar as it once lived but now does not (insofar, that is, as it no longer falls under the species *cow*).

And similarly, if not sheer senselessness, "divine mind" may well denote, not a mind of a determinate species, but a mind of any species insofar as it is divine. "Divine" may function, not as a *differentium*, but as an indication of preeminent exemplification, serving to modify, not the genus *mind*, but its "mode" of instantiation.

What inclines me toward the latter interpretation is not simply the apparent blasphemy of shackling the divine mind with essential difference while our own goes free. For the human can, with similar justification, be claimed to represent a determinate *species* of mind (distinct, perhaps, from avian mind or crustacean mind, or again, from angelic mind). Thus, our own mind-species could be equally, if differently, constrained. Were this the case, however, the divine would be separated from the human by a specific difference quite inaccessible to us in reflection. The "difference" could not be a difference *for us*. Qua mind, the divine would have its intelligibility. Qua divine, God would simply vanish, for us, into the noumenal. We could say nothing, think nothing, comprehend nothing of noumenal divinity—a fate visited upon *any* theological persuasion (not simply phenomenological theology) that, incoherently, casts the purported specific difference of God beyond human ken. If theology—*any* theology—is at all possible, "divine" cannot function as a *differentium*.

More decisive, and more profound, however, subtending the issue of subsumption, is the invariant and "polar" character of the world, entailing, as it does, an invariant and "antipodal" noetic activity of world-intending. Consciousness—all consciousness—would cease in the absence of conscious reference, mediate or immediate, to the world-pole. Thus, world-intending is, of eidetic necessity, ongoing, perpetually in progress. It never becomes "past," and thus never lies anesthetized under the scalpel of the phenomenological anatomist.

But return to my analogy of running. *In progress*, we cannot say *of the running itself* that it is swift or slow. Or if we do, we are speaking merely of a completed segment (from start to present). We can, however, say that the runner is running *swiftly*. What for *completed* action is "adjectival" description may be transposed, in *progressive* activity, into "adverbial" description.[28] And we must be wary of assuming that "swift running" is interchangeable with "running swiftly." In fact, the two modes of description, while intimately related, are incompatible. Activity in *progress* cannot be adjectivally described. *Completed* activity cannot be adverbially described. Hence, to say that Smith is running *swiftly* is not to say that Smith's running is *swift*.

Contrary to the lessons of elementary grammar, while adverbs may "modify" verbs, verbs thus "modified" do not signify (completed) actions. "Swiftly" characterizes, not *running*, but the *way* the running is presently proceeding. Even here, however, there lurks a danger of premature reification. For to say, as we must, that "swiftly" modifies a "way," is not to imply the substantive existence of a "way" that quite literally *instantiates* swiftness. If it is illegitimate to reify an activity in progress, it is also illegitimate to reify the "way" it is progressing. To substantialize an activity or its moments is to complete it. While completed action is "opaque" and substantial (a genuine substrate of predication), progressive activity is ineluctably "transparent." We can only say that "swiftness" appears *through*, not *in*, the ongoing activity.

"Mind," like "action," can, in one of its disambiguations, be understood as substantial and temporally complete. And in this acceptation, mind is amenable to the logic of subsumption. A particular mind may be subordinated to a given mind-species; only on this reading could sense be made of the supposition that "divine" is a *differentium* of mentality. Yet the noetic activity whereby God-as-object is brought to presence cannot be thus substantialized. God-intending is inescapably "verbal": "God *minds*," not "God *has* a mind." Progressive divine minding is "transparent." The ongoing activity of divine minding cannot *instantiate*, but can only *reveal*, divinity and mentality.

While our reflections will not permit the assumption that "divine" is a *differentium* of mentality, it by no means follows that the eidetically discernible structures of the completed intentional act are irrelevant to a description of progressive intentional activity. "Smith's running is swift" can be true only upon completion or segmentation of the act. Still, if every segment of the running up to the present is *swift*, then it is manifest to us that the present progressive activity is occurring *swiftly*. Indeed, the "way" the activity is progressing, its "direction" or vectorial character, is manifest *only* through the instantial features of the "segments." Again, in Husserl's pivotal commentary, *"the totality as totality* in its complete system of special forms . . . *must first be disclosed in order that . . . teleology can be manifested"* (italics added). Without the "segments" (the "special forms") and their "totality," the "adverbial" and thus teleological character of progressive activity would, of necessity, go unmanifest.

What, then, is the "way" of progressive divine minding? What is the vectorial character of a minding that occurs "divinely"? Or again, to what is the progressive activity of divine minding "transparent"? The answer, of course, is that a minding that progresses "divinely" is transparent to divinity, its "way" being a directedness toward the divine. World-minding progresses "divinely" precisely because the world-pole, as the objectual aspect of divinity, *is* divine. Yet since the activity of divine minding cannot "pass," cannot be completed, and cannot, without contradiction, be segmented, divine minding cannot provide the condition for its own manifestation. It is only through completed acts that the revelation of divinity through the ongoing world-directed activity of divine minding is possible. And acts that can be completed are not divine.

A minding that reveals divinity (the endless and incompletable "way" toward the divine) is thus manifested *only* through act-segments, which cannot themselves instantiate divinity because of their very completeness. *Divinity is not, then, a formal eidetic feature derived from "second-order" reflection upon "first-order" human intentional acts, but a "trans-formal," vectorial characteristic of the series of acts itself, available only in "third-order" teleological meditation.* It is only in the reflective closure of phenomenology, in the "phenomenology of phenomenology," that teleology, and hence divinity, is manifest. Given that our own acts exhibit a God-orientation, it cannot be simply this that constitutes divinity. *Divinity is manifest only in incompleteable activity.* Indeed, we may say, divinity—far from merely a fixed and reifiable "Nature" instantiated or self-instantiated by God—is rather the endless "Way" toward God. Human acts, while occurrent, take up this "Path." Divine intentional activity never leaves it.

Since teleology awaits morphology, the endless "Way" toward the world-pole revealed through divine world-intending is manifest *to us* only through the essential structures of *our own* mind. We know that Smith is running *swiftly* because the segments are swift. If *our* acts are intentional (with all that intentionality brings in its eidetic wake), the "Way" in which divine world-minding progresses is likewise intentional. God "minds" intentionally.

There remains, however, a lingering, and crucial, qualm. Even granting that the eidetic structures of our own consciousness comprise a template, a tinted glass, filtering our apprehension of divine minding, may it not still be that *deity-in-itself* bears little, if any, relation to *deity-for-us*?

The question, of course, is circumvented by the *epochē*. Phenomenology, it is sometimes claimed, simply does not address itself to the noumenal. Whether deity-in-itself exists, and if so, what its intrinsic extra-phenomenal properties could be, are issues of no interest to phenomenology as such. This answer, while concealing the proverbial kernel of truth, is nonetheless seriously misleading. For the Husserlian phenomenon is not *an appearance of the object*, but *the object as it appears*. The object (in itself) is at the heart of the phenomenon. The phenomenon embraces the noumenon, but embraces it as an "ideal," as an incompletely constituted *telos*.

God is at the core of the God-phenomenon. But a fully constituted God, the absolute presence of the world-pole, like our "finish line," spells the end of the race, and the consequent annihilation of consciousness, human and divine. Thus, God-as-object *exists* only *as presented*. The divine "Omega" *is*, and is *only*, phenomenal. It is not that phenomenology *first* admits the Kantian distinction between the phenomenal and the noumenal, and *then* simply confines itself to the phenomenal, dismissing the noumenal as irrelevant to its concerns, though presuming the possibility of its existence. The *epochē* imports an initial and decisive rejection of the distinction itself.

This has, of course, the effect of banishing Kantian realism. Indeed, the phenomenologist would issue a variant echo of Berkeley's challenge to the realist. Berkeley would demand that the realist submit even a single example of a thing existing "unconceived" or forego the possibility of evidential support for the theory. And of course for Berkeley, the satisfaction of that demand undermines the very theory it is intended to support. For in conceiving an illustration of the thesis, the realist is thereby, incoherently, "conceiving the unconceived." It is sometimes argued, and not without a certain cogency, that Berkeley's argument confounds "conceiving-that" and "conceiving-of." The realist may, without contradiction, conceive *that* realities not subject to conceiving-*of* may nonetheless exist. The objection seems incisive against Berkeley inasmuch as he implicitly assumed the Kantian framework, relegating mind-dependent objects to the category of "things-for-us." Nowhere concerned to deny the distinction, Berkeley seems simply intent upon demonstrating that the category of "things-in-themselves" is vacuous. "Conceiving-of," in the expansive Berkeleyan sense, is akin to our familiar "intending." Anything capable of intentional objectivity is phenomenal. If we can conceive *that* something exists that is not thus "phenomenal," we have, in the sense of the "A" Edition of the first *Critique*, come across something "noumenal." The objection is thus question-begging, assuming, in disguise, the very distinction it purports to establish. Whatever its fate in Berkeley's hands, the Kantian distinction has absolutely no place within the "brackets" imposed by the phenomenological method. For Husserl, the intentional object is phenomenal—or impossible.

But neither is subjective idealism the outcome of a phenomenological rejection of realism. Idealism, as we have seen, rests upon the very distinction that phenomenology eschews.

But even if the world-pole is "in itself" phenomenal, what guarantees that the way it is present *for us* is in any measure adequate to the way it is *in itself?* There is, after all, a "third party" to consider. Should we not suppose that God perceives the world in a way unimaginably more lucid, articulate, and comprehensive than our own—a way that by comparison, would render our own limited modes of presentation approximately "false"? We may, indeed, wish to suppose so—*if* it were possible for God to see the world "in a way" at all. Otherwise, there would be no strictly deific standard of adequacy, and consequently no question of degree of truthful approximation. *Ours* would be the *only* ways of world-presentation. But *can* God see "in a way"? Is divine seeing a "seeing-as"? The answer is twofold: *yes* and *no*. God cannot see the *world* perspectivally, as we can. But our *seeing* of the world is perspectivally disclosed to the "all-consciousness."

First the *no*.

Suppose I am told that an important letter awaits me at the office. In my eagerness, I drop my present concerns and drive to the department, all the while thinking of the letter. I imagine its appearance, muse over its possible contents, wonder who its author could be, doubt that it could be more than a subscription notice. One thing that I cannot do before reaching the office is to *perceive* it. In a welter of ways, I entertain the letter *in absence*. When I arrive, when the letter is in my hands, before my eyes, it is then *present*—present "in person," in the Husserlian idiom. I then recognize (recognize) *in presence* what was once available to me only *in absence*. My former "empty" intention has now, through "identity-synthesis," been (partially) "filled." Throughout the process of "filling," however, the "empty" intention remains in play. One cannot *fill* a cup with coffee if the cup vanishes while the coffee is being poured. Nor can empty intentionality achieve sensory fulfillment if it *ceases* in confronting presence. Filling demands that "form" remain while "content" is added. "Content" is variable and contingent. "Form" is invariable and required.

Divine progressive world-intending, being incompleteable, ineluctable, and transcendentally formal, can be understood neither as the activity of world-presenting nor as the activity of identity-synthesis whereby world-presence "fills" empty world-intending. Both activities are essentially contingent. Divine world-intending is of necessity "empty." But constitution, the "animation" ("besouling") of *hylē*, is not functional in the utter absence of its "raw material." Thus, it can be *only our* consciousness, not the divine, that discloses world-presence, and thus, *only our* consciousness, not the divine, that, in any immediate sense, constitutes the world. It is *we, the universal intersubjective community of finite minds, who collectively constitute the successive modes of world-presentation through which divine empty world-intending is manifest.* And this, in part, is the significance of Husserl's assertion that "God . . . sees the thing from one side (with *my* consciousness) and 'at the same time' from the other side (with the consciousness of the *Other*)." God emptily intends the world, but the constitutive fulfillment of divine world-intending is achieved only through us. It is *we*, not God, who see the world "in a way." But while God is not the *agent* of world-constitution, the world *as constituted* is nonetheless available to God through our eyes. God is the "patient" of our world-constitutive agency. God is the "cup." We pour the coffee.

Let us turn to the *yes*.

While world-presence is not the *hylē* upon which divine constitutive activity works, world-presencing is. The "stuff" for divine constitutive agency is found a level up, in our own activity of animation. We, as individuated modes of world-constitutive activity, are the "matter" in-formed by the divine besouling of the intersubjective community:

> God is not the universe of monads itself but rather the entelechy residing in the universe of monads as the idea of the infinite telos of development of the absolute.[29]

As "entelechy," as the primordial "principle" (*archē*) whereby monadic consciousness perspectivally approximates the world-*telos*, God cannot simply be identified with the monadic community.[30] God "resides" in the community, but not of course as a "resident." God is not simply one more mind.

God-as-subject is that agency whereby the universal community is, in the Aristotelian sense, endowed with a "soul." Yet *Geist* (the "I" that is a "we," and the "we" that is an "I," the unity-in-multiplicity informing our world-constitutive agency) is not, contrary to Hegel, straightforwardly to be identified with God. Just as we, in the progressive enrichment of our world-vision, synthesize the manifold of world-presentations, seeing each as a "mirror" of the whole, so, too, the divine synthesizes the ongoing phases of our world-constituting, seeing each as a mirror of a whole that Husserl occasionally calls the "God-world" (*Gotteswelt*), the *telos* of perfect intersubjective interpenetration, perfect reciprocal transparency. A hall of mirrors, each so situated as to reflect all others within it, would poorly illustrate the *Ineinander* structure of the *Gotteswelt*, if there were at its center an opacity preventing the reciprocal reflection of facing mirrors. *For us*, the obscuring "matter" at the center of the world is the world's inexhaustible potentiality for alternative presentation. *For God*, the monadic community, understood as the limitless capacity for profiled presentation of the God-world, forms the centralizing opacity. To animate the community with an intersubjective "gist" (*Geist*) is progressively to "de-opacitize" the "hall of mirrors." We are the "coffee." God does the "pouring." But what is the "cup"?

God-as-subject is, as we know, "emptily" aware of God-as-object. But this, of course, is an emptiness that we fill. Both world-pole and God-world are termini of divine vectorial awareness. Or since an "object" is that which occupies the mind at a given time, we are left not with a radical duality of objects, but with a unitary, though internally dirempted, "object"—describable indifferently as *God-World/World-Pole*, as *Logos/Telos*, or as *Reason/Truth*. In the ideal, the intentional tension between subject and object is resolved. Polarity becomes unity, for the teleological striving toward this unity has reached its consummation. In the "house of mirrors," our representation of an intersubjectivity so thoroughly integral as to comprise a unitary and comprehensive "subject," the "object" is the array of mirrors itself. The distinction between "subject" and "object" does not disappear, but becomes aspectual.

Moreover, *in the ideal*, God, as the "all-consciousness," the "all-of-monads," is inseparable from the system of mirrors itself. This "absolute ideal" is "the ideal of an all-person that infinitely transcends all contingency (*das Faktische*) as well as all becoming and all development of the contingent toward the idea; it is a pole which lies infinitely far beyond it; it is *the idea of an absolutely perfect transcendental total community*" (italics added).[31] The *Gotteswelt* is the ideal interpenetration of *all possible* (not merely all actual) monadic "standpoints." In the ideal, God can thus be envisioned as a single and continuous "reflecting surface," spherically molded, such that at each "point" all others, and the "all" of others, are reflected. In intending the God-world, the divine thus intends its ideal self. It is hopeless to look for a second "cup."

God-world and world-pole comprise a single, but complex, "object" of a single "dual-pronged" intentional activity. Approximative constitution of each *Geist*-informed phase of intersubjective life is divine self-realization. Through world-constitution, we approximate the comprehensive "reflection" exhibited within the God-world. Through the constitution of intersubjectivity, God approximates the "reflecting."

We arrive, then, at the "final" application of our phenomenological resolution of the "worst difficulty." While Socrates could not follow us in attributing internal structure to the Forms, we, at least, have seen that *"subject" and "object" are moments internal to transcendental subjectivity. The "absolute ideal"—embracing at once the ideal form of subjectivity (the God-world) and the ideal form of objectivity (the world-pole)— is the ideal illustration of this complex "form." God "exemplifies" this form, but, of course, does so "adverbially."* Divine empty intentional activity is informed by a "way" (not a property or structure), the endless "way" toward the absolute *telos* of self-realization, self-constitution, through human constitution of the world-pole.

Notes

Introduction

1. What about the cosmos before humankind appeared in evolution? There *is* a "cosmos before mankind" only *for* man. The implication of this is that "to be" can only mean "to be for consciousness." What *this* implies is a further question. The philosopher will recognize a parallel to this in the recent theory of natural science that the cosmos *must* be such that anthropos evolve in it. See John D. Barrow and Frank J. Tipler, *The Anthropic Cosmological Principle* (New York: Oxford University Press, 1986); George Greenstein, *The Symbiotic Universe: Life and Mind in the Cosmos* (New York: William Morrow, 1988); and P. C. W. Davies, *The Accidental Universe* (Cambridge: Cambridge University Press, 1982).

2. George Lakoff, *Women, Fire, and Dangerous Things: What Categories Reveal About the Mind* (Chicago: University of Chicago Press, 1987), and Robert G. Jahn and Brenda J. Dunne, *Margins of Reality: The Role of Consciousness in the Physical World* (New York: Harcourt Brace Jovanovich, 1987).

3. For example, Heidegger in 1949 wrote in the Epilogue to *What is Metaphysics?*: "Being never comes-to-presence (*west*) without beings" (Nachwort, *Was ist Metaphysik?* [Frankfurt am Main: Klostermann, 5th ed., 1949], p. 46). But earlier he had written: "Being indeed comes-to-presence without beings" (Nachwort, *Was ist Metaphysik?* [Bonn: Cohen, 4th ed., 1943], as reported in William J. Richardson, *Heidegger: Through Phenomenology to Thought* [The Hague: Nijhoff, 1963], pp. 563–65).

4. *Rep.* 476a–480a.

5. This is a possible interpretation of Heidegger (cf. Richardson, *Heidegger*, pp. 638–40). Sometimes Heidegger speaks as if the *Lēthē* of *Alētheia* were the latter's concealment from us in beings, oriented as we are toward beings. Sometimes he speaks as if the *Lēthē* in *Alētheia* were that out of which the process of *Alētheia* happens. How is one to interpret the following passage, for example? "Only what Alētheia grants is experienced and thought, not what it is as such. This remains concealed. Does this happen by chance? Does it happen only as a result of a carelessness in human thinking? Or does it happen because the Self-Concealing, the Concealment (*Verborgenheit*), the *Lēthē* belongs to *A-Lētheia*, not as a mere addition, not as

shadow to light, but as the Heart of *Alētheia*? And is it not the case that a keeping and preserving hold sway in this Self-Concealing of [= within] the Clearing (*Lichtung*) of [= which is] Presence-hood (*Anwesenheit*), out of (*aus*) which Disclosure (*Unverborgenheit*) can be granted in the first place . . . ?" ("Das Ende der Philosophie und die Aufgabe des Denkens" [1964], *Zur Sache des Denkens* [Tübingen: Max Niemeyer, 1969], p. 78).

6. Emmanuel Levinas, *Totality and Infinity: An Essay on Exteriority* [1968], trans. Alphonso Lingis (Pittsburgh: Duquesne University Press, 1969); *Otherwise Than Being or Beyond Essence* [1978], trans. Alphonso Lingis (The Hague: Nijhoff, 1981); and *Collected Philosophical Papers* [1948–1978], trans. Alphonso Lingis (The Hague: Nijhoff, 1987).

7. In response to this question, see Daniel Guerrière, "How Does God Enter into Philosophy?," *The Thomist*, 48 (1984): 165–87.

8. For a survey of the major authors up to the early 1970s, see Edward Farely, *Ecclesial Man: A Social Phenomenology of Faith and Reality* (Philadelphia: Fortress, 1975), pp. 235–72.

9. Gerardus van der Leeuw, *Religion in Essence and Manifestation*, 2 vols. (paginated continuously), trans. J. E. Turner, with Appendices by Hans H. Penner (New York: Harper & Row, 1963), pp. 23–539.

10. David Tracy, *Blessed Rage for Order: The New Pluralism in Theology* (New York: Seabury, 1975), pp. 91–203.

11. Mariasusai Dhavamony, *Phenomenology of Religion* (Rome: Gregorian University Press, 1973), p. 10.

12. See van der Leeuw, *Religion* esp. the Epilegomena, pp. 671–95 and Dhavamony, *Phenomenology*, esp. the Introduction, pp. 3–28. For an exposition of the problem of the unity or distinctiveness of a "science of religion"—though he comes to a skeptical conclusion—see Donald Wiebe, *Religion and Truth: Towards an Alternative Paradigm for the Study of Religion* (The Hague: Mouton, 1981). Against the skeptical conclusion, see: Donald A. Crosby, *Interpretive Theories of Religion* (The Hague: Mouton, 1981); Friedrich Heiler, *Erscheinungsformen und Wesen der Religion* (Stuttgart: Kohlhammer, 1961), esp. pp. 1–21 and 561–65; ed. Lauri Honko, *Science of Religion: Studies in Methodology* (The Hague: Mouton, 1979), esp. part 2, pp. 143–366; W. Brede Kristensen, *The Meaning of Religion* (The Hague: Nijhoff, 1960), esp. the General Introduction, pp. 1–23; Georg Schmid, *Principles of Integral Science of Religion*, trans. John Wilson (The Hague: Mouton, 1979); Ninian Smart, *The Phenomenon of Religion* (New York: Seabury, 1973); Jacques Waarenburg, *Classical Approaches to the Study of Religion*, 2 vols. (vol. 1, Introduction and Anthology; vol. 2. Bibliography) (The Hague: Mouton, 1973), esp. vol. 1, part 5; idem, *Reflections on the Study of Religion* (The Hague: Mouton, 1978), esp. parts 2–3, pp. 51–137; Joachim Wach, *The Comparative Study of Religion*, ed. Joseph Kitagawa (New York: Columbia Univer-

sity Press, 1958); idem, *Types of Religious Experience* (Chicago: University of Chicago Press, 1951), esp. part A, pp. 3–57; and Geo Widengren, *Religionsphänomenologie* (Berlin: Walter de Gruyter, 1969), pp. 1–4.

13. See E. C. Krupp, *Echoes of the Ancient Skies: The Astronomy of·Lost Civilizations* (New York: New American Library, 1983); and Giorgio de Santillana and Hertha von Dechend, *Hamlit's Mill: An Essay on Myth and the Frame of Time* (Boston: David R. Godine, 1977). There are many studies of the compactness—*sine* the word—of science, religion, philosophy, moral code, and so on. For example, on the compactness of scientific worldview and moral code, see ed. Robin W. Lovin and Frank E. Reynolds, *Cosmogony and Ethical Order* (Chicago: University of Chicago Press, 1985).

14. Louis Dumont, *Homo Hierarchicus: The Caste System and Its Implications,* trans. Mark Sainsbury, Louis Dumont, and Basia Gulati (Chicago: University of Chicago Press, rev. ed., 1980); Hajime Nakamura, *The Ways of Thinking of Eastern Peoples,* trans. Philip P. Wiener (Honolulu: East-West Center Press, rev. ed., 1964); and Troy Wilson Organ, *The Hindu Quest for the Perfection of Man* (Athens: Ohio University Press, 1970).

15. For a massive effort to specify them historically, see Mircea Eliade, *A History of Religious Ideas,* 3 vols. (Chicago: University of Chicago Press, 1978–1985).

16. On "ideology" and "representation" in this sense, see, respectively, Paul Ricoeur, *Lectures on Ideology and Utopia,* ed. George H. Taylor (New York: Columbia University Press, 1986), and Eric Voegelin, *The New Science of Politics* (Chicago: University of Chicago Press, 1952), pp. 27–75.

17. The work of Carl Gustav Jung is well-known in this regard. See also, for example, Leonard J. Biallas, *Myths: Gods, Heroes, and Saviors* (Mystic, Conn.: Twenty-Third Publications, 1986); Martin S. Day, *The Many Meanings of Myth* (Lanham, Md.: University Press of America, 1984); William G. Doty, *Mythography: The Study of Myths and Rituals* (University: University of Alabama Press, 1986), esp. pp. 131–66; Leo Schneiderman, *The Psychology of Myth, Forklore, and Religion* (Chicago: Nelson-Hall, 1981); and Ann and Barry Ulanov, *Religion and the Unconscious* (Philadelphia: Westminster, 1975). On biblical religion in this perspective, see Heinz Westman, *The Structure of Biblical Myths: The Ontogenesis of the Psyche* (Dallas: Spring Publications, [1986]); on Greek religion, see Arianna Stassinopoulos and Roloff Beny, *The Gods of Greece* (New York: Harry N. Abrams, 1983).

18. On Rousseau's "theories" as myths, see Madeline B. Ellis, *Rousseau's Socratic Aemilian Myth* (Columbus: Ohio State University Press, 1977); and Nina Rosenstand, "Rousseau and the Origin of Language," unpublished paper, delivered at the meeting of the Western Society for Eighteenth-Century Studies, California State University/Long Beach, February 1988 [available from author at CSULB]. On Plato's myths, see Julias A. Elias, *Plato's Defence of Poetry* (Albany: SUNY Press, 1984); Eric Voegelin,

Order and History, 3: *Plato and Aristotle* (Baton Rouge: Louisiana State University Press, 1956); and Robert Zaslavsky, *Platonic Myth and Platonic Writing* (Washington, D.C.: University Press of America, 1981). On the persistence of myth in general, see Leszek Kolakowski, *The Presence of Myth,* trans. Adam Czerniawski (Chicago: University of Chicago Press, 1989).

19. Already Aristotle said it: *epistēmē* begins in an *epagogē,* an immediate grasp of some universal (*An. Post.* II 19).

20. Edmund Husserl, *Ideas Pertaining to a Pure Phenomenology and to a Phenomenological Philosophy,* First Book [1913], trans. Fred Kersten (The Hague: Nijhoff, 1983), §§1–17; G. W. F. Hegel, *Science of Logic,* trans. A. V. Miller (New York: Humanities Press, 1969), book 2, the Doctrine of Essence.

21. Cf. the distinction that Max Scheler makes between "the concrete phenomenology of religions" and "the essential phenomenology of religion" (*die Wesensphänomenologie der Religion, die philosophische Wesenserkenntnis der Religion*) in *Vom Ewigen im Menschen* [this article, 1917–1920], ed. Maria Scheler (Munich: Francke, 5th ed., 1954), pp. 156–59 (= *On the Eternal in Man,* trans. Bernard Noble [London: SMC Press, 1960], pp. 159–63).

22. It is one of the four types of discipline. The types that have developed are: the sciences (formal, natural, and human); the art-criticisms (literary, musical, fine, architectural, cinematic, and so on); the philosophies (however divided); and the theologies (however divided). Of course it took many centuries of human effort for the theologies to differentiate out of more compact thought, just as is the case for the other disciplines.

23. This theology is possible in principle for any religion, especially if it be universal. It has been actual for the universal religions, especially in our day and especially for Christianity. Examples include: David Tracy, *Blessed Rage for Order;* John B. Cobb, Jr., *The Structure of Christian Existence* (New York: Seabury, 1975); Francis Schüssler Fiorenza, *Foundational Theology* (New York: Crossroad, 1984); Langdon Gilkey, *Naming the Whirlwind: The Renewal of God-Language* (Indianapolis: Bobbs-Merrill, 1969), esp. pp. 315–413; and Peter Hodgson, *New Birth of Freedom* (Philadelphia: Fortress, 1976).

24. William L. Rowe, *Philosophy of Religion: An Introduction* (Belmont, Calif.: Wadsworth, 1978), p. 2.

25. Typical is Rowe, *Philosophy,* and William J. Wainwright, *Philosophy of Religion* (Belmont, Calif.: Wadsworth, 1988). These textbooks witness to academic orthodoxy in North America.

26. The rediscovery of "truth" as manifestness is the work of Martin Heidegger; see *Being and Time* [1927], trans. John Macquarrie and Edward Robinson (New York: Harper & Row, 1962), §44. Before the coherence of discourse, before even the conformity of discourse to thing, there must be manifestness of thing.

27. See Herbert Spiegelberg, *The Phenomenological Movement: An Historical Introduction* (The Hague: Nijhoff, 3rd rev. and enlarged ed., 1982).

28. James G. Hart, "A Precis of a Husserlian Philosophical Theology," in *Essays in Phenomenological Theology,* ed. Steven W. Laycock and James G. Hart (Albany: SUNY Press, 1986); Steven W. Laycock, "Toward an Overview of Phenomenological Theology" and "The Intersubjective Dimension of Husserl's Theology," both in *Essays in Phenomenological Theology,* and *Foundations for a Phenomenological Theology* (Lewiston: Edmund Mellen Press, 1988).

29. See above, pp. 3–4 and Laycock's article below, chap. 11, note 17.

The editor is grateful to Merold Westphal and Charles Courtney for their encouragement at the initial stages of this project, to Louis Dupré and Dana Prom Smith for advice, and to Ty-Juan Lamb Markham for inspiration.

Chapter 1

1. Mahatma K. Gandhi, *Yeravda Mandir* in *Gandhi Selected Writings* (New York: Harper, 1972), p. 41.

2. He himself coined a new word based on truth-being to articulate his life project: *satyagraha* Because *agraha* means firmness, determination, we could understand it as "remaining firmly faithful to the truth of being." For Gandhi truth implies a single-minded devotion to authenticity in speaking, thinking, acting, as well as a willingness to suffer persecution for it. Only after having pursued it morally may we hope that it will reveal itself cognitively. See D. M. Datta, *The Philosophy of Mahatma Gandhi* (Madison: University of Wisconsin Press, 1953), p. 128.

3. "We are so steeped in an epistemological method that we feel compelled to begin with judgment and then introduce 'truth' as a relation to fact to distinguish knowledge from mere belief. But from Gandhi's metaphysical perspective we can within the more general view take account of individual facts as well as individual beliefs and then introduce correspondence as one of the several meanings of truth of judgment" (Paul Grimely Kuntz, "Gandhi's Truth," *International Philosophical Quarterly,* 22, 3 [Sept. 1982]: 150).

4. See Hans Urs von Balthasar, *The Glory of the Lord. A Theologial Aesthetics,* vol. 1, trans. Erasmo Leiva-Merikakis (San Francisco: Ignatius Press; New York: Crossroad, 1982), pp. 137–40.

5. *Confessions* V, 3. The reason is eloquently stated in *De vera religione:* "There is no lack of value or benefit in the contemplation of the beauty of the heavens, the arrangement of the stars, the radiant crown of light, the change of day and night, the monthly courses of the moon, the fourfold

tempering of the year to match the four elements, the powerful force of seeds from which derive the forms of measure and nature in its kind. But such a consideration must not pander to a vain and passing curiosity, but must be turned into a stairway to the immortal and enduring" (# 52).

6. Not until the high Middle Ages did Western theologians clearly accept *all* knowledge as intrinsically good and destined to find its fulfillment in God.

7. *De magistro*, ## 38–46.

8. *De diversis quaestionibus*, 83, 48.

9. *Cur Deus Homo?*, trans. Jasper Hopkins and Herbert Richardson, in *Anselm of Canterbury*, bk. 1, chap. 2 (Toronto: Edwin Mellen Press, 1976).

10. On the ambivalence of Anselm's attitude, see William Collinge, "Monastic Life as a Context for Religious Understanding in St. Anselm," *American Benedictine Review*, 35:4 (1984): 378–88.

11. *Summa Theologiae*, I q. 1, a. 8.

12. "For Thomas, neither Christian doctrine nor the miracles that attest to it would say anything to man without the *interior instinctus et attractus doctrinae (In John*, c. 6, i. 4, n. 7; c. 15, i. 5, n. 5; *In Rom*. c. 8, i. 6), which he also calls *inspiratio interna* and *experimentum"* (Hans Urs von Balthasar, *The Glory of the Lord*, 1: 162).

13. The pragmatist model has been omitted from this discussion as being more appropriate for evaluating methods of solving practical and scientific problems than for evaluating the theoretical truth of religion. The pragmatist tends to sidestep the issue of truth in favor of that of practical (moral, esthetic, psychological) value. William James himself, that most perceptive interpreter of religion, defends "the will to believe" on the basis of its beneficial effects rather than its intrinsic truth. He treats faith as a good rather than as a truth:

> We see first that religion offers itself as a *momentous* option. We are supposed to gain, even now, by our belief, and to love by our non-belief, a certain vital good. Secondly, religion is a *forced* option, so far as that goes. We cannot escape the issue by remaining skeptical and waiting for more light, because although we avoid error in that way *if religion be untrue*, we lose the good, *if it be true*, just as certainly as we positively choose to disbelieve [William James: "The Will to Believe," in *Essays on Faith and Morals* (New York: World Publishing Company, 1972), p. 57].

Absent in this passage is any appreciation of the intrinsic truth of faith and of the attraction, indeed necessity, of that alleged truth with respect to the believer. Even regarding faith as the result of a decision misapprehends the believer's situation, since the believer considers his assent to be a *response* to a transcendent attraction.

14. *Logische Untersuchungen* (Halle, 1913), 1: 228.

15. Oxford: Clarendon Press (1906), 1969, p. 68. The importance of Joachim's expression lies in its distinguishing "the determining characteristic of the 'significant whole' " from a logical nexus that secures a certain cohesion of various elements without intrinsically relating them.

16. In the words of William Christian: "If there are domains of truth, then philosophers, taken collectively, would have the following complex project, among others, on their hands. They would be responsible for (1) formulating principles of judgment in various domains of discourse, (2) formulating general conditions of truth and showing how truth conditions in various domains specify the general conditions, and (3) exploring patterns of relatedness among different domains" (William A. Christian, "Domains of Truth," *American Philosophical Quarterly,* 12 [1975]: 62).

17. C. D. Broad, *Philosophy and Psychical Research* (London: Routledge, Kegan Paul, 1953), p. 235.

18. Michel Foucault, *The Archeology of Knowledge,* trans. A. M. Sheridan Smith (New York: Pantheon, 1972), p. 32.

19. How little this effect is intended, however, appears in the fact that the creative power is restricted to the human being— the sole maker of words. Derrida himself supports his position in a passage that could have been written by an Italian humanist: "Consciously or not, the idea that man has of his aesthetic power corresponds to the idea he has about the creation of the world and to the solution he gives to the radical origin of things" (*Writing and Difference* [University of Chicago Press, 1978], p. 10).

20. "On the Essence of Truth," trans. John Sallis, in *Basic Writings,* ed. David F. Krell (New York: Harper & Row, 1976), pp. 129–33.

21. *Wahrheit und Methode* (Tübingen: J. C. B. Mohr, 2nd ed., 1965), p. xxvv.

22. *Vorlesungen über die Philosophie der Religion.* Part 1, *Der Begriff der Religion,* ed. Walter Jaeschke (Hamburg, 1981), p. 25 (*Lectures on the Philosophy of Religion.* Part 1, *The Concept of Religion,* ed. Peter C. Hodgson [Berkeley: University of California Press, 1984], p. 106).

23. *Vorlesungen,* p. 219; *Lectures,* part 1, p. 315.

24. *Vorlesungen,* p. 223; *Lectures,* part 1, p. 319.

25. Gerardus van der Leeuw, *Religion in Essence and Manifestation*

(New York: Harper, 1960), p. 61. See my own evaluation in *A Dubious Heritage* (New York: Paulist Press, 1977), pp. 76–79.

26. *Ascent of Mount Carmel*, trans. Allison Peers (Garden City, N.Y.: Doubleday-Image, 1958), II, 26, 1.

27. Ibid., II, 26, 5.

28. Ibid., II, 26, 8.

29. *Analytica Posteriora* B 19

30. *Wahrheit und Methode*, pp. 333–37.

31. Edward Schillebeeckx, *Christ. The Experience of Jesus as Lord*, trans. John Bowden (New York: Crossroad, 1981), p. 37.

32. I leave the complex case of the mystical vision out of consideration. Besides being highly exceptional, the precise nature of visions and locutions remains obscure even by the mystics' own accounts. They could hardly be more than expressions of a more intense but *still mysterious* experience of presence.

33. Of course, some of the older wisdom literature appears to have consisted of a series of maxims considered useful for promoting a career in court administration—a relatively "secular" affair.

34. Martin Buber identified the original meaning of faith as steadfastness—even more than trust in a person. He sees this symbolically represented in the story of Moses' prayer during the battle with Abimelek. As long as his hands remained steady, Israel retained the upper hand, but the hands of faith always grow weak and need support.

35. Ignace de la Potterie relates truth and law in a causal way: "La vérité est un concept plus large, plus enveloppant; elle désigne la révélation même de la volonté divine et du mystère de Dieu; par contre la loi, les commandements, les paroles de Dieu, sont autant d'expressions concrètes de la volonté divine" (*La vérité dans Saint Jean* [Rome: Biblical Institute Press, 1977], p. 152).

36. Even when revived in the Reformation, the older concept assumed a subjective quality that had been absent from the Hebrew notion of trust. Luther's explanation of the first commandment reads: "It is the faith and trust of the heart which makes both God and idol. If your faith and trust are true, then your God will be true as well; and again, where trust is false and baseless, there is no true God" (quoted in Wolfhart Pannenberg, *The Apostles' Creed* [*Philadelphia:* 1972], p. 33). An echo of this we hear in Kierkegaard's statement that to know God truly is not to know the true God, but to achieve a true relation to God (*Concluding Unscientific Postscript*, trans. David F. Swenson and Walter Lowrie [Princeton University Press, 1941], p. 178).

37. See Jacques Dupont, *Gnosis* (Bruges: Desclée de Brouwer, 1949).

Special thanks to Jacqueline Mariña who assisted me in research for this chapter.

Chapter 2

1. See Martin Heidegger, *Holzwege*, "Die Zeit des Weltbildes (1938)," in *Gesamtausgabe*, vol. 5 (Frankfurt: Klostermann, 1977), pp. 78f.

2. See Philip Clayton, *Explanation from Physics to Theology: An Essay in Rationality and Religion* (New Haven: Yale University Press, 1989), chap. 2.

3. See, among many others, Paul Ricoeur, *Hermeneutics and the Human Sciences*, ed. and trans. John B. Thompson (Cambridge: Cambridge University Press, 1981), and Ian Barbour, *Myths, Models and Paradigms: A Comparative Study in Science and Religion* (New York: Harper and Row, 1974).

4. See the excellent anthology edited by Maurice Natanson, *Phenomenology and the Social Sciences*, 2 vols. (Evanston: Northwestern University Press, 1973); and Elisabeth Strüker, *Husserlian Foundations of Science*, ed. Lee Hardy (Washington, D. C.: University Press of America, 1987).

5. See esp. Mary Hesse, *Revolutions and Reconstructions in the Philosophy of Science* (Cambridge: Cambridge University Press, 1981); see also Patrick A. Heelan, *Space-Perception and the Philosophy of Science* (Berkeley: University of California Press, 1983).

6. Namely, theoretical truth, truthfulness of expression, and normative rightness, respectively. See Habermas, *The Theory of Communicative Action*, trans. Thomas McCarthy, vol. 1, *Reason and the Rationalization of Society* (Boston: Beacon, 1984), e.g., pp. 302–9.

7. P. McHugh, "On the Failure of Positivism," in J. D. Douglas, ed., *Understanding Everyday Life: Toward the Reconstruction of Social Knowledge* (Chicago: Aldine, 1970), p. 329.

8. Think of Eliade's claim that ontology gives place to history, in *Myth and Reality* (New York: Harper, 1963), p. 108.

9. Joseph J. Kockelmans, "On the Problem of Truth in the Sciences," *Proceedings and Addresses of the American Philosophical Association*, vol. 61, # 1 (Sept. 1987): 5–26 (at p. 19).

10. This is a theme that Michael Polanyi has developed as well as any recent writer; see his *Personal Knowledge* (London: Routledge and Kegan Paul, 1958).

11. See T. S. Kuhn's essay, "Logic of Discovery or Psychology of Research?," which set off the highly influential discussion contained in ed.

282 NOTES

Imre Lakatos and Alan Musgrave, *Criticism and the Growth of Knowledge* (Cambridge: Cambridge University Press, 1970).

12. T. S. Kuhn uses the term "conversion" some four times in *The Structure of Scientific Revolutions* (Chicago: University of Chicago Press, 2nd. ed., 1970). Paul Feyerabend, in *Against Method: Outline of an Anarchistic Theory of Knowledge* (London: NLB, 1975), is even less reticent to speak of the "religious" nature of these shifts: he argues, for instance, that voodoo may be as rationally justified as Western science.

13. These themes have been developed by Gerald Holton in, e.g., *The Scientific Imagination: Case Studies* (Cambridge: Cambridge University Press, 1978); and by Michel Foucault in many works; for a brief introduction, see his "Truth and Power," in *Power/Knowledge*, ed. Colin Gordon (New York: Pantheon, 1980), pp. 109–33.

14. Paul Feyerabend develops this example in detail in *Against Method* in order to argue that there is no methodology of science, that "anything goes" even among those we hold up as our paradigms of scientific research.

15. Hans-George Gadamer, *Truth and Method*, trans. [G. Barden and J. Cumming] (New York: Crossroad, 1975), p. 409.

16. See, e.g., *The Other Dimension: A Search for the Meaning of Religious Attitudes* (New York: Seabury [Crossroad], 1972).

17. See his *An Introduction to Religion: A Phenomenological Approach* (New York: Harper and Row, 1968), pp. 12f.

18. This is a central thesis of Gadamer's hermeneutic theory of the human sciences in *Truth and Method*. Some of the implications of this inseparability for sociology and anthropology are explored in Bryan Wilson, ed., *Rationality* (Oxford: Basil Blackwell, 1970). Of course, the goal of objectivity remains in social science. We want to listen to our subjects; and if we could predict their behavior with mathematical accuracy, we would be all the happier. Perhaps, though, others are forever unknowable, and all attempts to grasp them ultimately and necessarily fail. Given the view of science developed in this section, this would not surprise us, because important limitations have revealed themselves in the very nature of the *human* scientific activity. Once again, is this not exactly the situation we observe (with less surprise) in religion? The forever unknowable human other is just as other as the Totally Other whom we speak of as transcendent.

19. Paul Tillich, *The Courage to Be* (New Haven: Yale University Press, 1952), pp. 48, 175.

20. Clifford Geertz, "Religion as a Cultural System," chap. 4 of *The Interpretation of Cultures* (New York: Basic Books, 1973), p. 112.

21. See Pannenberg's still unrivaled *Theology and the Philosophy of Science*, trans. Francis McDonagh (Philadelphia: Westminster, 1977); Hans Al-

bert, *Treatise on Critical Reason* [1980], trans. Mary Varney Rorty (Princeton: Princeton University Press, 1985); and Karl Popper, *Conjectures and Refutations: The Growth of Scientific Knowledge* (London: Routledge and Kegan Paul, 4th ed., 1972).

22. G. van der Leeuw, *Religion in Essence and Manifestation: A Study in Phenomenology,* trans. J. E. Turner (New York: Harper and Row, 1963), 2:680.

23. See Henry Duméry, *The Problem of God in Philosophy of Religion,* trans. Charles Courtney (Evanston: Northwestern University Press, 1969), and Louis Dupré, "Duméry's Reductions of Experience" in *A Dubious Heritage: Studies in the Philosophy of Religion after Kant* (New York: Paulist, 1977).

I am grateful to Louis Dupré, Attila Sala, and Bill Wootters for helpful discussions and criticisms during the writing of this paper.

Chapter 3

1. While the theme of truth can be and should be considered in the broad framework of religion and religions, this essay will limit itself to philosophies and theologies of Western Christianity. I shall use the term "religion" to mean the Christian religion and "theology" as Christian theology.

2. This Christian vision of reality is not synonymous with the great medieval doctrinal and cultural synthesis or the intellectual visions of Dante or Thomas Aquinas. It is very much at the heart of classical Protestantism, too, and continues in all forms of Christianity whose version of the Christian message unites these various themes into a comprehensive cosmo-historical narrative.

3. The best account of this erosion and the cognitive issues it poses for theology is Van Harvey's *The Historian and the Believer: The Morality of Historical Knowledge and Christian Belief* (New York: Macmillan, 1966).

4. The antimetaphysical tradition of modern philosophy occurs in two major streams, and Christian theology attached itself to both of them. The two are Continental philosophy from Kant (who exposes antinomies attending all speculative accounts of being) through deconstruction, and Anglo-American empiricist and pragmatic philosophy with roots in British empiricism.

5. This group, which in some ways is a continuation into the 1980s of the earlier radical theology movement, finds its starting point in the later Heidegger, Derrida, and deconstruction. For the theme, the end of theology, see Carl A. Raschke, *The Alchemy of the Word: Language and the End of Theology* (Philadelphia: Scholars Press, 1979), esp. chap. 5. In addition see Mark C. Taylor, *Erring: A Postmodern A/theology* (Chicago: University of Chicago Press, 1984), and Charles Winquist, *Epiphanies of Darkness: Deconstruction in Theology* (Philadelphia: Fortress, 1986).

6. A good example of this marriage of linguistic philosophy and Christian dogmatics is George Lindbeck, *The Nature of Doctrine: Religion and Theology in a Postliberal Age* (Philadelphia: Westminster, 1984).

7. The older dictionaries of philosophy carried this typology. See, for instance, ed. Dagobert D. Runes, *The Dictionary of Philosophy* (New York: Philosophical Library, 1942), "Truth."

8. There seems to be little agreement in current philosophical literature about a typology of approaches to truth. Perhaps this is because different things are attempted in the typologies. Albert Hofstader proposes a constructive, philosophical typology rather than an overview of existing approaches (*Truth and Art* [New York: Columbia University Press, 1965], chap. 5). Eliot Deutsch derives differentiated meanings of truth from usages or meanings of truth in the English language (*On Truth: An Ontological Theory* [Honolulu: University of Hawaii Press, 1979], p. 1).

9. For a modern Thomist formulation, see B. Lonergan, *Insight: A Study of Human Understanding* (New York: Philosophical Library, 1957), pp. 502ff. An excellent survey and summary of the literature and discussion in Anglo-American linguistic philosophy is A. N. Prior's "The Correspondence Theory of Truth," in ed. Paul Edwards, *The Encyclopedia of Philosophy* (New York and London: Macmillan and the Free Press, 1967), vol. 2. See also Alan R. White, *Truth* (Garden City: N.Y.: Doubleday, 1970).

10. Husserl anticipates the primordial sense of truth in several ways. First, he locates truth not in the outcome of scientific inquiry as mathematizing of the world but in the prescientific realm of the life-world, that to which the scientist must always repair for originary givens and confirmations. Secondly, he connects truth with the experience of evidentiality, and evidence is "nothing other than the 'experience' of truth" (Marvin Farber, *The Foundation of Phenomenology* [Albany: SUNY Press, 1943], p. 133). Thirdly, Husserl says explicitly that the truth of predicative propositions posits a relation to the original of the proposition—that is, to its truth, "which is given in consciousness of the original, which means self-evident consciousness" (*Experience and Judgment: Investigations in a Genealogy of Logic* [Evanston: Northwestern University Press, 1973], p. 297).

11. See Martin Heidegger, *Being and Time*, trans. Macquarrie and Robinson (London: SCM Press, 1962), # 44; and "On the Essence of Truth" in *Basic Writings*, ed. David Krell (New York: Harper and Row, 1977). For a careful study of the roots of Heidegger's approach in Brentano and Brentano's studies of Aristotle, see David Krell, *Intimations of Immortality: Time, Truth, and Finitude in Heidegger's Thinking of Being* (University Park: Pennsylvania State University Press, 1986), chap. 4.

12. Two recent works attempt to reconcile a philosophy of truth with the historicity of truth. Risieri Frondizi attempts to show how truth surpasses mere historical relativity. See "Are Truth and History Incompati-

ble?," in H. G. Gadamer, ed., *Truth and Historicity* (The Hague: Nijhoff, 1972), pp. 29ff. In addition see Hans Barth, *Truth and Ideology* (Berkeley: University of California Press, 1976), pp. 175–94.

13. For a fine study of Marx's philosophy of truth, see Czeslaw Prokopczyk, *Truth and Reality in Marx and Hegel: A Reassessment* (Amherst: University of Massachusetts Press, 1980), chap. 3. See also Hans Barth, *Truth and Ideology*.

14. "Similarly, the truth of liberation faith is rooted not so much in its correspondence with themes and practices of the church in the past, but in its power to liberate people in the present" (Sharon Welch, *Communities of Resistance and Solidarity: A Feminist Theology of Liberation* [Maryknoll, N.Y.: Orbis Books, 1985], p. 53).

15. See Martin Buber, *The Knowledge of Man* (New York: Harper and Row, 1965), chap. 3; and *Between Man and Man* (Boston: Beacon, 1955), "Dialogue."

16. This primordial reality is given a variety of descriptions in twentieth-century Continental philosophy. We should not identify, therefore, the dialogal, face-to-face account found in Martin Buber and Emmanuel Levinas with its focus on "face," meeting, and dialogue—placing otherness or alterity at the center of the interhuman—with more anonymous accounts of intersubjectivity found in Husserl, who finds a way to the other by analogy with the sphere of own-ness, and Heidegger, who gives a general account of *Mitsein*.

17. Paul Ricoeur provides a version of the location of truth in the interhuman in connection with his exploration of the truth of fictional narratives. Behind such narratives are the structures of historicity that ground all referential claims and the intersubjective field of temporal experience. Further, this is prior to the subject-object division. See "Can Fictional Narratives be True?" in A. T. Tymieniecka, ed., *The Phenomenology of Man and the Human Condition, Analecta Husserliana*, vol. 14 (Dordrecht, Holland: D. Reidel, 1983).

18. This view is expressed succinctly by Michel Foucault:

The important thing here, I believe, is that truth isn't outside power, or lacking in power: contrary to a myth whose history and functions would repay further study, truth isn't the reward of free spirits, the child of protracted solitude, nor the privilege of those who have succeeded in liberating themselves. Truth is a thing of this world: it is produced only be virtue of multiple forms of constraint. And it induces regular effects of power [Michel Foucault, *Power/Knowledge: Selected Interviews and Other Writings 1972–1977*, ed. C. Gordon (New York: Pantheon, 1980), p. 131].

19. Although a brief footnote cannot do justice to the very complex

and subtle analysis of Robert Scharleman's *The Being of God*, it seems to be the case that he distinguishes truth from perception itself (that is, "direct experience" as expressed in the phrase, "This is a tree") and reflective experience. While he does think that reflective experience is part of everyday experience, he seems to think that there is some sort of everyday perceptual experience that can occur prior to reflection and prior to truth intention and truth experience. If this be so, then the position I am taking here—namely, that direct experience itself (of trees as trees) is an experience of manifestness and therefore of truth—is not reconcilable with his view. See *The Being of God: Theology and the Experience of Truth* (New York: Seabury, 1981), p. 25.

20. Paul Ricoeur, "Truth and Falsehood," in *History and Truth*, trans. Charles Kelbey (Evanston: Northwestern University Press, 1965), pp. 166ff.

21. One of the most subtle and comprehensive analyses of the human surpassing of particularity is Maurice Blondel's 1893 dissertation, published now in English translation as *Action: Essay on a Critique of Life and a Science of Practice* (Notre Dame: University of Notre Dame Press, 1894). This work develops by tracking what could be called a whole series of surpassings, toward past and future, from and through organic drives, space, language, body, and culture.

22. The relating of truth and enduring is not absent in contemporary philosophy. Francis Schwanauer argues that the subject of truth-claims or statements or even the experience of truth is a situation expressible by a predicate joined with a subject. Further, truth does not arise unless there is an agent who grasps this situation and maintains it. Truth, then, refers to the status of something ("the day is windy") that is upheld. Even claimed disjunctions between what is and is not true ("it is or is not raining") are "kept true" or upheld. See *Truth is Neighborhood with Nothing in Between* (Lanham, Md.: University Press of America, 1977), p. 5. Something of an enduring is indicated in Robert Scharleman's formulation of the experience of truth as having to do with identity in difference. A more conventional formulation is offered by Gerard Smith, who argues that what truth refers to are universally intelligible features of any situation, features that do not vary as long as *that* situation persists. His example is a chess problem that has developed in the course of a chess game. See *The Truth that Frees*, Aquinas Lecture (Milwaukee: Marquette University Press, 1956).

23. For a study of expressions (universals) of enduring that are expressions neither of utter particularity nor of transhistorical universality, see the chapter on determinate universals in my *Ecclesial Reflection: An Anatomy of Theological Method* (Philadelphia: Fortress, 1982), chap. 13.

Chapter 4

1. For the following, see Daniel Guerriére, "Outline of a Phenomenology of the Religious," *Research in Phenomenology*, 4 (1974): 99–127.

2. Martin Heidegger, *Sein und Zeit* (Tübingen: Niemeyer, 1927), §§48–53.

3. John Bowker, *Problems of Suffering in Religions of the World* (Cambridge: Cambridge University Press, 1970).

4. See the great study of the symbols and myths of evil by Paul Ricoeur, *The Symbolism of Evil* [1960], trans. Emerson Buchanan (New York: Harper & Row, 1967).

5. A phenomenology of embodiment clarifies our experience that, although the body is reducible to the self, the self is irreducible to the body. See the patient investigations by Edmund Husserl, *Ideen, II: Phänomenologische Untersuchungen zur Konstitution* [1912–1928], ed. Marly Biemel (The Hague: Nijhoff, 1952), part 2; the study of the existential phenomenology of Marcel, Sartre, and Merleau-Ponty by Richard Zaner, *The Problem of Embodiment* (The Hague: Nijhoff, 1964); the scientific work of John Eccles and Karl Popper, *The Self and Its Brain* (Berlin: Springer, 1977); and the summary argument by Daniel Guerrière, "Foundations for an Axiology of Life," *Journal of Value Inquiry*, 18 (1984): 195–205, esp. 202–3.

6. The religious names must not be confused with the other names for it in *compact* experience. All the dimensions of existence that we modern Westerners experience as differentiated are, for the ancients, compact. The history of consciousness is its differentiation. On this matter, see Daniel Guerrière, "The Structure of Mythic Existence," *The Personalist*, 55 (1974): 261–72. In a tradition still somewhat compact, the properly religious other may be indistinct from some other religious matter such as nirvana (the salvational condition of man). On this further, see the next section, below. For both compact and differentiated humanity, it is easy to amalgamate the first principle in philosophic reflection or scientific vision and the religious other. On the question of their identity, see below, part 4, and Daniel Guerrière, "How Does God Enter into Philosophy?," *The Thomist*, 48 (1984): 165–87.

7. See below, part 4, under the discussion of antitheism.

8. See Heidegger, *Sein und Zeit*, §7.A.

9. The perforce symbolic appearance of salvational Power suggests an answer to the question of the unity of this Power or its plurality—monotheism or polytheism. Since salvational Power appears only symbolically, it is always a *surplus* with respect to its manifestations; hence it cannot a priori be exhausted in any *one* symbol. The "many gods" would then be the many symbols of a single Power. It is one because its function—to save—is one, and this is for us its only essence. There is no reason to suppose that it should not manifest itself in *various* ways, even to the same person. This phenomenological argument finds deep support in historical research. Almost all cultures acknowledge a High God, who is often the source of the other gods (i.e., they share his essence). See the massive evidence gathered

by Wilhelm Schmidt in *Der Ursprung der Gottesidee*, 12 vols. (Münster: Aschendorff, 1912–1955); also his summary statement in *The Origin and Growth of Religion* [1930], trans. H. J. Rose (1931; repr. New York: Cooper Square, 1972), esp. pp. 251–90; and the short analysis by Mariasusai Dhavamony, *Phenomenology of Religion* (Rome: Università Gregoriana, 1973), pp. 60–64 and 111–34. However, historical research cannot provide a decisive argument even if it could be complete; for it can attain only empirical, not apodictic, evidentiality. The only decisive argument for monotheism is ontological; it would show that Being is one, that salvational Power and Being are identical, and that therefore salvational Power is one. On this, see Guerrière, "How Does God Enter into Philosophy?," esp. pp. 172–73, 183–85. Here, we shall take for granted monotheism, although the argument is compatible with polytheism.

10. Gregory Baum, *Man Becoming* (New York: Herder & Herder, 1970), p. 185.

11. Mircea Eliade, *Patterns in Comparative Religion* [= *Traité d'histoire des religions*], trans. Rosemary Sheed (New York: Sheed and Ward, 1958).

12. Eliade, *Patterns*, chap. 1; Louis Dupré, *The Other Dimension* (Garden City, N.Y.: Doubleday, 1972), pp. 15–17.

13. The power, force, or plenitude that founds the cosmos need not be particularly religious—i.e., salvational. See, for instance, the myths recounted in Charles H. Long, *Alpha: The Myths of Creation* (New York: George Braziller, 1963). The science of religion has not always made clear what is specifically religious about the originative Power; philosophy can take a critical stance toward the deliverances of science.

14. See Ricoeur, *Symbolism*; and Wendy Doniger O'Flaherty, *The Origins of Evil in Hindu Mythology* (Berkeley: University of California Press, 1976; 2nd ed., 1980).

15. Again see Ricoeur, *Symbolism*, pp. 9, 161–64.

16. This is clear from the very fact that a fundamental moral code may be elaborated without reference to religion. Perhaps the first to do it was Aristotle. Kierkegaard recognized the difference in his concept of "the teleological suspension of the ethical." Contemporary antitheists do so explicitly (e.g., Kai Nielsen, *Ethics Without God* [Buffalo: Prometheus, 1973]). Nonetheless, religious motivations are still important for the social efficacy of moral codes.

17. The term *Bewahrheitung*, like its English "verification," means literally "bringing-about-truth" or "truth-in-becoming." Husserl associates this "truthing" with the "filling" of an empty intention. See *Analysen zur passiven Synthesis (1918–1926)*, ed. Margot Fleisher (The Hague: Nijhoff, 1966), §§19–20, 44. Cf. the "second" notion of "truth" in *Formal and Transcendental Logic* [1929], trans. Dorian Cairns (The Hague: Nijhoff, 1969), §46.

18. Paul Ricoeur, *Interpretation Theory: Discourse and the Surplus of Meaning* (Fort Worth: Texas Christian University Press, 1976), pp. 31–32.

19. William Luijpen, *Existential Phenomenology,* (Pittsburgh: Duquesne University Press, rev. ed., 1969), p. 159.

20. For further discussion, see Guerrière, "Outline of a Phenomenology," pp. 110–12.

21. This, of course, is the great contention of Modern atheism, given classic expression by Ludwig Feuerbach in *The Essence of Christianity* [1841], trans. George Eliot (1854; repr. New York: Harper & Row, 1957), Introduction.

22. See Guerrière, "How Does God Enter into Philosophy?"

23. See Thomas Molnar, *Theists and Atheists: A Typology of Non-belief* (The Hague: Mouton, 1980).

24. The classical conclusion to the speculative problem of human freedom and God was *not* that God could not exist but that *freedom* could not. The classical *speculative* refutation of the modern antitheistic argument was already given, in classical terms, by Boethius in *The Consolation of Philosophy,* part 5 (Corpus Christianorum Series Latina, 94) (Turnholti: Brepols, 1957), pp. 90–105; his argument is based on the conceptualization of salvational Power as eternal. For a recent *speculative* refutation in detail of speculative antitheism based on evil, see Bruce R. Reichenbach, *Evil and a Good God* (New York: Fordham University Press, 1982). The argument in the present essay is *phenomenological.*

Chapter 5

1. *Critique of Pure Reason,* A 731 = B 759.

2. Paul Ricoeur, *The Symbolism of Evil,* trans. Emerson Buchanan (New York: Harper & Row, 1967), pp. 19–24.

3. Biblical quotations are from the New American Standard translation.

4. C. K. Barrett gives the following almost Heideggerian account of seeing "in a mirror dimly":

> The fact is that the metaphor of the glass must take its sense from the context; always the glass is an instrument of revelation, sometimes the stress lies simply on the revelation, sometimes on its indirectness. The latter use obtains here, but the ambiguity of the metaphor accounts for the addition . . . of a further qualification, *obscurely* (literally *in a riddle* . . .). In this Paul is probably dependent not so much on Hellenistic usage as on Num. xii.8, where God says that he will

speak to Moses face to face (cf. verse 12b), not obscurely (*through riddles . . .*). But the expression would be fully comprehensible to Corinthians unfamiliar with the Greek Old Testament. The Chorus complains of Cassandra that she speaks in riddles . . . (Aeschylus, *Agamemnon* 1112); this is because she is inspired by Apollo, whose custom it is to deliver obscure oracles. Paul means that in the present age all knowledge of God (all *gnosis*) is incomplete and unclear [*The First Epistle to the Corinthians* (New York: Harper & Row, 1968), pp. 307–8].

The ellipses indicate that Aeschylus, the Greek Old Testament, and the New Testament all use the same term, from which our word "enigma" comes, to signify imperfect apprehension. Cf. Deut. 34:10.

5. The importance of this distinction in the political realm has been emphasized by Jürgen Habermas, who acknowledges a special debt to Hannah Arendt and Hans-Georg Gadamer in this connection. See especially *Theory and Practice*, trans. John Viertel (Boston: Beacon, 1973), chap. 1. I believe that the distinction has a largely unexplored fruitfulness for philosophy of religion.

6. I am following C. E. B. Cranfield here. He writes:

The equivalence for Paul of faith in God and obedience to Him may be illustrated again and again from this epistle. [He supports this claim in a footnote.] Paul's preaching is aimed at obtaining again from his hearers true obedience to God, the essence of which is a responding to His message of good news with faith. It is also true to say that to make the decision of faith is an act of obedience toward God and also that true faith by its very nature includes in itself the sincere desire and will to obey God in all things [*A Critical and Exegetical Commentary on the Epistle to the Romans* (Edinburgh: Clark, 1975), 1: 66–67].

In another footnote Cranfield refers to Schlatter's view "'that it is only when God's message is replaced by a doctrine offering instruction about God that a gap between faith and obedience appears.'"

7. Martin Buber expresses the particularity and participatory character of biblical knowing, in distinction from all claims to universality and distanciation, in these comments on the Decalogue:

What is said here to Israel as a whole, and so to each individual amongst the people, is not that there *are no* other gods: to say this would be to contradict the intentional sense and connection of the passage; Israel is told, that it is *forbidden* for other gods to exist. Forbidden that *they* should have other gods: but it only concerns *them*, who are addressed, and the whole reality of the subject under discussion is that of the relationship between YHVH and Israel. This is the significance of the fact that the Decalogue is prefaced by the reminder,

"I am YHVH thy God, Who brought thee out of the land of Eqypt, out of the house of bondage" [*The Prophetic Faith* (New York: Harper & Row, 1960), pp. 22–23].

8. In the second of the passages just mentioned, Rom. 16:25–26, Paul describes the preaching of the gospel as the "revelation" of a mystery long hidden but now "manifested" and "made known" to all peoples for the purpose of producing "the obedience of faith."

9. Abraham J. Heschel, *The Prophets* (New York: Harper & Row, 1962), 1: 211

10. J. A. Thompson, *The Book of Jeremiah* (Grand Rapids: Eerdmans, 1980), p. 479.

11. See also John 1:6: "If we say that we have fellowship with Him and yet walk in the darkness, we lie and do not practice the truth." In both passages the King James Version speaks, happily I believe, about doing the truth.

12. Rudolf Bultmann writes:

For just as "falsehood" has no merely formal meaning in John, neither does "*truth*" . . . as if it meant the nakedness of that-which-is in general or reality in the purely formal sense in which that can be predicated of any object (in contrast to a mistaken notion about it). Rather, the basic meaning of "truth" in John is God's reality, which, since God is the Creator, is the only true reality. The emancipating knowledge of the truth (8:32) is not the rational knowledge of the reality of that-which-is in general; such a knowledge would at best free one from the prejudices and errors occasioned by tradition and convention. No, this knowledge of the truth is the knowledge, granted to men of faith [notice again the lack of opposition between knowledge and faith], of God's reality; it frees one of sin (8:32–34). . . . So truth is not the teaching about God transmitted by Jesus, but is God's very reality revealing itself—occurring!—in Jesus [*Theology of the New Testament*, trans. Kendrick Grobel (New York: Scribner's), 1955, 2:18–19].

From this it follows, Bultmann argues, that to be "of the truth" (another Johannine construction) is to orient one's life around God rather than around the world, understood as those systems and lifestyles not oriented toward God (1 John 2:15–17).

13. Augustine regularly attributes the errors of the Manichees to their unwillingness to do the truth. See my discussion in "Taking Suspicion Seriously: The Religion Uses of Modern Atheism," *Faith and Philosophy*, 4 (1987): 33. But here the issue is not error but the distinction between correctness and truth.

14. *Confessions*, V,3 (Warner translation).

15. M. Merleau-Ponty, *The Phenomenology of Perception*, trans. Colin Smith (London: Routledge & Kegan Paul, 1962), p. viii.

16. Paul Ricoeur, *Freud and Philosophy: An Essay on Interpretation*, trans. Denis Savage (New Haven: Yale University Press, 1970), p. 32.

17. Edmund Husserl, *Cartesian Meditations: An Introduction to Phenomenology*, trans. Dorin Cairns (The Hague: Nijhoff, 1973), p. 2.

18. *Cartesian Meditations*, pp. 6 and 11.

19. Ludwig Landgrebe borrows a different metaphor (from Hegel) for Husserl's "reluctant departure" from Cartesianism. In his account, "the shipwreck of transcendental subjectivism," which occurs "before the eyes of the reader," takes place "behind Husserl's back." Because of his "reluctance" to see it, the full import of his findings is "partially obscured by the self-interpretation he gave it" "Husserl's Departure from Cartesianism," *The Phenomenology of Edmund Husserl: Six Essays*, ed. Donn Welton (Ithaca: Cornell University Press, 1981), p. 68. See the third paragraph from the end of the Introduction (*Einleitung*) of Hegel's *Phenomenology*.

20. It has been suggested that Heidegger and Merleau-Ponty take us beyond the hermeneutics of finitude to the hermeneutics of suspicion. I have tried to show that this is the case neither with Heidegger ("Socrates between Jeremiah and Descartes," *Philosophy and Theology*, 2/#3 [Spring 1988]: 199–219) nor with Merleau-Ponty ("Situation and Suspicion in Merleau-Ponty," *Ontology and Alterity in Merleau-Ponty*, ed. Galen Johnson and Michael Smith, forthcoming).

21. See Hans-Georg Gadamer, "Rhetorik, Hermeneutik and Ideologiekritik," and Jürgen Habermas, "Der Universalitätsanspruch der Hermeneutik" in *Hermeneutik and Ideologiekritik* (Frankfurt: Suhrkamp, 1971). The former essay is translated as "On the Scope and Function of Hermeneutical Reflection" in Gadamer, *Philosophical Hermeneutics*, trans. David E. Linge (Berkeley: University of California Press, 1976). In the same volume see also "The Universality of the Hermeneutical Problem."

22. *Cartesian Meditations*, p. 14.

23. Martin Heidegger, *Being the Time*, trans. John Macquarrie and Edward Robinson (New York: Harper & Row, 1962), pp. 191–94. Paul Ricoeur, speaking of Heidegger's notion of thrown projection, writes, "One small word separates Heidegger from Sartre: *already*" (*Hermeneutics and the Human Sciences*, ed. and trans. John B. Thompson [Cambridge: Cambridge University Press, 1981], p. 57). That may be unfair to Sartre's understanding of the situatedness of the for-itself, but the formula fits perfectly the relation between Heidegger and Husserl.

24. *Being and Time*, pp. 191–92.

25. *Cartesian Meditations*, pp. 19, 53, 63, and 76. This reflects the assault on naturalism and historicism in "Philosophy as Rigorous Science."

26. *Cartesian Meditations*, pp. 76–77.

27. Edmund Husserl, *Experience and Judgment: Investigations in a Genealogy of Logic*, trans. Churchill and Ameriks (Evanston: Northwestern University Press, 1973), pp. 41, 31, 42–43, 41.

28. Through the historical reduction an "attitude is arrived at which is *above* the pregivenness of the validity of the world." In this way "the gaze of the philosopher in truth first becomes fully free: above all, free of the strongest and most universal, and at the same time most hidden, internal bond, namely, of the pregivenness of the world. Given in and through this liberation is the discovery of the universal, absolutely self-enclosed and absolutely self-sufficient correlation between the world itself and world-consciousness. . . . But the world, exactly as it was for me earlier and still is . . . has not disappeared; it is just that, during the consistently carried out epochē, it is under our gaze purely as the correlate of the subjectivity which gives it ontic meaning, through whose validities the world 'is' at all." Of this gaze Husserl claims, "This is not a 'view,' an 'interpretation' bestowed upon the world. Every view about . . . [Husserl's ellipsis], every opinion about 'the' world, has its ground in the pregiven world. It is from this very ground that I have freed myself through the epochē; I stand *above* the world, which has now become for me, in a quite peculiar sense, a *phenomenon*. From these heights the 'mankind' which makes up the life-world can be recognized 'as a self-objectification of transcendental subjectivity' which is always functioning ultimately and is thus 'absolute' " [Edmund Husserl, *The Crisis of European Sciences and Phenomenological Philosophy*, trans. David Carr (Evanston: Northwestern University Press, 1970), pp. 150–53].

29. Kathleen Freeman, *Ancilla to the Pre-Socratic Philosophers* (Cambridge: Harvard University Press, 1966), p. 64, and Hans-Georg Gadamer, *Reason in the Age of Science*, trans. Frederick G. Lawrence (Cambridge: MIT Press, 1981), p. 52.

30. *Being and Time*, p. 206.

31. Hans-Georg Gadamer, *Truth and Method*, trans. [Garrett Garden and John Cumming] (New York: Seabury, 1975), pp. 258 and 261.

32. *Philosophical Hermeneutics*, p. 9.

33. *Phenomenology of Perception*, p. xiv, and *The Primacy of Perception and Other Essays*, ed. James M. Edie (Evanston: Northwestern University Press, 1964), p. 40. It is just this detachment that Husserl requires of the transcendental ego, which is to be the *"disinterested onlooker"* at the world and the "non-participant onlooker" at itself (*Cartesian Meditations*, pp. 35–37).

34. Paul Ricoeur, "Ethics and Culture: Habermas and Gadamer in Dialogue," *Philosophy Today*, 17 (1973): 157. This statement is a sympathetic summary of Gadamer. See also *Hermeneutics and the Human Sciences*, p. 68.

35. *Hermeneutics and the Human Sciences*, pp. 108 and 113.

36. For this interpretation of Hegel, see my *History and Truth in Hegel's Phenomenology* (Atlantic Highlands, N.J.: Humanities, 1979). See also "Hegel and Husserl: Transcendental Phenomenology and the Revolution Yet Awaited," in *Critical and Dialectical Phenomenology*, ed. Donn Welton and Hugh J. Silverman (Albany: SUNY Press, 1987), esp. pp. 110–25.

37. Martin Heidegger, *The Question Concerning Technology and Other Essays*, trans. William Lovitt (New York: Harper & Row, 1977).

38. Henri J. N. Nouwen, *A Cry for Mercy: Prayers from the Genesee* (Garden City, N.Y.: Doubleday, 1983), p. 95.

39. See David Tracy, *Plurality and Ambiguity: Hermeneutics, Religion, Hope* (San Francisco: Harper & Row, 1987). Tracy develops the plurality implied by the hermeneutics of finitude and the ambiguity indicated by the hermeneutics of suspicion in terms of our rootedness in language and history. I believe that there is an inward dimension to the ambiguity of faith not adequately captured by the notion of history, but would want to affirm with Tracy the public, corporate ambiguity to which he points.

40. I have developed this point in *God, Guilt, and Death: An Existential Phenomenology of Religion* (Bloomington: Indiana University Press, 1984), chap. 1.

41. Kant, *Critique of Pure Reason*, B xiii.

42. *Truth and Method*, pp. 274–305.

43. See, for example, Gerhard von Rad, *Theology of the Old Testament*, trans. D. M. G. Stalker (New York: Harper and Row, 1965), 2: 80–98.

44. Ricoeur, *Hermeneutics and the Human Sciences*, p. 109.

45. Ricoeur, *Freud and Philosophy*, pp. 457–58, my italics.

46. Ibid., p. 458. Ricoeur places this picture of thought in the service of desire, which emerges from even a casual reading of Freud, in a philosophical tradition that includes Spinoza and Leibniz, Schopenhauer and Nietzsche (*The Conflict of Interpretations: Essays in Hermeneutics*, ed. Don Ihde [Evanston: Northwestern University Press, 1974], pp. 211–12). He may well have added Bacon, Hobbes, and Hume to the list, along with Augustine, Rousseau, and Kant. The "masters" of suspicion, Marx, Nietzsche, and Freud, have a long list of luminaries on whom to draw.

47. Ricoeur speaks of "*a distanciation of self from itself*," which is crucial

to the appropriation of a text, something I can accomplish "only if I disappropriate myself" (*Hermeneutics and the Human Sciences*, p. 113). This is prior to the element of suspicion and corresponds to the idea of openness, receptivity, and response-ability vis-à-vis that which is to be interpreted. See Thomas Merton: "We do not detach ourselves from things in order to attach ourselves to God, but rather we become detached *from ourselves* in order to see and use all things in and for God" (*New Seeds of Contemplation* [New York: New Directions, 1972], p. 21).

48. See Ricoeur, *Conflict of Interpretations*, pp. 184–85.

49. Kant, *Critique of Pure Reason*, B xiv.

50. Sören Kierkegaard, *Concluding Unscientific Postscript*, trans. David F. Swenson and Walter Lowrie (Princeton: Princeton University Press, 1941), pp. 179–80.

51. Socrates' description in the *Gorgias* of sophistry as flattery and pandering is a good description of the kind of theology that needs a good dose of suspicion.

Chapter 6

1. Raymond Boudon, *L'Idéologie* (Paris: Fayard, 1986), pp. 40f.

2. Karl Marx and Frederick Engels, *On Religion* (Moscow: Foreign Languages Publishing House, 1955), p. 50.

3. Paul Ricoeur, "The Critique of Religion" (1973), in *The Philosophy of Paul Ricoeur: An Anthology of His Work*, ed. Charles Regan and David Stewart (Boston: Beacon, 1978), p. 215.

4. Rudolf Bultman, *The Theology of the New Testament* (London: SCM Press, n.d.), pp. 295ff.

5. In recent years this work of demythologization has perhaps been most effectively developed by the French religious thinker, René Girard. Girard holds that the most radical aim of Judeo-Christian revelation is to expose and overcome the mythic foundation of pagan religions in the ritual sacrifice of an innocent scapegoat. Imaginatively projecting the cause of all disharmony and evil onto some "externalized" innocent victim, society contrives to hide from itself the real cause of its *internal* crisis. True Christianity rejects the cultic mythologizing of the scapegoat, deployed by societies as an ideological means of securing social consensus. Only by demythologizing this ideological lie of sacrificial victimage—that is, by revealing the true innocence of the scapegoat Christ—can Christianity serve as a genuinely antimythic and antisacrificial religion. See René Girard, *Le bouc emissaire* (Paris: Grasset, 1982), particularly the chapter entitled "Qu'est-ce qu'un mythe?," pp. 36–37. See also my article, "René Girard et

le mythe comme bouc emissaire," in *Le Colloque René Girard* (Paris: Grasset, 1984).

6. Ricoeur, "Science and Ideology" (1974), in *Hermeneutics and the Human Sciences*, ed. and trans. John B. Thompson (Cambridge: Cambridge University Press, 1981), pp. 222–46.

7. Mircea Eliade, *Myths, Dreams and Mysteries* (London: Fontana, 1968), p. 24: "Myth is thought to express the absolute truth because it narrates a sacred history; that is, a trans-human revelation which took place in the holy time of the beginning. . . . By *imitating* the exemplary acts of mythic deities and heroes man detaches himself from profane time and magically re-enters the Great Time, the Sacred Time."

8. Ricoeur, "Science and Ideology," p. 225.

9. Ibid., p. 229.

10. Boudon, *L'Idéologie*, pp. 85f.

11. Ricoeur, "Science and Ideology," p. 227.

12. I have attempted to apply this critique of ideology as it operates in Irish myth and religion in two recent studies: "Faith and Fatherland," in *The Crane Bag*, 8/1 (1984), and *Myth and Motherland*, Field Day, Derry, #5 (1984), reprinted in *Ireland's Field Day* (London: Hutchinson, 1985).

13. Boudon, *L'Idéologie*, pp. 85f.

14. Ricoeur, "The Critique of Religion," p. 219.

15. Ibid.

16. Ricoeur, "Science and Ideology," p. 236

17. Ibid., p. 231.

18. Ibid. See Claude Lévi-Strauss, *Structural Anthropology* (New York: Basic Books, 1963), and Cornelius Castoriadis, *L'Institution imaginarie de la société* (Paris: Editions du Seuil, 1976). For a detailed critical commentary on Castoriadis's and Ricoeur's notion of ideology as a "social imaginary," see John B. Thompson, *Studies in the Theory of Ideology* (Berkeley: University of California Press, 1985).

19. Boudon makes this point in *L'Idéologie*, pp. 183f. It is also Recoeur's conclusion. The hermeneutics of suspicion runs the danger of assuming that it remains unscathed by the defects that it denounces. A totally nonideological science could be only a nonhistorical science—that is, a form of total and timeless knowledge disengaged from historical interests and limits. And, for Ricoeur, this is impossible—as it is for Heidegger, Sartre, Merleau-Ponty, and other exponents of the new phenomenological finitude

of understanding. All understanding of history—no matter how scientific— is itself historically conditioned and therefore incapable of ever escaping from ideology in any absolute manner. Moreover, this historical character of understanding accounts for the primacy of symbolic consciousness—that is, of mediated, indirect, and multilayered consciousness—over and above transparent scientific knowledge. Because human understanding operates in a hermeneutic circle, it cannot represent meaning in a timeless univocal fashion; it can do so only through a temporalizing process of representation. This means that our understanding of present reality is mediated by a recollection of the past (*wiederholen*) and a projection of the future (*entwerfen*). Perhaps the central discovery of phenomenological hermeneutics has been the priority of the figurative over the literal: the recognition that there can be no access to reality except through the hermeneutic detour of our intentional and symbolizing representation. We shall return to this question later. Suffice it to cite now Ricoeur's outline of the implications of this discovery for the relationship between ideology and our understanding of social reality. To quote a key passage from "Science and Ideology":

> If it is true that the images which a social group forms of itself are interpretations which belong immediately to the constitution of the social bond; if, in other words, the social bond is itself symbolic; then it is absolutely futile to seek to derive the images from something prior which would be reality, real activity, the process of real life, of which there would be secondary reflections and echoes. A non-ideological discourse on ideology here comes up against the impossibility of reaching a social reality prior to symbolization. This difficulty confirms me in the view that the phenomenon of inversion cannot be taken as the starting point for an account of ideology, but that the former must be conceived as a specification of a much more fundamental phenomenon which pertains to the representation of the social bond in the after-event of its symbolic constitution. Travesty is a second episode of symbolization. Whence, in my opinion, the failure of any attempt to define a social reality which would be initially transparent and then obscured, and which could be grasped in its original transparence, short of the idealizing reflection. What seems to me much more fecund in Marx's work is the idea that the transparence is not behind us, at the origin, but in front of us, at the end of an historical process which is perhaps interminable. But then we must have the courage to conclude that the separation of science and ideology is itself a limiting idea, the limit of an internal work of differentiation, and that we do not currently have at our disposal a non-ideological notion of the genesis of ideology. . . . Such is the fundamental reason why social theory cannot entirely free itself from the ideological condition: it can *neither* carry out a total reflection, *nor* rise to a point of view capable of expressing the totality; and hence cannot abstract itself from ideological mediation into which the other members of the social group are subsumed [pp. 237–38].

20. On this distinction between the "archeological" and "eschatological" (and "teleological") aspects of hermeneutics, see Paul Ricoeur, "Existence and Hermeneutics," in *The Conflict on Interpretations*, ed. Don Ihde (Evanston: Northwestern University Press, 1974), pp. 22–24.

21. On the analysis of symbol as a "double intentionality," see Paul Ricoeur, "The Hermeneutics of Symbols and Philosophical Reflection," in *The Philosophy of Paul Ricoeur*, pp. 36ff.; and *The Symbolism of Evil*, trans. Emerson Buchanan (New York: Harper & Row, 1967), Introduction and Postscript.

22. Paul Ricoeur in interview with Richard Kearney, "The Symbol as Bearer of Possible Worlds," in *The Crane Bag Book of Irish Studies*, ed. Richard Kearney and Mark Patrick Hederman (Dublin: Blackwater Press, 1982), and republished in edited version in Richard Kearney, *Dialogues with Contemporary Continental Thinkers* (Manchester: Manchester University Press, 1984). In this same dialogue, Ricoeur distinguishes three modes of language: (1) ordinary language as identified by much contemporary analytic philosophy (e.g., the late Wittgenstein and Austin); (2) scientific language as practiced by the structuralist model of textual autonomy and codification; and (3) the symbolic language of myth, religion, and ideology privileged by phenomenological hermeneutics. Ricoeur argues that this third level is indispensable. The philosophy of ordinary language recognizes the importance of communication but often reduces meaning to a one-dimensional realm (as Marcuse recognized) by not taking sufficient account of language as a place of prejudice and dissimulation. The scientific language of structuralism, for its part, exposes the immanent arrangements of texts and textual codes, but virtually ignores the *meaning* created by these codes. A phenomenological hermeneutics, taking its inspiration from Husserl and Heidegger, addresses this central question of meaning. It acknowledges both the critical and creative functions of language by disclosing how human self-understanding occurs in and through the mediating detour of signs whereby we understand ourselves as projects of possibility. Ricoeur concludes accordingly that we need a hermeneutic approach to language, one directed neither "toward scientific verification nor ordinary communication but toward the disclosure of possible worlds. . . . The decisive feature of hermeneutics is the capacity of world-disclosure yielded by symbols and texts. Hermeneutics is not confined to the *objective* structural analysis of texts nor to the *subjective* existential analysis of the authors of texts; its primary concern is with the worlds which these authors and texts open up. It is by an understanding of the worlds, actual and possible, opened up by language that we may arrive at a better understanding of ourselves."

23. Paul Ricoeur, "Hermeneutics and the Critique of Ideology," in *Hermeneutics and the Human Sciences*, pp. 63ff.

24. Ricoeur, *The Symbolism of Evil*, particularly the Introduction. Ricoeur also develops a related distinction between ideology and utopia as two aspects of the social imaginary. See my dialogue with Ricoeur in *Dia-*

logues, pp. 29–31; and part 3 of Ricoeur's *Du texte à l'action: essais d'herméneutique* (Paris: Editions du Seuil, 1986), 2: 379–93.

25. Ricoeur, interview with Kearney cited in note 22 above.

26. Ibid.

27. Ricoeur, "Science and Ideology," p. 224. Ricoeur calls for a surpassing of the conventional polar opposition between ideology (*mythos*) and science (*logos*) by placing the critique of ideology within the framework of an interpretation "which knows itself to be historically situated but which strives to introduce as far as it can a factor of distantiation into the work that we constantly resume in order to re-interpret our cultural heritage."

28. Ricoeur, "Hermeneutics and the Critique of Ideology," pp. 99–100.

29. Ricoeur, "Science and Ideology." p. 241.

30. Ibid., p. 243.

31. Ibid., p. 244.

32. Ibid., p. 245.

33. See *The End of Ideology Debate,* ed. Chaim Waxman (New York: Simon and Shuster, 1968).

34. Louis Althusser, "Ideology and Ideological State Apparatuses," in *Lenin and Philosophy, and Other Essays,* trans. Ben Brewster (London: New Left Books, 1971).

35. Fredric Jameson, "Postmodernism, or the Cultural Logic of Late Capitalism," in *New Left Review,* #145 (1984).

36. An earlier and shorter version of this article appeared in *The Irish Theological Quarterly,* 52/1–2 (1986).

Chapter 7

1 Thomas Sheehan, "Revolution in the Church," *New York Review of Books,* vol. 31, no. 10 (June 14, 1984): 35. It provoked a storm of controversy in three issues of *Commonweal:* August 10, 1984, pp. 425–33; September 21, 1984, pp. 490–502; October 5, 1984, pp. 518–34, which drew some notable Catholic scholars into the fray.

2. I use the following abbreviations throughout: FC = Thomas Sheehan, *The First Coming, or How the Kingdom of God Became Christianity* (New York: Random House, 1986). J = Edward Schillebeeckx, *Jesus: An Experiment in Christology,* trans. Hubert Hoskins (New York: Crossroad, 1985).

3. John P. Meier, "Jesus Among the Historians," *New York Times Book Review* (December 21, 1986): 19.

4. Schillebeeckx's approach, which approximates closely that of Rudolph Pesch, has been criticized by Francis Schlüssler Fiorenza just because it makes so much turn on this experience. See his *Foundatinal Theology: Jesus and the Church* (New York: Crossroad, 1985), pp. 18–55. Schillebeechx has responded to some of his critics in *Interim Report on the Books Jesus and Christ*, trans. John Bowden (New York: Crossroad, 1981). For the political troubles that Schillebeechx incurred, see *Authority in the Church and the Schillebeeckx Case*, ed. Leonard Swidler and Piet. F. Fransen (New York: Crossroad, 1982).

5. See my *Radical Hermeneutics: Repetition, Deconstruction and the Hermeneutic Project* (Bloomington: Indiana University Press, 1987), especially chap. 10. The last section of the present chapter moves within the framework of this book.

6. "May it not be that Simon Peter—and indeed the twelve—arrive via their concrete experience of forgiveness after Jesus's death . . . at the 'evidence for belief': the Lord is alive? . . . A dead man does not proffer forgiveness. . . . [This experience] thus became the matrix in which faith in Jesus as the risen One was brought to birth. They all of a sudden 'saw' it" [J, 391].

7. Meier, "Jesus," p. 16.

8. Emmanuel Levinas, *Totality and Infinity*, trans. A. Lingis (The Hague: Nijhoff, 1969), esp. section 3, "Exteriority and the Face."

9. Martin Heidegger, *Poetry, Language, Thought*, trans. Albert Hofstadter (New York: Harper & Row, 1971), p. 184. See my "Heidegger's God and the Lord of History," *The New Scholasticism*, 57 (1983): 439–64.

10. See especially Jacques Derrida, *Spurs: Nietzsche's Styles*, trans. Barbara Harlow (Chicago: University of Chicago Press, 1978).

11. Friedrich Nietzsche, *The Will to Power*, trans. W. Kaufmann and R. J. Hollingdale (New York: Random House Vintage Books, 1968), no. 1041, p. 536; cf. no. 990, p. 517, and no. 1052, p. 543.

12. Martin Heidegger, "The Fieldpath," trans. Thomas O'Meara and Thomas Sheehan, *Listening*, 8 (1973): 39.

Chapter 8

1. Franz Rosenzweig, *The Star of Redemption*, trans. William W. Hallo (Boston: Beacon, 1972; Notre Dame: University of Notre Dame Press, 1985), p. 388. Henceforth *The Star*.

2. This chapter was first given on March 14, 1988, as one part of a lecture series, directed by Professor Arno Munster, "Judaism and Philoso-

phy: Rosenzweig and Scholem," at the Collège International de Philosophie, Paris. I would like to thank Ron Goodman for suggestions in improving this version.

3. There can be no doubt about Rosenzweig's profound and pervasive influence on Levinas, who has written two long articles on Rosenzweig: "Franz Rosenzweig: Entre deux mondes," first published in 1959, which appeared in (an edited) English translation in *Midstream*, November 1983, pp. 33–40; and "Franz Rosenzweig, une pensée juive moderne," first published in 1965. Levinas has also written the Preface to Stephane Moses' *Système et Révélation: La philosphie de Franz Rosenzweig* (Paris: Editions de Seuil, 1982), to be published by Wayne State University Press in English. Along with several other articles (by Moses and Paul Ricoeur), Levinas's writings on Rosenzweig will all be published in English translation in a single volume, *On Rosenzweig* (forthcoming). One must'also note the celebrated acknowledgment that appears in Levinas's Preface to *Totality and Infinity*, trans. Alphonso Lingis (Pittsburgh: Duquesne University Press, 1969): "We were impressed by the opposition to the idea of totality in Franz Rosenzweig's *Stern der Erlösung*, a work too often present in this book to be cited" (p. 29).

4. Stephane Moses, in *Système et Révélation*, has also emphasized the connection between *The Star* and Jewish mysticism.

5. I should like to recommend a very sensitive study by Professor Megumi Sakabe (University of Kawasaki) on the role of the mask in Japanese culture: "Le masque et l'ômbre dans la culture japonaise," in *Revue de métaphysique et de morale*, July-September 1982, pp. 335–43.

6. Erwin Straus, *Phenomenological Psychology* (New York: Basic Books, 1966), chap. 7, "The Upright Posture"; reprinted in *Phenomenology and Existentialism*, ed. Richard Zaner and Don Ihde (New York: Putnam's, 1973), pp. 232–59.

7. *The Star*, p. 422.

8. Ibid.

9. See Emmanuel Levinas, *Time and the Other*, ed. and trans. Richard A. Cohen (Pittsburgh: Dudquesne University Press, 1987).

10. The *panim el panim* is found in Exodus 33:11, where God speaks face-to-face to Moses who is within his "tent of the meeting" at the foot of Mount Sinai ("And God spoke to Moses face to face"); and in Deuteronomy 5:4, where Moses reminds the people Israel of their covenant with God which was made in Horeb ("The Lord spoke with you face to face").

11. Readers of Franz Rosenzweig's *The Star of Redemption* know of this work's journey from death to life. Its first sentence begins with the conflict of two forms of death: the metaphorical deathliness of the All of idealist

philosophy and, in contrast, real death, which is said to be the "origin" of philosophical deathliness. The comfortable, comforting, but escapist metamorphosis effected by the abstract nothing of idealist philosophy is sharply jolted by the fear and fact of real death. The book then passes from critque to a variety of stages, from eros, to ethics, to ritual, to end in life in the everyday world with others (der Alltag des Lebens), life "beyond the book." Like Rabbi Simeon ben Yohai (of the Zohar), who is said to have died with the word "life" on his lips, The Star ends with the dramatic and emphatic words "INTO LIFE" (INS LEBEN). The book thus transcends textual closure, moves from the black and white page to variegated life, to end with several cleverly triangulated final sentences that seem graphically to depict the disappearance of reflective discourse by a leap into life. The discourse disappears neither into a pumped up conceptualization of the abstract nothing of traditional philosophy, which was rejected at the outset, nor into the solitude and subjectivism of the individual's ownmost death, which at first jolted the abstract nothing from out of its daydreams. Rather it moves into the temporal and moral life beyond the book, a life whose essential elements, structures, and movements the book itself has painstakingly characterized. Many if not most books, however, aspire to transcend the condition of textuality, to refer to the "concrete," to "move" the reader, to "incite" action, to "change" behavior, or in some way or other to go "beyond the book" or "beyond the word." Even consciousness dreams these dreams, inventing for itself a world of prereflective naivety or instinct.

12. Totality and Infinity represents the prime example of salient differences separating Levinas from Rosenzweig not only because of its lengthy treatment of the face, but because overall it is a book closer to Rosenzweig's The Star than any other book of its stature.

13. See my article, "Absolute Positivity and Ultrapositivity: Husserl and Levinas," in The Question of the Other, ed. Arlene Dallery and Charles Scott (Albany: SUNY Press, 1988).

14. The Star, pp. 422–23.

15. The figures would be better if they were each printed on a clear medium so that they could be laminated one on top of the other. With regard to these drawings, which are my own and not Rosenzweig's, it is of some interest that precisely at the time Rosenzweig was conceiving and writing The Star, William Butler Yeats and his wife were (automatically) writing A Vision (1925). In their work the Yeatses articulated a complicated "system" of symbolic thought based on two intersecting triangles (and a circle). The Yeats' triangles, however, form what they called a "double vortex," not a Mogen David. Their vision, furthermore, remained personal, claiming allegiance, unlike Rosenzweig's thought, neither to a revealed tradition nor to a philosophical justification.

16. The Star, p. 422

17. Both thinkers explicitly deny the label "mystic." But in these matters, affirmative or negative avowals are of little account. Such is the freedom or mystery of mystical thought.

18. See *The Star*, p. 408. See below, pp. 188–90.

19. This story appears in the Babylonian Talmud *Hagigah* 14b and in the Jerusalem Talmud *Hagigah* 2:3–4. For one version of this story with commentaries, see Louis Jacobs, *Jewish Mystical Testimonies* (New York: Schocken, 1977), pp. 21–25.

20. The other methods of interpretation, according to the schema known by the acronym *pardes,* are *peshat,* the "plain" meaning, *remez,* the "allusive" meaning, and *derash,* the "solicited" meaning. To a certain limited extent, one can consider *peshat* the level or method of philosophical interpretation, *remez* the level or method of haggadic interpretation, *derash* the level or method of halakic interpretation. I am suggesting that *sod* takes care of everything left over after the other three methods have produced their results.

21. See Paul Ricoeur, *The Symbolism of Evil,* trans. Emerson Buchanan (Boston: Beacon, 1969), esp. the conclusion, pp. 347–57.

22. For instance, Levinas's proximity to Rabbi Hayim of Volozhin, as we shall see below.

23. It can be quite a sobering thought to realize that for the Jews the classical period of Greek antiquity, indeed the entire epoch of Greek antiquity, appears late in sacred history. Jewish mystical sources, however, all appear long after the fall of Greece to Rome.

24. Martin Samuel Cohen, *The Shi'ur Qomah: Litugy and Theurgy in Pre-Kabbalistic Jewish Mysticism* (Lanham, Md.: University Press of America, 1963). One text of the *Shi'ur Qomah,* translated and annotated in detail by Martin Samuel Cohen, is found on pp. 187–266.

25. The first and relevant part of this book, "On the Soul and Repentance," can be found in English translation in *An Anthology of Jewish Mysticism,* ed. and trans. Raphael ben Zion (New York: Yesod Publishers, n.d.), pp. 129–204, 225–33. Raphael ben Zion's anthology also contains an English translation of Rabbi Cordovera's text, *The Palm Tree of Devorah* (pp. 9–85, 211–19).

Levinas has written the preface to the French translation of Rabbi Hayim's work, *L'âme de la vie,* trans. Benjamin Gross (Lagrasse: Editions Verdier, 1986), pp. vii–x; he has also written an article on Hayim's thought, "A l'image de Dieu: d'après Rabbi Haim Voloziner," which appears in *L'au-delà du verset* (Paris: Editions de Minuit, 1982), pp. 182–200.

26. See Moses ben Maimonides, *Mishneh Torah,* I, chap. 1; and *The Guide for the Perplexed,* I, chap. 36.

27. *The Star*, p. 421.

28. One might think here of what Kant says in the third Critique of the sublime, particularly the mathematical sublime.

29. It has been suggested that the mechanism is "childish." In his carefully researched study of the *Shi'ur Qomah*, Martin Samuel Cohen is doubtlessly correct to join Gershon Scholom in criticizing those scholars— Philipp Bloch (1844–1923) is named—who believed the *Shi'ur Qomah* was actually intended only for grade school children (see Cohen, *Shi'ur Qomah*, p. 18; Scholem, *Major Trends*, pp. 66–67). Nonetheless, given the content of the central idea of the *Shi'ur Qomah*—i.e., the bigness of God (which M. S. Cohen himself admits: "The bigness of the godhead is, of course, the key idea in the *Shi'ur Qomah*" [p.93]), something like Bloch's thesis must still be affirmed. Whether the *Shi'ur Qomah* was actually used in grade school or in advanced study, its "key idea" is undoubtedly childish.

30. They are collected in English translation in *The Anatomy of God*, ed. and trans. Roy A. Rosenberg (New York: KTAV, 1973).

31. See Joseph Dan, *Jewish Mysticism and Jewish Ethics* (Seattle: University of Washington Press, 1986), pp. 90–91. "The mystic . . . does not know the 'true' reasons, only the vague hints suggested by the symbols" (p. 91).

32. Emmanuel Levinas, *Time and the Other* (Pittsburgh: Duquesne University Press, 1987), p. 84.

33. Lawrence Fine, *Safed Spirituality* (New York: Paulist, 1984), p. xiii.

34. Gershom Scholem, *Major Trends in Jewish Mysticism* (New York: Schocken, 1961), p. 252.

35. Quoted by Lawrence Fine in *Safed Spirituality*, p. 31. See also Cordovera, *Tomer Devorah*, in *An Anthology of Jewish Mysticism*, ed. and trans. Raphael ben Zion (New York: Yesod Publisher, [n.d.]), p. 15. Louis Jacobs, in his Preface to Fine's collection, quotes the words of Dean Inge: "Religion is a way of walking, not a way of talking" (p. ix), to sum up the momentous change effected by Cordovera in the character of Jewish mysticism.

36. Lawrence Fine says this in *Safed Spirituality*, p. 84; he also puts the later eighteenth-century work of Moses Hayyim Luzatto, *The Path of the Righteous (Mesilat Yesharim)*, in this category of the most influential Jewish ethical works.

37. The anthropomorphic symbolism that appears most often in kabbalah is not the face alone but the figure of the whole human body, the *Adam Kadman*, which is at once divine cosmos above and human microcosmos below. Owing to the influence of Isaac Luria, ten *sepharot* or divine emanations are at this time especially emphasized and made to correspond to parts of the human body. The uppermost three *sepharot* correspond to

the head and shoulders: (1) *keter*, "crown," corresponding to the head; (3) *binah*, "understanding," and (2) *hokhmah*, "wisdom," corresponding to the left and right shoulders respectively. The next six *sepharot* correspond to the arms, trunk, genitals, and legs: (5) *gevurah*, "power" (or *din*, "judgment"), and (4) *chesed*, "mercy," corresponding to left and right arms respectively; (6) *tif'eret*, "beauty" (or *rahamin*, "compassion"), which harmonizes *gevurah* and *hesed*, corresponding to the trunk; (8) *hod*, "majesty," and (7) *nesah*, "endurance" (or "victory"), corresponding to the left and right legs respectively; (9) *yesod*, "foundation," corresponding to the phallus. The tenth and lowest *sepharah*, (10) *malkos*, "kingdom" (or *shekhinah*, "God's presence"), corresponds to the feet. The face, then, would have to do "only" with the uppermost *sepharah keter*, the crown or head. This location gives it, in addition, the special significance of being both top and bottom at once, for the ten *sepharot* are repeated in each of four worlds, which are serially and progressively distant from God.

38. Cordovera, *Tomer Devorah*, pp. 38–41, in Raphael ben Zion, *Anthology*.

39. See Fine, *Safed Spirituality*, pp. 119–21.

40. Ibid.; the text is from Poyetta's abbreviated version of Elijah de Vida's *Beginning of Wisdom*; it could just as well be from Cordovera's *The Palm Tree of Devorah* itself.

41. On the importance of the imitation of God—*hitdamut la'El*—in the ethics of halakah, see Rabbi Joseph Soloveitchik, "Imitating God—The Basis of Jewish Morality," in *Reflections of the Rav*, adapted from the lectures of Rabbi Joseph Soloveitchik by Abraham R. Besdin (Jerusalem, 1979), pp. 23–30.

42. Joseph Dan, *Jewish Mysticism and Jewish Ethics*, pp. 86–87.

43. See Rivka Horwitz, "Franz Rosenzweig's Unpublished Writings," *The Journal of Jewish Studies*, 20 (1969): 74.

44. *The Star*, p. 106.

45. Rivka Horwitz, "F. R.'s Unpublished Writings," p. 74.

46. Gershom Scholem, *Kabbalah* (New York: Quadrangle, 1974), p. 196.

47. *Nefesh Hahayim*, chap. 1, section 3.

48. Ibid., chap. 1, section 5.

49. Ibid., chap. 1, section 6.

50. Ibid., chap. 1, section 9.

51. Ibid.

52. Ibid., chap. 1, section 12.

53. For Levinas the term "being" itself is inadequate to express the exceptional relation of infinity to infinity.

54. Ibid.

55. Already in *Totality and Infinity* Levinas writes: "The calling in question of the I, coextensive with the manifestation of the Other in the face, we call language" (p. 171). And: "The face opens the primordial discourse whose first word is obligation" (p. 201).

56. Emmanuel Levinas, *De Dieu qui vient à l'idée* (Paris: J. Vrin, 1982), p. 51, n. 24.

57. Ibid. See Hans Vaihinger, *Die Philosophie des Als-Ob* (Berlin, 1911); *The Philosophy of 'As If'*, trans. C. K. Ogden (New York, 1924).

58. For a penetrating discussion of the important contrast between the rabbinic technique of *kal ve-chomer* and the related interpretive techniques in Greco-Christian thought, see Susan Handelman, *The Slayers of Moses* (Albany: SUNY Press, 1982), pp. 52–57.

59. Handelman, *Slayers of Moses*, pp. 54–55.

60. *The Star*, p. 424.

The editor lightly revised the original submission.

Chapter 9

1. Jacques Derrida, *Positions*, trans. Alan Bass (Chicago: University of Chicago Press, 1981), p. 5. This research was assisted by a grant from the American Council of Learned Societies under a program funded by the National Endowment for the Humanities; and by a grant from the Emory University Research Committee.

2. Paul Ricoeur, *Freud and Philosophy: An Essay on Interpretation*, trans. Denis Savage (New Haven: Yale University Press, 1970), pp. 27–36; see Ricoeur, *The Conflict of Interpretations: Essays in Hermeneutics* (Evanston: Northwestern University Press, 1974), pp. 440–67.

3. Freud's metaphsychology is often portrayed as a misguided effort to submit psychology to the laws of Helmholtzian physics. See, for example, Hans Küng, *Freud and the Problem of God*, trans. Edward Quinn (New Haven: Yale University Press, 1979).

4. But see the discussion of "the third moment of phenomenology" in the editor's Introduction, pp. 3–5, above.

5. Again cf. the In-between of subjectivity and objectivity, the com-

mon One out of which both differentiate, as given exposition in the editor's Introduction.

6. Husserl, *Logical Investigations*, trans. J. N. Findlay (London: Routledge & Kegan Paul, 1970), 1:342, italics added.

7. Husserl, *Formal and Transcendental Logic*, trans. Dorion Cairns (The Hague: Nijhoff, 1969), p. 233.

8. Husserl, *Logical Investigations*, 1:254.

9. Husserl, *The Crisis of European Sciences and Transcendental Phenomenology*, trans. David Carr (Evanston: Northwestern University Press, 1970), p. 189.

10. Husserl, *Crisis*, p. 159.

11. *Logical Investigations*, 2: 584.

12. Derrida, *Positions*, p. 41; *Margins of Philosophy*, trans. Alan Bass (Chicago: University of Chicago Press, 1982), p. 17.

13. Ricoeur, *Husserl: An Analysis of his Phenomenology*, trans. Edward Ballard and Lester Embree (Evanston: Northwestern University Press, 1967), p. 204, translation revised. Cf. "the two intentive processes (*visés*)" (p. 6).

14. Derrida, *Speech and Phenomena*, trans. David B. Allison (Evanston: Northwestern University Press, 1973), p. 90.

15. Ibid., p. 89.

16. Ibid., pp. 89–90.

17. Ibid., pp. 91–92.

18. Husserl, *Logical investigations*, 1:285–86; quoted by Derrida, *Speech and Phenomena*, p. 97.

19. *Speech and Phenomena*, p. 98.

20. A turning point in the *Crisis* is the inquiry into "Descartes as the primal founder not only of the modern idea of objectivistic rationalism but also of the transcendental motif which explodes it." The section concludes with the observation that "precisely those ideas which were supposed to ground this rationalism as *aeterna veritas* bear within themselves a *deeply hidden sense*, which, once brought to the surface, completely uproots it" (*Crisis*, pp. 73–74). The lines could almost have been written by Derrida.

21. Staten, *Wittgenstein and Derrida*, (Lincoln: University of Nebraska Press, 1984), p. 47; I am indebted to Staten's exposition of this aspect of the encounter between Husserl and Derrida.

22. From "Limited Inc, a b c . . . ," trans. Samuel Weber, *Glyph*, 2 (Baltimore: Johns Hopkins, 1977), p. 232.

23. *Crisis*, p. 299.

24. Derrida, *Writing and Difference*, p. 292.

25. The term "postmodern" has been used in a great variety of settings, sometimes simplistically, sometimes with subtlety. Here I have recourse to the term sheerly for purposes of exposition, to designate a specific position regarding the nature of language.

26. Derrida, *Writing and Difference*, p. 293.

27. In "White Mythology: Metaphor in the Text of Philosophy," Derrida shows not only that philosophy is irreducibly dependent upon a network of metaphors (a good "postmodernist" point), but also that the very notion of metaphor, especially when adopted as a fundamental explanatory device, is itself shot through with philosophic precommitments (*Margins of Philosophy*, pp. 207–71).

28. *Positions*, pp. 7, 9; cf. p. 29.

Chapter 10

1. Iso Kern, *Husserl und Kant* (The Hague: Nijhoff, 1964); and Steven Laycock, *Foundations for a Phenomenological Theology* (Lewiston: Edwin Mellen Press, 1988). Of abiding interest also is Paul Ricoeur's "Husserl and Kant," in his *Husserl: An Analysis of his Phenomenology*, trans. Edward Ballard and Lester Embree (Evanston: Northwestern University Press 1967).

2. Husserl, *Phänomenologische Psychologie*, Husserliana IX (The Hague: Nijhoff, 1968), p. 95; *Phenomenological Psychology*, trans. John Scanlon (The Hague: Nijhoff, 1977), #11.

3. Husserl, *The Crisis of European Sciences and Transcendental Phenomenology*, trans. David Carr (Evanston: Northwestern University Press, 1970), #37.

4. See, e.g., Husserl, *Ding und Raum*, Husserliana XVI (The Hague, Nijhoff, 1973), pp. 105–16.

5. Husserl, *Phänomenologische Psychologie*, 97; trans. #11.

6. *Crisis*, #37

7. Husserl, *Erste Philosophie*, 2, Husserliana VIII (The Hague: Nijhoff, 1959), p. 457.

8. See Husserl, *Ideen zu einer reinen Phänomenologie und phänomenologische Philosophie*, Husserliana V (The Hague: Nijhoff, 1952), #7; and Robert Sokolowski, *Husserlian Meditations* (Evanston: Northwestern University Press, 1974), #24.

9. Husserl, *Cartesian Meditations*, trans. Dorian Cairns (The Hague: Nijhoff, 1960), #22; hereafter, CM.

10. See, e.g., Husserl, *Zur Phänomenologie der Intersubjektivität*, 3, Husserliana XV (The Hague: Nijhoff, 1973), pp. 593ff. In CM (#38) Husserl states that infants must learn to see spatial objects but not objects as substances of predication. They must learn to see tables, but cannot learn sameness and difference.

11. Husserl, *Ideas*, I, #74; *Crisis*, #9a. I am indebted to the excellent discussion of Robert Sokolowski, "Exact Science and the World in Which We Live," in *Lebenswelt und Wissenschaft in der Philosophie Edmund Husserls*, ed. Elizabeth Stroeker (Frankfurt am Main: Klostermann, 1979), pp. 92ff.

12. The observation is Sokolowski's, "Exact Science," p. 98; see Aristotle's *Metaphysics* 996a 20ff.

13. See Kant, *Critique of Pure Reason* (CPR), B 672ff.

14. See Husserl, *Crisis*, p. 346; *Krisis*, p. 360.

15. Husserl, *Erste Philosophie*, 2, p. 496. Cf. Jacques Derrida's discussion of open and closed infinities in Husserl, in *Edmund Husserl's "Origin of Geometry": An Introduction* (Stony Brook, N.Y.: Hays, 1978), pp. 127–30.

16. Husserl, *Formale und Transzendentale Logik*, Husserliana XVII (The Hague: Nijhoff, 1974), p. 194; *Formal and Transcendental Logic*, trans. Dorion Cairns (The Hague: Nijhoff, 1969), #73.

17. See my "A Precis of an Husserlian Philosophical Theology," in *Essays in Phenomenological Theology*, ed. Steven Laycock and James Hart (Albany: SUNY Press, 1986), pp. 134ff.

18. See Kant, CPR, B 698ff. For much of my interpretation of Kant I am indebted to John Findlay's rich and provocative *Kant and the Transcendental Object* (Oxford: Oxford University Press, 1981), p. 126. But for this particular point, see his *The Philosophy of Hegel* (New York: Collier, 1966), p. 126.

19. Bruno Bauch, *Die Idee* (Leipzig: Reinicke, 1925), pp. 92ff.

20. See *Erste Philosophie*, 2: 412–13, and my "Constitution and Reference in Husserl's Phenomenology of Phenomenology," forthcoming in *Husserl Studies*.

21. Findlay, *Kant*, pp. 136ff.

22. See my "A Precis," esp. pp. 112–17.

23. See Karl Schumann, *Husserl-Chronik* (The Hague: Nijhoff, 1977), p. 295; see "A Precis," p. 117. The (transcendental-phenomenological) metaphysical reflection will be successful if it is able to avoid fusing the protorationality of passive synthesis with the equivalent of the "inauthentic" and blindly mechanical and automatic process that Husserl found typical in, e.g., "doing arithmetic." Manfred Sommer believes Husserl did not avoid this confusion. See his fine work, *Husserl und der frühe Positivismus* (Frankfurt am Main: Klostermann, 1985). Whereas in the case of arithmetical operations we are delivered over to a blind automatic power in which there is no intuitive presencing, in the original protorationality there is constituted the wakeful prepresential "dative of manifestation." Where for Husserl the former case approaches "heteronomy," the latter is a "theonomy." Iso Kern, in his excellent *Die Idee und Methode der Philosophie* (Berlin: de Gruyter, 1975), believes that Husserl ascribes the achievements of rationality to sensibility; thereby Husserl can claim that there are proper (passive) identity syntheses in a realm where in fact there is only fusion and a continuous flux of indiscernible differents. Both Sommer and Kern agree that Husserl, in the realm of "inner-time consciousness," conveniently but illictly joins what must be kept distinct, i.e., the hyletic and egological (or the *sensa* and intentional-apperceptive). Instead of the appropriate demonstration "from below" of *forma ex materia* (Mach and Sommer) or *forma super materia* (Kant and Kern), Husserl's position is one of *materia preformata*. These authors raise rock-bottom issues for phenomenological theology. I hope to do justice to them on another occasion.

24. See my "A Precis," passim, but esp. pp. 150–59, which is indebted to Kern and Held. See Iso Kern, *Husserl und Kant*, p. 298; also Klaus Held, *Lebendige Gegenwart*, Phänomenologica 23 (The Hague: Nijhoff, 1966), pp. 162, 165, 176–79. But see also Ludwig Landgrebe, "Faktizität als Grenze der Reflexion und die Frage des Glaubens" and "Faktizität und Individuation," in his *Faktizität und Individuation* (Berlin: Meiner, 1982).

25. Kant, *Critique of Judgment*, Hafner edition (New York and London: Hafner, 1966), #88; Meiner edition, p. 329.

26. Kant, *Religion Within the Limits of Reason Alone* (New York: Harper and Row, 1960), p. 182; Meiner edition, pp. 220ff.

27. *Critique of Judgment*, #88, p. 309; Meiner, p. 330.

28. Again this is a basic theme of "A Precis."

29. See n. 20, above.

30. This from MS K II 4, 109a/b, cited in Kern's *Husserl und Kant*, pp. 129–130. Excerpts from important theological manuscripts can be found in Alwin Diemer, *Edmund Husserl* (Meisenhim am Glan: A. Hain, 1965), pp. 313–15.

31. Robert Sokolowski, *The God of Faith and Reason* (Notre Dame: Notre Dame University Press, 1982).

32. MS K III 12; see also Husserliana XV, pp. 385–386.

33. *Aufsätze und Rezensionen,* Husserliana XXII (The Hague: Nijhoff, 1980), p. 210; *Erste Philosophie* (The Hague: Nijhoff, 1959), 1: 362.

34. F IO 26, 148b; cited in Kern, *Husserl und Kant,* p. 126.

35. Husserl, *Aufsätze und Rezensionen,* p. 210.

36. *Erste Philosophie,* 2: 469; Kern, *Husserl und Kant,* p. 127.

37. *Ideen zu einer reinen Phänomenologie und phänomenologischen Philosophie,* 2:85, Husserliana IV (The Hague: Nijhoff, 1952).

38. For a brief sketch of this possibility, see part 2 of my response to Sallie McFague's theology of the divine body, *"Models of God* and 'Evangellogic,' " *Religion and Life,* 5 (1988), 33 ff.

I wish to thank Professor Samuel IJsseling, managing director of the Husserl Archives in Louvain, for permission to quote texts from the Nachlass. *The editor divided and otherwise edited this article.*

Chapter 11

1. Plato, *Parmenides,* trans. F. M. Cornford, ed. Edith Hamilton and Huntington Cairns, *The Collected Dialogues of Plato* (Princeton: Princeton University Press, 1961), p. 928.

2. Ibid.

3. In Parmenides' words, "knowledge itself, the essence of knowledge, will be knowledge of that reality itself, the essentially real" (134a), ibid.

4. Ibid.

5. A far more detailed discussion of phenomenological-theological methodology than would be warranted here may be found both in the Introduction to my *Foundations for a Phenomenological Theology* (Lewiston: Edwin Mellen Press, 1988) and in my introductory essay, "Toward an Overview of Phenomenological Theology," in *Essays in Phenomenological Theology* (Albany: SUNY Press, 1986). However, I know of no essay more insightful or more helpful in this connection than James G. Hart's contribution to the latter volume, "A Précis of an Husserlian Philosophical Theology."

6. Paul Ricoeur, "Toward a Hermeneutic of the Idea of Revelation," *Essays on Biblical Interpretation* (Philadelphia: Fortress, 1978), p. 109.

7. Informally, the "law of factual separation" is the principle excluding the mastery of *Slavery* (or slavery to *Mastery*) by a particular master (or slave). Formally: "Such sensible particulars [x, y] are related to each other *via* an immanent character chain as follows: (1) x bears F-in-x toward G-in-y, y bears G-in-y toward F-in-x; (2) x cannot bear F-in-x toward [psi] or any other Form, y cannot bear G-in-y toward [phi] or any other Form" (Mark L. McPherran, "Plato's Reply to the 'Worst Difficulty' Argument of the *Parmenides: Sophist* 248a-249d," *Archiv für Geschichte der Philosophie*, 68 [1986]).

8. Ibid. See also McPherran's essay, "Plato's *Parmenides* Theory of Relations," in ed. F. J. Pelletier and J. King-Forlow, *New Essays on Plato, Canadian Journal of Philosophy*, Supplementary volume 9 (1983). The problem has also been discussed by F. M. Cornford, in *Plato and Parmenides* (London: Routledge & Kegan Paul, 1939), and by R. E. Allen in *Plato's Parmenides* (Minneapolis: University of Minnesota Press, 1983), and is addressed in the following: J. Forrester, "Arguments and [sic] Able Man Colud [sic] Refute: Parmenides 133b–134c," *Phronesis*, 19, 3 (1974); F. Lewis, "Parmenides on Separation and the Knowability of the Forms: Plato *Parmenides* 133a ff," *Philosophical Studies*, 2 (1979); S. Peterson, "The Greatest Difficulty for Plato's Theory of Forms: the Unknowability Argument of *Parmenides* 133c–134c," *Archiv für Geschichte der Philosophie*, 63 (1981); I. Mueller, "Parmenides 133a–134e: Some Suggestions," *Ancient Philosophy*, 3 (1983).

9. Hegel, *Faith and Knowledge*, an English translation of Hegel's *Glauben und Wissen*, ed. and trans. W. Cerf and H. S. Harris (Albany: SUNY Press, 1977), p. 169.

10. Robert R. Williams, "Phenomenology *And* Theology: Hegel's Alternative to Dogmatism and Idealism," in Laycock and Hart, *Essays in Phenomenological Theology*, p. 78.

11. Edmund Husserl, *Ideas Pertaining to a Pure Phenomenology and to a Phenomenological Philosophy*, trans. F. Kersten (The Hague: Nijhoff, 1982), §58, p. 133.

12. Ibid., p. 134.

13. Ibid.

14. Edmund Husserl, *Zur Phänomenologie der Intersubjektivität: Texte aus dem Nachlass*, part 1, ed. Iso Kern (The Hague: Nijhoff, 1973), p. 9. I am indebted to Professor James G. Hart for his translation of this and subsequent passages cited from the *Intersubjectivity* texts.

15. Ibid.

16. "The absolute perfection at which all beings aim through and beyond relative achievements is God" (René Toulemont, *L'Essence de la société selon Husserl* [Paris: Presses Universitaires de France, 1962], p. 276).

17. I am grateful to Professor Guerrière for drawing my attention to what may, without further clarification, seem a fateful inconsistency. Earlier, in an effort to resolve the Socratic "worst difficulty"—a problem that, unsolved, would render impossible the enjoyment of *Reality* as an object of noetic activity—I voiced the Husserlian claim that transcendental subjectivity is the full "reality" of phenomenology, thus implicitly affirming that transcendental subjectivity is an "object," and indeed the *ultimate* "object" of phenomenological investigation. While by no means wishing to identify transcendental subjectivity with the world-pole, I have at the same time claimed that the latter is the terminal referent of intentional consciousness: again the *ultimte* "object"! The apparent conflict is, of course, resolved by recognizing alternative dimensions of ultimacy, the single Subject/Object. Like length and breadth, the subjective and objective dimensions are, as it were, utterly "transparent" to one another. As length is present *in its entirety* through (and throughout) breadth (and conversely), the world-pole, having the character of "transcendence-in-immanence," is manifest through (and throughout) transcendental subjectivity (and conversely).

18. God is conceived by Husserl as the "absolute ideal pole—idea"— "the absolute logos, the absolute truth in its full meaning of the *unum verum bonum* toward which every finite being is oriented, while being united by the aspiration which includes every finite being" (MS. E III 4, p. 36, quoted in Stephan Strasser, "History, Teleology, and God in the Philosophy of Husserl," in Tymieniecka, ed., *Analecta Husserliana*, vol. 9, pp. 324– 50).

19. Edmund Husserl, *Drei Vorlesungen über Fichtes Menschheitsideal*, MS. F I 14, p. 43, quoted in Strasser, "History," p. 328.

20. Edmund Husserl, *Experience and Judgement: Investigations in a Genealogy of Logic*, trans. James S. Churchill and Karl Ameriks, ed. Ludwig Landgrebe (Evanston: Northwestern University Press, 1973), p. 82.

21. Ibid.

22. Ibid. "Interest" need not signify "positive" interest. Indeed, as Husserl tells us:

> It can also be that the object itself touches our feelings, that it has value for us, and that for this reason we turn to it and linger over it. But it can just as well be that it is disvaluable and awakens our interest just because of its abhorrent qualities. Thus the feeling which belongs to interest has an entirely peculiar direction. In either case— whether the object motivates our turning-toward by the value or by the disvalue we sense in it—as soon as we apprehend it, its sense content is necessarily enriched [ibid., pp. 85–86].

23. In Perry's view, "a *thing—any thing— has value, or is valuable, in the original and generic sense when it is the object of an interest—any interest. Or,*

whatever is object of interest is ipso facto valuable" (Ralph Barton Perry, *Realms of Value: A Critique of Human Civilization* [Cambridge: Harvard University Press, 1954], pp. 2–3).

24. In approaching Husserl's work, we must, throughout, discriminate the "logic of subsumption" from the "logic of synthesis," *formality* from *finality*. The formal belongs exclusively to those moments of mind over which we may exercise reflective leverage; while finality belongs exclusively to living and presently ongoing consciousness. Thus, Husserl can affirm, without contradicting the theory of teleological interest-value, that "a value has no position in time. A temporal Object may be beautiful, pleasant, useful, etc., and may be all this in a determinate time. But the beauty, pleasantness, and so on, have no place in nature and in time. These qualities are not what appears in presentations and presentifications" (Husserl, *Experience and Judgement*, p. 198).

25. While Perry's axiology is inescapably relativist, he balks at the epithet: "But suppose that one substitute the more colorless word 'relational' [i.e., "relational theory of value" for "relativism"] and, instead of rejecting it as a fault, boldly affirm it as a merit, since it provides not only for value, but for ambivalence and multi-valence" (Perry, *Realms of Value*, p. 12).

26. Strasser, "History," p. 329.

27. *Intersubjectivity*, 3: 380.

28. The terms "completed" and "progressive" action are borrowed from Milton Fisk's rewarding study, *Nature and Necessity: An Essay in Physical Ontology* (Bloomington: Indiana University Press, 1973), pp. 182–86. As will become evident, I vigorously endorse Fisk's view that "in the absence of progressive actions, there are no foundations for temporal relational properties. . . . So a complete action . . . exists through dependence on progressive action and has its extensiveness on the basis of progressive action" (ibid., p. 184).

29. *Intersubjectivity*, 3: 610.

30. Husserl very helpfully characterizes the divine entelechy in his rhetorical query: "May we not, or must we not presuppose a universal intentional drive which unifies each original present into a lasting temporalization (*stehende Zeitung einheitlich ausmacht*) and which propels it concretely from present to present in such a way that each content is content of a fulfilled drive?" (MS. E III 5, pp. 3–4, quoted in Louis Dupré, "Husserl's Thought on God and Faith," in *Philosophy and Phenomenological Research*, 29 [1968], p. 206). A well-nuanced discussion of the notion of *entelechy* as it functions in Husserlian philosophical theology is found in James G. Hart's essay, "Divine Truth in Husserl and Kant" (chap. 10, above).

31. MS. E III 4, p. 61, as quoted in Dupré, "Husserl's Thought," p. 208.

The editor divided the original submission into sections, entitled them, and lightly revised it.

Contributors

JOHN D. CAPUTO is Professor in Philosophy at Villanova University and Distinguished Adjunct Professor at Fordham University. He is the author of *The Mystical Element in Heidegger's Thought* (1978), *Heidegger and Aquinas* (1982), and *Radical Hermeneutics* (1987).

PHILIP CLAYTON studied at Munich and at Yale and is now Assistant Professor of Philosophy at Williams College. He is the author of *Explanation from Physics to Theology: An Essay in Rationality and Religion* (1989), and co-editor of *The Theology of Wolfhart Pannenberg: Twelve American Critiques* (1988).

RICHARD A. COHEN studied philosophy at Paris-Sorbonne and at SUNY Stony Brook and is now Associate Professor of Religious Studies and Chair of Judaic Studies at The University of Alabama/Tuscaloosa. He is the author of various articles in French philosophy, has translated two works by Levinas, is editor of *Face to Face with Levinas* (1986), and is now preparing *Levinas and Rosenzweig* for publication.

LOUIS DUPRÉ is Professor of Religious Studies at Yale University. He is the author of *The Other Dimension: A Search for the Meaning of Religious Attitudes* (1972), *Transcendent Selfhood: The Loss and Rediscovery of the Inner Life* (1976), *A Dubious Heritage: Studies in the Philosophy of Religion after Kant* (1977), *The Deeper Life* (1982), *Marx's Social Critique of Culture* (1983), *The Common Life* (1984). He is also co-editor of *Light From Light: An Anthology of Christian Mysticism* (1988).

EDWARD FARLEY is Professor of Theology at the Divinity School of Vanderbilt University. He is the author of *Ecclesial Man: A Social Phenomenology of Faith and Reality* (1975), *Ecclesial Reflection: An Anatomy of Theological Method* (1982), and *Theologia: The Fragmentation and Unity of Theological Education* (1983).

DANIEL GUERRIÈRE is Professor of Philosophy at California State

University/Long Beach. He studied at Duquesne University and the University of Louvain, Belgium. He is the author of numerous articles and reviews in the history of metaphysics and in phenomenology.

JAMES G. HART is Professor of Religious Studies at Indiana University. He is the author of many articles, has translated and commented on Heidegger in *The Piety of Thinking* (1976), and is co-editor of *Essays in Phenomenological Theology* (1986).

RICHARD KEARNEY is Professor of Metaphysics at the University College, Dublin. He is author of many articles, co-editor of *Heidegger et la question de Dieu* (1980), and author of *Dialogues with Contemporary Continential Thinkers* (1984), *Poétique du possible: Herméneutique de la figuration* (1984), *Modern Movements in European Philosophy* (1986), and *The Wake of Imagination: Toward a Postmodern Culture* (1989).

STEVEN W. LAYCOCK is Professor of Philosophy at the University of Hawaii. He is the author of various articles in philosophy, co-editor of *Essays in Phenomenological Theology* (1986), and author of *Foundations for a Phenomenological Theology* (1988).

WALTER LOWE is Professor at the Candler School of Theology, Emory University. He is author of many articles and of *Evil and the Unconscious* (1983).

MEROLD WESTPHAL is Professor of Philosophy at Fordham University. He is author of many articles, editor of *Method and Speculation in Hegel's Phenomenology* (1982), and author of *History and Truth in Hegel's Phenomenology* (1978), *God, Guilt, and Death: An Existential Phenomenology of Religion* (1984), and *Kierkegaard's Critique of Reason and Society* (1987).

Index of Topics

This index does not aim to record *whether* a certain topic has been mentioned. It aims rather to summarize *which* topics emerged as major, *however designated*. It may therefore be used to find the consensus among the contributors despite their various terminologies.

Index of Names

This index does not contain every mention of an author. It does cite authors when they are quoted, placed in context, or linked to major ideas.

Frondizi, Risieri, 284n.12
Freud, Sigmund, 110, 120, 124, 128,
    136, 168, 205, 206–7, 294n.46

Gadamer, Hans-Georg, 35, 37, 40,
    110, 113, 114, 115, 117, 124, 137,
    140, 141, 146, 162
Galileo Galilei, 52–53
Gandhi, Mohandas, 19, 277nn.2,3
Geertz, Clifford, 56, 127
Girard, René, 295n.5
Guerrière, Daniel, 13, 287n.6,
    288n.9, 313n.17

Habermas, Jürgen, 49, 132, 137,
    140, 144, 281n.6, 290n.5
Handelman, Susan, 200, 306n.58
Hart, James G., 15, 311n.5, 312n.14,
    314n.30
Harvey, Van, 283n.3
Hayim of Volozhin, Rabbi, 187, 193,
    196–200, 201
Hegel, George Wilhelm Friedrich,
    36, 114, 126, 234, 270
Heidegger, Martin, 3–4, 35, 38–39,
    45, 46, 62, 63, 64, 69, 89, 110,
    111, 112, 113, 115, 124, 137, 146,
    149, 162, 168, 171, 172, 273n.5,
    276n.26, 284n.11, 285n.16
Heschel, Abraham, 108
Hick, John, 58
Hofstader, Albert, 284n.8
Horwitz, Rivka, 195
Husserl, Edmund, 3, 15, 30, 37, 46,
    49, 63, 87, 88, 89, 109, 111, 112–
    13, 115, 116, 119, 124, 125, 155,
    205, 209–18, 221–46, 250, 284n.10,
    285n.16, 288n.17, 293n.28,
    307n.20, 310n.23, 313n.18,
    313n.22, 314n.24, 314n.30

Jacobi, Friedrich Heinrich, 255
James, William, 237, 278n.13
Jameson, Frederic, 144
Jaspers, Karl, 25
Joachim, Harold, 32
John of the Cross, Saint, 39

Jung, Carl Gustav, 275n.17

Kant, Immanuel, 30, 45–47, 54,
    105, 207–9, 216, 221–43 *passim*,
    251, 268
Kearney, Richard, 14, 298n.22
Kern, Iso, 221, 239, 240, 241,
    310n.23
Kierkegaard, Søren, 39, 124, 147,
    280n.36, 288n.16
King, Winston, 53
Kockelmans, Joseph J., 50
Krell, David, 284n.11
Kuhn, T. S., 52, 282n.12
Küng, Hans, 306n.3

Landgrebe, Ludwig, 292n.19
Laycock, Steven W., 15, 221, 232,
    311n.5
Leibniz, Gottfried, 245
Lenin, Vladimir, 126
Levinas, Emmanuel, 4, 14, 165–68,
    175–201 *passim*, 285n.16,
    301n.3, 306n.55
Lévi-Strauss, Claude, 135
Lessing, Gotthold, 26
Lindbeck, George, 284n.6
Lowe, Walter, 14
Luria, Isaac, 304n.37
Luther, Martin, 280n.36

McHugh, P., 49–50
McPherran, Mark, 253, 312n.7

Maimonides, 25, 188
Mannheim, Karl, 127
Marcuse, Herbert, 140
Marx, Karl, 63, 64, 66, 110, 120,
    124, 126–29, 131, 132–34, 136,
    137, 151, 168, 297n.19
Marxsen, Willi, 159
Meier, John P., 148, 159
Merleau-Ponty, Maurice, 3–4, 46,
    49, 109, 110, 114, 115, 124
Merton, Thomas, 295n.47
Moses ben Jacob of Cordovera,
    Rabbi, 186, 187, 190–95, 196, 197